SHAPING THE FUTURE

John,

with every best wish,

Marion

21 March 2012

Shaping the Future

a history of
The University of Lancaster,
1961–2011

Marion McClintock
Honorary Fellow and Honorary Archivist,
University of Lancaster
2011

Name of the university: in February 1989 a change was made to the visual identity of the university. Rather than the full legal title of The University of Lancaster, accompanied by the Grant of Arms, it was decided to make reference on much material in the public domain to Lancaster University, with an accompanying logo.

Published by The University of Lancaster

First published 2011

Designed and Typeset by Carnegie Book Production, Lancaster

Every effort has been made to trace and acknowledge holders of copyright of the illustrations used in this book. The publisher would be pleased to hear from copyright holders concerning any errors or omissions.
Printed and bound by 1010 Printing International

ISBN 978-1-86220-286-3

Contents

Foreword

THE MAKING OF A UNIVERSITY calls for inspiration and sustained enterprise. As the University of Lancaster approaches its fiftieth birthday, it is timely to put on record an account of the endeavours and devotion to the university of so many people that have led to the success and international pre-eminence that it now enjoys. From the care with which the Academic Planning Board considered the initial choice of subjects to the strength of the college system to the leadership across the globe of many of its research teams, the university and its members has sought to lay firm foundations on which our successors can build.

The period since our foundation has seen many changes in national education policy and a substantial growth to the university sector. In the 1960s UK higher education was a restricted experience available to a few and, in the decades since, the sector has been opened to a broader range of students. At the same time the global market has expanded as economies, especially in the eastern hemisphere, have developed. The demands on research are now greater as a result of regular evaluations of research output and rationing of scare resources. In this environment Lancaster has flourished. I attribute this to the quality of academic leadership at all levels, prudent management of resources and a tenacious grasp of the importance of institutional autonomy.

The author, herself a long-time member and servant of the university, has written a vivid story of events since the university's inception. Drawing on original sources, she shows how the government and strategic direction connect with its learning and teaching, the experiences of its students, and its research, and how they are in turn underpinned by the crucial infrastructure of our finances and estates. I commend her account to all our alumni, many of whom I have had the pleasure of meeting in person across the world, and to our staff, students, and all those with pride in the achievements of Lancaster and a care for its future. As the university's fifth vice-chancellor, I have been honoured to lead Lancaster through its fifth decade, and I shall watch its future development with affection and respect.

Paul W. Wellings, DL
Vice-Chancellor
July 2011

Acknowledgements

I AM MUCH INDEBTED to Paul Wellings for commissioning this volume, and for the discussions about form and content that followed. He, together with Jeffrey Richards and Peter McClintock, read through the whole text and made valued comments, particularly about additions to be made. Individual chapters were read by Paul Graves (1 and 2), Gavin Brown (3), Amanda Chetwynd (4), Trevor McMillan (5, and Appendix A), and Peter Fielding (6, and Appendix B). I have greatly benefited from their comments, and from discussions with them and with others indicated in the footnotes, as well as with Gavin Hyman, Bob McKinlay, Andrew Neal, Mark Swindlehurst, Alan Whitaker, and Michael Winstanley. Mark Bacon, Magnus George and Eleanor Hamilton gave me the necessary field map for Appendix 2, and Paul Graves and Peter Fielding, and their staff, provided me with the data for Figures 1 to 10. Many colleagues in University House have responded promptly to requests for factual information, especially the Facilities Division, the Press Office, and the Secretariat, and Gwen Ainsworth has been a true partner in the provision of illustrations, skilfully interpreting my objectives and applying her customary high standards to them.

Most intelligent five-year-olds these days have a level of instinctive technological competence that many of my generation can only trudge towards. I am therefore especially grateful to Olga Falko for making me believe that the resources behind my keyboard might become my ally, to the staff of Information Systems Services for their forbearance of my ineptitude, and to Simone Gristwood and particularly to Lorna Pimperton for bringing the footnotes and bibliography into good order.

Sarah Randall-Paley and Hilary Holt have deftly and benevolently managed the business side of the publication despite their very busy schedules, and Anna Goddard and her colleagues at Carnegie Press have been a pleasure to work with, combining high professionalism with a light touch for the author. Jacqueline Whiteside, David Summers, Clare Powne, Pamela Holme and Helen Clish, and past and present Library staff, have given me crucial encouragement and friendship as I set about creating an archive and writing a book from it, and my husband Peter has given me every support, while ensuring that I retained the resilience and determination to complete a complex task.

The copyright of the illustrations is held by the University of Lancaster unless otherwise stated. I am very glad to acknowledge the willing and gracious permission of the copyright holders of the illustrations individually listed in the captions, as well as to Sally Scott and Sue Thorn, for their reproduction.

Chronology

1947	Alderman Douglas Clift initiates a Lancaster University College Committee, but the discussions are later aborted.
1955	Mr J. D. Waddell, Lancaster Town Clerk, reactivates the idea of a university.
1959	UGC announces that four more new universities are to be recommended to HM Government.
6 March 1961	Patrick McCall, Clerk to Lancashire County Council, approaches the UGC, and a Promotions Committee is set up.
14 April 1961	First meeting of the Executive Committee of the Council for the Promotion of a University in North-West Lancashire.
2 May 1961	Decision taken by Executive Committee to put forward Lancaster to the UGC, rather than Blackpool.
12 May 1961	Formal submission by Promotions Council to the UGC.
14 June 1961	Visitation by UGC to Lancaster and Blackpool.
23 November 1961	Announcement in the House of Commons that a new university is to be established at Lancaster.
31 January 1962	Promotion Council dissolved, and two bodies replace it: the Executive Council for the Establishment of a University at Lancaster, and the Academic Planning Board.
1 April 1962	Bailrigg is taken out of Lancaster Rural District and included in Scotforth, within the City's boundary.
7 June 1962	The Executive Council is incorporated as a company, limited by guarantee and not having any share capital.
11 June 1962	Announcement made that HM the Queen to be the Visitor, HRH Princess Alexandra the first Chancellor, and the 18th Earl of Derby the first Pro-Chancellor.
20 July 1962	The Directors of the Executive Council meet together for the first time.
4 December 1962	Professor C. F. Carter of the University of Manchester meets the Executive Council; the following day an announcement is made that he is to be the first Vice-Chancellor.
January 1963	The lease of the Bailrigg site is received by the Executive Council for 999 years, at £1 a year.

1 April 1963	Charles Carter takes up the post of Vice-Chancellor Elect.
Summer 1963	The Vice-Chancellor Elect and senior officers move into Bailrigg House.
2 July 1963	The choice of site development architects, Messrs. Bridgewater, Shepheard and Epstein, is announced.
1 August 1963	Mr A. Stephen Jeffreys takes up the post of University Secretary.
1 September 1963	Mr A. G. Mackenzie takes up the post of Librarian.
1 October 1963	Professor B. H. P. Rivett takes up the chair of Operational Research.
21 October 1963	Mr Donald B. Smith takes up the post of Building Development Officer.
1 December 1963	Professor S. G. Sturmey takes up the chair of Economics.
11–12 January 1964	First meeting of the Shadow Senate.
1 April 1964	The following professors come into post: J. C. Bevington (Chemistry), T. E. Lawrenson (French Studies), E. R. Dobbs (Physics).
1 May 1964	The following professors come into post: W. A. Murray (English), A. H. Woolrych (History).
1 June 1964	Professor G. Manley takes up the chair of Environmental Studies.
1 July 1964	The following professors come into post: E. H. Lloyd (Mathematics), F. N. Sibley (Philosophy).
1 August 1964	Professor P. A. Reynolds takes up the chair of Politics and the post of Pro-Vice-Chancellor.
14 September 1964	The Great Seal is affixed to the Royal Charter of the University of Lancaster by order of the Privy Council.
18 September 1964	The first formally constituted meeting of the Senate takes place; Academic Advisory Committee replaces Academic Planning Board.
6 October 1964	The first student intake, of 296 undergraduates and 36 graduate students, is admitted to Lancaster, at St Leonard's House.
9 October 1964	A service is held at Lancaster Priory in the presence of HRH Princess Alexandra; address by the Archbishop of York, who also dedicates S. Martin's College later the same day.

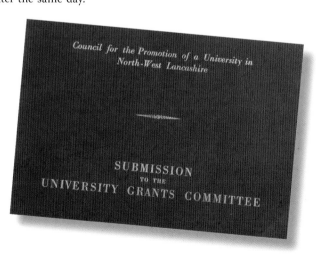

The slender brochure, with silver lettering on a maroon cover, that was submitted to the UGC in May 1961, over the name of Lord Derby, setting out the case for a university to be located in north Lancashire

A HISTORY OF THE UNIVERSITY OF LANCASTER

October 1964	The following academic departments open: Biology, Chemistry (laid down in 1990), Economics, English, Environmental Studies, French Studies, History, Mathematics, Operational Research, Philosophy, Physics, Politics, and Russian (laid down in 1982).
18 November 1964	HRH Princess Alexandra is installed as Chancellor at the Ashton Hall, Lancaster; some honorary degrees are conferred.
23 November 1964	The University Appeal is officially launched.
26 November 1964	Site work commences at Bailrigg.
5 December 1964	The inaugural meeting of the Court takes place.
15 December 1964	The authority of the Executive Council ceases, and the Council meets for the first time.
19 January 1965	The establishment of Bowland and Lonsdale Colleges is confirmed by the Council; the gift of £0.5 million by Lancashire County Council for the founding of a college (The County College) is announced.
18 May 1965	The purchase of Hazelrigg Farm is announced to the Council.
October 1965	Second intake of students is admitted, including some to take science subjects.
October 1965	The following academic departments open: Classics (as Classics and Archaeology, laid down in 1989), Marketing, and Systems Engineering.
4 December 1965	The first congregation for the conferment of one-year master's degrees is held in the Ashton Hall, Lancaster.
22 December 1965	Cartmel College is established by the Council.
October 1966	Grant of arms is made to the university.
October 1966	The first teaching, collegiate and administrative buildings open at Bailrigg: University House (Phase 1); Bowland main college.
3 January 1967	University Library (first phase) is opened by Sir Frank Francis, KCB, MA, DLitt, Director of the British Museum.
July 1967	The first bachelor degrees are awarded.
7 July 1967	Jennie Lee, MP, Minister of State for the Arts, lays the foundation stone of the Jack Hylton Music Rooms.
1 August 1967	The County College comes into being (with first-year students in residence from October 1969).
September 1967	School of Education at Lancaster approved by DES; teacher training qualifications validated and awarded for S. Martin's College and Poulton-le-Fylde College.
October 1967	Lonsdale main college opens; Physics and Chemistry Phase 1 available for use.
October 1967	The following academic departments open: Higher Education, Religious Studies.
December 1967	The Pavilion opens; recreation fields are available for use; the Indoor Recreation Centre opens.

1 August 1968	Furness College comes into being.
18 October 1968	Chemistry laboratories opened by Sir Harry Neville, KCB, FRS.
October 1968	The following academic departments open: Financial Control, Music.
October 1968	Student residences are opened in Bowland (including Bowland Tower) and in Cartmel colleges; Alexandra Square (including shops and banks) is completed; Fine Arts complex opens (including the Nuffield Theatre).
4 January 1969	The Physics building is opened by J. A. Ratcliffe, CB, CBE, FRS.
2 May 1969	The Chaplaincy Centre and its chapels are consecrated.
1 August 1969	Fylde College comes into being.
October 1969	The following academic departments open: Behaviour in Organisations, Computer Studies, Engineering, and Sociology.
October 1969	The Great Hall, the Learning Aids building (now the Round House), and the building for Biological Sciences and Environmental Studies open.
October 1969	The central workshops and the service station open.
October 1969	Furness main college opens; residences at Lonsdale, Furness and Fylde colleges open; Bailrigg House becomes the Medical Centre, and the Vice-Chancellor moves to Emmanuel House, Haverbreaks.
17 October 1969	HM the Queen visits the university (including The County College and the Chaplaincy Centre).
9 December 1969	Assistant Staff House and The County College opened by HRH Princess Alexandra.
11 October 1970	The Academic Advisory Committee is dissolved.
14 November 1970	Furness College is opened by Mr W. D. Opher, CBE.
April 1971	Lord Derby retires from the post of Pro-Chancellor.
October 1971	The following academic department opens: Central and South-Eastern European Studies.
January 1972	Lord Greenwood of Rossendale becomes Pro-Chancellor (to June 1978).
May to July 1972	Taylor Enquiry is conducted, and the report is published.
October 1972	The following academic departments open: Psychology, Theatre Studies.
October 1972	Students Bookshops takes over from R. Maxwell Ltd.
12 October 1972	Engineering and Systems Engineering Building opened by Professor Sir John Baker, OBE, FRS.
May 1973	The crown bowling green is established near the Library.
June 1973	The perimeter road is completed.
June 1973	The Student Representative Council offices move to the East Wing of Bowland Annexe.
October 1973	The following academic departments open: Arabic and Islamic Studies (laid down in 1982),Visual Arts, and the School of Independent Studies; scheme of study established in Ecology.
October 1973	Fylde main colleges and residences (Phase 2) open.

October 1973	Edge Hill College of Education transfers to Lancaster from the University of Liverpool.
October 1973	The playgroup and crèche open near the Pavilion.
March 1974	Fulcrum begins publication (to June 1990).
22 May 1974	Pendle College comes into being.
1 August 1974	German Studies becomes an independent department; the School of English is established.
October 1974	The following academic departments open: European Studies, Social Administration.
October 1974	Grizedale and Pendle main college and residences open; Visual Arts opens within that complex.
October 1974	The target of 3000 students within ten years is exceeded.
June 1975	Gillow House (now the Management School) opens.
1 August 1975	Grizedale College comes into being.
August 1975	Student Representative Council becomes the Students' Union.
October 1975	The department of Geography opens.
June 1976	School of European Studies is set up.
October 1977	County West opens (demolished in the summer of 2007).
October 1977	The Management Teacher Development Unit opens (subsequently the department of Management Learning, and in August 2005 of Management Learning and Leadership).
November 1977	The Richardson Institute becomes a centre of the university.
October 1978	Professor Philip Reynolds becomes Acting Vice-Chancellor.
October 1978	Mr W. D. Opher, OBE becomes Pro-Chancellor (to September 1980).
October 1978	The department of Law opens (and becomes the School of Law on 11 October 2000).
March 1979	Inaugural concert on Great Hall organ.
September 1979	Sir Charles Carter resigns as Vice-Chancellor (and receives an honorary degree in December 1979).
December 1979	The extension to the Biological Sciences and Environmental Science building opens.
January 1980	Professor Reynolds takes up the post of Vice-Chancellor.
26 April 1980	First Open Day is held, attended by 17,000 visitors.
September 1980	Sir Alastair Pilkington, FRS, becomes Pro-Chancellor (to September 1990).
2 December 1980	Swimming pool is opened by HRH Princess Alexandra.
May 1981	Substantial reduction in the universities' recurrent grants made by the UGC.
June 1981	University House Phase 2 (west wing) opens.

October 1982	The Sugar House in St Leonardsgate opens as a student social centre (lease from Mitchells Brewery from 1987 to 1999).
21 January 1983	The purchase of the boat house at Halton is completed.
February 1983	Emmanuel House is sold.
May 1985	Last UGC visitation takes place.
June 1985	The Croft is purchased as the Vice-Chancellor's residence.
1 October 1985	Professor Harold J. Hanham becomes Vice-Chancellor.
November 1985	Submission made for first research assessment exercise.
December 1985	Geography moves into Physics annexe.
January 1986	School of Independent Studies is designated as a department.
20 January 1988	School of Engineering, Computing and Mathematical Sciences is approved.
April 1988	Scott Gallery is re-named as the Peter Scott Gallery.
June 1988	Jarratt Report: Lancaster actions therefrom agreed for implementation.
1 June 1988	School of Management becomes The Management School.
1 June 1988	School of Creative Arts is approved; Visual Arts moves from the Pendle/Grizedale complex to Lonsdale Hall.
7 June 1988	LU Archaeological Unit set up in place of the Cumbria and Lancashire Archaeological Unit (and is transferred to Oxford Archaeology North in October 2001).
August 1988	The Bridging Summer School for Access is instituted.
August 1988	The School of Management becomes a faculty board (and replaces the School of Management and Organisational Sciences).
October 1988	The central well in the Library is roofed over.
12 October 1988	Institute of Environmental and Biological Sciences is approved.
October 1988	Enterprise in Higher Education is funded by the Department of Employment at Lancaster, for five years.
March 1989	Submission made for second research assessment exercise.
7 June 1989	Centre for Polymer Chemistry approved (and laid down in August 2000).
October 1989	Reception Building, with Careers above, opens.
October 1989	Extensions and additions made to Engineering Building.
February 1990	Environmental Science Phase 4 is completed.
31 July 1990	Department of Chemistry laid down: School of Physics and Chemistry set up (and reverts to Department of Physics in August 2000).
September 1990	72 residence rooms added to Fylde College.
1 October 1990	Sir Christopher Audland, KCMG, becomes Pro-Chancellor (to September 1996).
October 1990	Pilkington Teaching Award scheme is set up.
5 December 1990	The Graduate College (subsequently Graduate Hall; now Bowland Hall) opened by HRH Princess Alexandra.

20 March 1991	Institute for English Language Education constitution is approved.
1 April 1991	Centre for the Study of Environmental Change is established.
1 June 1991	Centre for the Study of Education and Training is established.
October 1991	Mezzanine floor is added to Engineering Building.
4 December 1991	Lancaster House Hotel and the Management Development Centre officially opened by HRH Princess Alexandra.
9 January 1992	John Creed Building opened by Mrs Jean Creed.
June 1992	Submission for third research assessment exercise: Lancaster in the top ten places.
1 September 1992	Charlotte Mason College becomes a college of the university (to 1996).
21 September 1992	Part of Storey Institute leased for LU Archaeology Unit and Adult Education.
September 1992	192 additional residence rooms added to Furness College.
28 October 1992	Commissioners' Statute for Lancaster comes into effect.
November 1992	HEQC academic audit unit visits Lancaster.
November 1992	CHP (Combined Heat and Power) plant comes on stream.
1 December 1992	Additional block added to the Graduate College (now used by CETAD).
January 1993	The enlarged and refurbished Peter Scott Gallery is re-opened within the Great Hall complex.
January 1993	S. Martin's College becomes an accredited institution.
May 1993	The cycle track between Bailrigg and Lancaster opens.
1 August 1993	Department of Management Science is formed out of: Operational Research and Operations Management; and Systems and Information Management.
October 1993	Part I Spanish inaugurated (and Part II one year later).
October 1993	Music building opens.
October 1993	Blackpool and The Fylde College receives associate college status.
8 December 1993	New Pendle College opens.
December 1993	George Fox Building is opened by HRH Princess Alexandra.
1 January 1994	Freehold of Bailrigg site purchased from Lancaster City Council for £500,000.
February 1994	Department of Continuing Education is established (and is laid down in June 2010).
7 March 1994	Lancaster receives one of the first round of the Queen's Anniversary Prize awards.
March 1994	New Pre-School Centre opened by HRH Princess Alexandra.
March 1994	Faculty of Education is established (and is laid down in 1996).
1 April 1994	Department of Mathematics becomes the Department of Mathematics and Statistics.

28 October 1994	School of Modern Languages is approved.
October 1994	The freehold of the Sugar House is purchased from Mitchell's Brewery.
January 1995	Chancellor's Wharf opens.
22 March 1995	Management School Graduate School opens; officially opened by HRH Princess Alexandra on 12 July.
March 1995	Records of the University approved to be housed in the Archive section of the University Library.
5 April 1995	Blackburn College receives associate college status.
April 1995	The £35 million 9.75% First Mortgage Debenture Stock 2025 is issued on the London Stock Exchange.
September 1995	Graduate College social centre opens.
24 January 1996	Professor William Ritchie, OBE, becomes Vice-Chancellor.
January 1996	The Department of Visual Arts becomes the Department of Art.
1 March 1996	Tower Avenue, Slaidburn House and Edward Roberts Court open.
20 March 1996	Ruskin Programme Centre approved (and becomes the Ruskin Library and Research Centre in August 2008).
April 1996	Submission for fourth research assessment exercise (RAE 96): results announced in September.
1 September 1996	Charlotte Mason College is transferred to S. Martin's College (with the initial teacher training provision).
October 1996	Mr J. B. Heron becomes Pro-Chancellor (to July 2003).
October 1996	SW Campus, aka new Graduate College, opens.
1 January 1997	Institute for Health Research commences its work.
1 January 1997	The four-year Recovery Plan period commences.
1 January 1997	Institute for Cultural Research is approved.
May 1997	CRILL report is published.
8 July 1997	Library and ISS extension, and the Sir Alastair Pilkington Reading Room, opened by HRH Princess Alexandra.
31 July 1997	The net book value of land and buildings at Bailrigg is valued at £125.6 million.
January 1998	LU Graduate School set up.
16 March 1998	Department of Politics becomes the Department of Politics and International Relations.
6 May 1998	The Ruskin Library is opened by HRH Princess Alexandra.
7 October 1998	Senior Management Team becomes the University Management Advisory Group (UMAG).
1 August 1999	Department of Communications Systems is established.
February/March 2000	QAA Continuation Audit visit takes place.

1 August 2000	Department of Philosophy is merged with the Centre for the Study of Environmental Change, to become the Institute for Environment, Philosophy and Public Policy.
11 October 2000	Departmental status is conferred on Institute for Cultural Research and the Institute for Women's Studies; Law becomes a School.
April 2001	Submission for fifth research assessment exercise (RAE 2001).
August 2001	The student residential accommodation project commences.
12 March 2002	Work commences on building of joint LEC building for NERC's Centre for Ecology and Hydrology and the Lancaster Environment Centre.
20 May 2002	Dame Kathleen Ollerenshaw Observatory is opened on the roof of the Physics Building by Sir Patrick Moore.
29 May 2002	Literacy Research Centre is approved.
19 July 2002	LUVU is opened by Hilton Dawson, MP.
16 September 2002	New custom-built Health Centre opens.
20 September 2002	Staff Learning Centre opens.
October 2002	Professor Paul Wellings becomes Vice-Chancellor.
9 October 2002	The Centre for the Enhancement of Teaching and Learning is established.
November 2002	The first Ordinances are approved.
13 November 2002	The Department of English becomes the Department of English and Creative Writing.
January 2003	Centre for Research in Human Development opens in the Whewell Building.
28 May 2003	Institute of Advanced Studies in Management and Social Sciences is approved (and becomes the Institute for Advanced Studies on 17 November 2004); and the Centre for Mobilities Research is approved.
1 August 2003	Mr Bryan Gray, CBE, DL, becomes Pro-Chancellor (to 2013).
August 2003	The Department of Behaviour in Organisations becomes the Department of Organisation, Work and Technology.
September 2003	The university enters into the residential accommodation transaction with Jarvis UPP (subsequently UPP (Lancaster) Limited) to build and maintain 3465 new and replacement residential rooms.
October 2003	Lancaster Leadership Centre (Management School) funded by NWDA.
2 October 2003	Institute for Entrepreneurship and Enterprise Development launched (and is approved as a department in November 2007).
10 October 2003	Centre for the Economic and Social Aspects of Genomics is launched.
4 November 2003	Pendle College extension opened by Right Worshipful The Mayor of Lancaster (Mr John Gilbert).
26 May 2004	Centre for Research and Human Development is approved.
June 2004	QAA Institutional Audit takes place.

6 July 2004	Lancaster Environment Centre building opened by Professor Paul Wellings and Professor John Lawton CBE, FRS.
August 2004	InfoLab21, funded by NWDA and ERDF, opens and houses Computing and Communication Systems, and a Knowledge Business Centre.
7 September 2004	40th anniversary party for all staff takes place at Leighton Hall.
24 September 2004	Charter Day dinner; unveiling of portrait of HRH Princess Alexandra.
September 2004	Lonsdale College moves to and reopens at Alexandra Park; Cartmel College moves to and reopens at Alexandra Park; naming of County South and Bowland North approved and operational.
October 2004	RLI Education Centre and LU Centre of Medical Education opened.
7 December 2004	HRH Princess Alexandra opens Barker House Farm (at Cartmel College) as her last official duty as Chancellor.
31 January 2005	Spade presented by HBG to mark the south extension of the Management School.
January 2005	Centre for Excellence in Teaching and Learning Postgraduate Statistics is funded by the HEFCE.
2 February 2005	InfoLab 21 is opened by Rt. Hon. Patricia Hewitt, CBE, MP, Secretary of State for Trade and Industry.
9 March 2005	Sir Christian Bonington is installed as the second Chancellor (to 2010 and, with reappointment, to 2015) at the Ashton Hall, Lancaster (preceded by a service at the Priory and followed by lunch in the Town Hall).
10 May 2005	Leadership Centre, Management School, opened by Sir Digby Jones, Director-General of the CBI.
25 May 2005	Careers Service becomes the Centre for Employability, Enterprise and Careers.
25 May 2005	InfoLab21 approved as a research centre of the university.
1 August 2005	Lancaster Institute for the Contemporary Arts is established, and includes the former departments of Art, Music and Theatre Studies; and the Nuffield Theatre, the Peter Scott Gallery and LU Concerts.
1 August 2005	The School of Lifelong Learning and Widening Participation is established (and is laid down in 2010).
November 2005	Lancaster wins second Queen's Anniversary Prize.
29 November 2006	Institute of Advanced Studies is opened by Frances Cairncross, CBE.
23 February 2006	Sir Liam Donaldson opens Clinical Anatomy Learning Centre.
March 2006	QAA Collaborative Provision audit takes place.
March 2006	Donation of £5 million by the Bowland Trust.
17 March 2006	First Ideas Festival takes place.
20 April 2006	First university honorary fellowships are conferred.
May 2006	Edge Hill is awarded university status.
18 September 2006	Sunway University College in Kuala Lumpur becomes an associated college of the university.

October 2006	The Centre for Medical Education takes in its first undergraduate students, and becomes the Department of Medicine.
22 May 2007	Gordon Manley Building (Phase 3 of LEC) is opened by Lord Rees of Ludlow, FRS.
October 2007	S. Martin's College is awarded university status as the University of Cumbria.
21 November 2007	Centre for Gender and Women's Studies approved (in place of the Institute for Women's Studies) but without departmental status.
13 November 2007	Bowland North is opened by Professor David Eastwood, HEFCE Chief Executive.
December 2007	Submission made for sixth research assessment exercise (RAE 08); results published in December 2008.
21 February 2008	The Postgraduate Statistics Centre is opened by Professor Sir David Cox, FRS.
18 April 2008	The Bonington Step is opened by Sir Christian Bonington.
1 August 2008	School of Health and Medicine is launched.
August 2008	Memorandum of Understanding signed with COMSATS Institute of Information Technology in Pakistan.
September 2008	Spectrum Centre for Mental Health Research opens.
September 2008	The County College town houses open.
October 2008	Departments of Biological Sciences, Environmental Science, and Geography are merged into the Lancaster Environment Centre, under a director, for full implementation on 1 August 2009.
12 May 2009	Centre for Organisational Health and Wellbeing is launched.
1 August 2009	Centre for Family Business is launched.
1 August 2009	The post of Chief Operating Officer is established.
August 2009	The £35 million 9.75% First Mortgage Debenture Stock 2025 is redeemed via the Royal Bank of Scotland for £80 million revolving credit facility, of which £45 million is the redemption price.
September 2009	Contract is signed for £20 million Sports Centre (for completion in 2011).
16 September 2009	45th Anniversary Dinner; portrait of Sir Christian Bonington is unveiled.
26 September 2009	Learning Zone in Alexandra Square opens.
16 October 2009	Grizedale College is relaunched by Dr Bob Bliss, former principal of the college.
November 2009	Lancaster wins third Queen's Anniversary Prize.
November 2009	ISS staff and equipment move to their new building.
9 December 2009	Lancaster Square (by County College) is inaugurated by Sir Christian Bonington.
15 January 2010	Learning Zone is officially opened by Sir Alan Langlands, Chief Executive of the HEFCE.

February 2010	Standard and Poor's give Lancaster a credit rating of A+ stable.
May 2010	Refurbishment of County South is completed.
10 May 2010	Lancaster City Council turns down a proposal for two wind turbines at Hazelrigg; a revised proposal for one turbine is approved in April 2011.
May/June 2010	League tables for student experience rank Lancaster as 8th in the *Independent*, 10th in *The Times*, and 6th in the *Guardian*.
15 June 2010	Sir Christian Bonington makes the first presentations of the Lancaster Award.
1 August 2010	Department of Politics, Philosophy and Religion comes into being.
1 August 2010	School of Computing and Communications comes into being.
September 2010	Lancaster is ranked 124th in THE World Rankings.
September 2010	The Lancaster Institute for the Contemporary Arts Building opens.
October 2010	Lancaster receives Best University Halls award (National Student Housing Survey).
12 October 2010	The review of higher education funding and student finance, chaired by Lord Browne of Madingley, is published.
21 October 2010	University acquires The Work Foundation.
10 March 2011	Charles Hendry, Minister of State for Energy and Climate Change, launches the university's Energy Centre.
29 March 2011	The LICA is officially opened by Professor Geoffrey Crossick, Vice-Chancellor of the University of London.
12 April 2011	The Charles Carter Building is officially opened by HRH Princess Alexandra.

Preface

I N AUGUST 2011 I shall have had the privilege of half a century of working within institutions of higher education, more than forty of them at Lancaster. I have therefore been enabled to observe at first hand the growth of one particular new foundation within an era of exceptional change, and to share in Lancaster's journey to a measure of success that would have delighted Lord Derby, chairman of the original Promotion Committee, Sir Noel Hall, chairman of the formative Academic Planning Board, and Sir Alfred Bates, chairman of the Executive Council for the Establishment of a University at Lancaster.

At the time that the Shakespearean Seven universities were being considered by the University Grants Committee, the growth in numbers and the extent to which students from all classes would enter universities were just taking off. In 1960[1] there were 123,500 UK students registered at university, of whom 22,700 were postgraduates and 29,533 were women. By 1990 the total student population had grown to 404,831, but was then more than tripled by the inclusion of the former polytechnics in 1992. By 2005 the total student numbers were 2.287 million, of whom more than half a million were postgraduates and the majority were women, and around that time there were suggestions that another thirty or more further education colleges might achieve degree-awarding powers.[2] The implications for class were no less startling. Notwithstanding the continuing twenty-first-century concerns about the proportion of students admitted from disadvantaged backgrounds, the situation has been transformed since the end of World War II. The Education Act of 1944 created the grammar schools that in the medium term would have a marked effect on movement between classes, but they were slow to admit a proportionate number of children of skilled and semi-skilled manual workers. The position was worse at tertiary level, for in 1955,[3] when it is estimated that about 70% of the population were manual working class, only a quarter of the 74,687 men registered with universities came from that 70%. A further dramatic change has taken place in the staff profile of universities such as Lancaster. In 1964 the great majority of academic and senior administrative staff were white, male, and middle class, with origins in the United Kingdom. There were two main categories: senior

---

[1] Malcolm Tight, *The Development of Higher Education in the United Kingdom since 1945* (Maidenhead: Open University Press/McGraw-Hill, 2009), Table 3.4(a), p. 55.

[2] Peter Kingston, "Further expansion on the cards", *Education Guardian*, 20 November 2007, p. 12.

[3] David Kynaston, *Family Britain, 1951–1957* (New York: Walker & Co., 2010), p. 141.

postholders in their 50s who had served in World War II, who became heads of departments and leaders of administrative areas, and a new generation of young staff who had mostly graduated from Oxford, Cambridge or the big civic universities. The science staff typically already had doctorates on appointment: those in the social sciences and humanities, if they had second degrees, tended to confine themselves to masters level. The assistant or support staff, meanwhile, were predominantly local people – an easy bus ride away – who were taking advantage of a new employment opportunity for Lancaster.[4] Fifty years on, almost all these characteristics have changed. The academic and professional staff span all ages, most nationalities, and both genders, and the support staff are just as likely to have distant as local origins, and to be themselves graduates. In the early days of the university, most people were obliged to undertake multiple tasks, a situation that brought opportunity and early responsibility to young staff: roles are now more specialised and there are formal performance criteria to meet. This book is therefore written about a single institution, but set against the background of larger changes in society and in higher education.

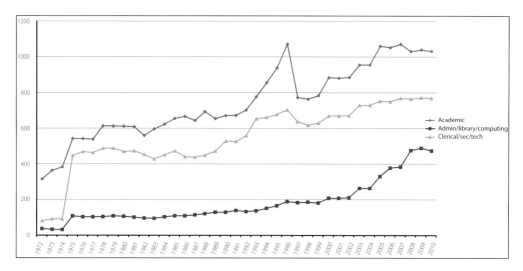

Figure 1. Staff numbers, 1972–2010

The move to set up seven new universities, fully formed from their moment of creation, was bold in the 1960s, but would surely be impossible in the early twenty-first century, when the bureaucratic, financial and legislative impediments would be insuperable. The seven, beginning with Sussex in 1961 and concluding with Kent and Warwick in 1965, opened their doors just in time for the intake of the post World War II baby boom and the output of the grammar schools. The 60s were also a time of aspiration, when at last the hardships

---

4 A significant number of early porters at the university, for example, were skilled craftsmen from the former Waring and Gillow factory at St Leonard's House.

of wartime and the first years of peace could fade from people's daily consciousness. While the converted colleges of advanced technology, such as Bradford, Brunel and Surrey, all founded in 1966, had a more technological slant than the so-called plateglass universities,[5] Lancaster and its peer institutions could follow a more traditional path of natural sciences and humanities with, in the cases of Lancaster and Warwick, the addition of business-related subjects as the principal innovation. In principle there were to be no favours shown to these young upstarts: in practice, they had the ready attention of senior ministers and civil servants.[6] Lancaster was deliberately located in an area of relative economic hardship and that choice, linked with its relative isolation at Lancashire South of the Sands, made it, in the words of a former colleague, always hungry for success.

As Lancaster set out on the steep path of becoming a national and international institution, the scope of higher education was not only increasing but diversifying. Crosland's Woolwich speech about removing the binary line was delivered in 1965, and in Lancashire other new institutions of higher education increasingly clustered around Lancaster: Central Lancashire and Manchester Metropolitan from 1992, Bolton and Chester from 2005, Edge Hill from 2006 and Cumbria from 2007, all of which achieved university status after periods of emergence from further education, or as institutes of technology that often linked together even smaller and more diverse tertiary colleges. Moreover, the expansion accelerated faster than expected, as additional student number targets proffered to institutions were accepted and filled more quickly than anticipated. Even if the Thatcher government of 1979–90 had not been ideologically bent on reining in the rate of growth, any other government of the period would probably have acted to restrain it. Furthermore, as heavy industry dwindled – in the cotton industry of Lancashire from the end of World War II – the moment when the nation realised its future would depend on living by its wits rather than by the production of exported goods heralded what has come to be known as the knowledge economy. In principle this is good news for higher education, when an educated workforce is seen as a valuable economic commodity: in practice, it means the universities have become part of a highly visible political scene that means the objectives and targets set for them are never stable.

Reflecting on this helter-skelter half century, I have come to realise how much continuity nevertheless remains. Just as across the world universities have more in common with each other than they have differences between them, so the underlying values expressed so trenchantly in Lancaster's Charter are what give meaning and purpose to their existence. As Harvard President Drew Gilpin Faust has indicated,

If we are to depend on a knowledge economy, how are we to understand what is actually knowledge, as contrasted with mere information? Education conceived only

---

[5] See chapter Nine of Michael Beloff, *The Plateglass Universities* (London: Secker & Warburg, 1968), in which Lancaster is epitomised as having a "reputation that burgeons on the Plateglass grapevine".

[6] Charles Carter's extensive correspondence with Sir John Wolfenden from 1963 onwards, for example, goes far beyond strictly Lancaster-related business.

as an instrument of economic growth … ignores that some things are not about 'facts', but are about meaning …

An overly instrumental model of the university misses the genius of its capacity. It devalues the zone of patience and contemplation the university creates in a world all but overwhelmed by stimulation. It diminishes its role as an asker of fundamental questions in a world hurrying to fix its most urgent problems. We need both.[7]

To that summation I would want to add the institutional self-confidence which ensures that each university is comfortable with the choices it has made about its perceived destination and its mode of travel, and the humility of an acceptance of both success and hardship as inevitable companions on the way. Perhaps the single most lasting lesson I have learnt is the fundamental importance of the people who make up the enduring community of the university, starting with the vice-chancellor of the day, who sets the tone and direction of the institution, and all the staff and students, who between them shape its present and hence the trajectory of its future. Their intelligence and drive, their priorities, and their interpretations of the university's objectives and significance, when combined together with a shared motivation for institutional success, form the true engine of any significant university.

This volume seeks, therefore, to show how a single institution charted its way from a tiny, new but already degree-awarding and research institution of 1964 to the medium-sized university of international standing today, as an account of intrinsic interest to its members and especially its alumni, and as a modest contribution to the higher education literature that draws on the particular to frame the general. Throughout, the opportunities and constraints introduced by external agencies are included, to show the extent to which Lancaster has been able to shape its own destiny, or not, and how the tensions between public and private, national need and institutional priorities affect policy. Documents written at the time that show staff and student views at the time of their composition, rather than through the glow of retrospection, are quoted from extensively. The main text can be read as a freestanding narrative, but the book is also designed to be a quarry for those who wish to explore topics in greater depth, using the footnotes and the index to pursue particular themes. Behind it is an archive of institutional documents available for reference and consultation, held in the University Library.

At the time that *Quest for Innovation* was published in 1974, most of the main actors were still in post and it was possible to ask them directly what had been meant by particular choices, or how they had reacted to certain events over a single decade. When Professor Paul Wellings commissioned this volume in 2006, it was clear that the fine-grained chronological detail of the earlier work should give way to a more thematic and analytical approach, taking as the period the time at which the establishment of a university at Lancaster was announced in the House of Commons in November 1961 and moving forward over the

---

[7] Drew Gilpin Faust, "No borders, only frontiers", Supplement to *Times Higher Education*, 16 September 2010.

following fifty years. This new work would again start from 1961, but provide an overview of selected topics for the fifty-year period to 2011. Thus the volume has begun with a chronology of principal events from 1961–2011, as a backdrop to whichever thematic chapter the reader then selects. An account of the governance of the university was an obvious first choice of treatment, not least because the form of governance and its implementation also informs the culture of an institution. In that context, the assumption common to Jarratt (1988), Dearing (1997), Lambert (2003) and Browne (2010) that their respective reports on efficiency, student profile, links with industry, or undergraduate tuition fees should also contain proposed interventions in the governance structures within the sector seems at best misplaced and at worst destructive.

Strategic planning is a close twin of governance and naturally follows: here questions of direction of travel, and how stratagem and action match each other, are of particular interest. The academic structures of the university, particularly in relation to learning and teaching, appropriately follow. There is then a change of style, for the chapter on student experience focuses on the students' perspective: not what was prescribed, but students' perceptions of it. Research, as the natural complement to learning and teaching, follows, and shows how Lancaster has come to excel in certain key fields, often those established by the university's pioneers: there is also a brief appendix of the crucial commercialisation of research and the consequences for the society in which the university is situated. Chapters on finance and on the physical domain complete the thematic tour. While the last two might by some readers be expected to be quite technical – even dry – Lancaster's history confounds this view in demonstrating how just as many twists and turns are to be found in these themes, not least in the appendix on the funding and building of the second generation of student residences in 2002–10. There is finally a codicil in the form of a brief epilogue. Throughout, the selection of evidence from the great body of available material, chosen to present a clear narrative and not to overwhelm the reader, has proved demanding. To all those readers whose favourite anecdote or larger theme is not included the author expresses her regret, while suggesting that it be written up for the Archive and kept for the future. Only by chronicling the past can we interpret the present or plan for the future.

Marion McClintock
Bailrigg
May 2011

CHAPTER ONE

Governance

I N MARCH 1963, three weeks before he was due to take up his post as Vice-Chancellor Elect, Charles Carter received a model Charter and Statutes from the Privy Council, which he was told was intended:

> to indicate the general layout and form which we would be glad to see adopted and which we feel would represent an improvement, from the drafting point of view, on several of the Charters granted to universities in recent years ... Since the requirements of Universities will inevitably differ, our 'model' can only serve as a very general guide in regard to substance, as distinct from form.[1]

Unlike institutions that had moved to full university status in the late 1950s or early 1960s, such as Keele or Leicester, or that had effected substantial changes, such as the move to create two universities of Newcastle and Durham out of the single University of Durham, it was known from the outset that no Act of Parliament would be necessary for the new university at Lancaster. Although as recently as the foundation of the University of Sussex, where its founders had to proceed by means of a special Bill to dissolve the University College of 1959, and to transfer its rights, properties and liabilities to the newly chartered university,[2] for Lancaster (in common with East Anglia, York, Kent, Warwick,

---

[1]   F. E. Leigh to C. F. Carter, 7 March 1963 (UA.1/16/8/6/2).

[2]   10 and 11 Eliz. 2 (UA.1/16/8/6/2).

and Essex), three apparently simple stages were all that were necessary. There would be a Humble Petition to the Queen's Most Excellent Majesty in Council, accompanied by the draft Charter and Statutes; a Warrant; and the application of the Great Seal. The Humble Petition was signed off for submission by Sir Alfred Bates on 31 October 1963 and, after due consideration by the Privy Council, a Warrant for a Charter was issued on 27 July 1964, and the Great Seal attached on 14 September 1964, the Charter Day. At this point Lancaster was immediately empowered to take responsibility for all the actions of a fully-fledged university, able to manage its own teaching, research and award of degrees, to sue and be sued as a corporate entity, and to manage its own finances, including its investments or entry into loans. From 14 September 1964, therefore, Lancaster was committed to functioning within the provisions of its Charter and Statutes, except inasmuch as it proposed amendments to the Privy Council, or when external bodies were authorised to intervene, as for example in the case of the Commissioners' Statute (see below).

The significance of governance arrangements within universities, including Lancaster's, cannot be over-emphasized. Because of the extent to which they are self-governing, the policies put in place by the chief bodies of the university directly and deeply affect the working lives and conditions of all staff and students on a daily basis. The relationship of central bodies to those who report to them, the role of officers in relation to statutory bodies and the committees that advise them, the extent to which structures enable or inhibit members of the university, and the clarity of the arrangements and the extent to which they

Sir Charles Carter, Vice-Chancellor from 1963 to 1979

are absorbed and understood by those affected fundamentally set the tone of an institution and have a direct bearing on the way that business at any level can be transacted, from the authority of a head of department or dean to sign off a purchase order to the way in which the Students' Union interfaces with the university. The discussion below of changes to the initial Charter and Statutes exemplify these considerations, while the account of times of difficulty (including finance or discipline), when the true mettle and quality of an institution are put to the test, should be read in the context of the governing structures of the university and the way they contribute to the solutions reached.

An understanding of changes to Lancaster's original Charter and Statutes relies on clarity about the original structure. In addition to the model provided by the Privy Council, the documents of other institutions were taken as examples, including those of Exeter, Liverpool, East Anglia, Kent, and Sussex. Charles Carter, when preparing the second draft of governance arrangements during his first summer as Vice-Chancellor (largely in his own neat hand), sought the detailed comments of all members of the Academic Planning Board. The Executive Council for the Establishment of a University at Lancaster was of course consulted, and the views of the University Grants Committee taken into account. It is, however, to Charles Carter himself that credit is due for the weight and sonority of the Charter's third clause: "The objects of the University shall be to advance knowledge, wisdom and understanding by teaching and research and by the example and influence of its corporate life."[3]

---

[3] Parenthesis to Outline of Charter and Statutes (undated, but circa April 1963) (UA.1/16/8/6/3), and University of Lancaster Charter, Clause 3.

The terms on which the university was empowered to make investments and the comparability of those terms with the other new universities was one point of debate during the drafting process. Another suggestion, that HM the Queen in person might, because of Lancaster's connection with the Duchy of Lancaster, appoint the successors to the first Chancellor, was mooted but, on advice, not pursued. Increasing refinement of the membership of the Court continued through the drafting period, including explicit approval by the Privy Council for the representation (at their request) of the House of Keys (Isle of Man). Generally there was enthusiasm for involvement in the new university, as shown for example by the response on behalf of the County of Cumberland: "The representation which you suggest on the Court of the University is certainly generous ... and I am sure that people in many parts of this County will feel a strong attraction towards the new university."[4]

Another discussion was about the relative role of the Court and the Council, for the Parliamentary Agents[5] had assumed that the Court of over two hundred members would be the governing body of the university. A letter of 12 July 1963 from Patrick McCall to Messrs. Sherwood and Company noted, however, that the

> Vice-Chancellor's comment was that this [i.e. the Council as governing body] had already been approved of by the Privy Council and that the precedent is contained in the Charter relating to the University of Sussex. In addition to that, the Vice-Chancellor points out that this new structure is one which is definitely being favoured now by the University Grants Committee.[6]

The separation of the respective powers and responsibilities of the Senate and the Council were progressively clarified during the drafting process, and the explicit decision was made that, while the Council would be the governing body, it should not be designated as supreme, in order to respect the powers reserved to the Senate.[7]

Particular care was taken to ensure that the chain of authority was maintained by the bodies already in existence throughout the period of establishment of the university. Thus the Humble Petition of October 1963 recited the steps taken from the setting up of the Promoting Council through to the acceptance "by your Majesty's Government" of the advice that a university be set up at Lancaster, how at that point the Promoting Council dissolved itself, "but before doing so it approved the continued existence of its Executive Committee (which was thereafter to be known as the Executive Council) ...", how that body in turn appointed the members of the Academic Planning Board, and how it had been decided it

---

[4] Letter of 19 June 1963 from G. N. C. Swift to C. P. H. McCall (UA.1/16/8/6/1).
[5] The Parliamentary Agents are a firm of solicitors (Sherwood and Company) who were approved by the Privy Council for work involving governance structures, both national and devolved.
[6] See UA.1/11/16/8/1. When the debenture stock was about to be floated on the London Stock Exchange in 1995, the primacy of the Court over the Council was again raised.
[7] Letter of 12 July 1963 from C. F. Carter to Messrs. Sherwood and Company (UA.1/16/8/3).

"would be fitting and helpful" to form a company limited by guarantee for the Executive Council.[8]

This level of care was reinforced by a set of Transitional Provisions that were included as part of the Statutes initially approved in 1964. The transitional arrangements brought into office both the Chancellor and Pro-Chancellor on Charter Day (14 September), and set out a timetable for the means by which the various bodies of the university could each be brought into existence. First, two colleges were to be established on the same day, and all full-time members of academic staff would be assigned to one or the other, in order to appoint syndicate members to the Senate. The Senate, in turn, was to meet not more than one month after Charter Day, and was to make its nine appointments to the Council. Next the Court was required to meet in the third month after Charter Day, and was to make its six appointments to the Council. Only then, up to one month after the special Court meeting, could the first meeting of the Council be held, and in the meanwhile the Directors of the Executive Council continued to be vested with the rights and powers of the Council. In addition, all staff already appointed, including the Vice-Chancellor, were required to be confirmed in their respective offices.[9] Not surprisingly, it was the end of the 1964 calendar year before all the steps had taken place in the correct sequence and the university's three governing bodies were complete, and June 1965 before the Executive Council was dissolved and the company wound up.[10]

The final piece of transitional machinery was perhaps the most important for the infant university. In common with its peer institutions, Lancaster was to have an Academic Advisory Committee, charged with "keeping under review the standard of education and research in the University, including the standard of the Degrees awarded".[11] This body was intended to remain in place until, on a motion of the Court and with the concurrence of the Council, the Lords of the Privy Council would decide a date by which the committee would be dissolved. As expected, the remaining members of the Academic Planning Board, with one or two additions, were appointed as members of this successor body.

The Academic Advisory Committee, chaired once again by Sir Noel Hall, continued to meet until 1970 and, although its later meetings were largely formal, there is no doubt that in the opening months of Lancaster's chartered existence the presence and the advice of its members were of quiet but substantial value to the institution and the founding Vice-Chancellor. The committee members had a personal stake in the success of the university they had done so much to establish, and were able to offer informed and sympathetic input on the whole gamut of academic-related issues, including those related to government funding.[12] Indeed, it was subsequently suggested by some members of the university that the committee might with

---

[8] Humble Petitition of the Executive Council for the Establishment of a University at Lancaster, Clauses 1 to 6 (UA.1/16/8/3).

[9] Statute 23, clauses (1) to (9) (UA.1/16/8/3).

[10] See UA.1/15/1/9.

[11] Charter, Clause 14(1) to (3), and Statutes 13, and 23(7)(a) and (b) (1964).

[12] Academic Advisory Committee papers, UA.1/15/8/3).

advantage have continued in existence long enough to have assisted the university when it faced external criticism during the period of student unrest in the mid-1970s, and when it faced the external financial pressures of the early 1980s.

Given the care with which the original Charter and Statutes were framed, the reader may feel some surprise at the volume of changes to Lancaster's governance structure that has taken place since 1964. In each case an understanding of the internal and external pressures for change is helpful. Thus, by early 1968 a Statute Revision Committee had been set up by the Senate, leading to changes that were finally approved by the Privy Council in May 1971, for backdated implementation to 23 March 1971.[13] Probably the most significant change at this stage related to the involvement of students in the governance of their universities, although an extension of membership of the university to include professional as well as academic staff was important to those affected.

The National Union of Students had initiated the debate about student representation in the mid-1960s, in part through a report that detailed the levels of representation that existed in certain universities throughout Europe, the rate of expansion in UK universities, and student representation at them up to 1966. The report presented arguments for the use of sabbatical student officers to be increased and for greater and more consistent student representation to be achieved:

> The National Union firmly believes that full student representation can make a vital and positive contribution to solving the problems created by expansion, to ensuring wider and fuller opportunities for all students in the future, and to gaining for students their rights and responsibilities both as members of their academic community and as members of society.[14]

Two years later a landmark joint statement, unimaginable just a decade earlier, was issued by the Committee of Vice-Chancellors and Principals and the NUS, covering areas of mutual interest from teaching methods to student discipline and written in the context of the legal age of majority being about to be lowered to 18. On student participation in university decision-making, the statement indicated that:

> We have no doubt that the machinery of student participation can and should be extended and improved. The means of doing this are likely to vary from one university to another. In those few cases where there is student membership of Council or even in effect of Senate, these will be watched with interest. The National Union of Students, itself, seeks student representation on these bodies ... Not as an alternative but to supplement this we would welcome the development of joint staff/student committees in new and more effective forms ... All such measures of student participation depend for their effectiveness on the

---

[13] The University of Lancaster, Charter and Revised Statutes (undated, but 1971) (UA.1/16/4/3).

[14] National Union of Students, *Student Participation in College Government* (London: NUS, 1966), p. 15.

willingness of students to take part ... They should, we believe, be student representatives in the real sense, understanding student needs and in sympathy with the aspirations of their fellow students ...[15]

At Lancaster, the ease of contact between staff and an initial student cohort of little more than 300 made consultation immediate and direct. Nevertheless, an informal Staff/Student Committee was put in place by Easter 1965, and formalised for the second academic year.[16] Chaired by the Vice-Chancellor in person, its remit was wide, ranging from defective roller towels at St Leonardsgate (five discussions) to student participation in a visit by the University Grants Committee (one). Students gradually made their way onto the obvious committees; Library, Bookshop, and Refectory, and college syndicates tentatively offered students first attendance and then membership. Students also took a full part in the colleges' disciplinary machinery, a practice that continues until today for incidents where the wrongdoer does not choose summary disposal. By June 1967, when the Staff/Student Committee laid itself down, students were being invited to attend both Council and Senate for items that were considered to be of special interest to them. Concurrently, student leaders were seeking a central student body for their own governance arrangements, in addition to the procedures for the running of junior common rooms within a federal structure.[17] While this issue of a single and central student body caused considerable controversy at the time, the Lancaster compromise described later in this chapter has proved durable and provides a satisfactory balance between student governance through the colleges, as intended by the Academic Planning Board, and the central union of the type found in many other universities.

Unsurprisingly, the Statute Revision Committee in early 1968 included a representative of the Student Representative Council,[18] and an explanatory memorandum by the committee to the Senate and the Council of September 1968 shows how far students at Lancaster were already pushing at an open door:

We believe that it is not in dispute that students should be informed and consulted about a wide range of subjects ... We do not, however, see this as a "right" ... but rather as a matter of common sense, likely to yield an understanding and cooperation which will improve the effectiveness of the University ...

---

[15] Committee of Vice-Chancellors and Principals and National Union of Students, *Joint Statement from the Committee of Vice-Chancellors and Principals and the National Union of Students* (London: NUS, 1968), pp. 3–4.

[16] Staff/Student Committee, minute book, March 1965 to June 1967 (UA.1/3/7/2).

[17] See Marion E. McClintock, *University of Lancaster: Quest for Innovation (a History of the First Ten Years, 1964–1974)* (Lancaster: University of Lancaster, 1974), pp. 357–66, on the development of a federal student union.

[18] Statute Revision Committee, Official Minute Book, 24 February 1968 to 22 December 1970 (UA.1/16/4/5): the Student Representative Council was a body that drew the Federation of Junior Common Rooms into an overarching governing body that subsequently evolved to become the current Students' Union.

It would be possible to inform and consult students through a system of consultative committees without decision-making power ... We think that the experience at Lancaster of the presence of students at Senate and Council, and their membership of many important committees, shows that there is an advantage in understanding and mutual trust to be obtained from first-hand contact, which would be hard to obtain through reporting links with a consultative body.[19]

Thereafter the debate was about how, rather than whether, students should become members of committees throughout the university. There were two models: first, that the Senate should continue as before, but should set up a board of itself on which students would sit and at which most business would be transacted; or, secondly, that students would be made full members of the Senate, except for items that were deemed to be reserved, mostly relating to the affairs of individuals, whether students or staff. Although the first model was used on an unofficial basis for a while,[20] it was the second that prevailed, and from 1971 onwards there has been a Senate and a Committee of the Senate, and a Council and a Committee of the Council, of which students are full members of the parent body. Student membership of the Court was also covered in the new statutes and, by the time that these were approved, the only bodies on which students did not sit were the Development Committee and committees dealing with individuals, such as staff promotions or student appeals.

However, a watchful external eye was being maintained. The Statute Revisions Committee was advised that revisions submitted to the Privy Council on 21 March 1969 were still held up in January 1970 because of "the receipt of a number of new Statutes governing student participation: the Privy Council does not want to approve one particular system without full consultation with the Government and the UGC."[21] Despite the Vice-Chancellor's expressed optimism that the delay was not expected to be long, reassurances from him were sought by the Privy Council in March to ensure that student participation would be genuinely representative of the student body, and that they would not participate in reserved business.[22] Even by the end of the calendar year, the Privy Council was reported as considering that ten students on the Senate would be "excessive", and the finally approved wording allowed for there to be "one student elected by and from the students of each college", as well as the President of the Student Representative Council.[23]

More than three decades later, the participation of students on governing bodies and their committees has become ubiquitous in the UK, although judging their impact on universities' policies and operations is more difficult. Michael Shattock, writing in 2006, was

---

[19] "Revision of Statutes: explanatory memorandum by the Statute Revision Committee", pp. 1–9 (G.68/334, September 1968) (UA.1/16/4/5).

[20] In subsequent chapters, some references to the short-lived Board of the Senate will be found.

[21] C. F. Carter to Statute Revision Committee, January 1970 (UA.1/16/4/5).

[22] C. F. Carter to Board of the Senate (VC/70/27, March 1970) (UA.1/16/4/5).

[23] Statute 11, Charter and Revised Statutes (1971): see also N. E. Leigh to A. S. Jeffreys, 18 December 1970 (UA.1/16/4/5).

rather dismissive of their influence and saw little evidence of active student engagement, even at a time when student fees were rising in quantity and political significance. For him, departmental staff/student liaison committees act as the main conduit for dialogue on academic matters.[24] His summation does not tally with experience at Lancaster, where student sabbatical officers share almost as many university bodies as do the university's senior managers. Their interventions are given significant weight; at times, it is whispered, even more than those of many staff. The Students' Union invests heavily in student representative training, and while students may not always attend the bodies of which they are members, or may come ill-prepared, such problems are not confined to their category of membership. At the major governing bodies, and on the working parties to develop policy that report to them, their impact is both plentiful and valued, and the anticipated effectiveness of their membership has been realised.

Other significant changes in the 1971 Revised Statutes included the definition of departments and the provision of *ex officio* seats at Senate for their heads, the extension of university membership to most categories of administrative staff, and the deletion of the transitional arrangements. These changes were not, however, sufficient to cope with new problems that faced the university. The long period of student dissent that originated at the University of California in 1964 and reached Paris in 1968 touched most British universities about the same time; at the London School of Economics, for example, in 1966–67.[25] Lancaster's principal period of student sit-ins and similar events occurred from 1971 onwards (see Chapter 4), and proved to be a particular challenge to a vice-chancellor and his staff who had believed in a liberal approach towards the management of institutional conduct. Such events also challenged the governance structures of the university, a consequence unintended by the perpetrators, for whom an occupation of the Senate Chamber was more a rite of passage than any serious attempt to undermine the university's management.[26] In 1972, however, following the so-called Craig Affair,[27] the Pro-Chancellor of the day commissioned Councillor Tom Taylor,[28] who had been involved in the early planning of the university, to hold an enquiry and present a report.[29] His findings, informally discussed by the Senate on 2 October 1972 and formally by the Council the next day, considered such matters as increased lay representation on major committees, including the Development

---

[24] Michael Shattock, *Managing Good Governance in Higher Education* (Maidenhead: Open University Press, 2006), pp. 79–80, 155.

[25] Ralf Dahrendorf, *LSE: A History of the London School of Economics and Political Science, 1895–1995* (Oxford: Oxford University Press, 1995), pp. 443–75.

[26] Lancaster alumni, now distinguished in their respective fields, often refer with nostalgic pleasure to their part in such events.

[27] See McClintock, *Quest*, pp. 393–4.

[28] Subsequently ennobled as Lord Taylor of Blackburn.

[29] University of Lancaster, "Report of the Taylor Enquiry, 18 May–5 July 1972", and the minutes of a special meeting of the Council convened by the Pro-Chancellor on Tuesday 3 October 1972 to discuss the Taylor Report and to determine action arising therefrom.

Committee, the appointment of a full-time deputy for the vice-chancellor, the creation of a post of information officer and an improvement of communication around the university, more precision about the roles of heads of departments and of principals of colleges, improvements in student facilities, the appointment of a student counsellor, the provision of a student social centre in the town, and the establishment of negotiating and consultative machinery with the trade unions. Some of his recommendations were accepted: a student counsellor was appointed, and the university's first Information Officer, Roger Grinyer, took up his post later in 1974 and initiated a fortnightly university newspaper, *Fulcrum*. Others, such as the students' social centre and a deputy vice-chancellor, came later. The issue of substance, however, was the report as a means by which the governing bodies of the university could be enabled to be effective in their management of the evolutionary and the non-standard. Because the machinery of governance is primarily reactive and dependent upon the material presented for consideration, important issues can become submerged. In this case, the Pro-Chancellor's action was timely in facing issues that needed thoughtful institutional consideration, whatever the consequential decisions that emerged.

No sooner was a line drawn under the Taylor Report, however, than the impending major reorganisation of local government led the University Secretary to begin a substantial body of work in preparation for the amendments relating to the composition of the university's governing bodies that were needed. These changes principally affected the membership of the Court, and to a lesser extent of the Council, and were wrapped into a statutory instrument that included the authorisation of the Lancaster amendments.[30]

Five years later yet another Statute Revision Committee was set up that, the Senate was later told,

> met eight times between June 1979 and March 1981. It considered the substantial number of detailed suggestions that were made in response to its invitation, and many of these have been incorporated in the revised Statutes now presented. It also considered, but was unanimous in rejecting, three different proposals for radical alteration of the governmental structure of the university.[31]

These proposals were, respectively: the introduction of a unicameral system – i.e. one body that would replace both Council and Senate; tricameralism, where Senate and Council were to be retained, although linked by a new planning body that would act as a bridge between them; or governance by elected persons.

The Vice-Chancellor took to the pages of *Fulcrum*[32] to argue the case for "a radical solution" for a "single governing body – remembering that the decisions about what to do

---

[30] Statutory Instrument 1974 No. 595, The Local Authorities etc. (Miscellaneous Provision) (No. 2) Order 1974, which was laid before Parliament on 29 March 1974 and came into operation on 1 April 1974, authorised amendments to Statutes 8 and 9 of the University of Lancaster.

[31] Document GM/81/196 (UA.1/16/4/5).

[32] *Fulcrum*, No. 32, November 1977, p. 2.

are not really distinct from the decisions about how to finance, house and staff it", and suggesting that the real reason for not going down such a road would be the "less reputable argument" that "we academics have got the essential powers in the university, and do not propose to share them". His proposals were not well received, and were seen as creating a single chamber, where

> The bursarial and general authority which a vice-chancellor and other senior officers now exercise by virtue of domination of the Council would be extended to academic matters by virtue of the continuing support that the laymen would bring to them. Far from making a university responsive to outside pressures, the single chamber would help to abolish scrutiny and refining criticism where academic proposals were considered.[33]

The University Secretary made a special journey to the University of Toronto to discover at first hand how unicameralism worked there, but members of the Statute Revision Committee were firm in their view that a subsequent report

> made it clear that whilst Toronto clearly did not want to make another change, nevertheless the experiment had been something of a disaster and had involved the university in a bureaucratic morass with members of the academic staff left with a definite sense of grievance and frustration … Since this meant it was now impossible to point to any university where unicameralism had proved a success, the committee, after considerable discussion, and not unanimously, agreed that it would be difficult to advocate it.[34]

At their request, the Vice-Chancellor and the University Secretary were asked to examine tricameralism, but the paper that came back, entitled "Three in One and One in Three"[35] and suggesting an academic council, a business council, and a policy council, was found to be impossibly complex.[36] A compromise body, initially named the Senate Planning and Resources Committee (SPARC), and subsequently simply PARC, that straddled the membership and the concerns of both the Council and the Senate, also survived only a short time before that approach was decisively abandoned.[37]

The third and last proposal to be rejected by the governing bodies of the university declared that:

> In our view the government of the University should be in the hands of elected persons … We believe that too many powers have been concentrated in the hands of one officer

---

[33] *Fulcrum*, No. 34, January 1978, p. 7.

[34] Document SU/73/4 of 27 February 1978 (UA.1/16/4/5).

[35] C. F. Carter and A. S. Jeffreys, 16 March 1978 (UA.1/16/4/5).

[36] *Fulcrum*, No. 37, April 1978, p. 2: the opposition of the incoming acting vice-chancellor (*Fulcrum*, No. 38, May 1978, p. 1) was also highly influential.

[37] Senate Planning and Resources Committee, and Planning and Resources Committee, 1989–93 (UA.1/16/4/5): see Chapter 2.

– the Vice-Chancellor – notably the chairmanship of Senate and of major committees. Our proposals aim at limiting the powers of the office of Vice-Chancellor. We also believe that heads of departments and the professoriat still have excessive powers ... We believe that the university should be accountable to the local community [and] Our proposals give special weight to the Court ...[38]

Its proponents asked that there should be proportionate representation on the governing bodies of the university for "teaching, administrative, research and assistant staff; postgraduate students; undergraduates", and opposed the continuation of the offices of Chancellor, Pro-Chancellor and Deputy Pro-Chancellors. While other, more minor changes were agreed and implemented during this round of governance debate, the episode is interesting in revealing at a single moment the complete gamut of views at a university like Lancaster, from rarefied central control to management by its membership acting together by consensus. It was also perhaps the final period, unbeknown to its members, during which the university was fully able to determine for itself how it wished to be run.

That a preoccupation with the conduct of the strategic planning process as a fundamental element of governance had not been misplaced was demonstrated when the Jarratt report[39] was issued to the universities by the CVCP, initiating a process designed to inquire into the efficiency and effectiveness of universities, including their decision-making processes and review of resources.[40] There was heightened talk of internal, external and operational performance indicators, and administrators learned, to the pleasure of some and the horror of others, to think of themselves as managers. The Department of Education and Science warmly supported these changes of approach, and Lancaster in common with the rest of the sector became engaged in discussions designed to bring the university into line with the Jarratt recommendations (see Chapter 2). Changes were to be implemented despite the warning of two of its staff, expert in the area, who cautioned that: "No one has yet devised even a *single* indicator of performance which commands wide support amongst the academic community", and suggested they should be used with "great caution and considerable humility".[41] Paradoxically, the Council was increased in size as a result of the Jarratt implementation, from 31 to 42 members, in order to accommodate additional lay representation, members of assistant staff and, building on earlier discussions, two registered graduates of the university.[42]

---

[38] L. Beier and C. Otley (September 1979) were lecturers in the departments of History and Sociology respectively, and both members of ASTMS (UA.1/16/4/5).

[39] Steering Committee for Efficiency Studies in Universities, *National Data Study [the Jarratt Report]* (London: Committee of Vice-Chancellors and Principals, 1985).

[40] See Jill Johnes and Jim Taylor, *Performance Indicators in Higher Education: UK Universities* (Buckingham: Society for Research into Higher Education and Open University Press, 1990), pp. 4–12.

[41] Johnes and Taylor, *Performance Indicators*, p. 185.

[42] "Special Resolution to Amend the Statutes", minute CO.87/7, Council meeting on 6 March 1987.

Another external intervention, leading to a limited but significant change to the Statutes, arose from the implementation of the Education Reform Act (1988). There had been concern in government circles, as the higher education sector was progressively enlarged and becoming a more visible and proportionately more costly part of the national economy, about the apparent inflexibility of academic tenure. Tenure was the system by which no officer of the university could be removed from office save for good cause: conviction of a criminal offence, mental or physical incapacity, conduct that was of an immoral, scandalous or disgraceful nature, or a failure to perform the duties of the post.[43] The cuts imposed by the Thatcher government in 1981 had brought this issue to the fore, and the remedy in the Act was to set up a temporary body of University Commissioners. They were to ensure that, while academic staff had freedom within the law to question and test received wisdom without loss of jobs or privileges, they could in future also be dismissed by reason of redundancy, subject to suitable procedures.[44]

The prospect of such changes stirred up strong passions in a profession where tenure of office was regarded as precious for its own sake and as compensation for what were perceived to be relatively low material rewards for service. Six Commissioners, headed by Sir John May, QC, began the work in 1989 of drafting a model statute that could be inserted into the statutes of all the qualifying institutions. It was intended to become effective for all contracts entered into on or after 20 November 1987, and for all contracts involving a promotion on or after that date, so that new entrants would not receive tenure, and the number retaining it would progressively dwindle. The CVCP took the lead in coordinating institutions' responses, and some of the finest academic legal minds in the sector were brought to bear on the detailed wording of the model statute. Lancaster, whose University Secretary, George Cockburn, served for a period on the CVCP working group, in turn set up its own working party.

The Commissioners' proposals, when published in September 1990, were found to be detailed both in enablement and in the establishment of disciplinary, appellate, and grievance procedures, including for the first time explicitly making recommendations about the post of Vice-Chancellor. In response to pressure from certain contributing institutions, however, and contrary to views put forward by Lancaster, staff on fixed-term contracts would not qualify for protection under the procedures. Lancaster had sought to reach agreement on a more succinct statement of general principles, and a report to the Council led to a motion being passed that regretted that the "briefest possible enabling and requiring Statute" had not been permitted,[45] while giving approval to the Commissioners' proposals except in matters of fine detail. It was March 1991 before the Commissioners were able to let vice-chancellors have the final model statute, and further time elapsed before it was incorporated into each university's statutes, leading in Lancaster's case to Statute 20, Academic Staff.[46]

---

[43] Statute 19(5), University of Lancaster, 1964: a form of words that was similar to many other universities.

[44] Education Reform Act 1988, Schedule 11, sections 202–8.

[45] Minute CO.90/100, Council meeting on 30 November 1990.

[46] University of Lancaster *Calendar*, 2006–07, pp. 29–41.

While there was a lull in the rate of statutory change at Lancaster in the 1990s, across the sector the style and forms of governance were changing at a rapid pace. "We cannot say conclusively that standards of behaviour in public life have declined", began the solemn prologue by Lord Nolan to his two reports on standards in public life, following the Eighth Report of the Committee of Public Accounts on the proper conduct of public business,[47] but "We can say that conduct in public life is more rigorously scrutinised than it was in the past … [and] there are weaknesses in the procedures for maintaining and enforcing those standards. As a result people in public life are not always as clear as they should be about where the boundaries of acceptable conduct lie. This we regard as the principal reason for public disquiet. It calls for urgent remedial action."[48] There had been a breakdown in governance at University College Cardiff in 1986–87,[49] and other institutions around this period faced a range of problems with implications for governance: Derby College, Wilmerton, reported in November 1994,[50] the University of Portsmouth (1997),[51] and Glasgow Caledonian University (1998).[52] From 1992 the Financial Memorandum, designed to manage the financial relationship between the Higher Education Funding Council for England and each institution that received HM Treasury funds, became progressively more prescriptive. Vice-chancellors were named as designated officers, accountable to their governing bodies for ensuring that the conditions of the Memorandum were met and answerable to the Chief Executive of the HEFCE for any actions incompatible with it.

Hard on the heels of these events, the Committee of University Chairmen (CUC), under the chairmanship of the Earl of Limerick and with Michael Shattock as secretary, published a guide for members of governing bodies, with a first edition in June 1995. By 2004 the document had almost tripled in length, and a comparison of different editions reveals that over the intervening nine years the guide had hardened from a set of fairly generalised precepts into "a voluntary [sic] code of practice to which, it is hoped, all institutions will be able to subscribe".[53] Lancaster's principal institutional focus in the mid-1990s was managing a severe cash flow problem (see Chapter 6), but by 1998 pressure from the CUC, coupled with the volume of internally identified issues, had grown to a level at which further

---

47 Committee of Public Accounts, *The Proper Conduct of Public Business: Eighth Report*, 1993–94 Hc154 (London: HMSO, 1994).

48 Committee on Standards in Public Life, *Standards in Public Life [the Nolan Report]*, vol. 1: report, Cm. 2850-I (London: HMSO, 1995), Summary, para. 2.

49 Brian Smith and Vanessa Cunningham, "Crisis at Cardiff," in *Managing Crisis*, ed. David Warner and David Palfreyman (Maidenhead: Open University Press, 2003), pp. 8–31.

50 Michael Shattock, *Derby College, Wilmerton: Report of an Enquiry into the Governance and Management of the College* (London: Further Education Funding Council, 1994).

51 National Audit Office, *University of Portsmouth: Report by the Comptroller and Auditor General*, 1997–98 HC 4 (London: Stationery Office, 1997).

52 National Audit Office, *Investigation of Misconduct at Glasgow Caledonian University: Report by the Comptroller and Auditor General*, 1997–98 HC 680 (London: Stationery Office, 1998).

53 The CUC Guide has been through four editions: June 1995, March 1998, April 2001, and November 2004. The final edition was in five parts, with a separate summary of Parts I and II.

changes were unavoidable. Moreover, the pro-chancellor in post at Lancaster from 1997 to 2003 was Mr Brian Heron, already a member of CUC and chairman of its working group on the second edition of the *CUC Guide*, who was well tuned into the direction in which university governance was moving.

A Statute revision working party, with members from both Senate and Council on it, was convened in 1998. More than four years were to elapse, however, before changes were agreed, approved, and implemented. Many of them were matters of detail, while other areas not significantly changed were the Charter, Statute 20 (the Commissioners' Statute) or the provisions relating to the Court. Considerable debate took place about extending the membership of the university to all staff, for

> While it was argued by some that membership was primarily symbolic, those who did not hold this view (and others in their support) argued strongly to the contrary. There was then considerable discussion about what effect the extension of membership might have on employment rights ...[54]

Much more substantial change took place in the membership of the Council, to ensure a lay majority and, in line with Recommendation 57 of the Dearing Report,[55] to have no more than 25 members, rather than the 42 reached in 1990. Many hours of debate resulted in a compromise of 32, with pro-vice-chancellors to be in attendance rather than as members, the deletion of representation from the two county councils of Lancashire and Cumbria, and reductions of other categories rather than their removal. The relationship between the Council and the Senate was rebalanced, with more emphasis being placed on prior discussion by the Senate of decisions that might have a substantial effect upon the academic life of the university or the welfare of its students. Such discussion was to include policy relating to the financial transactions into which the university might enter, its major building developments, and the terms and conditions of service of academic and academic-related staff. On the other hand, the Senate would no longer be able to act unilaterally on the creation (or the laying down) of colleges, departments or faculties, but would have to make a recommendation to the Council in each case.

The change with perhaps the most far-reaching effects, while apparently merely an alteration of nomenclature, was the stages between 1987 and 2005 in the movement from boards of studies to faculties. In 1963 the Academic Planning Board had seen boards of studies as entities in which teachers in different subjects would be grouped as the balancing of subjects for teaching or examinations required, and it consciously decided against the setting up "of orthodox Faculties with the tendency to rigidity which had been associated

---

[54] Text for consultation with the Privy Council Office, 8 January 2001 (with a commentary by Professor Peter Rowe) (UA.1/16/4/7).

[55] National Committee of Inquiry into Higher Education, *Higher Education in the Learning Society: Main Report [the Dearing Report]* (London: HMSO, 1997).

with them in the past".[56] Since it was expected that the boards would emerge from clusters of ideas, it was thought twenty or more might be set up, with non-professorial chairmen who would sit on the Senate (at a time when professors were members of the Senate *ex officio*), and with academic staff being able to sit on at least two boards each.

When it was proposed in 1970 that departments should be represented on the Senate, Charles Carter drew attention to what he saw as "an already excessive tendency to departmentalism. The Boards of Studies have not proved to be strong organs of government; and it may be that we should at least leave ourselves free to move towards a School system ... (A small start has been made already, with Business Studies.)"[57] A caricature of the boards, but one unfortunately not too far removed from the reality of staff views, was the description of the

> Boards of Study, organs representing the departments in the university. They were officially known as Board X, Board Y and Board Z and unofficially known as Bored Sick, Bored Rigid and Bored Daft. The Daft Board, Board Z, represented those subjects commonly described as the Inuitile Sciences or the Humanities. Your humble chronicler ... once went to a meeting of Board Z and found the experience so overwhelming, he was never tempted to go again.[58]

The reference by the Vice-Chancellor to business studies was significant, however, since it was there that the first moves towards a faculty-based structure emerged. Lancaster had been unusual amongst the plateglass universities in setting up business-based studies from the outset: Operational Research, and Economics (1964); Marketing, and Systems Engineering (1965); Financial Control (1968); and Behaviour in Organisations (1969). These departments tended to cluster together, and in 1974 a separate building, originally called Gillow House, brought them together under a single roof, and away from the salad bowl of mixed collegiate and departmental accommodation for all other non-science subjects. At the same time the name of a School of Management and Organisational Studies served to mark its distinctive identity, and while the existing Board of Studies F continued to be responsible for the validation of business-related subject areas, the usage of a School name became increasingly prevalent across the university to denote other activities and to create entities that gradually assumed partial responsibility for staffing and budgeting.

Winston Kwon, in a thesis on corporate reputation management that drew on the experiences of Lancaster's Management School for his case study,[59] has demonstrated the powerful external pressures being exerted in the late 1980s on business schools to

---

[56] McClintock, *Quest*, pp. 101–6.
[57] C. F. Carter, "Statute Revision Committee" (January 1970, GM/70/1), (UA.1/16/4/5).
[58] Olaf B. Dossier, "The Case of the Fossilized Board", *Lancaster Comment*, No. 39, 28 February 1974, pp. 6–8.
[59] Winston Kwon, "Reputational Objects: A Critical Re-Evaluation of Corporate Brand Management" (PhD thesis, Lancaster University, 2006), Chapters 4–7.

join the professional groupings for such schools that were springing up at the time. The vice-chancellor of the day, Harry Hanham, had identified the School as a key element in his plans to transform Lancaster into a world-class institution, and to have its strengths appropriately recognised nationally and internationally. His first step was to appoint a dean rather than a chairman, and the appointee, David Ashton, did not disappoint him. The School

> gradually became an intermediate administrative structure between the departments and the centre, and was given further autonomy over budget allocation and staffing decisions. This allowed the LUMS administration to effectively 'top-slice' from the departmental budgets in order to resource school or 'cross-departmental' programmes and activities. … Ashton's first initiatives were to make LUMS more like its competitors through the creation of: a) the Management Development Division: a vehicle to create and deliver bespoke executive education programmes for corporate clients; b) an MBA programme; c) the Dean's Advisory Board: a panel of senior industry figures … and d) the scaling back of departmental consultancy activities in order to free up resources for a shift in organisational emphasis on research.[60]

The School was also the first area of the university to take the initiative of presenting a separate constitution for approval by the Senate.[61] Other parts of the university followed – the social sciences first, and the sciences and the arts and humanities not long afterwards – and, while the Statutes retained the term 'board of study', the language used internally was increasingly of faculty boards, of which there came to be seven. Revised statutes of 2002 recognised this evolution, and the proposal made was that the term 'faculties' be used thereafter. At first the new structures had combined elements of the former boards of studies with the characteristics of intermediate administrative structure that were already in place in the Management School, the precedent that all the faculties have increasingly come to follow, but increasingly the relationship between the centre and the departments has become less horizontal and more vertical. While departments have retained membership of the Senate for their heads, the inclusion from 2005 of the deans on the University Management Advisory Group[62] inevitably led to a distancing between the chief officers of the faculties and the departments for which they increasingly take responsibility.[63]

Another significant shift that occurred late in the process of statute change was the use

---

[60] Kwon, "Reputational Objects: A Critical Re-Evaluation of Corporate Brand Management", pp. 109–10.

[61] Minute S.87/99, Senate meeting on 3 June 1987.

[62] The main function of UMAG, which includes the pro-vice-chancellors, four faculty deans and certain senior administrative managers, is to advise the vice-chancellor of the day on policy formulation and implementation.

[63] A striking feature of the first three decades or so of the university is the existence of correspondence files, in which the vice-chancellor of the day took an informed and direct role in advising and guiding the heads of departments, a role now taken by the faculty deans.

for the first time at Lancaster of ordinances. The founders of the university had advised against their inclusion, and in 1968 Charles Carter had suggested that, in the statutes, "the chance uses of this word may as well be eliminated".[64] The first group of ordinances in 2002 were principally about technical matters, including the procedures for student appeals or complaints and disclosures.

A review of the effectiveness of the Council in 2005 reopened the debate about the size and composition of its membership, and the reduction eventually made was to 22, including the removal *per se* of the representation of Lancaster's graduates and the removal of members elected by the Court. Feelings ran so high that a special meeting of the Court was held in October 2005, at which the ability of a deputy pro-chancellor to take the chair of Court at the invitation of the chancellor was confirmed. The right of external bodies to appoint members to the Council was also removed, with the exception of Lancaster City Council. The Senate was reviewed in 2006–07, when concern was expressed about the extent of removal of an increasing proportion of statute material to ordinances.[65] A letter from the Department for Education and Skills the previous year had made it clear, however, that there would be strong encouragement, supported by AHUA (the Association of Heads of University Administration), for some deregulation of the governance arrangements of higher education institutions that would include such matters as the powers, make up and meetings of Senates and Courts,[66] although the Senate was reassured that any changes to ordinances would be specifically earmarked for discussion. Finally, a review of the Court was carried out in which the membership was rationalised and all but an overarching definition of these categories was placed in an ordinance. The consultative nature of the Court's annual meeting was retained, however, as was a modest role through the Nominations Committee in the appointment of senior lay members of the Council. Lancaster's moves were in line with other institutions' changes to their governing bodies. Indeed, once Cambridge had voted through a lay majority on its council in 2008,[67] only Oxford was left with a minority of outside members and was coming under increasing pressure to conform with the rest of the sector.[68]

At the same time as the moves to restructure the governing bodies were taking place there were parallel discussions about changes to the terms and conditions of the staff of universities, and particularly to devise a set of procedures that would apply equally to all

---

[64] Document GT/68/334, 25 September 1968 (UA.1/16/4/5).

[65] Minute S.2007/29, Senate meeting on 23 May 2007.

[66] Letter from Bill Rammell, MP, Minister of State for Lifelong Learning, Further and Higher Education, to Vice-Chancellors, 6 February 2006.

[67] "Academics Lose Majority on Cambridge Council," *Times Higher Education* No. 1837, 20–26 March 2008, p. 7.

[68] For eight questions posed by the HEFCE to Oxford's Audit and Scrutiny Committee, "to explain to us how [Oxford's] corporate governance arrangements meet requirements for effectiveness and scrutiny given the very limited involvement of external individuals in its corporate governance", see *Cambridge University Reporter*, No. 6086, 17 October 2007, pp. 87–8.

categories of staff, whether junior or senior, fixed-term or continuing, full-time or part-time, academic or other. A process that began in 2004–06 by putting everyone on a single pay spine and discarding the different pay scales for different functional groups, laid the way open to conversations about common codes for dismissal, grievances, redeployment or capability. They in turn created pressure for a repeal of the Commissioners' Statute, or to change its status "to a lower level of regulatory importance",[69] a move noted to be strongly supported by AHUA. The discussions at Lancaster were protracted, continuing from 2006 to 2009, and there was also some division of opinion between the unions recognised by the institution, with UCU nationally[70] and locally pressing strongly for earlier qualitative distinctions to be retained. Proposals for the establishment of a standing Redundancy Committee were equally strongly resisted. In late 2009, however, the Council approved the replacement of Statute 20 with a single clause about upholding academic freedom, and a Redundancy Committee was set up that approved cases across the board of both fixed-term and continuing staff.

As at the time of the Nolan reports, misdemeanours at one institution have repercussions across the sector. A key example was the consequences that flowed from problems at London Metropolitan University[71] in 2009–10 that began with concerns about apparent inflation of student number calculations and escalated into the resignation of the vice-chancellor and of the chairman and lay members of the university's board of governors. A direct consequence of these events was a fresh reworking of the model Financial Memorandum between the HEFCE and English universities,[72] including a change of appellation from designated officer – normally the vice-chancellor of an institution – to accountable officer with effect from August 2010. In addition, heavier emphasis was laid on risk and its management, on actions that could be taken in relation to a university perceived to be failing, and on academic standards as part of an institutional framework in which the HEFCE would take a direct interest. Despite widespread protests across the sector, particularly about the latter addition, the agreed rewording remained controversial and there were lingering concerns about the terms on which the HEFCE could intervene in the business of a university.[73]

Another significant and externally provoked change, this time by the Charity Commission,

---

[69] Dennis Farrington, "[Letter]", *Times Higher Education*, No. 1965, 16–22 September 2010, p. 33.

[70] See, for example, Tony Tysome, "Stealth Attack on Employment Rights", *UCU Magazine*, January 2008, pp. 24–5.

[71] See the extended article by Melanie Newman, "Fallout Assessment", *Times Higher Education*, No. 1943, 15–22 April 2010, pp. 30–5. It sets out the successive steps of the London Metropolitan difficulties.

[72] Higher Education Funding Council for England, "Model Financial Memorandum between HEFCE and Institutions: Terms and Conditions for Payment of HEFCE Grants to Higher Education Institutions", 2010/19 (Bristol: HEFCE, 2010), http://www.hefce.ac.uk/pubs/hefce/2010/10_19/.

[73] Simon Baker, "Threat to Autonomy Remains Despite Revision, Expert Says", *Times Higher Education*, No. 1985, 29 July–4 August 2010.

was the move for the Students' Union to become a separate student-led educational charity. The changes, completed late in 2010, meant that while still part of the university and subject to the provisions of the Charter and Statutes, LUSU now has a small trustee board consisting of elected student officers and members, as well as four external trustees who were to oversee the administration, governance, and legal compliance of the union, and to receive reports from the chief executive (previously known as the general manager).[74] There are six full-time sabbatical officers and the governing body is the Union Council, on which students are represented through their junior common rooms. There is also an Academic Council that considers academic policies that affect students and student representatives sit on most major bodies of the university at central and faculty level. The views of students at large are obtained either by means of a General Meeting or by Union referenda of all student members. Participation in officer elections, at about 15% of those eligible to vote, is high relative to many other institutions, and e-voting was introduced for the first time in November 2010, a process not without its flaws but one that appears likely to increase voting turnout when it becomes tried and tested.

The university's governance has therefore undergone major shifts in its first half century, some of them to accommodate growth in numbers, some in response to external pressures, and some relating to a cultural shift that takes as a starting point a less participatory and more managed institution. The propensity to propose radical change across the sector, moreover, is not confined to the HEFCE, as the Browne review of 2010 revealed. While ostensibly about student funding and undergraduate tuition fees, uncertainty was increased by the unanticipated inclusion of summary proposals for the replacement of the HEFCE, the QAA, OFFA, and the Office of the Independent Adjudicator (OIA) by a single body, a Higher Education Council.[75] Once again the prospect of direct intervention in teaching quality by central government, at present managed through the QAA, an entity set up by the sector itself, had been raised. Given all these pressures, the ability of the university to determine the structures best suited to its particular circumstances is constrained. The faculties will take time to reach their full potential and the quality of their interaction with the central bodies and officers, in both directions, will be key to whether in the long term they are found fit for purpose. Continual efforts will be necessary to refine the decision-making processes and, while schedules of delegation are an important feature of this process, the tying of the whole structure together, including the colleges, so that information is appropriately channelled and shared and the direction of travel of the institution can be understood by all its members, will remain a continuing challenge.

---

[74] Lancaster University Students' Union, Annual Report and Financial Statements for the year ended 31 July 2010.

[75] "Securing a Sustainable Future for Higher Education: An Independent Review of Higher Education Funding and Student Finance [the Browne Report]" (2010). http://www.bis.gov.uk/assets/biscore/corporate/docs/s/10−1208-securing-sustainable-higher-education-browne-report.pdf, Chapter 6.1.

CHAPTER TWO
Strategic planning

S TRATEGIC PLANNING for universities is concerned with the analysis and evaluation of the current situation and the shaping of the future, in the context of the objectives of the institution and the constraints within which it works. This chapter will trace the strategic direction of Lancaster from 1962 onwards, including the locus of such activity and the means by which strategic intention translates into active policy and is monitored.

The reader might assume that strong planning is universal amongst universities. One attempt at a global review of tertiary educational planning, however, concluded that: "Many countries in the world do not have any kind of planning at all",[1] and included case studies to support that perhaps rather startling assertion. In the UK, however, the process, albeit by a variety of names, has been widely accepted for at least the last half century. Moreover, at the time when Lancaster and its contemporary institutions were being established, there was particular interest in the growth of tertiary education and attempts made to articulate the values that should be expected to appear as active ingredients of institutions designated as universities. Strategic thinking was seen as a key element of this process of evaluation and bedding down of the enlarging sector. The new University of Sussex, in particular,

---

[1] Victor G. Onushkin, ed. *Planning the Development of Universities*, vol. III (Paris: Unesco, 1974), p. 15. Earlier volumes had been published in 1971 and 1973 respectively.

was treated as an example of particular interest for contemporaneous study.[2] This broader national context of strategic planning will be referred to from time to time in what follows.

Lancaster, as already discussed, was the seventh and last of the new greenfield, plateglass universities to be announced, and Sussex had already opened its doors to its first students by the time that Lancaster's planning processes began, thus providing some precedents for Lancaster to adopt if appropriate. Alongside the Executive Council for the Establishment of a University at Lancaster, to deal with financial, staffing and estates issues, the academic planning process was to be undertaken by an Academic Planning Board. As the seventh such body, the procedures for its establishment had become more streamlined, and early in 1962 the University Grants Committee had secured as the board's chairman Sir Noel Hall, principal of Brasenose College, Oxford, and a former member of the equivalent body for the University of Kent. Of the seven members of the board, four had received their first degrees from Oxford, two from Cambridge, and one from the University of Sydney; and their current places of employment were Oxford (two), St Andrews, Liverpool, Manchester and Leeds (one each), while the seventh was at a national research station at Slough. These backgrounds were similar to those for the matching bodies at the other new universities:

---

[2]   For example, Hycel C. Jones, G. Lockwood, and Norman MacKenzie, " The University of Sussex", in *Planning the Development of Universities*, ed. Victor G. Onushkin (Paris: Unesco, 1971); David Daiches, *The Idea of a New University: An Experiment in Sussex* (London: A. Deutsch, 1964).

mainstream, strongly Oxbridge or large civic university, and UK-based. These were the people who, in the abstract and on behalf of all those subsequently employed at or students of the university, laid down its fundamental blueprint.[3]

The terms of reference of this body, and their ordering, are instructive.[4] First, they were to consider "the arrangements by which Universities may be assured of the maintenance of satisfactory academic standards at the University, on the assumption that it will award its own first and higher degrees". Thus, the board was to act as guarantor to the rest of the university system that the new university would match their standards. Secondly, they were to consider the range of subjects to be studied, thirdly to Petition for a Royal Charter and select the members of the first governing body, and fourthly to select and nominate the first vice-chancellor and the professors of the principal subjects.

Discussions of the assurance of academic standards and of governance are to be found in Chapter 3 and in Chapter 1 respectively. It is the selection of subjects and the initial staff appointments, the second and fourth of the board's tasks, that are of particular relevance to shaping the future of an institution, and it is instructive to compare the debate at Lancaster with those taking place at other new institutions of the time. Keele's foundation year, designed to give students the opportunity to broaden their intellectual range during their first year at university, had been widely applauded. This precedent was followed nowhere else, however, principally because it required a four-year first degree at an English university (Scottish universities require four years of study to reach honours level: only Keele was different). Lancaster's contemporaries all opted for admission to honours degrees, rather than to the honours and pass degree streams that had been deployed at preceding generations of institutions, such as Durham, Sheffield, Leicester, and London. Over time this led to the atrophy of previously widespread general degrees, which by the end of the twentieth century had essentially disappeared. Sussex and Lancaster made the most effort towards "crossing the Snow line",[5] forcing students in the sciences to study an arts subject and *vice versa*, but in both places the system was progressively eroded in use and later dropped. Similarly, the design of the first year at the new institutions was intended to give students broader access to subjects that were either unfamiliar to them or not taught at schools, and to offer breadth as well as depth in the major subject. Again, this initiative was gradually eroded. The stated objectives of the governance structures that supported these aims were initially not about faculties, but rather about schools or boards of studies, although Lancaster later adopted faculties and gave them increasing autonomy. All the staff involved in the seven new universities had a sense that they were, as Harold Perkin suggested, re-drawing the map of learning; and all aspired to greater interdisciplinarity

---

[3] McClintock, *Quest*, pp. 23–4.

[4] McClintock, *Quest*, pp. 21–2.

[5] C. P. Snow was both a scientist and a novelist. In his 1959 Rede Lecture, *The Two Cultures and the Scientific Revolution* (Cambridge, 1959), he propounded the thesis that the breakdown of communication between the sciences and the humanities was a major hindrance to solving the world's problems.

and to the refreshment of narrowly defined subject disciplines through contact with other academic specialisms.[6] In this context Lancaster's initial structures fitted well with those of its contemporaries: a three-subject Part I in the first year, with plenty of scope for students to switch their major subject as they moved to Part II; a compulsory breadth subject; an emphasis on interdisciplinary and joint degrees; and a set of boards of studies as linking mechanisms for subjects to make new connections with each other.

Perkin's 1968 volume also contained an interim analysis of subject choice in the seven new universities, together with Keele, Stirling, and Ulster, and Lancaster's direction is again consonant with the others: arts, social sciences, and pure sciences; a relative absence of professional subjects (medicine, law, architecture); and some technological subjects developing out of the pure sciences. He noted that the new universities had been discouraged from embarking on the so-called Hayter[7] subjects, including East European and Slavonic languages, while noting that Russian was widely available. As a consequence, the Comenius Centre at Lancaster for East European languages was required to be resourced entirely from appeal funds, while Arabic and Islamic Studies was to rely on generous donations from external sponsors.[8] While Perkin alluded to the significance of operational research and systems engineering at Lancaster, he did not identify a particular business or management emphasis for the institution, although with hindsight that particular priority is evident from the outset. In looking for distinctiveness at the new universities, he finds the government-sponsored data bank at Essex, set up to collect data from social surveys, as the only example of a new university holding a monopoly. He concluded his analysis with references to studies by the universities of themselves: in Lancaster's case, two research fellows were appointed to examine the methods of university teaching and examining respectively. It is clear from his account that the important distinctiveness of the new universities, from each other and from the rest of the sector, was likely, initially, to be mainly at the margins.

The other key function of the Academic Planning Board – the appointment of the first vice-chancellor and founding professors – brought Charles Carter to Lancaster.[9] The board's original choice had been J. B. Butterworth, who instead went to Warwick:[10] Mr Carter, already known to Sir Noel Hall as a fellow member of the Academic Planning Board for the University of Kent,[11] made an excellent impression on members of the panel that he

---

[6] H. J. Perkin, *New Universities in the United Kingdom*, Case Studies on Innovation in Higher Education (Paris: O.E.C.D 1969), "New maps of learning", pp. 115–32.

[7] Sir W. G. Hayter, HM Diplomatic Services and Warden of New College, Oxford, chaired a UGC sub-committee (1959–61) on Oriental, African, Slavonic, and East European Studies which recommended the creation of nominated centres of study for particular areas overseas.

[8] Perkin, Part II, Chapter 4, pp. 133 ff.

[9] Carter, Sir Charles Frederick (1919–2002) (Oxford, Oxford Dictionary of National Biography).

[10] Butterworth, John Blackstock (Jack), Baron Butterworth (1918–2003) (Oxford, *Oxford Dictionary of National Biography*).

[11] Graham Martin, *From Vision to Reality: The Making of the University of Kent at Canterbury* (Canterbury: University of Kent at Canterbury, 1990), p. 22.

met in December 1962, and an invitation to become the first vice-chancellor followed immediately. He took up his post in April 1963, and all subsequent senior appointments were made with him at the helm: the first university secretary (A. S. Jeffreys), the building development officer (D. B. Smith), the finance officer (R. S. Boumphrey), and the librarian (A. G. MacKenzie) were all in post by the end of the 1963 calendar year, together with the founding professors of economics (S. G. Sturmey) and operational research (B. H. P. Rivett). Ten further professorial appointments were made by the beginning of the first academic year, in biological sciences, chemistry, English, environmental studies, French studies, history, mathematics, philosophy, physics, and politics. It was these men,[12] and a smaller group of more junior staff, who were in post at the time that the first students were admitted and the Charter and Statutes bestowed in the early autumn of 1964.

Of course, the work of the Academic Planning Board was in practice very broad, and it is to their recommendations that we owe Lancaster's colleges, the interpretation for Lancaster of the Privy Council's model charter and statutes, and the academic course structure, with its emphasis on experimentation in the teaching of science and strength in the social sciences. At the same time there was extensive interaction between the Board and the Executive Council for the Establishment of a University at Lancaster. The expectation at this early stage was that business and management subjects would be provided for research and graduate level study[13] – an important marker for the future – and that there would be clusters of subjects: science with mathematics, operational research, economics, and philosophy; history with politics, philosophy, and principles of science; history with language and literature, and principles of science; classics with philosophy and principles of science; economics with politics, philosophy, and principles of science; and economics with mathematics, operational research, science, and principles of science. In this brief list it is already possible to see the many permutations of subjects that became a special characteristic of Lancaster's curriculum.[14]

The University Grants Committee accepted the proposals of the APB; and, against the national background sketched out above, their agreement seems inevitable. The new professors, and their first colleagues, came in their turn to Lancaster and began to develop

---

[12] All the initial administrative and academic posts were filled by men, with the exception of one assistant lecturer (Miss Ada Phillips) in Environmental Studies. The Vice-Chancellor was at pains in February 1965 to reassure colleagues that this scarcity was being addressed by the impending appointment of a further three women (*Staff Newsletter*, No. 4, February 1965, UA.1/9/3/6).

[13] McClintock, *Quest*, p. 135. See also Chapter 3(iii), Selection of subjects (pp. 128–37), for a more detailed account of the APB's evolving ideas, and further comparisons with Lancaster's contemporary institutions.

[14] "Interim Report of the Academic Planning Board to the Chairman of the University Grants Committee", paras. 21, 24 (University of Lancaster, March 1963, UA.1/15/1/3).

their own understandings of the subjects agreed in broad terms on their behalf.[15] The APB then switched its focus to concentrate on achieving the completion of the governance arrangements by the time the first students were due to arrive, their efforts being rewarded with success just a fortnight before the beginning of the 1964 Michaelmas Term. Meanwhile, the Executive Council was negotiating with the UGC on finance, launching an appeal for funds from private donors, appointing the professionals needed to undertake the physical development of the Bailrigg site, and ensuring that temporary accommodation would be ready by October 1964. All these actions had considerable strategic impact on the university, but at the time they were treated primarily as operational issues.

The first meeting of a Shadow Senate took place at Bailrigg House on Saturday and Sunday, 11 and 12 January 1964, with the Vice-Chancellor in the chair and ten members-to-be present (including some professors already appointed but not yet in post) and, in attendance, two senior lecturers and a research fellow in university teaching methods. A telegram from Sir Noel Hall came with

> Best wishes to you and the Shadow Senate and your wives. We hope you will have as much pleasure and satisfaction in working out and developing your own ideas for the University of Lancaster as we have had in preparing a little raw material for you.[16]

While this meeting was a key moment of transition, in practice the seventeen items of business tackled that weekend veered between broad policy, such as the strategic relationship between the university and the teacher training colleges in the area, to matters of detail, such as a representative for the City of Lancaster Regatta. A subsequent meeting on 7 March 1964 was not dissimilar, with discussions about the possible introduction of theology, law, and marketing, and long-term developments that might include medicine and technology, sat alongside, for example, a discussion about whether there might be a station at Oubeck Siding.[17] Some distinctive voices began to be heard. For example, Professor Gordon Manley voiced his view that

> "Environmental studies" appears to be the most convenient name at present for the objective study of the characteristics and evolution of the external physical environment at and adjacent to the earth's surface, and the consequences with regard to the life thereon,

while Professor Tom Lawrenson commented:

---

[15] See "The University of Lancaster", *Lancaster Guardian Special Supplement* (Lancaster, 1964, probably in October), in which each new head of department set out his blueprint for his area.

[16] Minute 1 of Shadow Senate, meeting on 11 and 12 January 1964.

[17] Minute 17 of Shadow Senate, meeting on 7 March 1964: a railway siding at Bailrigg, to connect the university with Lancaster and Morecambe, remains an aspiration for some members of the university to this day.

As you know, I am anxious to establish French Studies at Lancaster as a degree in the total culture of one country, rather than as an exclusive training in linguistic and literary studies,

Professor John Bevington noted:

I give here a suggested general plan [for Chemistry majors] followed by more detailed suggestions. I believe that the general plan would be equally suitable for other science subjects,

and Professor Roland Dobbs, of Physics, said:

In my opinion, we should admit our undergraduates to the University rather than to any particular courses *ab initio*, and to assist in this, we should offer as wide a choice of first year subjects as possible.

In May 1964 the members of the Shadow Senate and the Academic Planning Board gathered at Leamington Spa for a joint meeting that was notable for the attempts made to achieve a consensus on breadth of learning across the undergraduate curriculum and the creation of structures that would support those aspirations. The anxiety of the science professors not to give up teaching time that would detract from professional training in their respective subject areas left the APB members and the non-science professors in the uncomfortable position either of seeking compromises around this problem or of rationalising their colleagues' approach to make it appear that there was more movement in their views than initially appeared. Similar problems came to light when the timing of examinations within Part II was discussed. The uncompromising determination of the science professors not to give ground on annual examining procedures,[18] whether or not their determination could be considered as justifiable, was hugely influential in the subsequent gradual decline in the extent to which Lancaster students were compelled to work across the Snow line.

The discussion of future additional subject areas was perhaps more fruitful, including initial consideration of German, applied science, drama and television, marketing, accountancy, law, and (at the suggestion of the professor of mathematics) water resources. All these suggestions were later adopted (see Chapter 3), with the work on water, under the banner of hydrology, becoming a major research strength of Lancaster. A growing

---

[18] The heads of science departments wanted students to be examined at the end of each academic year, to ensure that there was confidence that material covered so far had been mastered; other subject heads, led by Philosophy but also including subjects such as History and Religious Studies, wished students to have the whole of Part II clear of formal examinations until the final term of the third year, so that they could continue to reflect on what they had already covered as they embarked on further courses.

emphasis on the desirability of professional subjects at this early stage, including medicine and architecture, is also of interest. However, the reader might be startled to learn that

> A small committee had been set up to report to the University Grants Committee on the University's need for a Computer. If the case failed, it would be necessary to find a private donor.[19]

Initially the resultant 16K machine, which was housed in a specially designed building, was the responsibility of the Mathematics Department.[20]

And so the baton passed from the external board members to the internal staff, and from the theoretical and the ideal to the pressures and predilections of the initial appointees and the persons whom they themselves helped to select. As the APB in late 1964 became transmogrified into the Academic Advisory Committee (see below), although in the main the same members continued on the successor body, their role would now be monitoring rather than shaping.

The above account, however, omits two key aspects of the strategic direction of the new institution. The first was the series of interventions by the University Grants Committee about funding decisions. For example, as early as March 1964 the Vice-Chancellor was writing to his small nucleus of academic staff about a rapid shift in policy from mid-1963:

> It now appears likely that we shall face considerable difficulties over recurrent grant for the three years commencing on 1st August, 1964. The U.G.C. speaks of dividing a limited sum between Essex, Lancaster, Canterbury and Warwick. We have no idea what this sum will be, but the treatment of York and East Anglia does not encourage optimism ... In conclusion, may I say how sorry I am to put members of staff, recruited in times of rosier expectations, in such difficulties. We have been very badly affected both by the continued parsimony of the Government towards universities, and by the line of policy which the U.G.C. is now following towards new universities.[21]

There was also considerable uncertainty about whether or not the college buildings would be funded by government, and much correspondence went to and fro on that subject.

The second important but easily overlooked aspect in the determination of strategy in the opening months of the university was the sheer weight of pressing business. The Shadow Senate of September 1964 had 36 separate items of business to consider, many of them concerned with setting up structures, procedures and regulations *ab initio* that had profound consequences for the future, not to mention ten report items from the Vice-Chancellor. And

---

[19] Minute 10 of the Joint Meeting of the Academic Planning Board and the Shadow Senate held at the Clarendon Hotel, Leamington, on Saturday 9 May 1964.

[20] University of Lancaster, *Lancaster Guardian Special Supplement*, p. 24 (Lancaster, October, 1967).

[21] C. F. Carter, "Recurrent grant 1964–65" (6 March 1964, UA.1/15/2/10).

yet, despite the turmoil, in October 1964 Lancaster admitted its first cohort of students to a functioning university, with the Vice-Chancellor congratulating staff on:

> ... what, in retrospect, has been an extraordinary effort. No other university has started with so many students ... no other new university has acquired from the beginning teaching facilities in so many subjects. We have consistently done better than our own forecasts.[22]

As the Senate took over from its shadow, and the Academic Advisory Committee from the APB, both in October 1964, so the Council followed suit in the December by formally assuming the former powers of the Executive Council. A significant newcomer from late October, however, was the body to be known as the Development Committee, consisting of the Vice-Chancellor and Professors Reynolds (politics; pro-vice-chancellor), Bevington (chemistry) and Murray (English). This committee, which continued to function in various forms until the end of the second vice-chancellor's term of office in 1985, was immensely influential in what can best be described as incremental strategy-making. Indeed, for a time and depending on the speaker's perspective about whether it was to be more respected or feared, little happened without the committee's intervention, including new subject areas, major staffing reviews, and plans for economies. In 1970, for example, there was debate about whether its members should be elected by the boards of studies, by all academic members of staff, or by the Senate. The customary point was made that members did not see themselves as representative, but there was concern that

> Although the Development Committee had taken substantial decisions on the University's behalf, little was generally known about its deliberations or decisions ... the prime need was not for wider representation but for improved channels of communication to and from the committee.[23]

No election process was instituted, and a memorandum from Professor Ninian Smart a couple of years later indicated that, while "not intended as a criticism of the heroic work undertaken" by the committee, he nevertheless suggested that it needed to be small and strong only for dealing with problems involving departments or individuals. For other forms of its agenda he recommended that it should be more open to general discussion and "should meet once a term in the presence of a Forum to which any member of a board or syndicate could go (and vote) ... Merits: a wider view of development and a revivification of thinking about the university".[24]

---

[22] *Staff Newsletter* No. 1: 1 October 1964 (UA.1/9/3/6).

[23] Section 4.1 of "Report of Proceedings at a Conference of the Board of the Senate, 26 to 27 September 1970, at the Hydro Hotel, Windermere" (GM/70/435, UA.1/15/2/15).

[24] Ninian Smart, "The Development Committee – some proposals, 16 February 1972" (GM/72/133; UA.1/15/2/10).

While the tight-knit Development Committee, meeting frequently and with a close knowledge about all aspects of the still small institution, often took the initiative, the strategic process was the responsibility of the Senate. Conferences took place for Senate members roughly on an annual cycle, and involved time away at venues in the Lake District; Borrowdale, Ullswater, Grasmere, Grange-over-Sands, and Windermere were amongst the chosen locations. Intermingled with these were periodic visitations to Bailrigg by the University Grants Committee, or one of its subject sub-committees, to discuss development in general or to talk about particular subject areas that were a cause for concern nationally, or that might be candidates for expansion. Naturally these visits, the first of which took place in January 1966 and which continued until the demise of the UGC, occasioned a great deal of work in order to present particular areas optimally or to devise plans for funding requests. Board of Studies C, the location of the social sciences, was a particularly fertile source of new ideas that would involve additional subject areas or re-groupings of what was already in place, but other areas of the university were not far behind. A document late in 1970, for example, summarised 17 possible developments that could begin as sections within existing departments, either in the sciences or non-sciences; and a further 22 that would originate with groups of staff from two or more existing departments, this latter list also including area studies, principally in language-related areas.[25] A few areas were developed quite rapidly; other suggestions fell by the wayside immediately; others commenced but were later discontinued; some were re-introduced for further consideration at later stages. And, of course, the list did not include some key subjects not synergistic with existing areas but already under discussion, including religious studies (rather than theology), law, and medicine, two of which were launched quite soon, while the third was destined to wait for implementation until the beginning of the twenty-first century.

The 1970 Windermere conference, which included 50 participants for most sessions, together with observers, student members, persons in attendance, and a secretariat, marked the end of inclusive gatherings on such a scale,[26] and indeed of meetings that would take place over a 12-hour period on a Saturday, with another 7 hours the following day. Since this proved to be the last of a series, its proceedings mark a useful milestone. Two sessions were led by the Vice-Chancellor, as *primus inter pares*, on the building programme and structure of the boards of studies; one by the pro-vice-chancellor (Professor Reynolds) on the future of the colleges; and one by the Development Committee on the quinquennial planning cycle for the UGC. A topic not previously included concerned progress in research, and was led by three staff, one each from social and natural sciences, and the third from business studies. This addition was welcomed as an area not previously given due attention by the Development Committee and as being fundamental for the future, since the research grant income for 1969 of £167,000 was tiny, even against a turnover of £2.1 million, and was almost

---

[25] "University development 1972–77" (GM/70/475).

[26] There is some evidence that, although subsidised by the university, participants were required to pay for their costs of hotel and food.

matched by consultancy income of £105,000 in business studies.[27] Nevertheless, a proposal that there should be a university Research and Consultancy Committee was hotly resisted, and more than a decade was to elapse before any central research policy committee was established. In the meanwhile, the freedom of departments to generate research proposals was upheld, and the single institution-wide change was the introduction of an annual listing of research publications and grants.[28]

Thus the 1970 conference represented a progressive widening of the strategic focus, which was now deemed to include the physical infrastructure, a strong emphasis on organisational structures, and an underlying and recurrent theme of balancing the academic shape of the university, especially between science and non-science. A further area of discussion concerned student numbers: the predicted range for student number growth for the period to 1975 was 4850 to 6000, comfortably in excess of the 3000 ten-year target, but nevertheless constraining in terms of the realisation by colleagues of broader ambitions for their subjects. The tone of the report of the proceedings can also be seen to have altered, leaving behind much of the optimism and idealism of the foundation years.

From time to time, however, major innovations slipped into the mainstream more quietly. A modest paper by Professor Smart to the Senate outlining some criteria for research centres and institutes, in which he attempted with his customary tinge of humour to define generic types, was immensely influential for the future, since it enabled interdisciplinary research ventures to gain institutional recognition and yet have significant autonomy to operate alongside the existing departmental and board of studies structures.[29] In considering strategic development, therefore, a close watch on apparently peripheral movements is also key to an understanding of the institution's evolution. Equally, attempts by external distractions to affect development had to be resisted: for example, a joint working party of the UGC and the Computer Board recommended that from 1972 *all* undergraduates should be taught computing, but without any release of resources to put this determination into effect. As the Vice-Chancellor noted, "one might wonder if *all* undergraduates should not, in like manner, be taught statistics, or economics, or French, or even English".[30]

After 1970 more modest strategic gatherings were held at Bailrigg at irregular intervals, but the main directions of the university were increasingly set by the Development Committee. The early years of the decade were characterised by rapid inflation, and the carefully constructed plans for measured growth were overtaken by the need to manage a situation in which annual inflation was in double figures. Internal costs, including

---

[27] The role of the university companies, such as LANCORD and ISCOL, to generate live projects for postgraduate students in business studies, is discussed in Chapter 6. They remained controversial, however, until their demise.

[28] This listing continued on an unbroken basis until 2006.

[29] Ninian Smart, "Centres, Institutes and So Forth", 23 November 1970.

[30] CFC, "Next quinquennium (second list)", memorandum to Development Committee, 14 September 1970 (UA.1/15/2/8).

student rent increases and staff salaries, had to keep pace,[31] while carefully garnered surpluses became meaningless as inflation wiped them away. The 1975 proposals for new areas of study were much more modest than five years previously, with consolidation or modest extension of existing provision being the principal theme. They were considered by a Development Committee to which all resource requests were now directed, whether involving consideration of a single female member of staff for the Indoor Recreation Centre, or the detailed financial provisions for major French students during their year abroad. There seemed little incentive to consider the broader picture, an attitude reinforced by the Vice-Chancellor's report at the end of the year that

> The old quinquennial system appeared to be dead. No memorandum of guidance was to be expected, and the usual planning for the quinquennium could be suspended. The U.G.C. was trying to negotiate a three-year grant 1976–9, possibly with a shadowy 'indication' for 1979–82.[32]

A hint to the university that increasing admissions numbers to attract more recurrent grant might be a sensible move was negated only two months later.

This sense of the university not being fully in control of its own destiny was not peculiar to Lancaster. Liverpool, after decades of successful growth, was in 1975 labelled as being merely a "steady state" university,[33] Durham had to make rapid adjustments to cope with the emergency action being taken by government,[34] while at Southampton the whole vice-chancellorship of Jim Gower, from 1971 to 1979, was dominated by the country's financial troubles.[35] These cutbacks, and those to follow after the election of the Thatcher government in May 1979, should be seen in the broader context of a cultural shift in the national position of universities well summarised by Peter Scott.[36] He points to the huge scale of increase in the student population during the 1960 to 1970 decade, rising from 179,000 to 446,000. This was followed by a further large increase in the 1970s, principally in the polytechnics, which coincided with both a more rigorous treatment by government of national expenditure and the diminution of the UGC's status and authority. There was a perceptible shift to pessimism in higher education under the influence, *inter alia*, of persistent student unrest, of a growing gap between modern universities and the lay society

---

[31] The Vice-Chancellor reported in May 1975 that the recurrent grant to the university for 1975–76 allowed for inflation of just under 30% for all items other than academic salaries (Development Committee, 10 May 1975, AR/75/62).

[32] Minute DG.75/82 of the Development Committee, 1 November 1975 (AR/75/118).

[33] Thomas Kelly, *For Advancement of Learning: The University of Liverpool, 1881–1981* (Liverpool: Liverpool University Press, 1981), p. 325.

[34] Nigel Watson, *The Durham Difference: The Story of Durham University* (London: James & James, 2007), p. 95.

[35] Sally Nash and Martin Sherwood, *The University of Southampton: An Illustrated History* (London: James & James, 2002), p. 80.

[36] Peter Scott, *The Crisis of the University* (London: Croom Helm, 1984), especially Chapter 4.

within which each must operate, and of a sense that the value of higher education lessened as a greater proportion of the population received either degrees or a host of related tertiary awards. This is a larger theme whose consequences will continue to be worked through in the twenty-first century.

The immediate breakdown of the quinquennial system was followed in June 1979 by cuts in the sector's building programmes, a further substantial and mandatory increase in overseas student fees, a cut in expenditures on university computers, a reduction in the funds available to the research councils, a cut in the recurrent grant to universities (other than the Open University), and increases in value-added tax and the cost of borrowing money.[37] Successive government announcements presaged a period when Lancaster's senior officers came to concentrate on survival first, with planning for the future pushed into the background, a situation that was to intensify in the succeeding months.[38] In the bleak words of the Expenditure Plans, 1981–82 to 1983–84:

> for home students in higher education the plans provide for a progressive reduction in expenditure so that by 1983–84 institutional expenditure (net of tuition fee income) will be rather more than 8 per cent below the level planned in Cmnd. 7841. This is likely to oblige institutions to review the range and nature of their contribution to higher education. It is also likely to lead to some reduction in the number of students admitted to higher education with increased competition for places.[39]

A. H. Halsey, in a lecture of 1984,[40] cited Charles Carter as being in 1971 "perhaps the last voice of confidence in an expansive future", but drew attention to the "endemic dyspepsia" as the universities were "rudely summoned in the summer of 1981 to the experiment of strength through starvation of public funding", especially at Aston, Salford, and Bradford, where the cuts disproportionately fell. For Lancaster there was unwelcome advice in the form of UGC recommendations for an overall decrease in arts and social science numbers, the discontinuation of archaeology and theatre studies, and the continued phasing out of Russian-based studies. Staff in European Studies were to be assisted in a move to the University of Kent, and those in Central and South-East European Studies, along with the stock of the Comenius Centre library, were to be transferred to the University of Oxford.

---

[37] Taken from the summary by the Acting Vice-Chancellor to the Development Committee, meeting on 13 June 1979, of the Chancellor of the Exchequer's budget speech the previous day (DC.79/95).

[38] M. E. McClintock, "The University of Lancaster: the First Thirty Years" (lecture to the Summer Programme, 27 July 1994, pp. 6–7).

[39] *The Government's Expenditure Plans 1981–82 to 1983–84*, Cmnd. 8175 (London: HMSO, 1981), Part 2, Section 10, para. 14. Tuition fees for most students at this date were still being paid by local authorities. The CVCP calculated the average cut in recurrent grant to be 15% rather than 8%; the chairman of the UGC was prepared to acknowledge a figure of 11%.

[40] A. H. Halsey, "The Idea of a University", Charles Carter Lecture 1984 (Lancaster, University of Lancaster, 1984), p. 1.

Within overall reductions of student numbers, however, there were to be increases in business and management, and in physical sciences, especially physics.[41]

For a time an atmosphere of near-desperation was experienced by staff, and for anyone reading with the benefit of hindsight the papers and minutes of the Senate, the Council, and the Development Committee, the sense of an institution struggling under severe external pressures to retain some control over its destiny is intense. Indeed, the Development Committee, seeking to mitigate internal criticisms of ignorant and wilful damage to the academic offerings of the university for which its members were felt to be largely responsible, undertook a series of much-dreaded visitations to departments to find out at first hand where the capabilities and the vulnerabilities were to be found. In parallel the Senate initiated an exercise of its own, conducted by colleagues not on the Development Committee, to carry out a review of the proposed cuts on its behalf and report to members of the university whether they were necessary if disaster was to be averted.[42]

The 1981 cuts caused serious and lasting damage at Lancaster, especially in the provision of modern languages outwith Western Europe, and of Arabic and Islamic Studies, as well as the subsequent but related demise of Classics and Archaeology. Nevertheless, the willingness of academic staff in particular to take premature retirement and unpaid leave of absence, as well as simply to work harder as posts were not replaced, was a significant element in the university's ability to regain its momentum. In other words, a bottom-up response, that included voluntary donations of salary from some staff, sustained the institution as much as the resolve and openness of senior officers. Student numbers, in line with the rest of the sector, fell from 5000 in 1980–81 to 4706 in 1984–85,[43] and the building programme came to a halt for the rest of the decade. Nevertheless, the university managed to break even on an annual basis, and while in 1982 the Vice-Chancellor told his staff that "We still therefore float about on a sea of uncertainty, which makes effective planning impossible",[44] the position was eased by the provision of a New Blood scheme launched by the UGC. There were to be 200 posts in science and technology across the sector, and 30 for other subjects, for which bids could be made and of which Lancaster gained in the second round more than its proportionate share. Furthermore, the university decided to set aside part of its scarce resources for internal research bids in each of the four main academic areas. In part this exercise was designed to accelerate research activity at Lancaster, but also in part to show evidence to the UGC that the institution was subscribing to a new term that was to become a watchword, the use of selectivity – that is, the rewarding of the already strong, or the funding of earmarked new developments in preference to weaker existing ventures. By

---

[41] Edward Parkes, attachment to Circular Letter 10/81 of 1 July 1981 (published in *News Sheet* No. 76, 2 July 1981 (UA.1/9/1/3).

[42] See *News Sheet*, No. 83 (19 October 1981), No. 84 (29 October 1981), and No. 85 (13 November 1981).

[43] Marion E. McClintock, *The University of Lancaster: The First Thirty Years* (Lancaster: Lancaster University, 1994), Fig. 9.

[44] Vice-Chancellor's letter to staff, 13 October 1982 (UA.1/9/3/9).

1985, as Philip Reynolds retired as Vice-Chancellor, he saw a university that was: "markedly stronger than it was in 1981, and there are several readily-identifiable areas of distinction".[45]

However, another major change in the culture and tenor of universities was about to take place. A key strategic shift towards managerialism in the sector was marked by the Committee of Vice-Chancellors and Principals in a report that arose from a working party it commissioned to examine the effectiveness and efficiency of universities. This review involved an investigation into the management structure and decision-making processes of universities, as well as their methods for examining their use of resources. The consequent Jarratt report[46] proved to be something of a Trojan horse for the universities, albeit fashioned from within their leadership structure.[47] The findings were immediately and warmly welcomed by the Department of Education and Science, especially the intended publication of comparative unit costs and other performance indicators.[48] Lancaster was no exception to the sector's readiness to absorb and internalise the implicit change in the standing and running of universities, although it would be ungracious to cavil at an institution only two decades old, and one that had not yet secured its reputation, for its lack of resistance. Indeed, its senior officers were reminded on what a short leash it was held, for the positive statement that Lancaster was not on any UGC hit list was qualified by a reminder that the institution would not be too far away if there was one, and should therefore avoid doing "silly things" (as the Vice-Chancellor wryly noted, "a sophisticated concept").[49] A joint Senate/Council Committee to consider the Jarratt report was set up and sat for a year, leading in 1986 *inter alia* to the establishment of a Senate and Planning and Resources Committee (SPARC) and a joint Senate/Council Strategy Committee. In addition, the duties of heads of departments were tightened, staff development and appraisal were introduced, and the concept of delegation of authority to officers of the university took on more formal shape.[50] The Strategy Committee was the first attempt by the institution to dedicate a senior body for the sole purpose of forward planning. The terms of reference were:

– to examine long-term trends and, in the light of these, to develop objectives and priorities (to be reviewed annually) beyond a five-year planning horizon;

---

[45] Vice-Chancellor's letter to staff, 15 May 1985 (UA.1/9/3/9).

[46] Steering Committee for Efficiency Studies in Universities, *National Data Study [the Jarratt Report]*.

[47] See Geoffrey Alderman, "Simplistic view of insider betrayal", *Times Higher Education*, No. 4907, 30 July 2009, p. 46.

[48] Johnes and Taylor, *Performance Indicators*, pp. 4–5: see also Chapter 10, setting out five proposed performance indicators that, while they included comparative degree results, did not mention measurement of teaching quality.

[49] Letter from the Vice-Chancellor to all staff, 18 May 1985 (UA.1/9/3/9).

[50] Agenda and minutes of the extraordinary meeting of the Council, 27 October 1986.

– to stimulate discussion of and to examine suggestions for major developments and changes.[51]

Not only was the committee set up by the Council, rather than the Senate, but the Pro-Chancellor was an active member, as were lay and Senate-appointed members and the President of the Students' Union. The practice of annual conferences away from Lancaster was resumed, although on the basis of invitations to attend particular sessions arranged by a core body rather than the previous inclusive model.

More confidence returned in the late 1980s, a period when university managers across the sector anticipated that they could shape their institutions' futures, provided that there was a clear corporate strategy.[52] This was a time when a Secretary of State would attend an individual university to give his view of substantial expansion in higher education over the next quarter century, as Kenneth Baker did in a speech at Lancaster in January 1989,[53] and when major shifts were taking place in the national funding regime. The balance between recurrent grant and student fees would, universities were informed, increasingly be weighted towards the latter, coupled with full compensation to local education authorities for their share and the introduction of a Government-backed loan system for students.[54] Furthermore, within the recurrent grant there was to be banding for particular groups of subjects (more for the sciences; less for the arts) and a separation for the first time between funding for teaching and research, apportioned in the light of the research assessment exercises of 1986 and 1989.

The changes in national funding regimes were also reflected in the move, in 1989, from the University Grants Committee to the short-lived Universities Funding Council, primarily to effect the implementation of the changes. Mary Warnock spoke for many in the sector when she wrote:

> In the same spirit [of absence of policy], the newly established University [sic] Funding Council, set up to distribute the money allocated by Government to the universities, has as one of its stated aims "to see that an increasing proportion of the ... incomes of universities should be derived from non-Government sources". This seems a somewhat perverse aim for a funding council to adopt. And while its adoption is defended in high-sounding phrases ... it is hard, well, impossible, not to think that it means simply

---

[51] Minute CO.88/52, Council meeting on 28 June 1988.

[52] See the bibliography in P. Temple and C. Whitchurch, eds., *Strategic Choice: Corporate Strategies for Change in Higher Education* (Reading: Conference of University Administrators,1989), pp. 90–1, for a survey of the profuse literature on corporate strategy of the period.

[53] *Fulcrum*, No. 132, 19 January 1989.

[54] Department of Education and Science, *Shifting the Balance of Public Funding of Higher Education to Fees: A Consultation Paper* (London: DES, 1989). The proportion of the relevant age group in higher education had by 1988 reached 15%: Science and Arts Committee Education, *Higher Education: Minutes of Evidence*, 1988–89 HC 87 I (London: HMSO, 1988), para. 25.

that they are to get less public funding. After all, they were never really going to become financially independent of Government, and Government itself neither seriously believes nor wishes that they should.[55]

From now onwards, universities were to be funded on the basis of the bids they made, rather than on the amount a central government body decided on their behalf that they should have. Although both parties continued to use historical data to determine both bid and consequent allocation, the intention was that there was to be more responsibility assumed by universities for their own financial stability. This situation was heightened by the introduction of the Higher Education Funding Council for England in 1992 and the inclusion of the post-1992 institutions as direct competitors with existing universities for resources.

Against the above backdrop there was no shortage of issues for the new Strategy Committee to consider, and it is instructive to compare its deliberations with the reports of the Senate conferences two decades earlier. Between 1989 and 1993 the Strategy Committee, on several occasions, concentrated on: growth in student numbers, with particular emphasis on the development of the sciences; physical planning and expansion in relation to student numbers, and requirements for additional teaching and residential accommodation; an over-view of research, including policy on European funding and the university's international reputation; and links with business and industry, with special reference to the North-West region. For the first time an attempt was made to prepare and agree a mission statement, setting out main aims and objectives for the next ten years, with priorities set in advance.[56] Another innovation was the first Academic Plan,[57] which included an introduction, some overall academic objectives, and a section on finance (i.e. the avoidance of deficits). Academic profiles by type of provision and individual area were given for the first time for science and technology, management, social sciences, and humanities, with explicit labelling of each subject discipline on a scale ranging from outstanding to below average, information to which all other areas of the university had access. The term "academic plan" had, however, two years later become a "planning framework", with more emphasis on statistical trends and targets.

The extent to which the dedicated Strategy Committee could be held to have shaped the future depends on an evaluation of its deliberations in conjunction with related bodies in the university. The UGC had expressed concern about the extent of Lancaster's implementation of Jarratt recommendations, and had pressed the Vice-Chancellor on:

i.   Actual changes that have been effected in Council lay membership (these were said only to be "probable" in the University's response);

---

[55]   Mary Warnock, *Universities: Knowing Our Minds* (London: Chatto & Windus, 1989), pp. 9–10.
[56]   "Mission (?)", 5 March 1987, SU/87/6.
[57]   Academic Plan, May 1987, GM/87/237.

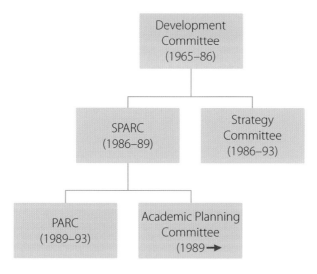

Figure 2: Strategic planning structures, 1965–93

ii. details of changes in the functions of Council (recommendations relating to these aspects were said to have been accepted only "insofar as change was necessary");

iii. the way in which planning, resource allocation and accountability are brought together ... and how the Senate Planning and Resources Committee is operating without lay members ... the Committee will wish to scrutinise particularly closely the first of your institution's annual reports on gains in efficiency and effectiveness.[58]

Under this pressure, the SPARC was divided into two bodies (see Fig. 2): a Planning and Resources Committee (PARC) and an Academic Planning Committee, solely accountable to the Senate.[59] The PARC was a small joint committee of the Council and the Senate, including lay as well as academic members. This move proved not to be a success: academic issues, such as the future of Chemistry at Lancaster, research strategy, and student recruitment, directly overlapped with the agenda of both the Strategy Committee and the Academic Planning Committee. Meetings of PARC were increasingly deferred or cancelled, and agendas were set and discarded, as the proper location of types of business became more problematic. The committee, while remaining on the books for a while, ceased to meet in 1993. By that time, however, the UGC and the UFC had given way to the Higher Education Funding Council for England, with different procedures

---

[58] Sir Peter Swinnerton-Dyer, letter to Professor H. J. Hanham, 4 December 1987 (UA.1/15/3).
[59] The APC at first held some ten meetings a year, and was directly and substantially influential in advising the Senate; latterly it meets only to consider revisions to the Strategic Plan.

and guidelines for a sector that now included the former polytechnics, and the former probing questions about lay involvement ceased for the time being. Furthermore, the Vice-Chancellor began to extend informal weekly chats with key officers to a somewhat wider circle of pro-vice-chancellors and senior administrators, and this group began to take on increasing significance. Its successor bodies, VCSAG and UMAG under the fourth vice-chancellor, continued this trend, with some echoes of the problems presented by the Development Committee in the university's early days.

In 1993 the Strategy Committee was also effectively suspended, but this did not preclude the holding of annual strategic conferences, and it has been the exception in the succeeding fifteen years that such a gathering has not been convened. The important difference, however, is that they were no longer growing out of the Senate's activities; they originated either in the Vice-Chancellor's office or from the Council. The 1993 conference, held soon after the announcement of Lancaster's outstanding achievement in the 1992 research assessment exercise, fell in line with the final Strategy Committee discussion, with a focus on industrial links, technology transfer, and the application of research to the community, including the management of the intellectual property generated. Student rights and organisation also featured, as well as an examination of institutional strengths and weaknesses, and the future research and teaching profile of the university.

The 1996 conference, at a time when the university was walking towards a cash flow crisis (see Chapter 6) during which its future would depend in part on the goodwill of external agencies, including commercial banks, might have been expected to concentrate on finance. Instead, it had as its theme the shape of the university by 2005, including the relative benefits of group and individual research, the organisation of teaching and learning, some regional, national, and international issues, and the impact of information technology on the university. The capital funding of the university, perhaps one of the most significant topics of the decade, did not feature either in 1993 or 1996. By the time of the 1998 conference, with the cash flow problem having largely been weathered, there was a strong emphasis on the role of the HEFCE, including its policies on widening student participation, on how to reward teaching, and on the future of research assessment. Thus, while the Academic Planning Committee was shaping the academic agenda for the Senate, the days were past when the Senate was leading the institutional strategic process.

By 2003, the opportunity presented by a new millennium alongside, first, a determination to put the vulnerabilities of the previous decade behind and, secondly, the appointment of a fifth vice-chancellor, Paul Wellings, made a fresh strategic start possible. The emphasis at the 2003 conference was on a review of the university's mission statement, and the key goals derived from it, together with the setting of fresh goals and strategies allied to specific targets for particular areas. The consequent document, now written primarily for external audiences, was expressed in a series of numbered bullet points, the significance of which at times relied heavily on insiders' knowledge. Visually handsome, being plentifully illustrated and professionally designed, the content was more generic and the somewhat coded statements, with a strong emphasis on positive achievement, required more interpretation

Professor Paul Wellings, Vice-Chancellor, 2002 to 2011

– a considerable change from the rawly self-critical documents of only a decade earlier. Seven main goals required the institution to maximise student achievement, recruit and retain high-quality staff, position itself at the cutting edge of research and teaching, apply its knowledge and skills regionally, nationally, and internationally, provide a supportive, fair, and safe working and living environment, be flexible and responsive to customers, stakeholders, and alumni, and deliver organisational excellence.[60] Objectives expressed in these terms were also to be found in similar documents at universities across the land, inevitably deadening the impact of any one of them, and of the sense of differentiation that each institution sought.

A follow-up conference the following year set off on the basis of more detailed preparation, including reports from a series of theme-based working groups that had already distilled major topics before the conference began. These included stakeholder management, student facilities, teaching and learning, commercialisation, and research. The conference resulted in a set of tasks so detailed and complex that priorities were hard to establish, and it was clear that a corrective would be needed for the next strategic statement. A series of working groups was again convened in advance of a conference held in January 2006, but on a more selective set of key concerns, and the conference itself was confined to a discussion of them.

---

[60] *Strategic Plan 2003–08* (Lancaster: Lancaster University, 2003), pp. 16–37.

The resulting plan extended to 2011,[61] and was careful to set the agenda for the reader on key aspects of the university, starting with the Lancaster hallmark, and on its vision and mission ("to pursue research at the highest international level, to create a stimulating and innovative learning environment for all students and staff and, in international, national and regional collaborations, to enhance economic, cultural and social well-being"). Beliefs and values, its strategic planning framework, student-centred learning, the research focus, its staff, financial sustainability, the campus and support services, international, national, and regional partnerships, its key performance indicators and their monitoring, and key challenges for the future were all briefly summarised. It stated that:

> Lancaster University is characterised by excellence and innovation in its endeavours, and by the combination of features listed below [high calibre staff, the quality of research, exacting teaching quality standards, contributions to economic development, the college system, a beautiful campus setting, a disciplined financial regime] that set us apart. Our success is based on the vision and foresight of the University's leaders over the years, as well as to the quality, commitment and loyalty of our staff and students.[62]

While this statement appeared at the time of writing to be a sound platform from which to move to the future, the financial turmoil of late 2008 again placed the values implicit in the statement under strain. A further strategic plan was issued in the following year[63] to take account both of the "global economic turbulence" and of the increased emphasis on the internationalisation of both the student body and the academic staff. The message being conveyed was that the university was fully prepared to steer a steady path through a troubled period. This statement, coupled with Lancaster's achievement of high league table positions in 2010, led to the setting of objectives to be first in the North West, in the top ten for the UK, and in the top hundred in the world. Strategic plans seem likely to be overtaken with increasing rapidity, however, as they are undercut by a rapidly moving external environment. In 2010 a combination of the Browne review[64] of undergraduate student funding, a change of UK government, and a highly controversial Comprehensive Spending Review once again altered the parameters of higher education. The stated intention of waiting until 2013 for a review of the university's 2009–15 plan seems unlikely to remain in place.

Fortunately, however, work of a more directed kind, led by the Vice-Chancellor, took place over the summer of 2010, culminating in two documents[65] that gave a richer picture of Lancaster's strengths and potential vulnerabilities. The first, on financial sustainability, ruled

---

[61] Lancaster University, *Strategic Plan 2006–11* (undated, but late 2006).

[62] Lancaster of University, *Strategic Plan 2006–11*, p. 3 (published late in 2006).

[63] University of Lancaster, *Strategic Plan 2009–15* (published late in 2009).

[64] "Securing a Sustainable Future for Higher Education: An Independent Review of Higher Education Funding and Student Finance [the Browne Report]".

[65] Financial Sustainability and Academic Regeneration Working Group Reports, discussed by the Council on 8 October 2010 (minute CO.10/74).

Geoffrey Clarke (1969), three of a set of sterling silver vessels, with appliqué decoration, from a set donated to the new university by the Goldsmiths' Company

out three options: no voluntary severance scheme open to all staff would be introduced; no search to change the academic structures and shape of the university would take place; and the entry standards for students would not be reduced. A further working group on academic regeneration usefully probed further into issues surrounding the renewal of the academic community at Lancaster, especially the trends in their numbers and turnover, the consequences of the university's recruitment and retention practices, and steps to maximise the quality of the staff profile to 2020.[66] While the recommendations from the group broke no new ground, the focus on these core staff was welcome and important.

This chapter began with an assertion that strategic planning is about how an institution shapes its future, and has demonstrated how often that objective is challenged by external forces. It concludes on a note of uncertainty for higher education, as institutions face their biggest challenges for fifty years.[67] Lancaster, perhaps in part because of previous buffetings it has faced, is as strongly positioned as any of its peers for the current period of turmoil, during which its ability consistently to shape its own future will once again be put to the test.

[66] For example, the report demonstrated that while Lancaster is strong at recruiting and developing staff early in their careers, and retaining high fliers who become distinguished professors, it is less good at attracting academics in mid-career.

[67] A comment made by Professor Wellings in his address at a Staff Assembly on 2 November 2010.

CHAPTER THREE

Academic culture

IN THE EARLY YEARS of the university the greatest proportion of time and attention was properly given to the establishment of the academic structures around teaching and learning, including the setting up and staffing of departments, the determining of the degree structure and student assessment, and making of provision for related services, including the Library, laboratory space, and lecture theatres. This emphasis is reflected in *Quest for Innovation*,[1] where there is a detailed description of how academic choices were made, both before the first students were admitted and for the first decade of the university's existence, and some of the consequences of those choices. Public lectures in 1994 and 2004 brought the story up to date.[2] This chapter will therefore be more of a discussion around selected topics that carry the story forward, rather than a detailed chronological account of subsequent small but significant changes, bewildering in their frequency even to current staff and students. In common with other UK universities where teaching and learning are fundamental to the institution's purpose and continually in a state of evolution and development, it is a story both of success and of constant striving for improvement.

Lancaster has also been fortunate in having had leaders of national debates about learning

---

[1] McClintock, *Quest*, especially but by no means exclusively Chapter 3.

[2] Marion E. McClintock, "University of Lancaster: The First Thirty Years": lecture to the Summer Programme, 27 July 1994; Marion E. McClintock, "University of Lancaster: Forty Years Young: A Lecture at the Storey Institute", 23 April 2004.

and teaching on its staff, including at different times Oliver Fulton, Peter Goodyear, Peter Knight, and Paul Trowler.[3] The steady succession of Lancaster winners of the National Teaching Fellowship Scheme,[4] launched in 2000 to recognise excellence in teaching at UK universities, is indicative of the importance paid to teaching at Lancaster. Members of staff across many departments have helped to frame the agenda of a shift from the more didactic style of earlier years to a greater emphasis on the importance of enabling students to acquire career-related skills as well as subject content. There has been an increasing focus, growing out of early interactive seminars that became workshops and shared student projects, towards more collaborative styles of teaching and learning. This move towards more peer-centred learning, initially at postgraduate level but increasingly for undergraduates as well, is reflected in the spaces created for students in the Management School, in the Learning Zone, and in the Postgraduate Statistics Centre (see Chapter 7). These changes were reliant on excellent teaching that gave confidence to students, and ways in which that attribute is rewarded include teaching being treated as a fundamental component of academic staff promotion and the establishment of the Pilkington Teaching

---

[3] All these people have been or are members of the Department of Educational Research.
[4] 2000: Mick Short; 2001: Susan Armitage; 2002: Mike Winstanley; 2003: Eric Evans; 2004: Moira Peelo; 2006: Andrew Folkard; 2007: Jane Sunderland; 2008: Deborah Mawer.

Awards, initiated in 1990.[5] Staff across departments have taken a keen interest in these developments: just four examples of such colleagues are Nick Abercrombie, as first dean of undergraduate studies and later as pro-vice-chancellor and deputy vice-chancellor; Richard Carter in Engineering; Gordon Clark in Geography; and the late Nigel Whiteley in Art.

Biology	1964
Chemistry	1964
Classics	1965
Economics	1964
English (and Linguistics)	1964
Environmental Studies	1964
French Studies	1964
History	1964
Marketing	1965
Mathematics	1964
Operational Research	1964
Philosophy	1964
Physics	1965
Politics	1964
Russian	1964
Systems Engineering	1965

Figure 3: Founding subjects at Lancaster, 1964–65

A chapter about academic structures, and how they support learning and teaching, requires a brief recapitulation of their origins.[6] The Academic Planning Board, established by the UGC under the chairmanship of Sir Noel Hall of Brasenose College, Oxford, recommended to the UGC that the initial subject areas for first degrees should be in the arts, including languages, and in the natural and social sciences, including business subjects (see Fig. 3), with the intention that undergraduates should take three subjects at Part I, including non-school subjects and those not taken at Advanced Level. At Part II they would follow a single or combined major[7] that would flow from their Part I choices, but they would also be compelled to study across disciplinary boundaries, particularly across the Snow line,[8]

---

[5] Minute S.90/113, Senate meeting on 10 October 1990: the awards were funded from a generous donation to the university from funds available to Sir Alastair Pilkington (Pro-Chancellor 1980–90).

[6] Material taken from McClintock, *Quest*, especially Chapter 3.

[7] There were also triple majors, involving three Part II units from each of three separate major subjects, e.g. Philosophy and the History of Science with one of Physics, Mathematics or Chemistry (S.72/159), but they proved too onerous, even for the best students, and did not persist.

[8] See footnote 5 (Chapter 2) above.

to ensure breadth of study. The core academic unit was to be the department, and from there all members of academic staff would be members of one or more interlinked boards of studies. The initial functions of these boards were to recommend schemes of study, with the associated syllabus for each major or combined major; to keep under review the inter-relationship of courses within a scheme of study, the teaching methods involved, and the training of university teachers; to nominate internal and external examiners and keep examination methods under review; to receive the results of examinations from the examiners and authorise their publication; to inform college tutors when candidates should be discouraged from continuing (with an alternative scheme where possible); and to approve special or shortened schemes in special circumstances.[9] The emphasis was on flexibility and wide student choice, and the first year was to be qualificatory, in preparation for the two years of Part II, where nine units of assessment were to be taken on which the degree classification would be based. Although there was heavy reliance on three-hour final written examinations, from the outset there was allowance for coursework assessment to count in agreed proportions for each unit. All degree schemes were to be assessed within a framework of unified degree regulations.[10] These elements of the Lancaster degree structure were taken so much for granted that it is important to recognise how far universities such as Lancaster had moved by the early 1960s, away from a set canon of material that must be followed in common, and in a particular sequence, by all students, towards a more open-ended curriculum and the use of continuous assessment rather than a judgement based solely on formal final examinations.

At postgraduate level, twelve-month masters courses and three-year research degrees, and their part-time equivalents, were available from the outset in areas related to staff expertise. There was a degree of MA that was to be obtained by coursework on which examinations would also be set, and parallel degrees of MSc and MPhil that would require a thesis embodying research and directed study, alongside an option for some coursework. Candidates for the degree of PhD were required to be graduates or persons of equivalent qualification who could show evidence of exceptional ability,[11] and the award was to be made on the examination of a thesis that would be judged by the examiners as a contribution to knowledge at a higher level. Higher and honorary doctorates were also specified.

However, the boards of studies were not to be involved in graduate studies, for a Board of Graduate Studies was agreed in principle at the first official meeting of the Senate.[12] Some members demurred, not at the weighty regulations for graduate study included in the agenda but at the Vice-Chancellor's proposal for a separate body. They preferred that the Boards of Studies A to D look after masters courses, with a Board of Research Studies for research degrees, but were won round to the idea of a special board on which all departments would be represented. The full regulations came back in November, together with the terms of

---

[9]   Document S.64/198, meeting of the Senate on 18 September 1964.
[10]   Initially all first degrees led to the award of Bachelor of Arts.
[11]   University of Lancaster, *1965–66 Prospectus 1966–67*, pp. 108–9.
[12]   Minute S.64/3/5, Senate meeting on 18 September 1964.

reference for the BGS, and not for the first or last time nine crisply expressed folio pages from the Vice-Chancellor laid firm foundations for all graduate regulations thereafter, from the management of students studying away from the university to regular supervisors' reports and the conditions for the submission of a thesis. The difference in structure meant, however, that taught postgraduate courses at Lancaster have continued to maintain a certain distance from first degrees, even after a Committee for Undergraduate Studies was established in 1989 that included a requirement to work in common with the BGS. The two populations have to some extent co-existed rather than become integrated, including within the college structure (The Graduate College) and the Students' Union (The Graduate Students Association).

The position of research students, then and now, crosses even more boundaries. They are students who require training, supervision, and examination, all of which fitted naturally within the Board of Graduate Studies and its successor bodies: many, however, also contribute substantially within research teams and through them to the university's research output, and are relevant to the Committee for Research and within the research assessment exercises; some of them are part-time staff, whether as demonstrators or assistant lecturers for undergraduate programmes, and the boundaries of their involvement therefore become relevant to undergraduate studies. They contribute actively to college and student life, and often act as a catalyst in their home departments for new approaches and ways of shaping the curriculum and its delivery, while at the same time relying on committed support from supervisors and departmental support networks. The effort to integrate them in all these spheres is worthwhile but also something of a challenge.

The lines of academic authority for the above arrangements were established in the Charter: "the University should be both a teaching and examining body and ... [shall] provide instruction in such branches of learning as the University may think fit, whether for members of the University or others",[13] with wide powers to admit students, to grant academic awards (and to deprive persons of them if necessary), to recognise the awards of other places of learning, and to institute and award fellowships, scholarships, studentships, and prizes. The principal vehicle for the exercise of these responsibilities was to be the Senate, which was to direct, regulate and promote teaching and research, conduct examinations and appoint internal and external examiners, grant degrees and other academic distinctions, regulate student discipline, and exclude students if necessary.[14]

The manner in which these powers were to be further transmitted or implemented was left open, although all full-time officers with teaching duties were to be members of a college syndicate and at least one board of study.[15] The definition of departments and their functions made no reference to teaching duties, although an "adequate method of consultation between its members and students taking courses in the Department"[16] was

---

[13] University of Lancaster, Charter Clause 4 (1964).
[14] University of Lancaster, Statute 12 (Charter and Revised Statutes, June 1971).
[15] University of Lancaster, Statutes 14 and 15 (1964).
[16] University of Lancaster, Statute 15 (1964).

stipulated. In this framework the departments took the lead, particularly in the malleable early years, and it was there that the academic structures were honed and augmented. For example, a university-wide teaching timetable was necessary for an institution where students had so much choice, and the so-called clash list of what Part I courses could occupy the same time slot was an important determinant of choice. Similarly, there was earnest debate about starting lectures on the hour and finishing them ten minutes before the hour so that staff and students could move to any point of the university in time to reach a lecture on a wholly different subject for the next hour. The organisation of seminars, workshops, and tutorials, however, was at the discretion of departments, and increasing differences grew up as the years went by, about for example, the extent of one-to-one interaction between a student and a full-time academic member of staff. Similarly, anyone perusing the early papers of the university will look in vain for general regulations about handing in coursework[17] or expectations about marking periods or feedback to students. It was the departments, under increasing pressure from student load, that in the main sought to standardise practices for their own major and minor students, while not disadvantaging combined major students working across departments. Yet there were also exceptions to this emphasis on departmental autonomy, such as institutional policy on and administration of admissions, for which a special sub-committee of the Senate was established; or the regulation of non-academic student discipline, where a more centralised approach was deemed appropriate. Intercalation – a break in the period of study for periods of up to a year – was in the early years regarded as something of a privilege, and there are instances of individual cases being considered by the whole Senate.

One example of a consistently centralised approach relates to academic discipline, where successive debates have taken place in the context of a university whose commitment to its students' success, particularly once they clear Part I, is strong, the presumption being that virtually all of them will continue to Finals. When the Senate was invited at its first fully constituted meeting to consider some General Regulations for students, members were told they were intended to be as few in number and as liberal as possible, of a nature that could not be ignored and were likely to be enforced, and written in a language that aimed "to convey the need for cooperation and should not suggest that students are delinquents or children or both".[18] They were approved, but rather oddly on the basis that separate regulations would be provided for graduate students. Non-academic discipline was also to be treated separately, as a matter for college disciplinary deans, who would be supported by college disciplinary committees. On the matter of academic discipline, a matching role was framed for the boards of studies, to which the heads of department would report on failure of "reasonable diligence" or an unsatisfactory record of attendance. In either case exclusion was available if necessary. Less than a year later, however, the Senate reverted to the topic

---

[17] The single exception was a cut-off date mid-way through the Summer Term for coursework that would count for final degree classification.

[18] Para. 4 of General Regulations for Students and Student Discipline (unreferenced document: see minute S.64/1/8, meeting of Senate on 18 September 1964).

of exclusion on grounds of academic failure and, notwithstanding the express approval already included in the Statutes for its delegation, resolved "That Senate should itself exercise the power of excluding students because of academic failure and should not delegate this power."[19] In practice this meant that the unfortunate Vice-Chancellor had to make decisions about the fate of individual students, and the Senate minute books contain examples of his notification to members of some of the results of those hearings. This procedure was not sustainable, and it comes as no surprise that by early 1966 further consideration was being given to "responsibility for disciplinary action in cases where undergraduates were reported for academic indiscipline, consistent refusal to produce work or contravention of academic regulations (including unfair practices at examinations)".[20] What had provoked the debate was the failure of four students to attend a January examination on the first term's work in their distant minor of Biology and Man, while a fifth had used unfair means in a biology examination. Four senior professors – Murray (English), Piggott (Biology), Reynolds (Politics), and Sturmey (Economics) – therefore sought approval for a standing body "to consider and act upon cases of unsatisfactory academic performance, breaches of academic regulations, and individual cases of academic difficulty",[21] with the power to make binding decisions on the fate of individuals. Students called before the committee would, it was suggested, be required to wear academic dress and to be accompanied by their college tutor. And thus the dreaded Standing Academic Committee was brought into being and, in an expanded form that includes postgraduate taught and research degree students, continues to the present day,[22] with exceptional powers to exclude or to allow continuation on strict conditions.

Subject and disciplinary groupings

While the first generation of subjects at Lancaster (1964–66) was mainly determined before any academic staff were appointed, the second (1967–78) was principally the outcome of their deliberations about what should be added, and there were many such debates (see Chapter 2). Charles Carter was keen to introduce further business subjects; some science departments quickly put out additional feelers for ecology, biochemistry or geography; Board of Studies C (for social sciences) was prolific in its suggestions, including of such broad-based schemes as Philosophy and the Arts, an umbrella for ambitious combinations of philosophical and creative arts courses. The second generation of subjects was also more eclectic (see Fig. 4), and established over a longer time-scale. It is instructive to see what became of these choices and to bring the picture up to date. Of the 16 founding subjects, 4 continue within the same

---

[19] Document S.64/198, meeting of the Senate on 18 September 1964.

[20] Minute S.66/2/18, Senate meeting on 2 February 1966.

[21] Minute S.66/3/9, Senate meeting on 2 March 1966: three of the four reprobate students had to sit a special paper and the fourth received a zero, while the student in biology was "reprimanded in severe terms".

[22] See terms of reference in *Staff Handbook* 2006–07, pp. 169–71.

departmental structure as they began (Economics, History, Marketing, and Physics), and a fifth, Mathematics, has become Mathematics and Statistics. Three have been discontinued: Chemistry, as a subject accredited by its professional body (see also below); Classics (which for a time also included Archaeology); and Russian (latterly Russian and Soviet Studies). English spawned Medieval Studies and Linguistics and became briefly a school; when the school was laid down, the main subject became English Literature,[23] and the department is now called English and Creative Writing.[24] Environmental Studies, later Environmental Science, joined Biological Sciences within the Institute of Environmental and Biological Sciences (IEBS), and is now part of the Lancaster Environment Centre; while French Studies became part of a department of Modern Languages, now called European Languages and Cultures. Operational Research absorbed another early subject, Systems Engineering, and is now termed Management Science. Philosophy, having in the early 1990s briefly formed an institute that included research on the environment, reverted to a single department, and has now joined with Politics (later Politics and International Relations) and Religious Studies to become the department of Philosophy, Politics and Religion. Biology, later Biological Sciences and then a part of the IEBS, has split to join the Lancaster Environment Centre (as Biological Sciences and Cell Biology) and the School of Health and Medicine (as Biochemistry and Life Sciences).

Of the 21 second generation subjects, 4 continue unchanged (Engineering, Law (now a school), Psychology, and Sociology), while a further 4 have had a change of appellation; Accounting and Finance (formerly Financial Control), Applied Social Science (formerly Social Administration), Educational Research (formerly Higher Education), and Organisation, Work and Technology (formerly Behaviour in Organisations). Four have been discontinued: Arabic and Islamic Studies, Central and South-Eastern European Studies, European Studies, and Independent Studies. Visual Arts, which later became Art, has joined Music and Theatre Studies in the Lancaster Institute for the Contemporary Arts (LICA), Computer Studies (later Computing) has been combined with Communications Systems to become Computing and Communications, Geography has become part of the Lancaster Environment Centre, German Studies and Italian Studies (the latter now available only as a combined major) have combined with French and Spanish in European Languages and Cultures, Religious Studies is joining Philosophy and Politics in the unitary department of Philosophy, Politics and Religion, and the Management Teaching and Development Unit greatly expanded its remit and is now the department of Management Learning and Leadership.

---

[23] Medieval Studies, which drew on History, Music and French Studies, was for a short time a separate organisational entity, but was gradually phased out structurally, although not academically.

[24] Creative Writing began as a single course in English, developed within a short-lived School of Creative Arts to the status of a combined major, was briefly an independent department, then moved to Independent Studies, and is now back with English, where it started, but with separately designated staff.

Financial Control	1968
Arabic and Islamic Studies	1973
Visual Arts	1973
Behaviour in Organisations	1969
Central and S.E. European Studies	1971
Computer Studies	1969
Higher Education	1967
Engineering	1969
European Studies	1974
Geography	1975
German Studies	1971
Independent Studies	1973
Italian Studies	1974
Law	1978
Management Teacher Development	1977
Music	1968
Psychology	1972
Religious Studies	1967
Social Administration	1974
Sociology	1969
Theatre Studies	1972

Figure 4: Second generation subjects at Lancaster, 1967–78

The pattern in the third generation of subjects, set up from 1989 to the present, is even more varied. Some schemes of study, such as Combined Science (now in the Lancaster Environment Centre with Combined Technology) or Spanish (now in European Languages and Cultures), did not gain sufficient critical mass to become departments, and the brief experiment of teaching Chinese and Japanese (1993–95) was even more transitory. The Centre for Training and Development (known as CETAD), which emerged from the faculty of Teaching and Education in 1996 to become part of the Bailrigg offerings, was included with Continuing Education in the School of Lifelong Learning and Widening Participation (SLLWP), and is now included within the School of Health and Medicine; while Continuing Education, initiated in the mid-1970s, and made a department in 1994 and a member of the SLLWP in 2005, was disbanded in 2010. Communications Systems, which grew out of Engineering in 1999, has joined Computing in a new school of Computing and Communications in 2010. American Studies was transferred from History to the Institute for Cultural Studies; the institute later merged into the Department of Media, Film and Cultural Studies that in 2010 became part of LICA, while modules in American Studies have reverted to History and the scope for a year abroad in North America no longer exists. An even more striking cycle involves Women's Studies, which evolved from Sociology in the early 1980s, and became a research institute, a flagship of Lancaster research strength, and a provider of undergraduate and postgraduate teaching and research supervision. It was made a department of the university in 2000, but recruitment fell away and in 2010 women and gender studies was once more absorbed within Sociology. On the other hand, an Institute of Entrepreneurship and Enterprise Development, set up under the aegis of the Management School as part of its outreach to the North-West, expanded from research strength to postgraduate and first degree teaching, and was made a department of the university in 2007.

The biggest single new development in the first decade of the twenty-first century has been the establishment of the School of Health and Medicine, thus fulfilling a long-standing aspiration of successive vice-chancellors. It was a difficult road, and indeed Professor Hanham in 1991 had noted "that earlier attempts to become involved with medicine had turned out very badly", while suggesting that there were now possible opportunities for the university to work with consultants and the health authorities in selected areas of postgraduate medical research.[25] In the following year a medical research trust was set up:[26] although this proved abortive in raising funds for an immediate research presence, Lancaster staff and consultants at the Royal Lancaster Infirmary became increasingly involved in mutual collaboration in the context of a growing critical mass of health and medicine-related research in the natural and social sciences and in management subjects. In 1996 an Institute for Health Research[27] was set up to draw together health-related research across the university, by then involving some sixty members of staff. The institute was later responsible for bringing D.Clin.Psy. students to Lancaster in place of Bangor, and became increasingly renowned for its work in end-of-life care and the hospice movement.

Background discussions, tentative approaches, and hard-nosed bargaining across the region led in 2003 to a decision that Lancaster should make a joint bid with the University of Liverpool to the HEFCE for 50 undergraduate medical places, to be based at Bailrigg from October 2005,[28] for students who would be admitted and graduated by Liverpool, and follow a Liverpool curriculum, but be based and taught at Lancaster. Professor Abercrombie told a rather nervous Senate that John Hutton, MP for Barrow-in-Furness and minister for health education, had drawn attention to the Morecambe Bay NHS Trust as "the only one of its size that did not include a medical school, in an area where there were special issues of provision, including remote and rural areas. The view in London was that Lancaster had the ability to make the scheme work, including for mature students." Although subsequent negotiations became stretched out, a Centre for Medical Education, with Professor Anne Garden as its first director, was approved early in 2006,[29] in time to admit the first students later in the year. After a brief period as the Department of Medicine it was absorbed into the School of Health and Medicine, which was set up in 2008 with Professor Tony Gatrell as its founding dean and

---

[25] Minute S.91/96(ii)(a), Senate meeting on 9 October 1991.

[26] Minute S.92/107, Senate meeting on 7 October 1992: see also UA.1/13/2/1 for the Cumbria and Lancashire Foundation for Medical Research.

[27] Minute S.96/35, Senate meeting on 20 March 1996; see also document AR/96/504.

[28] Minute S.2003/78, Senate meeting on 19 November 2003.

[29] Minute S.2006/15(e), Senate meeting on 22 February 2006.

LICA meeting rooms in the woods, spring 2011

almost at once was able to declare an outstanding result in RAE 2008 (see Chapter 5). The school in all but name functions as a small faculty and consists of four divisions: biomedical and life sciences (including staff from biological sciences); health research (including end-of-life care, organisational health and well-being, and mental health research); and medicine, which takes primary responsibility for the teaching programme; and CETAD. Degree programmes are offered in biochemistry, biological sciences, biomedical science, biological science, and cell biology, and the first students will graduate in the summer of 2011.

From the above summary of academic evolution it will be seen that, at a point not too far from its first half century, the university has sustained some three-quarters of its founding and second-generation disciplines and departments, albeit with combinations into larger clusters for the sake of critical mass in some instances (LEC and LICA being the most notable examples), and has progressively added to and developed from areas of strength. The relative proportion of science and non-science activity is approximately the same as in the founding years, despite a wobble in the early 1990s when Chemistry was fragmenting and the future of Physics was in doubt (see Chapter 5). The loss of languages is perhaps the most striking feature of the disciplines no longer covered, although Lancaster is far from alone in finding recruitment to foreign languages difficult. The laying down of Classics inevitably also had an adverse effect on subjects such as Philosophy, and the alliance of the latter with study of and research into the environment within society was made problematic by the rejection of that emphasis in the research assessment exercises, particularly in the 1992 round. Another example of this critical relationship was Chemistry, where poor RAE results in 1986 and 1989 became linked with weakening student recruitment. Despite the strength of a polymer group, which after some anguished debates[30] eventually transferred to the University of Sheffield, the university felt unable to resource the subject sufficiently for it to retain key staff and its Royal Society of Chemistry accreditation. This decision in turn had a negative impact, particularly on Physics and to a lesser extent on Biological Sciences, although it has been possible to continue environmental chemistry as a programme within LEC.

The overall impression of Lancaster's subject coverage, despite the losses and the movements in organisational positioning that demonstrate the porosity of subject boundaries, is therefore one of continuity and disciplinary stability across the institution. Although the subjects least able to move their boundaries seem to be those with the strongest external professional bodies, such as engineering and law, areas of teaching have emerged from research activity, and *vice versa*. Students also vary greatly in their allegiance to disciplinary areas, for while some wish to stay at the heart of long-established disciplines, others relish the opportunity to work across subject areas, either for career reasons in ways that allow them to build up a diverse portfolio of knowledge and skills, or because they wish to shape their own study; for example, medicine with law, or theatre studies with social work. How the university is organised, where it sets the boundaries or allows them to move, can be just as central to the development of teaching and learning, and to the self-identity of academic staff, as having excellent teaching facilities. The apogee of student choice was the ability within Independent Studies to propose and have approved undergraduate schemes of study centred round their personal intellectual interests. Equally popular in the early years of the university were the non-standard schemes of study, where students at Part II could combine courses from subject areas for which they had qualified at Part I, together with one-unit minors not requiring pre-requisites. Both these options provided exceptional opportunities for first degree students, but both were resource-intensive, requiring a level of individual supervision that was not economical and for which the home department of particular academics could not be adequately remunerated. The students involved also increased their level of risk: there was a notion, not too far from reality, that students in Independent Studies could expect to obtain a First or a Third, but little in between. The school catered well for students who were already sufficiently mature to take a specialist topic and broaden out from it, but there was little fallback if a study ran into the sands. Similarly, the most experimental non-standard schemes relied heavily on the student to

---

[30] See minutes S.1999/87 and S.1999/105 of the Michaelmas Term 1999, and S.2000/2(F) of 19 January 2000.

supply the coherence between units selected from different subject areas.[31] For a while the university set up specific consortial schemes of study that drew on units from a variety of departments, but the resources required to make them run well meant that only some integrated science schemes now remain.

From boards to faculties

The kaleidoscopic changes in departmental and disciplinary profiles give one indicator of institutional growth and coalescence: another is the principles by which the university groups them. Initially there were the four boards of studies, A to D, and the Board of Graduate Studies: in 1967 Board of Studies E, for the School of Education, was added. By 1969 the four mainstream boards were organised into natural sciences (A); mathematics, technology and business studies (B); social, historical and philosophical studies (C); and language, literature and area studies (D).[32] Two years later, however, a special board was set up for the School of Business and Organisational Studies (Board F).[33] While the early and main function of the boards was as a forum for interdisciplinary coordination and educational discussion, after five years of the university's full-scale operation, the Senate had ceased to consider new schemes of study in full conclave and proposals were being routed through the Development Committee. When that vehicle in turn became overloaded, they were directed through a special Senate Courses Committee, despite the separate decision to deem the boards to be committees of the Senate and hence in principle to have the ability to act on its behalf.[34] That the tension between centralised control of academic approvals and the effective functioning of the boards of studies was difficult to resolve can be seen in a rather testy report written in preparation for the Senate conference of 1979, in which the authors stated a wish to

> restore to the boards the powers which, constructively at least, have been moved to powerful central committees. It was brought to [our] attention, particularly by the academic registrar, that the central committees came into being because the boards were thought to be scrutinising inadequately proposals for new courses and new methods of assessment. [We are] not persuaded that the degree of uniformity that the academic registrar thinks essential is either desirable or in reality possible ... Above all [we] recognise and hope that the Development Committee and the Senate will recognise that the real guarantees of academic standards and of fairness of treatment of students (as far as it is attainable) reside in the academic standards and integrity of the teaching and

---

31 For a discussion of these issues, see Paul Trowler, "Beyond Epistemological Essentialism: Academic Tribes in the 21st Century", in *The University and Its Disciplines: Teaching and Learning within and Beyond Disciplinary Boundaries*, ed. Carolin Kreber (New York: Routledge, 2009), pp. 181–95.

32 Document GM/69/89, to Senate on 12 February 1969.

33 Minute S.71/132, Board of Senate meeting on 3 March 1971.

34 Document GM/71/659, to Board of Senate meeting on 29 November 1971.

examining members of staff of the university and of the external examiners carefully appointed by the Committee of the Senate. With good teachers and good external examiners the university has nothing to fear; without them it will find that bureaucratic scrupulosity is not only tedious and irritating but also ineffective.[35]

The subsequent debate marked a shift of responsibility to the boards of studies for the final approval of courses. The compromise reached was that the Academic Registrar should bring to the Senate's attention proposals he thought it should examine, while the Senate Courses Committee was to be laid to rest but the Committee on Examinations and the Board of Graduate Studies were to continue.[36]

In 1983 Economics moved from Board B to Board F, more because it wanted to be part of management and organisational studies than because of discontentment with its home board of studies.[37] However, it was not many months before the transfer had caused Board B to crumble and its remaining departments were also moved; Computer Studies, Engineering, and Mathematics to Board A (the science board), and Geography to Board C (the social sciences board). Equally, however, there could be moves in other directions, for Law was initially intended to be part of business studies and the department was briefly located in Gillow House for the purpose, before it moved organisationally and physically to join the social sciences.[38]

The growing self-identity of business and management led to months of internal debate resulting in a form of constitution, novel for Lancaster, that was equivalent in staff numbers and disciplinary spread to a board of studies, but which was internally initiated. The new School was:

1. to provide a focus for and to encourage planning of joint academic provision (especially resources and staff facilities) pertaining in the area of management and organisational studies, without prejudice to final discussion within Board F;
2. to make provision for the operation of consortial academic activities;
3. to foster research (particularly cross-disciplinary research) within the area of management and organisational studies ...,
4. to act as a unified body for purposes of external representation and publicity ...,

so that Board F was in effect being treated as the senior body that approved the academic

---

[35] Document GM/79/227, to Senate at its meeting on 28 June 1979: by authors A. Mercer (Operational Research), R. M. Hogg (Linguistics), C. A. Lyas (Philosophy), R. H. Tredgold (Physics), and S. M. Warren (Student Representative Council).
[36] Section III of the record of the Conference of the Senate held on 12 April 1980: reports of items deemed to be of note continued to appear in the Senate agenda until the opening years of the twenty-first century.
[37] Document GM/83/13, to Senate on 19 January 1983.
[38] Law was a member of the school from 1978 (S.78/26) to 1989 (S.89/48).

provision and discussed the affairs of the School. This dual structure was approved by Board F and the Senate in late 1984.[39] With the appointment of a dean of the School in 1987 (see Chapter 1), a shift in the balance of authority occurred, with a revised constitution that, while it left the board and the School running in tandem for some time to come, positioned the School as the body to which the university looked for policy decisions.[40]

A precedent for a faculty-like structure had thus been set and, within the context of the university's discussion of the Jarratt report (see Chapter 2) and strongly encouraged by the Vice-Chancellor and by pressure from SPARC, the boards of studies for the social sciences and for the humanities were the next to jump. In June 1989 proposals came to the Senate for faculty boards in both areas that would replace the boards of studies and that had not dissimilar stated objectives as those in the Management School template.[41] The Senate was not wholly convinced and in response

> to uncertainties expressed about what the expected benefits were from faculties and what had been the expectations of the most senior levels of the university in initiating the debate about them, the Vice-Chancellor explained that in the case of the social sciences, he was looking for a leader who would work on the creation of a stronger staff community to respond to national initiatives, as a head of intellectual development, to draw people together when funding becomes more interdisciplinary. In the case of the humanities, the funding imperatives were not quite the same, but there was a need to work more closely together and to have a spokesman to articulate their agreed position.[42]

Both faculty boards were to have elected deans and associate deans, and both were to follow the Management School in having a policy and resources committee, while the social sciences also added committees for teaching and research.

The sciences, however, were moving in the opposite direction, and Board of Studies A was dissolved in favour of three new bodies for the sciences: the Institute of Environmental and Biological Sciences; the School of Engineering, Computing and Mathematical Sciences; and the School of Physics and Materials. Their sole link was a Joint Courses Committee. It is interesting to reflect on the consequences for the sciences of this fragmentation, which probably did not help any of the departments involved when the time for difficult choices about the sciences occurred in the early 1990s. In 1994 a faculty board of Education was established to cater for the Charlotte Mason departments that had come into the university through the short-lived department of Teacher Education and Training, and to this were

---

[39] Documents GM/84/292 (amended); GM/84/36 (amended); minute S.84/169, Senate meeting on 21 November 1984.

[40] School of Management, Interim Constitution, document GM/87/234, approved by the Senate on 3 June 1987 (S.87/99).

[41] Documents GM/89/105 (Social Sciences) and GM/89/202 (revised) (Humanities); see also GM/89/204 and GM/89/233, to the Senate on 7 June 1989: the term "faculty board" was used to allow the new entities to exist without an immediate change to the Statutes.

[42] Minute S.89/81, Senate meeting on 7 June 1989.

added Continuing Education, the LU Archaeological Unit, and the Institute of English Language Education.[43] The university had thus acquired seven bodies by which to manage its academic affairs, and it comes as no surprise that, in the process of re-establishing financial stability a couple of years later, close attention was given to university structures and procedures. The transfer of Charlotte Mason College to S. Martin's College in 1996 led to the breakdown of Education, and the three science groupings were clustered into two faculty boards: Environmental and Natural Sciences, and Applied Sciences.[44]

While the five faculty boards thus remaining continued in place for the best part of a decade, changes within them were continuous. There was increasing devolution of budgetary responsibility to faculty boards; shifts in the method of selection of deans from election to appointment; and changes in the relationship between heads of departments and deans that increasingly made the faculty boards, rather than the departments, the main channel of communication between central governance and administration, including in matters related to academic programmes and the teaching and learning policies of the institution. This process was heightened in the course of a strategic review in 2003. The Senate was invited[45] to approve a project intended to devolve more authority and responsibility to the faculties in respect of budgets, appointments, promotions, and quality assurance, and to move resources from departments, and from central offices, to the faculties. There was also to be more delegated authority to senior postholders, including the deans, in order that areas of risk could be treated uniformly. A report in October re-asserted the objectives of the exercise and bluntly stated that there would be "three faculties with fully functional faculty offices", since the university

> no longer had the resource necessary to support five faculties, but could support three. In addition, three would help Lancaster in efforts to be more visible externally and would assist the drive to efficiency and speed. There were risks for the institution in moving to relatively less direct central control, particularly in such matters as staff appointments, but steps would be taken to manage the risks.[46]

The Senate, again sceptical, asked its working party to test the respective merits of both three and five faculties, but not to look at alternative structures, such as clusters of schools.[47]

The reconvened discussion, in March 2004, matched in length and complexity the significance of the proposed changes,[48] and although proposals for three faculties were

---

[43] Minute S.94/30, Senate meeting on 16 March 1994.

[44] Minute S.96/106.25, Senate meeting on 13 November 1996.

[45] Document VC/03/R163 to the Senate, meeting on 28 May 2003: see also minute S.2003/36(b).

[46] Document VC/03/R225, to Senate on 8 October 2003: an appendix demonstrated that the annual income of the three would roughly be in equilibrium, although the student load was highest for arts and social sciences, and the staff numbers for the sciences (VC/03/332).

[47] Minute S.2003/65, Senate meeting on 8 October 2003.

[48] Minute S.2004/18, Senate meeting on 10 March 2004.

Charles Carter and Hugh Pollard walking into Lancaster Priory, 9 October 1964 (copyright, *Lancashire Evening Post*)

agreed – an unchanged Management School, a faculty of Science and Technology that included both Psychology and Geography, and a faculty of Arts and Social Sciences – the timescale for implementation was extended to August 2005. Some of the potential drawbacks were freely acknowledged. First, there would be overt competition for resources between the three faculties, but it was stated to be preferable for that debate to take place between the faculties, rather than at UMAG, which would in its turn attempt to take an oversight of the whole institution; secondly, some senior and research-active staff would be diverted to become deans and associate deans; and, thirdly, a forthcoming QAA institutional audit would be framed in the context of an institution in the midst of major structural change. The intention was that the deans would be full-time, for periods of five years, renewable once at the discretion of the Vice-Chancellor, and that they would be members of UMAG[49] and would have to balance their roles both as members of a senior management executive

---

[49] See also S.2004/37, Senate meeting on 26 May 2010.

A HISTORY OF THE UNIVERSITY OF LANCASTER

and as protagonists for their faculties. There would also be associate deans who would be relieved of teaching but not research duties.

And so, a year later, the new structures came on stream, and were joined by the School of Lifelong Learning and Widening Participation to encompass Continuing Education and CETAD. In 2008 they were joined by the new School of Health and Medicine (see above): in 2010, however, the School of Lifelong Learning and Widening Participation was laid down at the demise of Continuing Education. The four workhorse thematic committees, the Lancaster Graduate School and the committees for Undergraduate Studies, for the Associated Institutions, and for Lifelong Learning, Widening Participation and Outreach, were also disbanded, leaving behind two advisory groups for the deans of undergraduate and postgraduate studies respectively. Given this rate of change, and the propensity at Lancaster for frequent alterations to structures, the three main faculties are almost certainly not the last word and, however rational a choice for external presentation they are, they do not fully lend themselves to assisting the infinitely complex networks and alliances of Bailrigg departments. The faculties continue the process of internalising their new responsibilities, even as the central services make adjustments in relation to a process of devolution that, while far-reaching, cannot remove ultimate responsibility from the university's governing bodies and senior officers.

Collaborative provision

When Charles Carter and Hugh Pollard walked side by side to Lancaster Priory on the occasion of a service of thanksgiving for both university and college in October 1964, their destinies seemed quite separate. Lancaster had less than a month earlier received full degree-approving and degree-awarding powers, while S. Martin's courses were to be validated by the University of Manchester, the institution that would also award their degrees. Yet these divergent paths soon came together, for in 1967 Lancaster set up its School of Education under the direction of Professor Alec Ross,[50] with Area Training Organisation status delegated by the DES from Manchester to Lancaster. By 1973 not only had S. Martin's College been brought under the validating wing of Lancaster, but so had Edge Hill College of Education at Ormskirk, as well as smaller institutions at Chorley and Poulton-le-Fylde. Charlotte Mason College at Ambleside,[51] which had initially not been included in these arrangements, made further overtures in 1973 and had its courses validated by Lancaster from 1979. Another, five-year, validating relationship with the C. F. Mott campus of Liverpool Polytechnic also featured in the School's work.[52] These arrangements could become very complex: Edge Hill, for example, had special regulations drawn up so

---

[50] McClintock, *Quest*, pp. 183–9: a separate board of studies – initially E but later enlarged and re-termed H – reported direct to the Senate.

[51] See J. P. Inman, *Charlotte Mason College* (Winchester: Cormorant, 1985), pp. 68–86.

[52] Minute S.85/12, Senate meeting on 23 January 1985: see also the attached text of a letter to P. A. Reynolds from the Rector of Liverpool Polytechnic.

that some part-time students taking a BA in combined studies validated by Lancaster could also take a minor with Lancashire Polytechnic.[53] Successive secretaries and their staff of the School of Education and the later Office for the Associated Institutions[54] had to show exceptional dexterity in managing the fine grain of these validating relationships, including the negotiation of appropriate regulations and their correct interpretation and application. Lancaster became acknowledged as a major player in the field, both quantitatively and qualitatively.[55]

In 1986 Lancaster was invited, in common with a rationalisation of small colleges that also involved the universities of Leeds and Nottingham, to enter into still closer association with Charlotte Mason College, one of the "monotechnic teacher training institutions which are too small to offer the range and depth of subject studies which are essential within the B.Ed. degree",[56] and increased numbers for the college were made conditional on progress in this direction. The Charlotte Mason students, all of whom were training for primary school teaching, were to spend their first year at Ambleside, following an area of subject study taught by the college's staff. In their second year the students would come to Bailrigg and follow the same subject area alongside Lancaster Part II students, and then return to Ambleside for their third and fourth years of the B.Ed. degree. They would, by this means, reach the level of subject study appropriate to qualification as primary school teachers.[57] Funding of £2000 per student was to be paid to the university, and an allowance of £1 million was also allocated by Cumbria County Council to enable the Charlotte Mason students to be resident at Bailrigg rather than in lodgings (see Chapter 7).[58] The first cohort of students would reach the university in October 1988, and were to be eligible for the award of B.Ed. with honours.[59] These arrangements proved not to be wholly satisfactory. The students involved – some 120 a year – found themselves plunged into a much larger and more challenging institution than the environment to which they were accustomed and, while some individuals achieved conspicuous success, there were numerous comments at boards of studies about their need for additional tutorial support and their tendency to be grouped towards the lower end of the range of marks. The arrangement was thus further developed, under the watchful eye of Professor Alec Ross, to the attainment of full incorporation of

---

[53] Minute S.85/112, Senate meeting of 5 June 1985.

[54] The change from school to office was made in August 1990, and this was the point at which Professor Walter Fairbairn became the dean: see minute S.90/67, Senate meeting on 6 June 1990.

[55] See, for example, the terms of Lancaster's response to Further Education Unit, *FEU Response to Academic Validation of Degree Courses for Higher Education [the Lindop Report]* (London: FEU, 1985), tabled at the Senate on 5 June 1985, and subsequent discussion of the consequential code of practice (S.86/157).

[56] DES letter of 14 May 1986: quoted in document GM/86/152, Senate meeting of 4 June 1986.

[57] Minute S.86/104, Senate meeting on 4 June 1986.

[58] Minute S.86/125, Senate meeting on 21 June 1986.

[59] Minute S.87/54, Senate meeting on 25 March 1987.

the college from August 1992, to give further protection to teacher training in particular and higher education in Cumbria more generally.[60]

The early 1990s were a period of rapid change in further education, particularly once the former polytechnics took on the mantle of university status from 1992. Lancaster did not stand still, but successfully steered the way for the associated colleges to move from the BEd to a BA or BSc with Qualified Teacher Status.[61] A particularly significant change, initiated by Lancaster, was for the post of assessor to move to the role of course consultant,[62] a term that brought with it the attribute of direct partnership. Lancaster staff thus became involved with informal discussions about new courses and issues surrounding validation, and they attended examination boards to advise on practice and precedent, as well as visiting students and staff on Lancaster-validated awards to talk through their experiences. It was an appropriate and timely step that, during the operation of the scheme for the better part of two decades, built up a knowledge base and dissemination of good practice between institutions linked with Lancaster, as well as within them, and one that regularly received plaudits in external reviews. It was also part of a general philosophy that supported the development of greater autonomy for the institutions associated with Lancaster, both existing and to follow. Another change was to invite the associated institutions to take more responsibility for their research students,[63] for whom the university had made shared supervision arrangements since 1987, especially for their supervision and welfare. Yet another was the decision to ask the associated institutions to set up their own Part I examination boards, without university representation,[64] that would make binding decisions about which students could proceed to Part II.

These steps were evolutionary, but important for institutions that wished to gain increasing independence. Informal overtures by the new director of Edge Hill College, Ruth Gee, developed into a formal request for accredited status, a term that Professor Fairbairn sought to define, as he

> stressed the crucial importance of ensuring that the status and standard of the degrees in the accredited institutions must be the same as those of the university, and thus the university's retention of the responsibility to appoint external examiners and the submission of their reports to the vice-chancellor as well as the head of the accredited institution were fundamental safeguards ... the expectation was that the accredited

---

[60] See minute S.91/101, Senate meeting on 9 October 1991. This incorporation in turn came to an end in 1996: see William Ritchie and Marion E. McClintock, "Capital Building and Cash Flow at the University of Lancaster", in *Managing Crisis*, ed. David Warner and David Palfreyman (Maidenhead: Open University Press, 2003), pp. 37, 41–2.

[61] Minute S.91/19, Senate meeting on 23 January 1991.

[62] Minute S.90/84, Senate meeting on 6 June 1990.

[63] Minute S.91/44, Senate meeting on 20 March 1991.

[64] Minute S.91/51, Senate meeting on 20 March 1991.

institutions would be brought within the scope of national agreements on academic audit and quality control.[65]

The Senate agreed that an inspection group should be set up to work with Edge Hill on the formulation of accreditation proposals, and this was followed by a matching group for S. Martin's College.[66]

All the parties involved entered the discussions in the expectation that any issues encountered could readily be resolved. In practice the process became increasingly protracted, as the extent to which the validating university could properly cede authority for the quality of its awards became uncertain. Behind the courteous rhetoric of the official record, the increasing frustration that a solution satisfactory to all could not be found is apparent, culminating in a Senate meeting of March 1993[67] when the recommendation of the accreditation panel was that "accreditation should not be granted at this time" to Edge Hill. Professor Gee, while accepting the report, expressed particular disappointment at the lack of common ground about what the term accreditation should imply, noting that the college's application for this status two years earlier had been seen as a step towards obtaining degree-awarding powers. As these differences of interpretation between the CNAA model and Lancaster's implicit definitions were highlighted by Edge Hill, similar sentiments were voiced by Professor Edenbry for S. Martin's College.[68] Further discussions took place, alongside further devolution of specific processes, under the aegis of the Committee for Associated Institutions. The pragmatic solution reached was that the existing, highly devolved partnership agreements with Edge Hill and S. Martin's should in principle be redesignated as *de jure* accreditation for both colleges,[69] in order to "assist the colleges in identifying their status and clarify it in relation to similar institutions in other parts of the country, but [it] would not denote any change in the nature of the relationship with the university nor any further devolution of authority or responsibility". The two colleges were thus enabled to prepare themselves for moves towards degree-awarding status.

Meanwhile, two other major developments had taken place. The first was the establishment of an International Committee,[70] primarily for links across Europe. The university was fortunate that one of its early forays into formal links with overseas organisations was the validation of a master's degree in sociology at the Central European University, initially situated in Prague,[71] a relationship that in an evolved form continues to this day. The numbers were manageable, the students of high calibre, and the staff generally well prepared

---

[65] Minute S.91/102, Senate meeting on 9 October 1991.
[66] Minute S.92/15, Senate meeting on 22 January 1992.
[67] Minute S.93/56, Senate meeting on 17 March 1993.
[68] Minute S.92/82, Senate meeting on 3 June 1992.
[69] Minute S.94/83, Senate meeting on 1 June 1994.
[70] Minute S.90/108, Senate meeting on 10 October 1990.
[71] Minute S.93/140(E), Senate meeting on 10 November 1993: see also S.96/73 of 5 June 1996 for renewal of the relationship with CEU, now relocated to Warsaw.

for partnership arrangements with Lancaster. It was an auspicious start to the process of learning how to support high quality of provision at long distance. Internally at Lancaster the relationship was managed through the Office for the Associated Institutions, with input from the postgraduate committee of the social sciences faculty board.

The second was approaches by two further education colleges in Lancashire that offered some higher education: at Blackpool and The Fylde, in Bispham and central Blackpool; and at Blackburn, in the heart of the town by that name. Unlike that of S. Martin's and Edge Hill, most of their provision was pre-degree level and, furthermore, the higher education work was not conducted on the basis of an exclusive relationship, for Blackburn in particular had validating relationships with universities at some distance. Blackpool excelled at hospitality management and at art, with growing areas of strength in information technology: discussions there, building on existing validations, fairly quickly reached the point where the college could be awarded associate status with Lancaster.[72] Blackburn's special strengths lay in engineering, in selected areas of business studies, and in criminology and in applied social sciences, and its student body included not only (like Blackpool) a large number of part-time students but also a substantial proportion of ethnic groups and women within those groups. The negotiations were protracted while the extent to which Blackburn would retain its existing validation relationships elsewhere was debated, but an institutional evaluation of April 1994 led to a recommendation that Blackburn should become an associate college, "a relationship ... formed on the assumption of partnership. Since this implies a more equal relationship than the college has enjoyed hitherto with other validating institutions, the college would need to accept that the relationship with Lancaster University will need to develop over time so that it is characterised by ... a greater maturity on the part of the college in the development and delivery of higher education programmes."[73] The formalities were completed a year later, with a three-year review built in.[74] By the time the review took place the college was pressing for closer links with Lancaster, including the possible transfer of Blackburn-funded student numbers to Lancaster, but there were sensitivities involving Lancaster's Management School, and the proposals fell away.[75]

Further incremental changes were made to the processes involving both Edge Hill and S. Martin's colleges. Their accredited status was ready for major review in 2000, by which time their joint undergraduate population was larger than that of Bailrigg. The review process, chaired by Professor Bob McKinlay, was extended and exhaustive, and undertaken in the context of QAA guidance on collaborative provision. The focus was on the quality of the output: issues such as equivalence of student experience and unfair competition were, however, also identified as critically important. The intention was to set up systems that took the colleges' distinctive missions and their growing maturity into account, and when new instruments of accreditation were approved for the five years to July 2005 it was

---

[72] Minute S.93/122, Senate meeting on 6 October 1993.
[73] Minute S.94/84, Senate meeting on 1 June 1994.
[74] Minute S.95/41, Senate meeting on 22 March 1995.
[75] Minute S.99/43, Senate meeting on 24 February 1999.

agreed that there would be an Accredited Colleges Committee that would be equipped to deal appropriately with their evolving autonomy.[76] Another device was to run a series of academic equivalence reviews that looked at particular subjects taught in at least two of the three institutions (Edge Hill, S. Martin's, and Lancaster), in order to test their equivalence of academic standards.

An account of the accredited status of the two colleges formed part of Lancaster's submission to the QAA for the 2000 Continuation Audit (see also below). Another part of the collaborative provision that was causing interest was the partnership arrangements with selected universities overseas, and reports were included about an MA programme with the Chinese University in Hong Kong and a BBA in European management that involved three European partners, in Germany, France and Spain, for a dual award. The 2000 review also took note of an increasing series of bilateral arrangements with overseas universities that enabled students who were successful on initial programmes at their home institutions to progress direct to Part II at Lancaster.[77] Other overseas collaborative arrangements at the time included an MA with the University of Lodz and a PhD for Romanian students, both in linguistics; an MA in Management for senior managers in conjunction with McGill, Insead and the Indian Institute of Management at Bangalore; an MSc in communications with DEL, Thessaloniki; and an interesting but short-lived overseas placement arrangement for an MRes in geography.[78]

Another national challenge to higher education came with the introduction of Foundation Degrees, to enable students to receive a completed award at the equivalent of the end of the first year of Part II.[79] After some painstaking discussion about how Lancaster should appropriately respond, both for its Bailrigg departments and its regional partners, a decision was forced over the summer of 2000 by the need to bid (or not) for funded numbers. Professor Fulton, as Dean of the Associated Institutions, explained to the Senate in October[80] that a bid for numbers in applied guidance, teaching assistants, and technology had been despatched; in other words, in subject areas with applicability to the accredited and associated institutions. He was strongly supported by the Deputy Vice-Chancellor, who emphasised the duty of the university to its partner colleges and to the region and its employers. The bid was successful, and over the next five years the range and extent of such awards at the colleges developed rapidly. Enormous effort was put into the validation

---

[76] Minutes S.2000/27, Senate meeting on 23 February 2000; and S.2000/58, Senate meeting on 31 May 2000.

[77] R. Cook, Letter and enclosures to Nicola Channon of the Institutional Review Directorate, 22 June 1999.

[78] Appendix 2 Quality Assurance Agency for Higher Education, "University of Lancaster Quality Audit Report", http://www.qaa.ac.uk/reviews/reports/institutional/lancaster/lancaster.asp#47. No feedback on these activities was given to Lancaster.

[79] The original intention was that a further one and a third years of study would be required to reach honours degree standard.

[80] Minute S.2000/84, Senate meeting on 11 October 2000.

Professor Philip Reynolds, Acting
Vice-Chancellor and Vice-Chancellor, 1979
to 1985

of each scheme, on the basis that each approved programme would be available for delivery at any of the colleges. Tripartite arrangements that involved one of the four initial partners extending the provision to other further education colleges in the region, however, proved more difficult for the university to manage.

Institutional approaches to Lancaster, as a university known to have both a high reputation and the infrastructure to manage complex arrangements, were regularly received from within the UK and around the world. Some of these approaches did not come to fruition; others fell away after a brief period, so that the enduring relationships are by no means the whole picture of Lancaster's involvement. Some of the range and diversity of these activities is reflected in the Self-Evaluation[81] of November 2005 for an Audit of Collaborative Provision held early the following year, where no less than 51 institutions were cited, ranging from Westlakes Research Institute in Cumbria, where a single master's level module was run, to Grimsby College of Higher Education at Hull for two schemes of study, to Knowsley College in Liverpool for Foundation Degrees, and overseas from mainland China to Korea and Hong Kong, and through most countries in west and east Europe, and in level from Foundation Degrees to doctoral study. Two case studies were undertaken, one of the IMPM in management, and the

---

[81]   Document AR/2005/871, November 2005.

other of the BBA in European management. Three visits to partner institutions were made, two of which were virtual (by means of video-conference), and the Students' Union produced a statement about their support of international students. Other documents included the 2005 re-accreditation reports for S. Martin's and Edge Hill and a dozen accounts of academic equivalency reviews. The QAA visit itself lasted from 27 to 31 March 2006, and the verdict of broad confidence[82] in present and future management and capacity was a fitting culmination to much investment by Lancaster staff in collaborative provision.[83]

Quality assurance

Lancaster might be thought to bear some responsibility for the national system of quality assurance that has developed at higher education institutions over the last quarter century. Professor Philip Reynolds, Lancaster's second vice-chancellor, chaired a CVCP group of distinguished members of universities across the system that in 1984 published a brief paper entitled "External involvement in the maintenance and monitoring of academic standards",[84] following on from earlier publication of his code of practice on the external examiner system for first degree and taught master's courses. Unabashed by the involvement of their own vice-chancellor, members of the Senate reacted sharply to the CVCP paper and to guidance from the Development Committee about it.[85] Concern was expressed at the extent "to which accrediting bodies, some of which had no senior academic persons on them, influenced or might influence academic activities in universities, in moulding syllabuses, in changing modes of teaching, in appraising modes of assessment". A "general antipathy" to external advisory committees was voiced, and it was felt that external assessors on appointing committees should have "neither a veto nor a dominant voice in the making of decisions".

However, the paper was in practice the first leaf in a blizzard of such documents, initially from a CVCP that felt it necessary to anticipate moves by government for greater monitoring of academic standards, and by a UGC that turned the debate on academic standards towards the broader issue of performance indicators, and thus to the Jarratt report (see Chapter 2). Little more than a year later the Senate was prepared to acquiesce to a proposal from its Steering Committee to accept a further report and to say that

> the university welcomes the document, which has been given careful consideration …
> These discussions made it clear that the proposed procedures closely reflect existing

---

[82] Quality Assurance Agency for Higher Education, *University of Lancaster Collaborative Provision Audit*, RG 264 08/06 (Gloucester: QAA, 2006).

[83] See below for the most recent developments in collaborative provision, including the so-called hybrid review of 2009.

[84] Committee of Vice-Chancellors and Principals, *External Involvement in the Maintenance and Monitoring of Academic Standards* (London: CVCP, 1984).

[85] Minute S.85/71, Senate meeting on March 1985.

practices within the university. The Senate, however, noted the need to devise procedures for monitoring courses from departmental level upwards ... [and] has recently established a working party to examine the effectiveness of its teaching styles ...[86]

Once the HEFCE was in place, the national debate about the assurance of quality in higher education increased. In summary, the White Paper of 1991[87] and the Further and Higher Education Act of 1992[88] required the HEFCE to ensure that provision was made "for assessing the quality of education in institutions for whose activities [the three funding councils] provide, or are considering providing, financial support". The HEQC, set up to manage these new responsibilities, would accordingly make "academic quality audits of institutions of higher education in the whole of the United Kingdom. The scope of the audit is wide",[89] and was to include privately and publicly funded provision at undergraduate and postgraduate levels. Two parallel auditing practices were to be used: individual subject reviews in each institution, initially graded as excellent, satisfactory and so on, but later using a 24-point scale that lent itself all too readily to the compilation of crude league tables and a series of institutional audits. In 1996 a Joint Planning Group for Quality Assurance in Higher Education recommended that the two streams be merged into a single body, leading to the launch of the QAA at Gloucester in April 1997. The Dearing report, published later that year, made recommendations that led to the expansion of the QAA remit, adding the provision of public information on quality assurance, verification of standards, and a heightening of the external examiner role. Until 2001 subject reviews and academic audits continued in parallel, with the intention to merge the two thereafter in a single academic review process, deploying a three-year cycle that became a six-year rotation in 2005. In England, for the period to 2011, the current processes are:[90] institutional audit; collaborative provision audit; integrated quality and enhancement review (for higher education delivered in further education colleges); and access to higher education for access-validating agencies that award certificates and diplomas.[91] A supporting academic framework includes manuals on higher education qualifications, subject benchmark statements, programme specifications, and a code of good practice. The QAA can also commission thematic reviews.

As the HEFCE bedded in during 1992, Lancaster's Senate entered into debates about the contextual issues relating to academic quality assurance, including the enhancement

---

[86] Minute S.86/107, Senate meeting on 4 June 1986.

[87] Department of Education and Science, *Higher Education: A New Framework*, Cm. 1541 (London: HMSO, 1991).

[88] Section 70(1)(a), *Further and Higher Education Act* 1992.

[89] Higher Education Funding Council for England and Higher Education Quality Council, "Joint Statement on Quality Assurance," http://www.hefce.ac.uk/pubs/hefce/1994/m1_94.htm.

[90] http://www.qaa.ac.uk/reviews/default.asp (15 July 2010).

[91] Lancaster was open to review by all these means until the Open College for the North West became disengaged from the university in 2009. It now takes sole and total responsibility for its own quality assurance.

of staff development, the initiation of departmental reviews, a more structured framework for relationships with the associated institutions, and degree schemes for the sciences that allowed for four years,[92] including one year of advanced study. Lancaster was one of the first institutions to experience the new institutional audit, and the new developments, together with much other factual information, were included in documents coordinated by the Planning Office for invited guests from the Division of Quality Audit of the HEQC. The process was untried, and somewhat exploratory and tentative for all the parties involved, as well as lacking the intense preparation and rehearsal that characterised its successors. As a result, the institutional portrait in the subsequent report[93] has the merit of immediacy, depicting an institution showing

> obvious commitment at all levels in the University to maintaining and enhancing academic quality. This was evident in the concern to provide a favourable teaching and learning environment as it was in the research area.

Accolades included the success of the Enterprise in Higher Education programme and its continuation in the Unit for Innovation in Higher Education, the involvement of students in the teaching and learning processes, the departmental codes of teaching practice, the care over probationary academic staff, and the inclusion of a teaching profile in academic staff promotions. Criticisms included inconsistencies of practice, overcrowded teaching rooms, and the need to structure staff development. In the following year the first of the subject reviews took place, and these were complemented by professional body reviews; the one for mechanical engineering, for example, was described as "not painful".[94] Internal reviews of all academic departments were undertaken in the early 1990s, under the aegis of the Planning Office, and although in practice there was a heavy emphasis on research, the reviews had important consequences for the future staffing of departments and hence an obvious bearing on teaching quality.[95]

Despite all these actions, however, there was concern that Lancaster was lagging behind other institutions in the design of its first degree, and in the way that support services were organised, and in June 1997 the Senate received reports from two working parties designed to tackle both problems. The first was about a proposed simplification of academic structures, involving a decision to change the number of Part II units from nine to eight, each equating to 30 CATS points, and combining this with the adoption of notional learning

---

[92] Minutes S.92/102; S.92/110; S.92/109; S.92/108(b), all from a meeting of the Senate held on 7 October 1992.

[93] Higher Education Quality Council, *University of Lancaster: Quality Audit Report*, Quality Audit Report (Birmingham: HEQC, 1993).

[94] Minute S.93/70(d), Senate meeting on 2 June 1993.

[95] See, for example, the discussion of the Geography review (minute S.94/28, Senate meeting on 16 March 1994. This cycle of reviews was not completed until the end of the 1996 calendar year.

hours,[96] less student choice and more core units, and a determination that all Part II units should be examined in the Summer Term of the year in which they were taught, so that second year examinations would take place across all schemes of study.[97] By a series of closely contested votes, and with much strength of feeling expressed on both sides of the argument, the proposals were passed[98] and sent away for further work and implementation. The second report was more explicitly designed to respond to

> growing pressure from national bodies, including the HEFCE and the HEQC, to develop formal policies on teaching, learning and assessment and to demonstrate that [higher education institutions] have structures in place through which these policies can be implemented. The outcomes of audit and assessment are increasingly widely publicised to potential students and those who advise them ... and if Lancaster graduates are to be attractive to potential employers, then the University must play a clear role in developing transferable skills, including self-reliance and information skills [and] the identification of a portfolio of such skills will also represent an important contribution towards the development of a distinctive Lancaster sense of 'graduateness'. Measures of the success of our graduates in the employment market will be a further indicator ... The forthcoming Dearing Report will almost certainly add to these pressures, for example in the area of training for academic staff.[99]

The intention was therefore to draw together within a single organisational structure the services covering staff development, teaching innovation, learning technology, short courses for senior and middle management, study support, and pre-sessional academic support for overseas students. The Senate was not minded to agree at once[100] and it was only in October, and after an away day of the groups most closely involved, that Professor Fulton presented revised proposals for a structure that would integrate staff development, the Unit for Innovation in Higher Education, and the Higher Education Professional Courses Unit.[101] The Staff and Student Teaching Development Unit was established a few months later,[102] subsequently changing to the Student Learning Development Centre.

In the meantime the Deputy Vice-Chancellor, Professor Abercrombie, was keen to ensure that the Senate was left in no doubt that the new system being introduced by the QAA would be "more draconian" than the existing arrangements, would "be likely to have a profound effect on the way the university's academic business was conducted", and would

---

[96] Notional learning hours included hours of study invested by the student in addition to the contact hours.

[97] Document S.R.97/248 (revised), submitted to the Senate on 4 June 1997.

[98] Minute S.97/55, Senate meeting on 4 June 1997.

[99] Para. 2.2 of report to the Senate of the Working Group on Teaching, Learning and Assessment Structures (OAI/97/149 (revised), to Senate on 4 June 1997.

[100] Minute S.97/57, Senate meeting on 4 June 1997.

[101] Minute S.97/73, Senate meeting on 8 October 1997.

[102] Minute S.98/27(G), Senate meeting on 18 March 1998.

"be more extensive and more robust".[103] The difficulty was that while the QAA's founding director, John Randall, was making waves around the sector, no definitive proposals had been promulgated, leaving scope for some universities to make their dissent plain. Since Lancaster was to face an institutional audit in 2000, which would cover both the Bailrigg departments and its collaborative provision, there was some sensitivity about the position that the university might wish to adopt.

The analytical account required of the university was despatched in late 1999,[104] and the subsequent visit involved 13 meetings with staff and students and a volume of supporting documentation that occupied most of the Senate chamber. The exercise was thus hugely resource intensive, both for the QAA and the university. The outcome was positive, however, citing an institution that "has evidently sought, in a methodical and cumulative manner, to develop appropriate frameworks for the management of quality and standards",[105] that had sought to systematise its degree structure, and had used its faculty board structures as a means of managing the tension between departmental autonomy and "the provision of sufficient institutional steer and direction to assure the standards of the University's awards".[106]

Even while the report of the audit was awaited, however, there were further discussions by the Senate[107] about what was expected of the sector, a question not necessarily easy to answer while the QAA itself underwent changes of direction and policy, and the merits of deeper intervention or a lighter touch were debated. Responsibility for quality assurance at Lancaster passed from the Planning Office to a Quality Standards Office which was later augmented to become the Centre for the Enhancement of Learning and Teaching (CELT). Internal processes were developed that mirrored those imposed from outside. In addition to the annual departmental reviews, the reports from which were channelled through faculty teaching committees to the relevant thematic committee and thence to the Senate, once every sixth year departments would be "asked to undertake a systematic and thorough review of their undergraduate and postgraduate ... provision and of the way in which quality and standards are assured at departmental level".[108] Review teams would be set up, including at least one external member, and departments would be asked to write a critical self-evaluation in advance. Since the initial reviews in 2002–03, which for a time threatened to become as onerous as any external visitation, a lighter touch has been

---

[103] Minutes S.98/3(E) (21 January 1998); S.98/26(F) (18 March 1998); S.98/82(F) (7 October 1998).

[104] University of Lancaster, "Continuation Audit 28 February to 3 March 2000: Analytical Account" (AR/99/1259).

[105] Para. 94 Quality Assurance Agency for Higher Education, "University of Lancaster Quality Audit Report".

[106] Para. 97 Quality Assurance Agency for Higher Education, "University of Lancaster Quality Audit Report".

[107] See, for example, minute S.2000/19 of 23 February 2000.

[108] Lancaster University, "Periodic Quality Review: Guidance to Departments" (QSO, August 2002).

developed and greater efforts made to facilitate departmental access to relevant data on their own performance.

By the time the university was preparing for a further institutional audit in 2004 programme specifications had been written for all taught degree schemes in every department and approved by the relevant teaching committees; annual programme reviews took place at the end of each academic cycle (summer for undergraduate programmes, and autumn or winter for postgraduates). In addition, four projects had been launched as part of a learning, teaching, and assessment strategy designed to improve assessment practices; to help students develop their skills, awareness, and capabilities for their later careers; to develop cost-efficient and flexible teaching practices; and to improve student-related data.[109] In addition to seven general meetings with staff and students, the audit included four disciplinary audit trails, for Accounting and Finance, Engineering, English, and Sociology, and a thematic review of student responses at departmental level. The outcome[110] in 2004 was again of broad confidence, especially in the level of student involvement and the reflective approach to course design and teaching, but some loss of momentum was suggested.

The most recent QAA institutional audit, in 2009, was of a type described as hybrid, since it combined an overview of both Bailrigg departments and collaborative provision. The same broad confidence was upheld, with the report noting that the system was based on a "mutual interest principle" that involved "a flexible approach ... devolving greater responsibility to some partners than to others, and in some cases creating bespoke committees for specific partnerships. Underpinning this is an institutional commitment to capacity building among partner institutions ..."[111]

Recent years

Edge Hill achieved its ambition to become a university, by that name, on 9 May 2006.[112] For S. Martin's, the route was a little longer. Reports in 1995[113] and 2000[114] had pressed the case for Cumbrian higher education and had discerned significant unmet need. The college had responded by establishing a campus at Carlisle in addition to those at Ambleside and Lancaster, and the case was reinforced by Sir Martin Harris in 2005, who stated that an institution would be established to combine S. Martin's and the Cumbria Institute of the

---

[109] Lancaster University, "QAA Institutional Audit June 2004: Self-Evaluation Document" (February 2004), Chapters 2 and 4.

[110] Quality Assurance Agency for Higher Education, *University of Lancaster Institutional Audit*, RG 092 10/04 (Gloucester: QAA, 2004).

[111] Quality Assurance Agency for Higher Education, *Lancaster University: Institutional Audit*, RG 504 06/09 (Gloucester: QAA, 2009), para. 92.

[112] Minute S.2006/31, Senate meeting on 24 May 2006.

[113] Dale Campbell-Savours, *The Case for the University of the Lakes* (self published [1995]).

[114] DTZ Pieda Consulting, *Higher Education in Cumbria* (s.l.: Advisory Group for Higher Education in Cumbria, 2000).

Arts.[115] The new University of Cumbria came into being on 1 August 2007, and was formally inaugurated at Carlisle Cathedral that October.

Lancaster joined with its two associated colleges, Blackpool and The Fylde and Blackburn, to bid for Strategic Development Funding for each of them. Dedicated higher education accommodation has been built at the Palatine site in Blackpool for the former, and alongside Barbara Castle Way in Blackburn for the latter, and both colleges had their partnership with the university confirmed until 2013.[116] The university has also worked with the universities and colleges of the region on the setting up of lifelong learning networks, for which some HEFCE funding was initially available, that are intended to permit students to move between institutions according to their academic needs and to encourage greater involvement in higher education in parts of the region where participation is below – in places substantially below – the national norms. In the autumn of 2009, however, a shift of strategic direction took place, documented in a Senate decision to terminate relationships with most of the university's regional partners.[117] What will remain are the relationships with Blackpool and Blackburn and the engineering degrees with Furness College at Barrow-in-Furness. The Office for Associated Institutions was dissolved into the Secretariat[118] and the committee structure overhauled and simplified.

On the international front, further partnerships have been established and, most recently, have become the main responsibility of the faculties. There are three particularly significant links. The first is with Sunway University College, a private university within an educational trust at Kuala Lumpur, which became an affiliated college of the university in 2006[119] for the award of dual degrees. Malaysia has made a commitment to becoming the Asian hub of English higher education in its region, and has regarded its private university colleges as critical to achieving this objective,[120] while at the same time Lancaster was seeking to extend its network of high-quality overseas collaboration, although not to follow the example of universities such as Nottingham that have established satellite campuses overseas. The match in shared aspirations between Lancaster and Sunway was helpful to both institutions in the necessarily protracted discussions, which included a full review team going to Sunway in March 2006.[121] The initial academic programmes, at undergraduate level, were in management and information technology: subsequent programmes have included postgraduate provision and subject coverage that extends across all three Lancaster faculties.

---

[115] Minute S.2005/70, Senate meeting on 12 October 2005.

[116] Document OAI/2008/636, reported to Senate on 21 May 2008.

[117] Minute S.2009/59, Senate meeting on 7 October 2009.

[118] The Secretariat, headed by the University Secretary, has particular responsibility for institutional governance and academic quality.

[119] Minute S.2006/49, Senate meeting on 24 May 2006.

[120] Section 2 of document OAI/2005/651, reported to the Senate on 23 November 2005.

[121] Institutional approval report, document AR/2006/308, reported to Senate on 14 May 2006.

The second link is with the G. D. Goenka Institute,[122] set up by a private company in Delhi that planned to extend its educational programme from schools to higher education. As a new institution, a site was being developed and Lancaster and Goenka were able to work together on the quality of academic staff appointments, marketing, and student entry standards. Initially three undergraduate degree programmes in management subjects for Lancaster awards were launched in October 2009, although there are plans for enlargement both of the subject base and of student numbers. The third link is with the COMSATS Institute of Information Technology in Lahore which had initially involved the institute sending its staff to Lancaster to study for higher degrees. More recently[123] agreement has been reached for the development of dual degrees at undergraduate level, managed primarily through the faculty of Science and Technology.

The university is therefore continuing to develop its internal structures and its collaborative provision in places around the world where there is congruence of aims and objectives with partner institutions. The appointment of Professor Steve Bradley as pro-vice-chancellor in October 2010 specifically for international relationships is a further indication of Lancaster's commitment to its overseas partners, and further international developments are in progress.

---

[122] Document GAP/2008/0914, reported to Senate on 8 October 2008.
[123] Minute S.2009/60, Senate meeting on 2 October 2009.

CHAPTER FOUR

The student experience

A NY ACCOUNT OF STUDENTS' EXPERIENCES must begin with a cautionary note about why generalisations in this area are fallacious. Students range across and beyond almost any characteristic deployed to summarize them: in age from 17 to more than 70; from distant lands or the local area; in study of academic disciplines whose requirements are widely dissimilar; in mode, as full-time, part-time or visiting; and in the level of the award they are seeking, from a level below an honours degree and as far as a higher doctorate. Because the experiences of students are so disparate, groupings that aggregate and homogenize accounts of student life at Lancaster should be read with an understanding of their limitations. Thus this chapter will seek to examine some aspects of the life and work of Lancaster's students in the opening years of the university, drawing on their individual voices wherever possible, and to compare them with students in the first decade of the twenty-first century.

By March of 1964, when the university had very recently begun the process of recruiting its first cohort of students, the university had received 318 acceptances out of a thousand applications,[1] already in excess of the "up to 250" predicted in the modest 20-page prospectus issued late in 1963.[2] Entrants were warned:

In the year 1964–65 there will be no first-year courses in the experimental sciences,

---

[1] "State of Applications – 4th March 1964" (Lancaster, Academic Office, 4 March 1964).
[2] University of Lancaster, *Prospectus 1963–64* (Lancaster, October 1963).

although there will be provision for research in certain fields of Chemistry. Facilities for research degrees, and for Masters' degrees by examination on graduate courses, will be provided from the beginning in any subject where the basic library or laboratory facilities are available. The methods of teaching will be deliberately experimental and varied.[3]

While the university in time expected to provide a "full range of subjects in Arts, Social Sciences, Pure Science and Technology", the curriculum was to be devised "so as to encourage the study of interlocking groups of subjects, rather than specialisation on a narrow front. An educated man [sic] should have some idea of the habits of thought both of science and of the humanities; to this end particular attention is to be given to studies that cross traditional faculty boundaries ..."[4]

From its opening day, Lancaster was authorised under its Charter and Statutes to offer academic awards at all levels. All first degrees initially led to the degree of BA, taught postgraduate courses to the degrees of MA, MSc or MPhil, and research study to the degree of PhD. There were significant changes from university programmes of even a decade earlier, including students' ability to defer choices about their major subject until the end of their first year and the use of coursework as a contribution towards their final degree

[3] *Prospectus 1963–64*, p. 12.
[4] *Prospectus 1963–64*, p. 11.

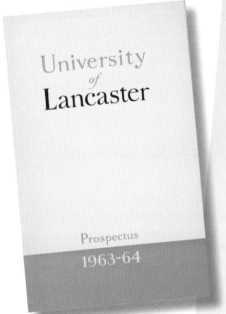

The 20-page, A5 university prospectus published in late 1963, setting out the chief officers of the university and the courses available, and stating that "An educated man [sic] should have some idea of the habits of thought both of science and of the humanities; to this end particular attention is to be given to studies that cross traditional faculty boundaries."

Circular letter from Charles Carter to headmasters, May 1964, encouraging further applications to be made to the university for entry in October that year

classification.[5] Because Lancaster stipulated that three discrete subjects were to be followed at Part I, and made nine units of assessment the fundamental building blocks at Part II, there was a dazzling array of permutations that could be devised from within the initial fifteen disciplinary areas on offer. One of the Part II units was also intended to be in an area well outside the student's major or minor subject areas, to be known as the distant minor and later as the free ninth unit. A degree of sophistication was therefore required by students to assess the likely consequences of their choices at each stage and to select units

---

[5]   University of Lancaster, "Outline of First Degree Courses, 1964–65, 1965–66" (Lancaster, June 1964).

that, taken together, matched their personal interests and their career aspirations, as well as ensuring academic coherence.

Great efforts had been made during the 34 months between the announcement of the seventh new university and the entry of the first students to create a satisfactory working environment for them within temporary accommodation. St Leonard's House, on the site of a medieval leper hospital and more recently the location of the Waring and Gillow factory (the final form of the famous Lancaster furniture-making firm founded in the eighteenth century), had been leased by the City to the university. The three blocks of the factory together provided 69,000 sq.ft.[6] The central and oldest block, six stories high and with a basement, revealed cast-iron pillars that supported large timber beams, and timber-boarded floors surfaced with asphalt. A library for up to 70,000 volumes was placed in the basement, with reading space on the ground floor.[7] There were lecture and seminar rooms and office space for academic and administrative staff. Teaching and research laboratories (including the provision of specialist gases) were to be placed on the second and third floors, with a staff common room on the fourth. A common room for students, also used by clerical and junior library staff,[8] was located near to the refectory. The bare-faced brickwork was lime-washed, and new lifts and two fire escapes were installed, while across the road there was parking space for 250 vehicles. Lecturing space was available at the late eighteenth-century Grand Theatre, just opposite St Leonard's House, thus helpfully augmenting the funds of the Lancaster Footlights Club.[9]

While opportunities for choice of subject matter had been greatly expanded by comparison with earlier student generations, and despite statements made about new teaching methods, in practice lectures were similar to those at existing universities: students in gowns being addressed by a lecturer also wearing a gown and standing at a lectern. The essays they submitted now contributed to their final degree classification, but the material they worked with was largely primary texts, since the era of extensive textbooks and quick guides was still in its infancy. Almost all of the students admitted had taken three subjects at Advanced Level, and hence had been accustomed to learning conditions at school not dissimilar to those they now experienced, especially in the first year.

At the final count, 296 undergraduates were registered in the first week of October 1964, of whom 174 were men,[10] and they signed up for 41 different Part I combinations, including some across the arts/science divide: for example, English, History and Environmental Studies, or Economics, History and Mathematics. There were also 36 graduate students,

---

[6] Information derived from "Temporary buildings to serve early needs of the university", *Lancaster Guardian* Special Supplement, April 1964, p. 31.

[7] An even earlier form of the Library existed for a few months in a former stained glass factory on Castle Hill.

[8] Personal recollection of Mrs Pat Foy (December 2008).

[9] "Varsity lectures will help the Footlights Club finances", *Visitor*, 7 October 1964.

[10] Undated and untitled document from a file compiled by the Vice-Chancellor, entitled "Statistics".

spread across nine subjects, a quarter of whom were studying Operational Research.[11] All students had been nominally assigned either to Bowland or Lonsdale, the only two colleges for which shadow syndicates had so far been formed, and each was given a college tutor who was also assigned to the same college. The undergraduates came from all over England and ranged in age from 17 to 21, which meant that, at a time when the age of majority was 21, most of them were minors.[12] There was one overseas student, from Zanzibar. UK students were funded from the late 1950s by means-tested grants from their local education authorities, but in any case only £75 per annum was required to cover registration, tuition, examination, and graduation, plus a small college fee. Many of the students had all their fees covered and most of their maintenance. With hindsight, the grant provision in the early 1960s to 1980 is likely to prove to have been the most generous student funding regime ever available in UK higher education.

Reporters from the regional and local press, after some weeks of printing stories about the conversion of the former furniture factory to a university, were at last able in October to meet actual students, including a line-up of female undergraduates.[13] While coverage was given to the plans for building on the Bailrigg site, the main focus of attention was on the facilities at St Leonard's House, where begowned students, the men mostly wearing collars and ties, and the women in skirts and court shoes, were to be found in the library or the refectory:

> Where laboratory benches now stand, craftsmen made treasured antiques. The decorative woodwork for the Queen Mary and the Queen Elizabeth was fashioned here. So, for that matter, was that large and very special table at the United Nations on which Mr Kruschev once hammered his shoe.
>
> Through the square leaded windows [the students] will be able to look across the crowded roofs of Lancaster to John of Gaunt's old castle on the hill ... Yet despite the wonders that have been done with gay two-tone paints and strip lighting and sound-proof flooring, the old 'factory' atmosphere remains.[14]

HRH Princess Alexandra came to Lancaster twice during the first term, once in October to attend a service at the Priory and officiate at the opening of S. Martin's College, and again in November to be installed as Chancellor. Each time part of her itinerary involved meeting students bent diligently over their work tables. An article at the time of her installation attempted to sum up the prevailing atmosphere:

> Talk of Lancaster being our university is not just talk, whether East Lancashire gets its own university or not.

---

[11] "The University of Lancaster, Graduate Students", 26 October 1964 (UA.1/3/2/8).

[12] "Note to Heads of Departments", 8 October 1964 (UA.1/3/2/8).

[13] "An attractive line-up of some of Britain's newest undergraduates", *The Sun*, 8 October 1964.

[14] *Manchester Evening News*, 9 October 1964.

St Leonard's House, the former furniture factory where the university was initially housed, on 8 November 1964. The Congregational Church can be seen at the far end of the street, and the Grand Theatre to the left (copyright, *Lancaster Guardian*)

Lancaster is already running departments which will help East Lancashire in very tangible ways: operational research, which will show industry and local as well as national government how mathematics can help in practical day-to-day decision-making problems.

And most important of all to young people, the new university is being run by people in the prime of life, not old timers. Most of the staff are in their twenties, thirties and forties, and the impression is, for once, one of youth brimming with new, unstuffy ideas ...

From the top downwards, the young idea is at the helm.[15]

Students at the university and at S. Martin's College soon began to make a positive impact on their surroundings:

... this sudden influx of young blood into a town that can trace its history back more seven and a half centuries has done nothing to spoil its charm.

---

[15] David Sheppard, "It's Such a Go-Ahead University", *Lancashire Evening Telegraph*, 18 November 1964.

Student Representative Council meeting at St Leonard's House, 1965 (copyright, *Lancashire Life*)

They have already begun to approach music, drama and other cultural organisations in the town with a view to joining ... The public library is busier now and Mr E. H. Lowe, city librarian, said that since the opening of the university and the St Martin's Teachers' Training College ... just over 200 students had joined the library.

Mr Clive Jones, manager of one of the two cinemas in the town, said that he had definitely noticed an increase in audiences in recent weeks, and a snack bar proprietor also said business had taken an upward trend.[16] A student journalism survey,[17] however, came to a rather less buoyant viewpoint, for when townspeople were asked what they thought of the new university, they replied that 300 students had made a "slight difference" to their trade. Generally, the students were informed, Lancaster was "Sleepy Valley", "a slow town ... it's backward", and sympathy was expressed that the university had come to such a "poor town", whose own schoolchildren planned to go somewhere more exciting. The editorial concluded rather ruefully by hoping that the student body would be accepted as "a cultural boost to a hitherto dead area".

[16] *Liverpool Daily Post*, 8 November 1964.
[17] Editorial, *John O'Gauntlet*, No. 3, April 1965.

Of course, the facilities taken for granted in a fully functioning university had to be fashioned from scratch at Lancaster. For example, the Lancaster and Morecambe College was prepared for the first year to let the university's students use their games pitches, and initially the local swimming baths offered advantageous rates to students, while the John O'Gaunt Men allowed the Rowing Club to use its facilities. The University of York, older by one year, acted as host for the first Roses[18] match in May 1965. A table tennis room was set up at St Leonard's House, but there was noted to be a lack of shower rooms for players; additional reading and study space was rented in nearby Great St John's Street; and there was a student production of Anouilh's "Waltz of the Toreadors" at the Grand Theatre early in 1965.

Students' arrangements for their own organisations had to be worked out from first principles and agreed with university officers. The first meeting of the Student Representative Council, at which there were joint officer posts to ensure equal representation of both colleges, took place on 22 October 1964.[19] Its first action was to change the designation of the joint chairmen and vice-chairmen to become presidents and vice-presidents, and its second to appoint a Dance Chairman. A further meeting the following day pressed for negotiations with the Ribble Bus Company for a reduction in student fares between Lancaster and Morecambe, although without success. By the beginning of the second term the first student officer resignation had been received, while an impressive list of societies and clubs had been formed, including a Conservative Association, a Labour Club, and a Marxist Reading Group. There were societies for arts, orchestra, literature, film, music and records, history, cross-country running, bridge, hockey (including a separate ladies' team), boats, sailing, and cricket. Two student newspapers: *John O'Gauntlet* and *Carolynne*, were established,[20] while groups such as the Flowerpot Men aimed to make their own musical records and to play at special events.

Students spent long days at St Leonard's House, for once they had endured the lengthy bus ride from Morecambe and over the eighteenth-century Skerton Bridge, which still in 1964 took two-way traffic ("a morning penance"),[21] it made sense to continue their round of lectures, seminars and social activity until fairly late in the evening. They then returned to their approved lodgings, mostly in Morecambe, and because Saturday mornings often involved further teaching or examinations, only Sundays were spent away from the centre of Lancaster. The Superintendent of Lodgings had the task

of searching for and securing suitable lodgings in Lancaster, Morecambe, and surrounding districts. He must carry out regular inspections of all University lodgings to ensure that

---

[18] The vice-chancellors of York and Lancaster had agreed to hold this latter-day sporting version of the War of the Roses, to be held in York and Lancaster on alternate years. For a time the event was known as the Lancaster–York Sports Weekend, but subsequently simply as Roses.

[19] University of Lancaster, Student Representative Council, Minutes 1964 (unpaginated).

[20] SRC Minutes 1964: *Carolynne* published both a university and a town edition.

[21] Frank Rawes, "Bridging the Gap", *John O'Gauntlet* (No. 5, May 1965), p. 3.

they provide satisfactory standards of accommodation. He also has responsibility for the general welfare of students in lodgings ...

Over 200 students were lodged in Morecambe, with the balance almost all residing in Lancaster. Rent was set at a uniform rate of 70 shillings (£3.50) a week, but the circumstances in which the students found themselves were far from uniform. A survey, conducted in 2006–07, of the initial students' reactions to residence in Morecambe over 40 years earlier[22] gives a vivid picture of the vagaries of differing conditions that students faced. Some accounts are very positive:

> In digs with two other students, with family of parents and 8 year old boy and 4 year old boy, plus maternal grandmother. Visited landlady last week ... I shared a room with one of the others, the third had a small room to himself. Rooms had washbasin, shared other facilities with the family. Downstairs they had the front room (where we were after a while invited to watch TV in the evenings ...). We were given a full English breakfast ... That was seven days a week ... On Sundays we were given a Sunday lunch – roast meat and two veg, plus rice pudding or apple tart or similar. Then high tea ... We were also entitled to a hot drink each night if in before 10 p.m. and a biscuit or two,[23]

or again:

> First year in residential house with very 'motherly' landlady. Shared bedroom with one other student. Just like being at home but study facilities not too good. Years 2/3 at large boarding house on West End with 6/7 others. Own bedroom. Dedicated study space. Great landlord/landlady, good rapport with students. Bar in basement open every night. What more could you want?[24]

or again:

> Life in 1964 at home was very much as it was in the immediate post-war austerity period. The swinging 60s was something that happened somewhere else. So going to university was a great release and an opportunity to meet young people from all walks of life. Staying with Nellie [the landlady] allowed this process to start in a stable environment which felt a little bit like home but without parental restrictions.[25]

Others were less fortunate:

---

[22] Emma Jean Carnell, "A discussion on the relationship between Lancaster University and the seaside resort of Morecambe using student-based perceptions" (dissertation in partial fulfilment of the requirements of the degree of BA, May 2007): (hereafter the Carnell Archive: quoted with permission).

[23] Carnell Archive, respondent 37.

[24] Carnell Archive, respondent 43.

[25] Carnell Archive, respondent 38.

1st year was boarding house – twin bedded room – only heating was 1 bar electric heater – no drying facilities, 6 or 7 of us – meals typical of a boarding house – no cooking facilities for self. Pretty grim as only suitable for summer accommodation. By next year turned into bedsits. The local boarding house owners began to see how [they] could make money by adapting to needs of students rather than holiday makers.[26]

Students who were based in Lancaster for their first year could find themselves at Morecambe for the second:

In year 2, I stayed in a sea front B and B hotel in Morecambe which had 8 other students. The rooms were poorly heated, had utility furniture, and were scruffy in presentation. Breakfasts were often served cold. The rule was "out by 10.00, back by 10.00". Landlord/landlady best described as unfriendly.[27]

The accommodation in Lancaster was more varied. One student lived in an old farmhouse in Greaves Drive with a "great landlady, freezing cold. Tea on Sunday worth looking forward to ... My fellow lodger, my landlady and myself sang in the church choir (church next to the Shakespeare – think it's demolished now)". The same student, who had grown up in Kenya, also went to Morecambe, revelling in double features at the cinema where she could stay as long as she pleased. Lectures at the Grand Theatre, however, involved wearing a gown, "which always seemed a bit strange – bright, clean gowns in a flea pit like the Grand".[28]

While staff and students were settling into St Leonard's House, building work had begun three miles away at Bailrigg. Despite *John O'Gauntlet* suggesting that "Many students have either forgotten about Bailrigg, or dismissed as unlikely the possibility of their ever seeing it even partially completed",[29] a comment by the Vice-Chancellor about "the danger involved in carelessly walking around the site",[30] and the need for prior permission to visit, suggests that there was keen interest in what was taking shape in the rain-sodden fields to the south of Lancaster. Because the Vice-Chancellor and his senior officers were located at Bailrigg Mansion, meetings of the Staff/Student Committee usually took place there, and included an ever-widening range of issues about which students were to be consulted.

One such recurring topic was sport. The Rowing Club was active in recruiting members and setting up training for a race that would form part of the first Lancaster/York contest,[31] to be held at York, and a local supporter offered £5000 to build a boat house. In the event this sum proved to be insufficient, and an existing boat house upstream at Halton was converted for the purpose, and continues to this day. Students pressed for pitches to be

---

[26] Carnell Archive, respondent 15.
[27] Carnell Archive, respondent 16.
[28] Carnell Archive, respondent 18.
[29] *John O'Gauntlet* (No. 3, February 1965), p. 1.
[30] Staff/Student Committee, 16 May 1965, p. 3.
[31] *John O'Gauntlet* (No. 3, February 1965), p. 12.

Student sport in Alexandra Square, with students clustered on the steps to the north side of the square to watch this and many other informal events

made available at Bailrigg as quickly as possible, and temporary playing areas were created while pitches were being prepared. An Athletics Union was formed during the first year, and quickly became an important lobbying organisation for sporting activities.[32]

The 1964 student entrants were involved in the design and implementation of the Introductory Week for October 1965, although the term 'week' was a courtesy for the three days – Friday to Sunday – that were provided for the second intake, with a University Service at Lancaster Priory on their second Sunday. The initial students also organised themselves to take their share of responsibility for welcoming and integrating their immediate successors. Early hopes of a formal ball or a Rag Day during the first year, however, proved logistically impossible,[33] and there were complaints about a general lack of social facilities and events. Perhaps that was one reason why student high spirits included the removal of four flags from the top of a social club at the White Cross mills of a local manufacturer, Storey Brothers. Lancaster City magistrates convicted the four students involved of theft, but fortunately an appeal at Lancaster Quarter Sessions was successful, and the chairman, Mr

[32] Staff/Student Committee, 10 May 1965, p. 2 (UA.1/3/7/2).
[33] *John O'Gauntlet*, May 1965, p. 1.

The Bailrigg campus from the east, 2009, showing Alexandra Park to the left

W. H. Openshaw,[34] accepted their contention that the episode was a joke and that the flags were intended merely to be repositioned elsewhere.

The lack of an active social scene also fed into an increasing demand for undergraduates to be allowed to live in flats:

> The only social facility offered by the town consists of a bad selection of public houses. A bar in the University would provide a focus for social life, but we have been told repeatedly that this was out of the question ... The granting of flats would help to make a stable student community a more likely proposition.[35]

An initial proposal that students be allowed to occupy flats after their first year was turned down although, after an intervention by the syndicates of Bowland and Lonsdale colleges, a compromise was reached that students over 21 on entry could choose to live in flats rather than approved lodgings, as could those who attained the age of 21 during their time at Lancaster. In addition, students in their third year who were not yet 21 could apply for permission to live in flats, but the application had to be accompanied by the written

---

[34] "Varsity students' appeal is allowed", *Lancashire Evening Post*, 9 April 1965.
[35] *John O'Gauntlet*, May 1965, p. 1.

consent of their parents and a recommendation from their tutors. It was stipulated that undergraduates who chose to live in flats would be responsible for payment of the rent, and the college disciplinary committees had the power to revoke permission.[36] Despite this wealth of caveats, these new arrangements proved sufficient to manage the situation until residential accommodation at Bailrigg became available in 1968.

A more serious problem was the decision to increase rental levels to 84 shillings (£4.20) a week for 1965–66, with a retainer of 10 shillings (£0.50) a week at Christmas and Easter. The Vice-Chancellor explained at the Staff/Student Committee that a condition of setting up the initial lodgings arrangements had been the inclusion of a review before the start of the 1965–66 academic year, that the university would continue for some time to depend on the goodwill of Morecambe landladies, and that not only had the cost-of-living index risen but the landladies were well aware that students' maintenance grants from their local education authorities were to be given a "fairly substantial increase".[37] While students signed a petition against the increase, Mrs Hilda Charlesworth of the Morecambe Hotels and Caterers' Association commented that: "Personally I don't think the present fee is a fair return. When items like food, heating and lighting are taken into consideration, it is getting pretty near the bone."[38]

The first Summer Term ended with a garden party at Bailrigg Mansion, attended by HRH Princess Alexandra, for over 2000 guests, including local landladies[39] and the president of the MHCA. Despite the apparent resolution of the revised lodgings charges, and the approval of the Senate for them, the issue rumbled on over the summer. The Superintendent of Lodgings was content that agreement had been reached with the Association,[40] and an upbeat account of lodgings in Lancaster included one landlady who declared: "It's a lucky bag – you don't know what you are getting. But one thing I can be sure of is plenty of laughs. There's always a good deal of fun for a landlady …"[41] Hints of trouble to come were heard in September,[42] and on arrival back for the new term students planned a mass refusal to pay extra unless there were differential rents according to facilities, student involvement in future rent negotiations, revision of the regulations concerning flats, and encouragement for a unified association of landladies to cover both Lancaster and Morecambe.[43] Students

---

[36] "Regulations for students living in approved lodgings: revised regulations", Senate, 24 June 1965 (document GM/65/532).

[37] Staff/Student Committee, Minute 1 of 14 June 1965 (UA.1/3/7/2): grants for students outside London, and living in college or lodgings, were raised to £340 a year from September 1965, up from £310 to £320 (The *Times*, 25 May 1965).

[38] *Lancaster Guardian*, 11 June 1965.

[39] "Primrose Princess at the University Garden Party", *Visitor*, 30 June 1965.

[40] "Varsity 'digs' to cost more", *Lancashire Evening Post*, 20 August 1965: see also *Visitor*, 25 August 1965.

[41] Anne Fitzgibbon, "Students' landladies are not dragons", *Lancashire Evening Post*, 20 August 1965.

[42] "Students may revive row over lodgings fees", *Visitor*, 8 September 1965.

[43] *Visitor*, 6 October 1965.

were themselves divided over tactics, however, and the student president of Bowland College, Carole Barker, resigned over the refusal to pay.[44]

By this time the Senate had become involved.[45] Thanks to an almost Hansard level of Senate record at this period, we can read of an extended report by the Vice-Chancellor at a special meeting, followed by the entry of four students representing their Lodgings Committee. Discussion between them and the Senate members took place and they then withdrew. On re-admission a statement was read to them to the effect that the new rent would have to be paid, was less than the landladies had demanded, and would remain unchanged for three years. The Vice-Chancellor also undertook to involve student representatives in further discussions on rent levels, while reminding the students of the Staff/Student Committee's earlier discussion. Once the four students had again withdrawn, the two student editors of *Carolynne* and *John O'Gauntlet* were brought in and told that both publications must carry a statement from the Secretary of the University. A statement from the Vice-Chancellor also emphasized that strict surveillance of the two papers would henceforth take place:

---

[44] *Carolynne*, No. 10, 14 October 1965; "Student row flares again", *Lancashire Evening Post*, 4 October 1965.

[45] Senate, Section B agenda, meeting on 6 October 1965: see also G.65/761; G.65/775.

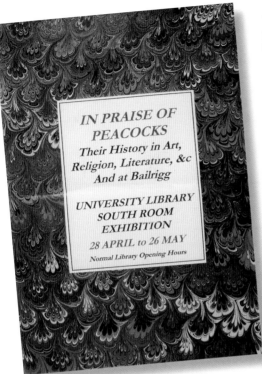

The poster advertising an exhibition in the Library about peacocks, May 2000, including a family of them that took up residence in the university grounds for some years

> With regard to the good name and well-being of the University as a whole especially in its early years of development ... The University cannot allow one generation of students to jeopardise the interests of future students.[46]

The Secretary's statement was duly issued, the rent was paid, and the first significant rift between students and staff came to a close. There were clearly lessons to be drawn from it about how the university could reconcile the conflicting perspectives of landladies and students, and the issue demonstrated just how much resources of time and energy had to be spent on the housing of students before residential accommodation became available.

An even more significant matter, relating to academic standards, was not picked up by the local or student press. As early as March 1965 there was evidence of some nervousness about the likely results of the first Part I examinations, to qualify for admission to Part II, in the minds of Senators.[47] In April 292 undergraduates sat written examinations in all three of their Part I subjects, and between 30 and 45 of them were identified as likely, even before re-assessment by the end of term,[48] to be "irredeemable failures" who would be subject to the procedure for external re-examination and potentially to the termination of their

---

[46] Statement by the Vice-Chancellor, Senate, 6 October 1965 (G.65/777).

[47] Minute S.65/3/2 (iii), (iv), (v), Senate meeting on 4 March 1965.

[48] Agendum 20, meeting of Senate on 3 June 1965.

Nine invitations and programmes from a great range of special university occasions between 1964 and 2004

university careers. The heads of departments, moreover, were said to have taken account of all possible factors in each candidate's favour, and the Part I Board of Examiners felt that reference to the Senate was essential.[49] The Senate was therefore faced with a result that, as the Vice-Chancellor pointed out, would give a potential first-year wastage rate of between 10% and 15%, as against a national average of 6% to 10%. Charles Carter continued, with his characteristic blend of pragmatism and compassion:

> Although the British universities may move to a system of freer entry and greater first-year wastage, this clearly cannot apply to a year [i.e. 1964–65] of acute pressure of demand. There is, in fact, much criticism (not least in Government circles) of the present wastage rates, and a belief that they show an insufficient feeling, in some universities, of responsibility for their students ... A first-year wastage of between 10 and 15% would be so exceptional as to lead inevitably to adverse criticism by the U.G.C., and to a weakening of our case for the next quinquennium: to bad relations with the schools and very probably to hostile public comment. Nevertheless, we would have to face these disadvantages if we could *prove* that it was in the interests of the students concerned, and necessary for

---

[49] CFC, "Failures in Part I", Agendum 2(b), Senate meeting on 30 June 1965 (G.65/426).

the maintenance of academic standards in the future, that so large a number should be ejected. But I do not believe that we can prove any such thing.[50]

He went on to list six possible explanations for poor performance that could not be attributed to students – bad selection; badly timed examinations; difficulties either in settling down in a new institution or in establishing the right levels of teaching and examination; inexperienced staff; and inadequate disciplinary procedures – and just one that was attributable – their "unusual idleness" – which he did not feel could be "the dominant reason, when so many other possibilities exist". Instead, he suggested, one difficulty was the provision of a wholly inadequate opportunity for redemption. He therefore proposed that the re-assessment be delayed until September, thus giving a realistic period for revision.

Other Senate members weighed in: Professor Sturmey, as Admissions Officer,[51] gave statistical evidence to show that the entry of some 55 students with comparatively low A Level scores had not contributed to the high failure rate, and Dr Oldfield[52] pointed out the absence of standardisation of assessment methods between departments, ranging from 100% examination to 70% "term work" (i.e. course work), a situation that had led to large differences of marking range between subjects, but not within them. What no Senator appears to have highlighted were the discrepancies in staff:student ratios between subjects in a young institution with varying staff complements, ranging from 16:1 in Mathematics to 54:1 in English.[53] The causes suggested by the Vice-Chancellor were, however, substantiated in a report[54] by the Research Fellow in Teaching Methods, Mr W. T. Koc, based on an enquiry conducted during the Lent Term. This revealed student anxiety related not only to overwork, but to unsatisfactory study conditions in lodgings, poor working conditions in the Library, the absence of an induction period at entry or sufficient prior information about subjects on offer or methods of study, and the requirement quickly and early in their first term for students to produce written work, including in subjects of which they had no previous experience. They felt unable to reconcile the conflicting demands of the different departments or to identify staff members whom they could consult about their difficulties.

The outcome of these difficulties was, however, beneficial for students. In October 1965 the second intake of undergraduates were given at entry a clear statement of assessment procedures that would apply to them:[55] Part I written examinations would be held in the

---

[50] CFC, "Failures in Part I".

[51] S. G. Sturmey, "Comparison of A Levels and University Examination Results", Senate, 3 June 1965 (G.65/447).

[52] F. Oldfield, "To All Members of Senate" (2 June 1965).

[53] W. T. Koc, "Preliminary statistical analysis of the April assessment results" (May 1965, and included in the papers of the Senate on 3 June 1965).

[54] W. T. Koc, *Annual Report of the Research Fellow in University Teaching Methods* (Lancaster: University of Lancaster Department of Higher Education, 1965), pp. 6–10.

[55] A. S. Jeffreys, "Note for undergraduates: Examination and assessment procedure in Part I, 1965–66", paper to the Senate on 6 October 1965 (G.65/764).

second half of June, and the assessment would be a combination of examination and of "such other evidence as the department concerned may determine at its discretion", including essays and practical results, with their relative weightings also being determined at subject level. Students were to be required to achieve a minimum aggregated mark across all three subjects, as well as minimum grades within each one that varied according to their choices of major and minor subjects. The results would be published in early July, and Senate had the discretion to permit undergraduates to take resits in September, with further discretion for one external reassessment and a statutory right of appeal against exclusion. Taken together, and with some refinements, these procedures became standard for the university thereafter.

Meanwhile, consideration of individual cases led to the retrieval of the university careers of almost all the failed students. Commendation also came from the Academic Advisory Committee for the "Great care and trouble [that] was taken in the organisation and conduct of examinations at the end of the first year".[56] Furthermore, a senior lecturer in English, Dr David Craig, was commissioned by the Senate to prepare an introduction for new students[57] about habits of study, full of sound advice on reading matter, note-taking, choice of courses, making the most of lectures, seminars and laboratory work, the best approaches to written work and examinations, and how to optimise the vacations academically. It concluded with words that still carry force for academic staff:

> In coming to university you are joining a guild of specialists, who wish to teach you their craft. They go on the assumption that people who have chosen to come here have been moved partly by personal intellectual interests, and do not have to be allured by gimmicks or the expectation of instant results to keep at a subject. The staff are also constantly learning themselves, partly by trying to add to knowledge and partly by trying to become better at communicating what they know. In this quite literal sense the senior members of a university are themselves students along with the research students and undergraduates, and part of their learning takes place in teaching you. This is no demagogic slogan ... The more the relation between teachers and taught becomes one of co-operation and friendship, the more genuine will be its intellectual results.[58]

Lancaster's second academic year opened in October 1965 with 780 students, including a further 428 undergraduates selected from over 4000 applicants, and with some students following laboratory-based subjects for the first time.[59] There were now 80 graduate students, and an academic and research staff complement of 96. The university had acquired a small computer, with a larger one promised for the coming months. To create the space for this doubling of numbers, the university took a lease on the Centenary Congregational

[56] Noel Hall, "Academic Advisory Committee Report to Council for the Academic Year 1964–65" (Senate, 27 September 1965, G.65/689(b)).

[57] David M. Craig, An Introduction to University (Lancaster: Lancaster University, 1965), which publication, further expanded, went through several editions, the final one in 1972.

[58] Craig, An Introduction to University, pp. 16–18.

[59] "Scientists figure in university intake 'bulge', Lancashire Evening Post, 4 October 1965.

Bowland North courtyard in the spring, 2010

Church, at the end of the street in which St Leonard's House is situated, together with 109 St Leonardsgate for extra staff rooms.[60] In addition, Skein House at 4 Queen's Square in Lancaster was briefly leased from Mr Barton Towneley (the former owner of Bailrigg Mansion) to house the departments of Marketing and Operational Research. The new generation was perceived by the veterans of 1964 thus:

> They came issuing out of the wet and gas-lit station. Some called for taxis, some waited for buses, and some, more mindful of their financial future, walked. The other half, they were.
>
> They came from the unsunned skies of Bolton or the Tory wastes of London SW 3 ... Some went mackintoshed and wet down to the front [at Morecambe] to stare bleakly at the wistful wastes of the gun-metal sea, and tried to see the distant hills of Westmorland, but couldn't, because it was raining. Some sat cocooned in soft-bedded double rooms, amid their files, transistors, and copies of yesterday's Guardian ... In sheets of rain they came on Thursday too. Some found it difficult as they walked beside the closed and glassy super-market, to believe there really was a story beneath every stone; others gently dropped their illusions about "varying and interesting" landscape as they huddled near St Leonard's Gate, staring at uncompromising and bechimneyed factories.
>
> It rained, and dripping students wandered into the squashed and universal J.C.R. to sit amid their contemporaries in the Great Adventure ... And Monday morning, they rose

---

[60] "Former church to become lecture hall", *Lancashire Evening Post*, 15 April 1965.

Degree certificate and case. Honorary degrees are awarded by the university to persons of special distinction, normally at the degree ceremonies in July and December.

for the First Day ... And in distant Morecambe, college-scarved bodies clutching their desperate copies of Eliot, Auden and "Mathematics for the Simple Minded", raced like startled thrushes to catch the 8.40 train. The other half had arrived.[61]

The second intake of students experienced the same variety of lodging and living experiences as their predecessors. They recall[62] dances at the Winter Gardens in Morecambe, beach football at Half Moon Bay in Heysham, playing darts in the Shakespeare at St Leonard's House, and taking local jobs; for example, with the promenade photographers for Morecambe tourists. One Londoner who shared rooms with two others at Sunset House in Morecambe recalls a hand coming round the bedroom door at 10.00 p.m. to turn the lights off, and the trouble there was about hairwashing because it was thought to damage the drainpipes. When she and the others went to the Accommodation Office to complain, however, who should they find already in the queue but their landlord and landlady, waiting to complain about them.[63] Fortunately the house to which they were then transferred had a "nice cheerful lady who provided huge breakfasts and seemed to enjoy having students there". A science student recalled sharing an attic room 12 ft by 10 ft on Albert Road,

[61] Robert Fisk, "The Other Half", *Carolynne*, No. 10, 14 October 1965, pp. 6–7.
[62] Carnell Archive; summary of numerous replies.
[63] Carnell Archive, Respondent 67.

The original ranks of card catalogues in the Library foyer, now replaced by on-line catalogues that can be accessed from around the world

Morecambe, with a blanket on the wall for their pictures.[64] At first he could take a train to Green Ayre in Lancaster, but when the line was closed and the service ended, there was a rather cheerless bus. Nevertheless, the academic programme suited him well:

> Lectures were impressive – after Year 1; especially the investigation-based programme run as practicals, field trips, enquiry sessions, the trial dissertation, and especially the micrometeorology. The initiative was given to students and it was much the most useful I ever did – the attitude and confidence from this enquiry-based appraisal staying with me for life.

The students were allowed to run a second-hand bookshop within St Leonard's House, and to organise themselves in the larger junior common room space of the converted Congregational Church on the corner of St Leonardsgate and Rosemary Lane. There was also talk of appointing a careers adviser. Study space remained a problem, particularly when the Quiet Room at 3 Great John Street was commandeered for use as an examination hall.[65] Another inevitable issue was whether there could be a licensed bar, and a ditty in the style of John Betjeman concluded:

---

[64] Carnell Archive, Respondent 10.
[65] *John O'Gauntlet*, No. 16, May 1966, p. 8.

Mid trials and tribulations
The ancient church was sold
What yielded confirmations
Now yieldeth only gold.
But hearken all ye faithful!
Take heed! Though from afar,
The Church's voice still thunders,
"Thou shalt not have a bar".[66]

After months of negotiation, however, a bar was approved by the church's trustees.

The Michaelmas Ball, held at the Town Hall and attended by a quarter of the students and some 30 staff, was judged to be a success,[67] but the Boat Club suffered defeat, using a borrowed shell, in the Northern Universities' Regatta at Newcastle-upon-Tyne.[68] Despite this setback, Lancaster nevertheless in the spring won the first Roses weekend to be held at Lancaster.[69] The first Charities Week included a fashion show, a rag ball and a parade of nineteen floats through the city centre,[70] and was even the subject of a laudatory letter from the Lancaster manager of Lloyds' Bank about the students' behaviour.[71]

The third year, 1966–67, was transitional. Students in arts subjects attended lectures and seminars at Bailrigg and some fortunate students were assigned study rooms in Bowland College, while the bookshop (run by Maxwell's) was located in the college's basement. The Library at Bailrigg was open for use, although only the basement and the top floor had been completed in July when book stocks were being transferred from St Leonardsgate.[72] Students whose subjects cut across arts and sciences could, however, be expected to attend at both St Leonard's House and at Bailrigg on the same day and, with a return to their Morecambe boarding houses, the most important work of reference was the local bus timetable. The second Charities Week was marked by a flour fight in Market Square during the rag procession, in which spectators were injured by flying eggs and apples. Plentiful recriminations followed, as well as a letter of reproach from Mr Waddell at the Town Hall. Moreover, York won the third Lancaster–York sports weekend by four points. Students campaigned against increases in overseas student fees in meetings of the Federation of Junior Common Rooms, and a Student Representative Council (SRC) newspaper, to be called *Scan*,[73] began publication on a weekly basis, using distinctive yellow duplicating paper, at a cost of £6. 5. 3. for 500 copies.

[66] William Smethurst, "The Church's Restoration", *Carolynne*, No. 8, June 1965.
[67] *John O'Gauntlet*, No. 11, December 1965, p. 1.
[68] *John O'Gauntlet*, No. 11, December 1965, p. 8.
[69] "Lancaster thrashes York", *John O'Gauntlet*, No. 16, May 1966, p. 8.
[70] *John O'Gauntlet*, No. 14, March 1966, p. 1.
[71] Staff–Student Committee, 25 April 1966, minute 3 (UA.1/3/7/2).
[72] University of Lancaster, Report of the Librarian, 1965/66.
[73] "Scan" stands for Student College and Administrative News: see the SRC Agenda, November 1967. See also: Marion McClintock, "You Scallywags!", *Scan,* 14 February 1997, Issue 8, for an account of its first 30 years of publication. The complete collection is to be found at UA.1/9/3/1.

At the end of the year, in July 1967, the first undergraduate degrees were conferred at Ashton Hall by HRH Princess Alexandra: 264 students who graduated in non-laboratory subjects as bachelor of arts. The profile of the awards – 3 with a I, 46 with a II(i), 138 with a II(ii), and 60 with a III, was not uncharacteristic of other universities of the period.[74] The ceremony began with the conferment of six honorary degrees, by Professor Tom Lawrenson as Public Orator, then the higher degrees of PhD and MSc, and finally the bachelor of arts graduates by college (Bowland, Cartmel, and Lonsdale, in that order).

This was also the year in which David O'Dell of Berkhamsted had accepted an offer of a place at Lancaster from Mr W. G. Fuge, Senior Administrative Assistant, to read Economics. To this he added History at Part I registration, and was thinking of taking Environmental Studies as his third subject, "but the queue is rather long and it's lunchtime. The Politics queue is much shorter and so I join it, beginning a 40+ year career studying, teaching and examining the subject."[75] His Politics seminar group contained three Lancashire policemen in their 40s, a trades union official, the chairman of the Lancaster University Conservative Association, and an ex-monk, and lectures "are in Centenary House ... in blocks of two hours. Two hours spent sitting on the polished wooden church pews taking notes on Aristotle's teleology. Seminars are at Bailrigg. Painters continue their work on the outside of the window frames as steam rises from our damp duffle coats and we desperately try to work out what Mill meant by 'self-regarding conduct'."[76] After Christmas he was allocated a study work room in Bowland College that he was nominally to share with 45 others. This sense of enjoyable semi-anarchy, reflected in his account, is echoed in the pages of *Carolynne* and *John O'Gauntlet*, while the Senate, more soberly, was considering the detail of assessment policy and the procedure to be followed for the exclusion of students from the university.[77]

The fourth year, 1967–68, with an undergraduate population of about a thousand, also continued the shift from an institution based at the centre of Lancaster and occupation of the new site at Bailrigg. In addition to Bowland College, Lonsdale College was becoming available for staff of non-science departments to occupy, and the Faraday complex came on stream for science teaching. The residence rooms in the two colleges were used for study space, now notionally with four to rooms that included desks and locker space.[78] Students took up residence by small stages, starting with third year undergraduates, while all first year students continued to be housed in lodgings.[79] Local landladies were simultaneously nervous about the approaching loss of their student market and keen to increase rents to keep up with rising student grants. The second phase of the Library had been built, and the

---

[74] The proportions of II(i) to II(ii) developed over the years to 1973 to a ratio of 2:3 by the end of the period: see McClintock, *Quest*, Appendix xiii, pp. 426–9.

[75] David O'Dell, *1966 And All That* (David O'Dell, 2009), Chapter 1: this and other extracts quoted with permission.

[76] David O'Dell, *1966 And All That* (David O'Dell, 2009), Chapter 3.

[77] Minute S.66/10/4, Senate meeting of 12 October 1966.

[78] Ernest Phillips, in *Lonsdale College 30th Anniversary Reunion* brochure (1994), p. 4.

[79] Barry Lucas, in *Lonsdale College 30th Anniversary Reunion* brochure (1994), p. 7.

Margaret Eddershaw in a performance of "The Duchess of Malfi" at the Nuffield Theatre, early 1970s
(copyright, Leslie Stringer)

first phase of the Indoor Recreation Centre was open for student use, albeit down a short
dirt track because the South Spine had not yet reached much beyond the end of the Library.
Cartmel and County colleges were in the process of being built, and at County College David
O'Dell was elected as the first full-term president of the JCR, although his executive's office
was a room by courtesy of Bowland. Charities Week from 1 to 9 March 1968

> ends with a Grand Parade through Lancaster which, unlike last year's, does not end in a
> pitched battle. The streets are lined with hundreds of cheering students and Lancastrians
> and as JCR President I play Clyde Barrow in County's Bonnie and Clyde. To our surprise,
> we come third behind Cartmel's inspired Magic Roundabout and the Rugby Club's
> Flintstone Special.[80]

As the centre of gravity shifted from Lancaster to Bailrigg there was nostalgia for Centenary
House and 112/114 St Leonard Gate, and affection for Dolly's Bar and its presiding bar
lady,[81] together with a call for there to be some kind of social space for students provided

---

[80] David O'Dell, *1966 and All That*, Chapter 7.
[81] *John O'Gauntlet*, No. 35 (February 1968), pp. 3, 8.

in Lancaster. It would, however, be more than a decade before such provision was made and students, meanwhile, became accustomed to using their college junior common rooms as the core of their social lives.

As the second, and larger, group of finalists moved to the end of their three years in 1968, there was a wave of student uncertainty about the assessment of their degrees. *John O'Gauntlet* investigated the use of continuous assessment in 14 departments, and revealed considerable disparities in the amount and significance of its use, from 20% to 50% for each Part II unit out of nine. Indeed, Professor Sibley was not prepared to give a percentage for the Department of Philosophy, and was quoted as saying that the amount varied from student to student.[82] The system was not helped by the use of letter grades in some departments, with the difference between a D–? and a D(–) being indistinguishable, particularly when unaccompanied by a written comment.[83] Dr Noel Entwistle, Director of the Joseph Rowntree Research Unit, thought that there was "a measure of adequacy in any type of assessment: the problem is in trying to make inadequacies as small as possible".[84]

The biggest controversy of the year, however, blew up suddenly when *Carolynne* published a short news item[85] about a confidential meeting of Cartmel College syndicate at which the idea of mixed corridors when the college became residential was discussed. The proposal was supported by Dr David Craig, dean-elect of the college, who also expressed a personal view that students should have mixed bedrooms if they wished (see Chapter 7). As a consequence of the *Carolynne* article, the university had a sudden and unwelcome taste of negative publicity,[86] and special meetings of the Student Representative Council took place on 15 and 16 May. Dr Craig resigned his college position, *Carolynne* was banned from its office in University House, and the Student Representative Council issued a statement expressing "in the strongest possible terms its disapproval of this aspect of *Carolynne's* editorial policy", while also deploring the attitude of the national press and the "inaccurate, biased and sensational manner in which many newspapers have treated this and other events which recently taken place at this University".[87] Both Senate and Council became involved, and the incident brought the year to a subdued conclusion. Charles Carter, reflecting on these events,[88] noted the "dangerously distorting influence of the morbid public interest in student problems, as it affects the attitudes of press and television", that included BBC correspondents waylaying students and questioning them about their sex life. He saw the

---

[82] *John O'Gauntlet*, No. 36 (February 1968), p. 5.

[83] A. Bruce (Lonsdale College), letter to *Carolynne*, No. 32, 9 May 1968, p. 17.

[84] *Carolynne*, No. 32, 9 May 1968, pp. 10–11.

[85] *Carolynne*, No. 32, 9 May 1968, p. 5.

[86] There must have been a dearth of news at the time, for a short report of the controversy appeared as far away as the *Durham Morning Herald* in North Carolina in May 1968 (personal recollection of the author).

[87] *Scan*, Special Edition, 16 May 1968.

[88] University of Lancaster, *Fourth Annual Report* presented by the Vice-Chancellor to the Meeting of the University Court, 7 December 1968, pp. 3–4.

whole press campaign as starting "from a report of an individual's personal view expressed at a private meeting, which was never within miles of representing any actual policy".

By 1968–69 undergraduates were in residence at Bowland and Cartmel colleges, and the university was unambiguously located at Bailrigg. Now that shops and banks had opened in Alexandra Square, most students could if they wished spend the whole term on campus, and perhaps that is one reason why there was a high rate of demand for coach places to London at the weekends. Furness College had a functioning membership for its junior common room as its buildings went up, and Fylde College was being planned and electing its first JCR officers, including Bill Corr as first president.[89] He was also seen to be leading a group of about 50 students for the first over night sit-in of the Senate Chamber in support of student unrest at the London School of Economics. The Vice-Chancellor made them welcome, but the atmosphere was spoilt by the discovery of the theft of two of his personal possessions.[90] The Nuffield Theatre Studio had opened for performances, including a promenade performance of Jonson's *Bartholomew Fair*, and the Chaplaincy Centre was at an advanced stage of construction under the benign supervision of Father John Turner. The Medical Centre moved to Bailrigg House, and office space thus vacated in University House was occupied by the Student Representative Council. Student sporting activities and societies, clubs, and associations numbered close to 70, and were perpetually in danger of dissolution as they all jostled for members amongst a still small student body.

At County College, David O'Dell completed his privileged existence as JCR president, and he and two fellow students who shared a rented house in Lower Dolphinholme found that:

> Without student politics to divert us, we all begin to work harder and more steadily. And, to our surprise, our essay marks got better: after 2.5 years I get my first 'A'. Work harder, get better grades. Who would have thought it? And why didn't anyone tell us?[91]

Fortunately this new regime did not prevent him from performing in *Lash Me to the Mast*, a musical loosely based on *The Odyssey*, at the Grand Theatre and, after a monastic period of intensive revision, he graduated with the best County performance of the year, in the shape of a II(i), and a college prize of £4. 10. 0. for his work on *Pendragon*, the college magazine.[92] After his final presentation to the Chancellor, David O'Dell, BA, was ready to leave Lancaster for pastures new.

The year ended with further journalistic controversy, however, when *Carolynne* published its so-called Black Issue in June 1969, describing students taking soft drugs, removing Library books on a large scale, and having problems with communal living,[93] including

---

[89] *Steps* (University of Lancaster, Winter 2010), p. 17.
[90] *Carolynne*, Vintage 5 (undated, but summer 1968) shows Bill Corr, with placard, and also other students jeering at the occupiers (unnumbered pages).
[91] David O'Dell, *1966 And All That*, Chapter 10.
[92] David O'Dell, *1966 And All That*, Chapter 11.
[93] *Carolynne*, "Black Issue", Tuesday 24 June 1969.

Visit of HM the
Queen, the Duke of
Lancaster and Visitor
to the university
on 17 October 1969
(copyright, Brian
Carter)

noise and drunkenness. The Vice-Chancellor, mindful of the previous year's rapid escalation of media coverage, wasted no time in appointing an investigatory committee of two senior professors and the University Secretary, and the Federation of Junior Common Rooms approved a proposal from Bill Corr that noted with grave concern the "misleading, erroneous and damaging picture of the University", and demanded that all university facilities be withheld from the producers of *Carolynne*.[94] By late July the Vice-Chancellor was able to report that the more lurid allegations were largely unfounded,[95] while noting that "the sexual behaviour of certain students has been such as to cause grievous offence to others". He went on to recommend that more senior members might live in the colleges, that the imbalance between student years should be altered so that there were proportionately more Part II students in residence, and that there should be more regulated behaviour at night. A digest of the fuller report came to the Board of the Senate in October,[96] when senior members declined to accept or enforce regulations about night-time visits. Instead a Committee on Discipline was proposed, starting with the general proposition that

Members of the University may not act so as to unreasonably to disturb or offend other

---

[94] University of Lancaster Federation of Junior Common Rooms, Minute 4 of an emergency meeting held on 26 June 1969.

[95] C. F. Carter, "The *Carolynne* accusations: report to the Council" (23 July 1969, VC/69/55). In particular, a case study of a suggested Lancaster drug taker was found to be about a student at the University of Sussex.

[96] ASJ, "A Digest of the Lawrenson Committee Report" (9 October 1969, SU/69/72).

Officers of the Court, early 1980s, in Cartmel College Lecture Theatre. Front row, L to R, Dame Kathleen Ollerenshaw (Deputy Pro-Chancellor), Professor Philip Reynolds (Vice-Chancellor), Lord Taylor of Blackburn (Deputy Pro-Chancellor), Mr Geoffrey Thompson (Treasurer); back row, student officers and Mr George Cockburn (University Secretary).

members or the general public or by example to encourage others to break the regulations of the University or the law of the land.[97]

From this time onwards there were published rules,[98] reminding members of the community "of the ways in which they should exercise self-discipline, for the benefit of all". Included were rules for college, departmental, Library,[99] and car parking use, and bodies were set up to deal with miscreants: college and university tribunals, and a Committee of Appeals and Equity. Discussion of disciplinary structures and procedures continued, however, to occupy the time and energy of both junior and senior members of the university for some years to come.

The 1969–70 academic year began with a short visit from HM the Queen[100] on 17 October. After a walk from University House, into the Library, and along the south side of Alexandra Square, she visited the County College and unveiled a commemorative plaque before looking in on the Great Hall, the Jack Hylton Music Rooms, and, finally, the Chaplaincy Centre. All

[97] Section 1.9.1 of Unconfirmed Draft Report of the Board of Senate Conference, 29–30 September 1969 (GM/69/504).
[98] For example, University of Lancaster, *The Rules of the University* (1972).
[99] This was the period at which strips of magnetised steel were inserted in all Library books (the Diver Detection Device) to set off an alarm if a book had not been officially issued: heavy in relation to the glue holding them in place, they were, however, capable of being manually removed in large numbers.
[100] HM the Queen made a personal visit to each of the new universities opened in the 1960s.

went smoothly, the royal visitor being unaware of the installation by Bill Corr of a toad as the Archduke of Lancaster on the opposite side of Alexandra Square, a brief incident that was naturally highlighted by the press and that entered the Bailrigg mythology.

This academic year was the first in which students from North America came to Lancaster for all or part of their Junior Year Abroad. Initially the arrangement was with the University of Boulder at Colorado, who each year sent 40 to 50 students, accompanied on the first few occasions by their own resident Colorado tutor. They were able to take courses for credit that would be transferred to their home institution, a system that proved so popular that similar arrangements with other universities followed.[101] Subsequently matching arrangements were set up so that Lancaster students taking certain major subjects could spend the first year of Part II in the USA, and the credit obtained counted fully for up to as much as half of their final degree classification. The American students, with their outgoing approach to seminar participation and student life and sports, added spice to Bailrigg, and UK students who went abroad in a reciprocal arrangement benefited greatly from the experience, both at the time and in their subsequent careers.

---

[101] See University of Lancaster, *Junior Year Abroad Handbook* (published annually).

A HISTORY OF THE UNIVERSITY OF LANCASTER

The Federation of College Junior Common Rooms was active. There was support for a Theatre Project, later known as the Umbrella Project (see Chapter 7). And heated discussion took place, for example at a meeting held at Quernmore Park,[102] about the allocation of local authority grants for general student funding between the junior common rooms and the Student Representative Council, for behind the technicalities of the choice of procedures lay a continuing tension about whether the junior common rooms were paramount in student government, or whether the SRC should take an increasing role in managing student affairs. The latter body was involved in the refusal of a contribution for local industrial strike action – the beginning of an *ultra vires* debate that continued for some years – and in coping with the deficits relating to *John O'Gauntlet* and the LU Conservative Association. A prescient debate centred around the famous 13 Points proposed by Shirley Williams to aid a doubling of the student population by 1981, including the then novel suggestions of the reduction or removal of student grants coupled with a system of loans, restrictions on the numbers of overseas students, shorter or correspondence degree programmes, more intensive use of equipment and buildings, increases in staff–student ratios, and more students living at home and attending local universities.[103]

An annual cycle of events for the SRC had by now been established, starting with active participation at Introductory Week in October and concluding with the Graduation Ball in June. *Carolynne* and *John O'Gauntlet* both faltered and declined before their final disappearance, in 1971 and 1972 respectively, and although the joint staff–student *Lancaster Comment*[104] took up some of their campaigning ethos, *Scan* remained as the sole official student newspaper. The work of the SRC increased as student numbers grew, and a full-time administrative officer was deemed to be necessary as annual turnover approached £25,000 and the number of societies and activities diversified. There was pressure for a student counsellor, and a group of parents set up a privately run Playgroup.[105] In 1971–72 much time and energy was taken up with the so-called Craig Affair in the English Department,[106] but students were also concerned about a range of external political issues, ranging from the miners' strike to events in Northern Ireland. Repeated SRC meetings passed motions in favour of the chairman of the SRC becoming a sabbatical post – Tim Hamlet's rueful comments about the effects on his academic work, as a result of serving in this capacity in 1971–72, contributing to the sense that the current load was unsustainable – and a

---

[102] University of Lancaster Federation of College Junior Common Rooms: meeting of the Standing Constitutional Committee on 25 October 1969 (SRC/69/215): Quernmore Park, a couple of miles to the east of the university, was at the time occupied by an Anglican order of monks who rented out meeting space.

[103] Mark Smith, External Affairs Vice-Chairman, "University Development in the 1970s" (SRC/69/260).

[104] *Lancaster Comment* was published from 1972 to 1985.

[105] The Playgroup was subsequently brought under official university provision, and was later developed into the Pre-School Centre as part of its welfare services: see Chapter 7.

[106] See McClintock, *Quest*, pp. 393–4.

special meeting of the Senate in June 1972 approved a proposal from the Federation of Junior Common Rooms that Jerry Drew, elected as SRC chairman earlier in the day, could intercalate during his period of office.[107]

By 1973–74 eight colleges had either been fully established (see Chronolgy) or had set up shadow syndicates, and they came on stream in the following order: Bowland, Lonsdale and Cartmel, County, Furness and Fylde, and Grizedale and Pendle. All of them initially had undergraduates and postgraduate members, and all were governed by syndicates of senior members, to which junior members were increasingly added, with smaller college councils to run the day-to-day business. Undergraduates could be sure of residence in their first year, but were required to be in lodgings for their second year and usually for their third. Postgraduates were more often to be found in lodgings, although if they took on particular college posts, such as assistant dean, residential accommodation followed. In addition, under Simon Westerman's presidency, a Graduate Society was set up as a first step towards recognition of the distinctive needs of second and higher degree students. Unfortunately, and in part because of the long period before students could come into the colleges from the temporary accommodation at St Leonardsgate, the practice of dining in hall had not been adopted, although County made a brave attempt in that direction. Instead, there were three rather large and cheerless refectories, where people came and went as they wished, and a growing trend towards self-catering, while the core of each college's social existence was destined to be a junior common room, closely associated with a licensed bar. Senior members of the university, led by John Bevington and Malcolm Willcock at Bowland, Tom Lawrenson and Emlyn Lloyd at Lonsdale, John Creed at Cartmel, and Roland Dobbs and Brian Duke at County, strove to become involved with the colleges, and the preponderance of young and junior staff in the earliest years undoubtedly helped develop close bonds between staff and students. They were aided by some exceptionally strong-minded domestic bursars, especially Elizabeth Livingston (Bowland), Hilda Salmon (Lonsdale), and Audrey Robinson (Cartmel), who combined iron and velvet in the fists with which they managed their empires.

Nevertheless, despite their initiation from the outset, the colleges were never wholly confident of their role in the university. An extended statement of intent of 1966 from Lonsdale College, unsigned but showing evidence of Tom Lawrenson's imprint,[108] defined the colleges' main aims as being: to provide a means of expression for the academic staff in general matters of university policy, and a basis for an academic life transcending that of the department; to provide a focus of communal life, so that the university could expand without the evils of mass and over-centralised organisation; to create the means for a genuine corporate life, both academic and general, in which all could share and which would

---

[107] Minute S.72/243, extraordinary meeting of the Senate held on 28 June 1972. Pressure quickly mounted for other posts to be made sabbatical, but further approvals followed slowly and incrementally over several years.

[108] Document G.66/596, presented by Lonsdale Syndicate to the Senate on 6 July 1966.

A copy of the students' official newspaper, *Scan*, for January 1976, the headline demonstrating that some issues never go away

develop real loyalties; and to provide for the welfare of junior members through both the tutorial system and the maturing influence of corporate life, while avoiding the sacrifice of their personal liberty. The document recommended that there should be provision for senior, middle and junior common rooms, and an internal system of governance that enabled all three elements to work together for the common good.

Perhaps because of this uncertainty, the colleges have probably been the most frequently scrutinised and analysed element of Lancaster life. As early as 1970 a Conference of the Senate was considering papers on the future development of the colleges.[109] In 1972 the Taylor Report,[110] citing "a fair amount of disappointment with the collegiate system in its present form, not only as regards disciplinary matters, but because (as is often alleged) the colleges are not fostering (as they were intended to) a virile community life for both staff and students", recommended "separate and really thorough investigation by a small working party", including the question of remuneration for senior college officers. The proposal was agreed,[111] and the Secretary for College and Student Affairs, Rod Martindale,

---

[109] See, for example, "Colleges in a University of 6000 – and beyond" by Philip Reynolds, pro-vice-chancellor and founding principal of Furness College.

[110] University of Lancaster, *Report of the Taylor Enquiry* (8 May–5 July 1972).

[111] Minute CO.72/69 of the Special Meeting of the Council held on 3 October 1972.

worked energetically to canvass views across the institution and to return with meaningful and affordable recommendations. The consequential report[112] urged a review of the tutorial system, an introductory guide to college services for senior members, more coherent grouping of departments with colleges, the earlier establishment of planning committees for future colleges, a higher priority of provision for postgraduate students, and means by which a limited number of college officers could spend more time on the role. In part because of financial constraints, but also because practices had become all too quickly fixed in departments and elsewhere, only minor changes came about as a result of this round of consultation.[113]

During the period 1968–1974 there was a particularly high level of academic staff recruitment, many of whom would see out the twentieth century and beyond, and probably the most abundant choice of subjects in the history of the university, particularly as the Department of Law came on stream. A welcome addition to student life was the appointment of Barry Lucas as Social Manager.[114] He had been admitted to Lancaster, and to Lonsdale College, to read English and History in 1968. Two years later, as college social officer and with the Great Hall now open, he persuaded his Bowland and Furness JCR counterparts to pool their funds with Lonsdale, giving a fund of £1000 with which – without having informed their JCR presidents – they booked The Who, and attracted 1350 people at £1 each. In November 1972 the SRC sensibly agreed to give him a university-wide remit that included "booking of all groups engaged in any social function organised by the SRC", including the colleges when agreeable. From that time Lancaster became renowned for the groups that it managed to attract and pack into the Great Hall, in which it was aided by access to the motorway, good local ticket agencies, and support from a young generation in Lancaster itself who were eager for change. Barry urged the use of the Winter Gardens in Morecambe as a larger venue, but in vain. A listing for autumn 1977, for example, advertises 14 concerts between early October and mid-December, including Eddie and the Hot Rods, Elvis Costello and supporting groups, the Boom Town Rats, and The Jam + Support. His favourite coup was bringing Paul McCartney to Lancaster, with his newly formed band Wings, and his greatest regret was having to turn down the Rolling Stones because their gig would have coincided with the use of the Great Hall for Finals. It all came to an end in 1984, when tighter fire regulations made the use of the Great Hall impracticable and the Sugar House

---

[112] J. R. Martindale, "Report of the Working Party appointed to investigate the working of colleges" (JRM/75/15), report to Senate of 5 February 1972.

[113] The Vice-Chancellor had expressed concern to Professor Reynolds early in the review, pressing for "practical solutions" and suggesting that "trivial solutions" would only make matters worse.

[114] See: Contract for Barry Lucas, Social Manager (March 1972), University of Lancaster Federation of College Junior Common Rooms, Minutes 1972); Barry Lucas, "Sorry ... House Full" (SRC/73/140, SRC Minutes 1973); Interview (undated, unnumbered, but *Scan* (3rd Issue, Michaelmas Term 1973); Lonsdale College, *30th Anniversary Reunion* (1998); *The Visitor*, 17 November 2004, pp. 6–7; *Steps* (Winter 2009, pp. 6–7). The title lapsed in 1980 and was never re-activated.

accommodation was insufficient to pick up the role, but these events remain a favourite memory of the generations of alumni fortunate enough to have been at Lancaster at the time.

The range of other facilities was constantly expanding, from the eight cinemas in Morecambe and Lancaster to the Film Society at Bailrigg. The Grand Theatre was somewhat in the doldrums in this period, but in the 1970s The Duke's Playhouse [sic] and the Nuffield Theatre Studio vied in their choice of experimental theatre and dance, and a growing range of pubs and restaurants in Lancaster were eager for student trade. Trials for team sports were held by the Athletic Union as soon as students appeared in October, with provision for football, hockey, rugby, lacrosse, and cricket, as well as a bowling green. Students had to go to the Kingsway Baths in Lancaster to swim, but the Centre for Physical Education, under its ever-energetic director, Joe Medhurst, provided badminton, judo, dance, roller skating, squash, and weight training indoors, as well as snorkelling, canoeing, speleology, climbing, and sailing at a distance. There was a Conservation Corps, dedicated to tree planting, digging, and rubbish clearing, and a Community Welfare Group whose members worked in Lancaster[115] for groups needing support. And, as the range of colleges expanded, there was more scope for shared events, or for inter-sport rivalry.

Student rents became an increasing issue as the inflation of the early 1970s took hold (see Chapter 6). Lancaster students were involved in a series of rent strikes coordinated by the NUS, and its president, John Randall, came to speak in the Great Hall during Introductory Week 1973. In an interview[116] with this "small and rotund" student officer, he was quoted as anticipating a national demonstration, but only when support had been built up for it during the first term of the year. The SRC set up a Grants Action Committee to coordinate action in this area, a body attended with great regularity by Pete Elliott, a first year student from Bowland College, who became SRC Treasurer at the end of the Michaelmas Term.[117] The university adopted a low-key policy towards the campaign, and the SRC organised a system of rents being paid into funds held securely against the time when the phases of the campaign were complete and the money would be handed over to the university.

In 1974–75, however, a more difficult situation put the relationship of students and central officers to the test in ways that transcended the payment of rent. A brief summary of these events begins with NUS demonstrations about increases in rent levels that, across both London and Edinburgh, brought out some 40,000 students.[118] At the same time an unprecedented and sharp mid-year rent increase at Lancaster precipitated a rent strike that attracted widespread support amongst students in residence, of whom up to a half were

---

[115] The group enjoyed a long existence under the name of the Community Action Group.

[116] *Scan*, unnumbered and undated, but the second issue of Michaelmas Term 1973, pp. 13–14. Mr Randall subsequently became the first director of the Quality Assurance Agency (see Chapter 3).

[117] *Scan*, 11th issue of Michaelmas Term, 10 December 1973, p. 20. Mr Elliott filled a number of SRC posts during his time as a student: he subsequently became the General Manager of the Students' Union, and is now the Chief Executive of the charity formed in 2010.

[118] *Scan*, 18 November 1974.

John Chambers, tile panel of about 1908, with a rosehip design
(John Chambers Collection)

Gordon Forsyth (1919), lustre bowl, peacock blue
(John Chambers Collection)
Miniature vase of about 1905, with blue flambé glaze
(John Chambers Collection)
Richard Joyce (1919), lustre vase, with hares on a floral ground
(John Chambers Collection)
William Mycock (1913), lustre vase, "Contingent Bona Bonis"
(John Chambers Collection)

calculated to be joining in.[119] Some sanctions were imposed to discourage further student take-up, and in the eighth week of the Lent Term, the senior tutor of Cartmel College, in line with college policy, refused a college loan to a student who had applied on grounds of hardship. On 7 March, three days later, the SRC President, Dick Soper, led an occupation of University House. The university, for the first time, applied for an injunction against its students, and on 12 March Mr Justice Hollins at the High Court in Manchester made an order that "possession of University House be restored to the University",[120] which was executed in the early hours of 18 March.

Over 1000 students had been involved at some time or other, and the establishment of a Disciplinary Committee by the Senate on 17 March to hear charges against just 30 of them quickly ran into difficulties. In the Summer Term there were appeals against the penalties, particularly for students who were to be excluded. In May the Committee of Appeals and Equity met: no student representative was prepared to act, and the cases were heard by Lord Morris of Grasmere, in the chair, and two lawyers; one internal, and the other an external assessor. On 3 July Lord Morris issued a statement that said[121] "We accept the advice of the legal assessor that if any one of the four propositions put forward by Professor Griffith[122] is correct, the appellants are entitled to succeed on their appeal." The extended text of the decision, issued the same day, indicated that there were at least four procedural grounds on which the university had erred, principally because there were no standing members of the Committee for Appeals and Equity who could be kept apart from prior decisions. The Vice-Chancellor at once indicated that "Any fault of earlier procedure revealed by the decision … will now have the urgent attention of a committee appointed by the Senate, with student participation." The Senate in June was also disrupted, as were the proceedings of an Additional Tribunal held in Gillow House, although some fines were subsequently imposed on some students who had been individually identified. In the following academic year, in which the SRC was led by memorable student officers that included Victor Adereth and Maggie Gallagher, the university again addressed its disciplinary procedures in the face of student opposition, but the Committee of Appeals and Equity never again sat, and in 2002 was erased from the Statutes.

This prolonged period of tension can reasonably be said to have been the most difficult ever experienced at the university, and drew in most students and staff, whether as participants, negotiators, or members of disciplinary proceedings. The university was still at a size where a single topic could seize the attention of everyone at Bailrigg, and there was a rich crop of ephemera, with new fliers being distributed on tables and chairs across

---

[119] *Scan*, 4 February 1975.

[120] University of Lancaster, "Militant March", 24 March 1975, p. 3.

[121] *NewsSheet* No. 16, 3 July 1975.

[122] The reference was to Professor John Griffith (1918–2010), a controversial academic public lawyer, who was an active member of the Council of Academic Freedom and Democracy, and who had taken a keen interest in the procedures surrounding the cases: see obituary in *The Times*, 20 May 2010, p. 63.

the university at least once or twice a day.[123] The NUS was actively involved throughout, with the presidency moving from John Randall to Charles Clarke[124] during the course of the proceedings, although media coverage was regional rather than national, for by this time other universities were working through not dissimilar situations. The events had raised questions about how disciplinary machinery was to be designed and implemented, how far students could exercise their dissent without penalty, and how the principles of natural justice were to be satisfied in working through in subsequent disciplinary hearings.[125] They also demonstrated how exhausting and wasteful such protracted episodes could be, and how damage to working relationships between staff and students, once made, took time and effort to repair.

In 1980 the long-anticipated swimming pool in the Indoor Recreation Centre was opened to students, and, two years later, the perseverance of the Students' Union President Al Gordon and his executive led to the opening of the Sugar House at St Leonardsgate. This student social centre has been a successful and popular venue ever since, nimbly responding to changes in student taste and providing a useful source of income for the Students' Union. Nevertheless, the early 1980s were a rather muted period, for the substantial reduction in universities' recurrent grant brought about a temporary fall in student numbers at Lancaster. Some subjects were laid down (see Chapter 3), and considerable care had to be taken to ensure that all those admitted to degree schemes that were discontinued were enabled to complete the degrees for which they were registered, either by special arrangements at Lancaster, or in a few cases by agreed transfers to other institutions.

The return of institutional confidence in the second half of the decade included increases in student numbers. There were more overseas students,[126] including at undergraduate level, where the implementation of full cost tuition fees in 1980–81 had caused the biggest falls. The earlier decline in numbers had also created a buoyant market for graduate careers. The associated institutions were admitting more students who were eligible to take Lancaster degrees, and each year some 120 students from Charlotte Mason College were living and working at Bailrigg for the first year of Part II (see Chapter 3). The university's boundaries in this area would further expand in the early 1990s, when Blackburn and Blackpool and The Fylde students joined Edge Hill and S. Martin's colleges as associated students. There were growing numbers of part-time students, principally recruited through the Office of Adult Education.[127] The numbers of visiting students also increased, as the university, after

---

[123] See UA.1/3/5/10.

[124] Subsequently sometime Home Secretary in the Labour Government of 1997–2010, and currently Visiting Professor of Politics and Faith in the Department of Politics, Philosophy and Religion.

[125] The last student occupation, in 1991, was also about student rents, although the disruption of a day conference in 2005 (the George Fox Six) led to considerable controversy and to a further examination of the permissible boundaries of student protest (minute S.2006/53, Senate meeting on 24 May 2006).

[126] University of Lancaster, *Twenty-Second Annual Report*, 1985–86, pp. 24 ff.

[127] Lancaster University, *Annual Report 1993*, pp. 25, 26.

a decade of experience of North American students at Lancaster, felt able to be more flexible about the periods of their stay, so that, for example, they might attend for the equivalent of single semesters if that was their choice. The rate of student success was highly satisfactory, for at Part I 90% of students were qualifying for Part II at their first attempt, rising to 98% after resit examinations. At Part II, almost 5% were awarded first class honours degrees in 1985, and 44% either a first or an upper second.

From October 1988 undergraduates were also able to take enterprise units as part of their assessment for a classified degree.[128] Lancaster was the first UK institution to sign up with the Department of Employment's Training Agency for the Enterprise in Higher Education initiative, with Dr John Wakeford of Independent Studies as the academic coordinator and Mrs Janet Clements as the project coordinator. The key principle was that externally directed, practical work also merited one or two units out of the nine at Part II, whether it was developing physics apparatus for local secondary schools, studying diet and food availability amongst ethnic minorities, the role of nurse managers in community health centres, or the oral history of lime kiln workers.[129] One project, on student political and social attitudes, was sponsored by Guardian Newspapers for a run of years and proved particularly popular for the growing practice of group working. Numbers of students participating gradually built up over the five years of funding and it was a matter of regret when the scheme came to an end. However, the university agreed to fund internal projects for departments through the Unit for Innovation in Higher Education,[130] and the work undertaken there in turn informed fundamental shifts in teaching and learning at Lancaster (see Chapter 3). The university was also awarded two projects for teaching innovation by the UFC in the early 1990s,[131] and the Vice-Chancellor took a keen personal interest in the externally funded Regional Academic Summer School for talented school leavers, an accelerated route for undergraduate and postgraduate entry into subjects in the sciences, including engineering, mathematics, and computing.

As the university expanded, so did the cultural activities,[132] strongly encouraged by Professor Hanham. The Medici Quartet was in residence, and at the Peter Scott Gallery the exhibitions ranged from Picasso's late etchings to the work of Reginald Farrer, a Yorkshire botanist plant hunter. Extra gallery space was obtained by the conversion of music practice rooms, enabling displays from the Irene Manton bequest to be shown in dedicated space and associated with complementary collections from the university's own

---

[128] A useful account of this activity is given in Peter Wright, "Learning through Enterprise: The Enterprise in Higher Education Initiative", in *Learning to Effect*, ed. Ronald Barnett (Buckingham: Society for Research into Higher Education; Open University Press, 1992), pp. 205–23.

[129] "Outlook on Enterprise", First Edition, December 1989.

[130] Unit for Innovation: see UA.1/18/5/11.

[131] Lancaster University, *Annual Report 1992*, pp. 18–19.

[132] Lancaster University, *Annual Report 1991*, pp. 36–8.

Figure 5: Students numbers by year, 1968–2010

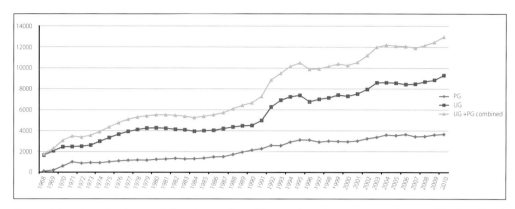

Figure 5 is based on a headcount of all students registered for a undergraduate or postgraduate qualification offered from the Bailrigg campus as of the 1st December in each year
It includes:
    Students on work and study placements
    Students at Bailrigg taking the Liverpool University Medical degree
    Study abroad students
    Students who are intercalating
It does not include:
    Part-time students taking short courses offered by the Department of Continuing Education and the Centre for Training and Development (CETAD)
    Students taking Lancaster validated degrees at the regional associated institutions
    Students taking Lancaster validated degrees at overseas partner institutions
    Students taking the Study Group international foundation course
    Members of staff taking staff development courses validated at undergraduate or postgraduate level
    Full and part-time students (excluding part-time students taking short courses offered by the Department of Continuing Education and the Centre for Training and Development)

early embellishment fund, such as Terry Frost, Miro, and Max Ernst.[133] The Nuffield Theatre was granted a public performance licence in 1992,[134] enabling it to expand its audiences and its repertoire, with dovetailing of travelling professional events and student productions in theatre, music, and dance. A further acquisition in 1994 was a fine and historic collection of Royal Lancastrian pottery, and in 1995 Leeds University generously donated other works previously owned by Professor Manton, including her international print collection to those already left to the university.[135] Furthermore, as the Ruskin Library rose from the ground, Mr (later Professor) Stephen Wildman was appointed to conserve, display, and manage the Whitehouse Collection of John Ruskin's books, manuscripts, and drawings, with an opening exhibition in May 1997, while an electronic edition of Ruskin's *Modern Painters*, Volume 1 was funded by the Leverhulme Trust.[136]

---

[133] Lancaster University, *Annual Report 1992*, p. 23.
[134] Lancaster University, *Annual Report 1993*, p. 26.
[135] The process by which the Irene Manton Collection came to Lancaster is detailed in UA.1/13/4/2.
[136] Lancaster University, *Annual Report 1995*, p. 10; see also *Annual Report 1996*, pp. 6–7, 8–9.

After years of building up the postgraduate student population, and with a growing number of them coming from overseas, the university in 1990 finally took the bold step of setting up a Graduate College. The intention was to give them a distinctive organisational and physical presence in the university, and to ensure that year-round provision for people working intensively from early October to the following mid-September could be better satisfied, whether in terms of twelve-month residence, office accommodation, library provision, and a full range of welfare facilities. The first building was positioned at the north end of the university (see Chapter 7), but the lack of college and social amenities and the cramped site led to a reconsideration, with the result that the college was relocated to the South-West Campus in 1996 and greatly enlarged as part of the Alexandra Park development in 2004. The first principal was Professor Chris Park, who also became the second dean of the Lancaster University Graduate School, and he was succeeded by Professor Maurice Kirby, previously Provost of Colleges, and then by Mr Jo Hardman, LUSU Business and Development Manager. The university could now guarantee residence for all new graduate students from overseas whose acceptances of places had been received by a set date, and also offered a limited amount of married student accommodation. The officers for the college were fewer than for the eight undergraduate colleges, reflecting the college's different needs: only a principal, a vice-principal, a dean, and an international officer. At the same time, the Students' Union undertook a series of discussions – and at times negotiations – about the standing and authority of the Graduate Students' Association. Whether the facilities on offer can ever precisely match graduate students' distinctive needs is a more elusive quest: a report of 1999[137] suggested that there was still ground to make up, and considerable efforts have been made in succeeding years to fill the gap.

The early 1990s was also the moment at which the most thorough examination ever of the colleges took place. Chaired by the Pro-Chancellor, Sir Christopher Audland, and with Paul Graves as its secretary and report writer, a joint committee of Senate and Council held twenty meetings between April and December 1993, took evidence from people and groups inside the university, visited Durham, York, and Nottingham, and commissioned interviews of 400 students via the School of Independent Studies. The report,[138] issued in January 1994, concluded that, just as major institutional effort had been made in improving research and teaching, the same energy should be put into improving student care, and hence:

> In this context, the University must reaffirm the importance of the college system, and redefine what is expected from the colleges. They should be given clearer mission statements and clearer organisational guidelines; and they should have modest but real resources under their control. The University should make clear by deed as well as word that it places high value on service to colleges by its members.

---

[137] Jennie Henley and Hilary Simmons, "Survey on Facilities Available to Postgraduate Research Students" (Lancaster University, undated but 1999).

[138] University of Lancaster, "Report of the Committee for the Review of the College System to the Senate and the Council" (SASA/93/1593, January 1994).

We need a new approach to the tutorial system, which has come in for both internal and external criticism. There is a place here for both colleges and academic departments, but the interface between the two must be clear and complementary, and both must relate well to centrally supplied student services: we cannot afford any waste of resources.[139]

The 38 recommendations covered college membership, college constitutions, officers and committee structures, tutorial and student support systems, physical organisation, JCR college finances, and the relationship between colleges and the departments and central offices of the university, and proposed both more separation (for example, of different kinds of student support, and of the financing of the colleges *per se* and of residential accommodation) and more integration (for example, a Colleges and Student Affairs Board). There were to be template job descriptions for the key college posts, principals were to be bought out for up to 50% of their time, and more modest remuneration for senior tutors and college deans was arranged. Unfortunately the recommendations were discussed at a time of growing financial difficulty for the university, particularly as the former college fee was finally absorbed with the HEFCE recurrent grant, and it is to the credit of the senior officers of the time that they were not extinguished altogether. The buyout levels for the principals, for example, were implemented at 50%, but soon afterwards reduced to 25%, and while £113,000 was allocated in 1996–97 for all college officer payments, this was reduced in 1997–98, first to £90,000 and again to £71,000. Nevertheless, even as the cuts were made, the review group set up to consider them drew attention to "the strength of support for the College system from all those who either submitted written responses, or were interviewed".[140]

By 1996 the total number of students just topped 10,000, of whom one-third were postgraduates on masters and research degrees. A much wider range of degrees had become open: first degrees now included BA, BSc, BBA, BMus, BEng, LLB, and BEd, as well as MPhys, MEng, and MMath. At postgraduate level, besides MA and Diploma, there were the degrees of MBA, LLM, MRes, MPhil, and PhD. By 2004, as the university celebrated its first 40 years, student numbers slightly exceeded 11,000, of whom just over a quarter were postgraduate.[141] In 2008–09, as the university approached its half-century, and after the closure of the Department of Continuing Education and with a small reduction in the postgraduate population, student numbers have stabilised at just over 12,000, of whom more than 90% are full-time and a quarter are postgraduate.[142] To the degrees already available has been added an MD.

---

[139] Paras. 3.1.2 and 3.1.3 of "Report of the Committee for the Review of the College System" (1994).

[140] University of Lancaster, "Report of the Review Group on the Buyout and Remuneration of College Officers" (PCO/97/143, undated but late 1997).

[141] "Celebrating 40 Years of Excellence, 1964–2004" (University of Lancaster, 2004), p. 3.

[142] Lancaster University, *2010 Report and Accounts*, pp. 44–5. The numbers cited do not include the students in the School of Health and Medicine who are registered for degrees with the University of Liverpool.

Finally, a brief glimpse of student life at the end of the first decade of the twenty-first century can stand as a marker against which future changes can subsequently be measured.[143] We have seen how the 1960s were years in which the young university relied on the extempore, the *ad hoc*, and the improvised solution, and how these measures were essential for the operation of the institution before all the requisite procedures had been put in place. The situation in the early twenty-first century could hardly be more different, since the student body is now codified, regulated and managed in ways that would have been inconceivable, even in a mature institution, half a century ago. Students (and their families) also to some extent see themselves as consumers of higher education, rather than the apprentices to whom David Craig once referred, and have ever higher expectations of what they will receive in return for the fees and maintenance for which they are personally responsible. Nevertheless, below that layer of consumerism there remain the intrinsic purposes of a university education: to enable students to become proficient in both subject-specific and general learning, to fit them for their future careers, and to equip them with the ability to respond creatively and intelligently to whatever challenges they face for the rest of their lives.

Another major difference, running as a theme through the continuing narrative of student experience, is the dependence of contemporary students on forms of electronic communication that had not been remotely imagined when the university began. As student generations enter universities whose members are already running their lives through mobile telephones, laptops, and other forms of electronic equipment now pouring onto the market, so they have an expectation that the university will engage with them through those and subsequent media. They have led the moves, for example, for on-line registration before entering the university as new Part I undergraduates. Blogs and websites are used by many staff to encourage peer learning at all levels, coursework is scanned electronically for plagiarism, learning materials are placed on and taken from the web, and personalised examination timetables are issued electronically. All student rooms in the colleges have internet access and there are well-publicised wi-fi hotspots across the campus. There are, of course, both advantages and disadvantages to this process. Face-to-face contact, of students with staff, and with each other, is still a critically important component of student learning, and the move to greater electronic contact is accompanied by the demands of undergraduates for guaranteed contact hours.[144] Furthermore, while many students thrive on electronic communication, others draw heavily on the availability of office hours with academic staff; for example, because they wish to embark on non-standard or complex projects, or because they are falling behind and need assistance to retrieve their position.

The imaginary tour again begins with admissions. While from 1965 onwards applicants had been required to use UCCA (Universities' Central Council on Admissions), entry qualifications

---

[143] But see the Epilogue for an introduction to the second decade.

[144] "Commitments on academic contact time", minute S.2008/4 of 16 January 2008. There are concerns across higher education that the close pedagogical relationship that students in the UK have enjoyed is under threat in an era of mass education: see, for example, Rebecca Attwood, "The personal touch", *Times Higher Education*, No. 1895, 7–13 May 2009, pp. 32–7.

were stated in the most general terms for undergraduates, while for postgraduates the original prospectus simply stated that each application would be considered on its merits.[145] No interviews or open days were offered, and the first that most students saw of Lancaster was on their arrival at Lancaster Castle railway station, it being unheard of at the time that their parents would have travelled with them. Two years later candidates for graduate study at masters level were required to be "graduates of approved standing or equivalent", while for doctoral study they were to be "graduates or persons of equivalent qualification who show evidence of exceptional ability or who have demonstrated their ability in graduate studies".[146]

Instead of the slender A5 brochure issued in the 1960s, with its understated red and grey lettering on the cover, the Lancaster experience for the twenty-first-century student begins with an Undergraduate Prospectus of 176 A4 pages, in full colour throughout and with an electronic version also on line. There are 33 pages of general introduction that markets the university to its potential future cohort, their families, and their teachers: of course, all faces are wreathed in smiles and the sky is always blue, or tinged tastefully with a few wisps of white cloud. "It's where you belong", it proclaims, "You'll never be short of things to do at Lancaster. Our college-based activities, sports and arts facilities, cinema, clubs and societies are a great way to get involved and make the most of your time here",[147] a message supported by direct quotations from named and pictured students. Programmes are listed alphabetically by subject area, and applicants apply through the more streamlined UCAS system. Each person receives a conditional offer that specifies both the grades they must meet across the wide range of pre-university qualifications now open to candidates, as well as specific requirements for the programme identified by the UCAS code. For example, Engineering programmes range from ABB for a four-year Electronic Systems Engineering programme to BBC for Sustainable Engineering 1. All applicants are strongly recommended to visit the university, either on pre-arranged annual visit days that are organised to bring cognate departments together in one venue, or on days when departmental visits, linked to campus tours conducted by students, are available. Parents regularly accompany the candidates, and departments often provide special question and answer sessions for the former. Since the introduction of tuition fees, universities provide some financial assistance to families below certain income levels or to students with high entry qualifications: the pattern is fairly consistent that about one-third of undergraduates or their families are able to pay the full amount, about one-third receive full financial assistance for both tuition and maintenance (involving the maximum loan support), and the remaining third fall in the middle ground.[148] Student earnings during term-time either

---

[145] University of Lancaster, *Prospectus 1963–64*, p. 37.

[146] University of Lancaster, *1965–66 Prospectus 1966–67*, pp. 108–9.

[147] University of Lancaster, *Undergraduate Prospectus Entry 2010* (Lancaster, 2009, p. 9).

[148] For the first couple of years of the new student tuition fee regime, there was also some financial support for students applying to subject areas that were perceived to be economically vital but lacking in candidates. That facility has come to an end, partly on grounds of complexity, but also because its availability did not have sufficient desired effect on the subject areas so designated.

Sally Scott and David Peace (1989), engraved doors in the Peter Scott Gallery, donated to the university by Michael and Jean Argles. The verse is from "Henry the Eighth", Act III, Scene 2, and begins: "Orpheus with his lute made trees / And the mountain tops that freeze / Bow themselves when he did sing …"

contribute to the lessening of the burden of debt or enable students to spread their expenditure a little more widely. Work obtained through the LUSU Job Shop is to some extent tailored to the needs of full-time students: other paid activity is less well regulated, and can be a matter of concern for directors of study who watch students struggling to reconcile academic study with paid employment.

The Postgraduate Prospectus is even weightier, at 224 pages, and covers both taught masters and research degrees. In line with the relative proportions within the student population, there is a much greater emphasis on provision for overseas students, including an accommodation guarantee that

> If you are a full-time postgraduate student from outside the European Union, you are guaranteed single on-campus accommodation for your first year of study, provided that
> – Your residence application form has been received by a specified date in August
> – You have notified your firm acceptance of a place and fulfilled conditions of acceptance
> – You are registered on a full-time course of at least 9 months, starting in September/ October.[149]

Programmes are grouped by faculty rather than by department, and applications are received on-line, direct to faculty contact points. There is a widespread recognition that word-of-mouth recommendation is the most effective way of recruiting from around the world, especially for doctoral students. As Lancaster overseas alumni take up increasingly senior positions in their home countries, the experiences they remember from their time in the UK is critical to the reputation that underpins other recruiting activity, including appearances at overseas fairs and introductions by a few respected agents.

Entry qualifications for masters degrees are normally an upper second class honours degree or equivalent, and the required level of English language proficiency; those for research degrees are more variable, and may include a masters level degree in the relevant area and/or professional qualifications. Applicants for postgraduate study, who are expected to apply at least six months before entry, may be invited for interview; often, of course, such a procedure is not feasible. Each applicant receives an offer letter, which may include conditions still to be met.[150] For some programmes applicants are required to pay a tuition fee deposit, particularly for the Management School, although this procedure does not necessarily deter students from taking up places at other institutions. The fees are now, of course, substantial: a minimum of £4170 per annum for masters degree students from the UK and EU, and £10,500 per annum for those from overseas. Actual fees may be higher: £14,000 for overseas students wanting a diploma or masters degree in Accounting and Financial Management, while the full-time MBA costs £18,500 for all students, irrespective of domicile.

A further constraint on overseas recruitment was signalled to universities late in 2008 by the UK Border Agency, requiring them to implement a student-related version (Tier 4)

---

[149] University of Lancaster, *Postgraduate Prospectus*, Entry 2011–12 (Lancaster, 2008), p. 21.

[150] From October 2009 it is intended that the relevant faculty office will issue the offer letter.

of a points-based system for immigrants to the UK in order to identify bogus students and institutions.[151] From March 2009, each university would have to apply for a sponsor licence and applicants would have to not only demonstrate evidence of their funding and qualifications, as before, but also convince the immigration authorities of their *bona fides*. More intensive record-keeping, particularly of visa status and attendance records, was to be introduced. There was inevitable concern about students being discouraged from applying to UK institutions under this regime, coupled with disquiet about the change in relationship between staff and students that such an inquisitorial approach was likely to bring.[152] The strength of feeling across the sector was shown, for example, by a letter from 37 academic staff across several institutions detailing the ways in which they personally were not prepared to cooperate in practices that they believed to be "discriminatory and [to] distort academic freedoms".[153] Since, however, overseas recruitment is so fundamental to the mission and economy of higher education institutions, including Lancaster, it seemed unlikely that in practice any university would be able to decline becoming involved in a process solely designed to assist the government of the day.

Once students have been admitted, the university's responsibilities to them multiply. Lancaster has retained the system of three terms rather than the two semesters adopted in some universities; new undergraduates come up for a full week before the Michaelmas Term begins in early October and postgraduates slightly later. These initial days are a period when all new undergraduates have privileged access to every kind of advice and support from staff and fellow students, as they are taken through the processes of entering residence, confirming their registration for their Part I courses, paying or making arrangements for payment of their fees, obtaining their vital Library card, and attending a Freshers' Fair and the multiplicity of social events based around the colleges and the Students' Union.[154] For postgraduates there are similar events, based around particular faculties and the Graduate College. Each year there is concern about the balance between events involving the consumption of alcohol and those that do not. An additional issue was identified in 2008–09 in relation to the Freshers' Fair, at which sporting and non-sporting clubs and

---

[151] Eversheds Educational Briefing, 11 November 2008.

[152] See: Senate S.2008/54(D) of 8 October 2008; University and Students' Union USU.08/51 of 11 November 2008; Graduate School Committee GSC.08/93 of 2 December 2008; Learning, Teaching and Assessment Committee LTA.009.004 of 19 January 2009; and Undergraduate Studies Committee of 26 January 2009.

[153] "Boycott these checks on students", letter in *The Guardian*, 14 April 2009. The damage is not confined to undergraduate study: see the comment on impediments to students and visitors from overseas in Mathias Brust, "Our learned foreign friends no longer seem to be welcome here", *Times Higher Education*, No. 1889, 1 April 2009, pp. 24–5.

[154] See the insert guide in *Scan*, Intro week, 30 September 2008, for all the societies available in 2008–09, from Muay Thai Kickboxing to a Gospel Choir.

The "You said, we have, 2010/11" leaflet widely circulated to students, and setting out how the university has responded to student requests on such matters as career guidance and feedback on student coursework

societies recruit members: there was evidence that the number of commercial stalls was on the increase while student-organised clubs and societies were in decline.[155]

The days when several students shared a single coldwater basin in Morecambe have, of course, long been forgotten. About two-thirds of all Lancaster undergraduates live either on the campus in accommodation provided by the university, or at Chancellor's Wharf in Lancaster, as members of one of the eight undergraduate colleges. Much of the accommodation has been built since 2000, via UPP (Lancaster) Limited (see Chapter 7), and there is deliberately a wide range of facilities and hence price bands from which students can choose, from as little as £64.75 a week in 2008–09 for a standard, unrefurbished room with a wash basin, to over £100 for a new studio apartment.[156] Most students expect *en suite* accommodation, and this has been allowed for in the mix. The majority of letting periods are for 40 weeks, meaning that students can stay in residence over the Christmas

---

[155] Minute 3(i) of the Student Support and Welfare Policy Committee, 9 February 2009. The problem of alcohol at the core of student social life is, of course, not confined to Lancaster: see, for example, the views of Sidra Hussain at Manchester University, *The Times Magazine*, 25 November 2008, pp. 55–7.

[156] "What accommodation?" lancs.ac.uk/depts/cro/whataccom.

and Easter vacations, either because they are from overseas or because they wish to continue their academic work. The rest of the students seek houses to share, usually in Lancaster, and the Students' Union housing office ensures that all premises to let are kept to appropriate standards.[157] Most students who wish to live in university-owned accommodation are able to do so for all three years. For graduate students there are 850 rooms in the Graduate College for 2055 full-time students, all based in Alexandra Park, while the remainder live in the city or nearby areas. Diploma and masters degree students, who have only 12 months in which to complete their studies and who are under severe academic pressure, tend to make weaker attachments to their college than either undergraduates or research students.

Once undergraduates have completed the admissions process, the Student Registry becomes the all-important nerve centre for programme and module registration, the teaching timetable, the verification of student information, the payment of fees, and access to university awards and loans. There is, in turn, a crucial interface with the Colleges and Residence Office for the allocation to colleges. By the Monday morning of week one of term time all new and returning students are able to begin their round of fully organised lectures, workshops, practicals, seminars, and tutorials. The teaching regime is, of course, tightly regulated, with approved university policies on, for example, academic regulations and procedures, academic contact commitments, e-learning, student support, plagiarism and progress files, assessment and learning hours, and much, much more.[158] The approval, implementation, and monitoring of these processes is discussed elsewhere (see Chapter 3), but the feedback from the National Student Survey, that students found that "staff are highly professional, enthusiastic about their subject and genuinely interested in the academic development of their students",[159] is reinforced by the Students' Union written submission to the QAA. Their perspective was that, "Based on our own research, feedback from students and external sources, the majority of Lancaster University students have a high quality academic experience and good pastoral support. This view is supported by good retention and pass rates",[160] even if most students would probably not make such self-conscious statements as they concentrate on imminent coursework deadlines or how they will spend the coming weekend.

Student views of the teaching provision, at all levels, are constantly monitored, in part for the purpose of feedback to departments, colleges, and central services, but also for the purposes of the forementioned annual National Student Survey. Despite the many shortcomings of external ratings and league tables, the consequences of the survey for the brand and reputation of the institution, and hence the quantity and quality of the recruitment, are profound. In the early years student feedback consisted of lively and

---

[157] The office handles a list of at least 700 properties each year.

[158] See the list of "Support Documents to Institutional Briefing Paper, QAA Institutional Audit, 9–13 March 2009", pp. 73–4.

[159] "you said, we have", leaflet of January 2009 widely circulated to students.

[160] QAA Student Written Submission, Lancaster University Students' Union, 27 October 2008, p. 46.

pointed pen portraits of individual staff in *Carolynne*,[161] and later of information collected in successive years for the Alternative Prospectus by the Students' Union.[162] Increasing pressure grew for the departments themselves to collect more systematic data on their own teaching performance, and these results formed part of departmental review processes. More recently a policy to standardise such information across the institution was agreed, and by 2006–07 a pilot, on-line process was being run: the Lancaster University Module Evaluation System (LUMES), which drew Registry data from the student records system (known as LUSI) to automate the delivery of module evaluation forms to students, and subsequently to provide summary analyses of the feedback customised to the recipient. The process is now highly refined and has a direct bearing on the ratings with which staff enter the promotion stakes.

Students' academic experiences, while critically important, are not the whole story of student life at Lancaster, even if other information is more elusive. A Student Experience Survey, run from the office of the Pro-Vice-Chancellor for College and Student Experience in 2006–07, noted that surveys about students' academic experiences were already well provided, and approached all second year undergraduates and all campus-based postgraduates on taught and research degrees in order to review the range and quality of the campus facilities and services.[163] The questions covered recreation, opportunities for democratic involvement, college facilities, support services, learning spaces, health services, shops, catering, and careers. Background questions were included to identify differences between different student categories, whether by gender, domicile, level, or ethnicity. The response rate of 45% for undergraduates and 30% for postgraduates was encouraging, and many respondents also made free comments. Broadly, the vast majority of the facilities and services were rated good by over 80% of respondents, although with actions identified for sports facilities, group learning spaces, department-specific careers talks, catering, and laundrettes. Some differences were clear: for example, when asked to name aspects of Lancaster life they particularly liked, 62% of UK white undergraduates put the collegiate system top: but the colleges were not mentioned by non-UK postgraduates, who instead emphasized the pleasures of the local area and the opportunities to meet students from other countries. The departments, on the other hand, consistently featured and were liked by between 22% and 34% of all students across all categories.

The transition from school or other pre-university education has always been a major step for undergraduates, and the university's intention is, of course, to produce graduates

---

[161] See, for example, "The professors", *Carolynne Vintage Two*: The Lancaster Year (June 1966), no page numbers; and "The professors", *Carolynne Vintage Three*: The Lancaster Year (Summer 1967), no page numbers.

[162] The Alternative Prospectus was issued annually by the Students' Union from 1980 to 1994 (UA.1/23/6/2).

[163] "Student Experience Survey", April 2007, pp. 1–19. I am grateful to Professor Amanda Chetwynd for these data.

who are proficient in subject knowledge and also "independent learners".[164] The teaching staff encountered by students are highly proficient in their respective disciplines and are subject both to training at junior level (including those postgraduates who undertake some limited teaching and assessment) and to updating throughout their careers. There are also institutional monitoring processes, including periodic quality reviews (see Chapter 3), to ensure that students are being given the best opportunity to develop their own sound academic practices within the parameters of particular subject areas.[165] The university has invested heavily in the upgrading of its teaching spaces and of the associated information technology, the Library is well-equipped to assist students, and seminar and tutorial sizes are kept under review when considering staffing levels in particular areas.

Nevertheless, UK students who have come through a school system that in recent years has broken subject knowledge down into ever smaller discrete elements and assesses them sequentially, rather than concurrently, can find the broader and deeper tertiary learning harder than did their peers in the post-war period, when school and university learning were more of a continuum. There are also specific difficulties. Students from overseas, for example, may have satisfied the formal language requirements but still have difficulty in relating to the give-and-take repartee of a UK seminar. Other students may have learning difficulties, of which dyslexia is one example, that are exacerbated in a university setting, particularly in a culture that increasingly relies on peer learning and hence on a high level of social and interactive skills. And all students are reliant on prompt and informative feedback on their assessed work, to give them direction for the next stage of their personal intellectual development.[166] For a time there was a dedicated member of staff to whom students could be referred if they were faltering in the learning process.[167] As the university grew larger, however, such *ad hoc* provision became over-stretched and was in practice available only to a minority of the students who might have benefited. Instead, the current policy is to place the emphasis on the departments to ensure that they have the appropriate faculty infrastructure to discern students' difficulties before they become entrenched and to give them appropriate support, coupled with access to limited personal student support on an individual basis in special cases.

From the above it will be seen that the university continues to be committed, once

---

[164] The principle of independent learning was strongly pushed by Professor Nicholas Abercrombie and colleagues from the early 1990s onwards.

[165] I am grateful to Dr Gavin Brown and Dr Moira Peelo for assistance with the preparation of this section: see also "Institutional Briefing Paper, QAA Institutional Audit, 9–13 March 2009", paras. 181 to 187.

[166] See the leaflet "you said, we have", issued widely within the institution in March 2009, for a commitment to the return of all coursework (but not larger projects) within four weeks of submission.

[167] One earlier device, the demise of which is still regretted, was a mid-year report on students who were falling behind, especially at Part I, that was sent both to colleges and departments for follow-up action.

Students at work in the Involve Office, June 2011

students have been accepted, to their success, and the rate of withdrawal of undergraduates, especially during Part II, is in tiny numbers. A powerful network of support and welfare services is in place to ensure that students can be helped via a variety of entry points. The colleges have already been mentioned in this regard, and the Bowland Project of 2006–07[168] was a good example of how college-based support can make a significant difference, both to decisions to withdraw and to appearances before the Standing Academic Committee.[169] Indeed, the colleges are akin, in the view of the Acting Head of Student Services,[170] to a family setting, particularly at times of student crisis: students in difficulties receive immediate and personal help, and there is also support for students who become heavily involved in looking after a friend.

Lancaster has been fortunate in the people who have headed the several versions of student services over the years for their commitment, ability and willingness to treat students as individuals and to work closely with departments and colleges.[171] Some areas

---

[168] For information about the Bowland Project, see www.lancs.ac.uk/celt/celtweb/bowland_project.

[169] The committee has delegated powers from the Senate to exclude students, either temporarily or permanently, who, in spite of all efforts by departments, colleges, and central services, demonstrate that they can no longer benefit from a university education. As a further safeguard, there is an appeal against exclusion to the Vice-Chancellor or an officer acting on his behalf.

[170] Discussion with Christine Quinn, 6 April 2009.

[171] Alumni of the university will recall with gratitude the hands-on help of, *inter alia*, Rod Martindale, Cora Martin, Colin Adams, Sylvia Brennan, Kathleen Bird, Chris Quinn, and their staff.

of welfare support, in particular, have ballooned in recent years. Financial advice is one example, where, as tuition fees were to be paid by students or their families, the complexities of the financial support arrangements put in place by the university had to be understood, updated, and negotiated, and where the financial support for disabled students both developed but also became more bureaucratic. Applicants for admission with disabilities enter into extended discussions, involving university officers as well as Social Services, about what specialist provision might be made for them and how they are to be funded, but may in the end not select Lancaster out of several places they initially approach. Issues of mental health are also important, and the case load increases year by year, partly because some applicants who might previously not have considered university can now do so, but also as students and their friends become more accustomed to talking openly about such problems and feel able to seek support to continue their studies, rather than dropping out of university.

A modelled undergraduate gown, worn for lectures and other academic occasions from 1964 to 1966

The concept of a network of services that will catch students regardless of their point of entry and guide them to the most appropriate personal support relies on close and harmonious working patterns and mutual respect between all the offices involved, from the Health Centre to the Chaplaincy Centre to the Counselling Service to the Students' Union, and has been achieved despite the absence of co-location.[172] There is, however, anecdotal evidence that some students tend to graze the services, sampling here and there but not engaging closely with lasting but perhaps demanding solutions. The approaches are numerous: in 2007–08, for example, 4314 enquiries from students, staff or immediate family were initiated, leading to follow-up telephone calls (2592) and e-mails (8276), and to one-to-one conversations.[173]

Some undergraduates continue to take the opportunity go abroad for a year to a university, most commonly in North America, for courses that form an integral part of their Part II programme of study, or for a period of subject related work experience. Most, however, are based at Bailrigg for their three years of study. Their university life centres around lectures, seminars, and the Library, and their increasing maturity and self-confidence grow out of their engagement with their chosen subjects and with the staff and fellow students with whom they have daily contact. Their development of academic maturity is, of course, fundamental, and is taken account of in the final examination regulations that make allowance for the so-called exit velocity: the spurt that some students produce, often well into their third year, that marks a higher level of personal achievement and intellectual prowess, betokening a graduate who merits separate recognition in determining their degree classification.[174] At the same time, students' involvement in sporting or non-sporting societies, in their college junior common rooms, or as representatives on departmental or university committees give them other forms of invaluable personal development. Thus, while students can if they wish pass most evenings in an alcoholic blur while taking advantage of special offers at places such as the Carleton in Morecambe on a Wednesday night, or Toast, Fusion, Hustle, or Revolution in Lancaster, in the longer run that approach misses the opportunities for the acquisition of many other skills; a stint as a journalist for *Scan*, for example, or taking on the organisation of a college extrav[175] at the end of the academic year, or leading campus tours for the next undergraduate generation.

Another highly developed set of opportunities is available through the LU Volunteering Unit, first set up in July 2002 on the basis of external funding facilitated by the then local MP, Hilton Dawson. The unit, under its energetic and forceful manager, Ben Matthews, enables students who want to undertake voluntary work to do so within a framework that safeguards both them and the people they seek to help, and is now an integral part of

---

[172] The establishment of The Base in 2010 was made to improve the interaction of services and ease of access to them for students.

[173] University of Lancaster, "Student Services Annual Report 2008–08".

[174] This distinguishing feature is likely to disappear if universities move, as many urge they should, solely to transcripts of separate module marks.

[175] These extravs (extravaganzas) are organised by the colleges, either on their own or cooperatively with each other, and enable the end of the academic year to be marked festively without the level of formality of the Grad Ball held for final year students.

the LUSU facilities.[176] Training support is given and the experiences gained are material for the all-important curriculum vitae. There are team projects with local primary and secondary schools (the Schools Partnership), work with the Lancashire Constabulary to reduce locally the occurrence and the fear of doorstep crime (titled Safe), or help for young people to become the social entrepreneurs of the future (Voltage). Moreover, some of the work undertaken also attracts units of credit that contribute to the students' degree results; Geography, English, Music, and Medicine are amongst departments whose students can obtain such credits. Even more exciting is a scheme called Create,[177] whereby students are encouraged to develop start-up businesses of their own, supported and encouraged by a central team who discuss and test ideas over a ten-week period. Feedback and advice, together with decisions about who is eligible for modest seedcorn funding is given by the Create Panel ("similar to Dragons Den ... only kinder! ... Create Panel Members will never disclose or steal your ideas"), which includes Lancaster graduates who have successfully set up their own businesses. Recent case studies selected from 23 Create successes include financial brokerage (Dashwood and Foxx), web design (Ice Cube web design), biodiesel (Ethical Fuels), soup production (Souped Up Ltd) and a chocolatier (Chez Joie Chocolat Ltd).

Students are, of course, becoming increasingly concerned about their future careers. As the recession of late 2008 tightened, questions were being raised in the national press about the extent to which a degree added value,[178] and Lancaster students were echoing this uncertainty.[179] The university takes the careers of its students very seriously and the Centre for Employability, Enterprise, and Careers (CEEC) is a very different operation to the single person in a small and remote office that was thought to be sufficient in the late 1960s.[180] Over a dozen staff now occupy a prime site immediately adjacent to Alexandra Square at the heart of the university, and students are strongly urged from Intro Week onwards to become involved with the service: the value of involvement with clubs, societies, and Involve, and the critical importance of building up a curriculum vitae that inspires confidence in potential employers, are emphasized.[181] There are careers workshops to help students improve their self-confidence, build up their interview skills, demonstrate how to make good job

---

[176] See: http://www.luvu.org.uk/ as at 24 April 2009. The scheme has recently been renamed as Involve.

[177] See: http://create.lusu.co.uk as at 24 April 2009.

[178] See, for example: "Value of gaining a degree plummets", *Sunday Times*, 31 August 2008, or "Does a degree set you up for life?" *The Observer*, 9 November 2008, or "Recession brings new reality to final-year students", *The Times*, 24 April 2009.

[179] See: "An Angry Graduate" (about the apparent lack of recognition by employers of Lancaster degrees), *Scan*, 30 September 2008, p. 9; or "Lancaster students satisfied, but graduates left grieving", *Scan*, 14 October 2008, p. 3.

[180] Mrs Jean Argles, who as Miss Jean Owtram had worked for the Appeal in 1963–64, was the first Careers Adviser for the whole university.

[181] See: "... but I'm only a first year!", *Futures*, Issue 6, Summer 08 (Lancaster, University of Lancaster).

The rear view of the Chancellor's robe, made
for HRH Princess Alexandra by J. Whippell and
Company of Exeter from a hand-woven silk
brocade, ornamented with gold oak leaf lace,
and showing the detail of the royal train

Sir Christian Bonington on the day of his installation as the
university's second Chancellor, 9 March 2005

applications, and be confident about what psychometric testing is all about, as well as giving advice on postgraduate opportunities at Lancaster and around the world. There is, however, a limit to what even the most dedicated service can offer, and as recently as the 2009 meeting of the Court there was mention of visits by big employers being cancelled for lack of student take-up.[182] In addition to appealing directly to students, therefore, departments are being asked to clear some precious teaching time for careers-related discussion that is subject-specific. A further inducement is the Lancaster Award, which from October 2009 was designed to

encourage and recognise the skills acquired through co-curricular activities. To qualify for the (non-credit bearing) award, a student must engage with activities in four key areas

---

[182] Court, 31 January 2009, where the employment prospects for Lancaster students were described as "still the Achilles heel of the university".

Sir Christian Bonington addressing staff in the Great Hall on the day of his installation as Chancellor, 9 March 2005. Behind him, from left to right, are Vice-Chancellor Paul Wellings; Pro-Vice-Chancellors Cary Cooper, Ray Macdonald, Bob McKinlay, and Alan Whitaker; Deputy Pro-Chancellor Claire Hensman; Pro-Chancellor Bryan Gray; and Deputy Pro-Chancellor Gordon Johnson

(employability/career development, campus community and social development, work experience and additional skills (such as language and IT courses)). The award has the backing of many major employers who, with Lancaster staff, will also be interviewing the students as part of the assessment relating to the award.[183]

The number of recruits to this scheme is rapidly increasing year on year.

With the advent of student tuition fees, student debt became an increasingly contentious issue in the relationship between universities and their students.[184] With the Browne review of 2010, and the autumn Comprehensive Spending Review, universities in the early months of 2011 were facing urgent decisions about how high to raise their undergraduate tuition

---

[183] Teaching and Learning Newsletter, Issue 3 (April 2009), p. 1.

[184] "Broke and broken funding system needs to change, says NUS", *Scan*, Week 1, Summer Term, 21 April 2009, pp. 6–7.

fees to compensate for significant reductions in funds,[185] and the consequences of those choices will be critical to institutional health and to their relationship with their students for the future. Students increasingly take term-time, part-time jobs that may, if their time management is not good, become deleterious to their studies. The acquisition of a large debt also inhibits students from moving on to postgraduate studies that are likely to involve further debt without necessarily, in many subject areas, any increased certainty of paid graduate-level employment. Lancaster's Students' Union runs a Job Shop from which students can obtain employment in a variety of campus positions, including catering and the Library, while other students are to be found within the city of Lancaster, in the bars or shops.

As will have already been observed from the above account, the Students' Union is a vital part of the university governance and welfare structure. The six sabbatical officer positions – recently revised to be a president and five vice-presidents for media and communications; finance, events, democracy, and societies; academic affairs; equality, welfare, and diversity; and sports[186] – neatly encapsulate the main areas of student focus, while a business with an annual turnover of £5.4 million[187] is capable of making a considerable impact within the university and itself demands significant management skills.[188] LUSU sees its direction as being the key point of connection between students, the institution, and the community, to act as the independent and campaigning voice for students, and to be a strong supporter of the college system. The Union's permanent officers provide representation and advice, coordinate and promote the course representative system (including through the Academic Council), play an active role in the style of and facilities for teaching assessment, run annual campaigns that may range from responsible drinking to the induction of new students, provide a range of commercial shops and services, and take responsibility for the fortnightly publication of *Scan* and for Bailrigg FM. The union has a major involvement with sport, including inter-college competitive events (especially for the annual Carter Shield contest) as well as the recruitment of university teams, and in the organisation of the continuing Roses competition against the University of York. Clubs and societies are both encouraged and kept on track, there is a wide range of training for college JCR officers, and the long-standing LUSU-owned nightclub in the city, The Sugar House, is attended by over 85,000 student customers a year. Welfare services are also provided, with an emphasis on such matters as plagiarism and how to avoid it, council tax, student complaints, consumer rights, including landlord responsibilities, and welfare benefits for international students.[189] Close

---

[185] Lancaster University, 2010 Report and Accounts, p. 3.

[186] "Sabbatical review passes at packed GM", *Scan*, Week 10, Michaelmas Term, 9 December 2008, pp. 1, 4–5.

[187] See: LUSU, "Report and Financial Statements for the Year Ended 31 July 2008" (GAP/2009/0055).

[188] The Union has a permanent General Manager (from late 2010 a Chief Executive) who is responsible for ensuring that a small team of permanent officers both supports the student body and gives the university confidence in LUSU operations.

[189] See: collection of leaflets from Slaidburn House, February 2009.

liaison with the central student services is critically important in order to avoid overlap, conflicting advice, or waste of resources, and this is coupled with a professionalism that sets out what is akin to a service level agreement, spelling out what students can expect (relevant information; signposting to other services; development of possible solutions) and what LUSU officers should receive (mutual respect; non-aggressive behaviour; and honest and accurate information about students' situations).[190]

Time passes all too quickly for most undergraduates. All too soon they have completed all the modules that contribute to their degree, undertaken fieldwork and more specialised final year projects, or competed for Short Loan volumes or public access machines on which to complete their coursework. Their ninth and final term centres around final coursework submissions and final written examinations during a designated Quiet Period that allows for revision and examinations without the distractions of loud music, raucous parties, or noisy building operations. It marks a difference in pace and style of activity, and during the examination period processes have been increasingly refined and tested to deal with any student eventuality that could be imagined, as well as the novel ones that still occur from time to time.[191] Academic staff move into temporary purdah, marking scripts and discussing results, and examination boards meet to move the assessment process forward swiftly and smoothly for the final confirmation of results at the special meeting of the Committee of the Senate in early July. Only ten days later there is a week of degree ceremonies at the Great Hall, presided over by the Chancellor, Sir Christian Bonington, or one of his deputies. Suddenly the jeans and teeshirts give way to neat suits and tidy haircuts, as families and friends assemble in the Great Hall to see each graduand separately cross the stage for a handshake and perhaps a brief conversation. For just a few students, because of illness or other grave cause, or of failure leading to re-assessment for a pass degree, their time as undergraduates is prolonged by some weeks or months. For the rest of each student cohort, the new graduates step out as life-long alumni of the university and members of it in perpetuity, bent on making the best of their future careers.

---

[190] See: www.lusu.co.uk/advice/about/confidentiality.

[191] University of Lancaster, "Student Registry: Examinations and results, summer 2009" (7 March 2009).

CHAPTER FIVE

Research

T HE UNIVERSITY'S obligation to research is enshrined in a single, powerful clause in the Charter, stating that: "The objects of the University shall be to advance knowledge, wisdom and understanding by teaching and research and by the example and influence of its corporate life." These words make explicit and unmistakeable the indivisibility of teaching and research, the continuum between knowledge, wisdom, and understanding of scholarship with research, and the necessity of the dissemination of research as part of the example and influence of the institution's corporate life.

Inevitably, much of this chapter[1] will focus on the university's strategic direction, on revenue generation, and on institutional reputation, and these are all important considerations in relation to the research activity that is paramount for the university's standing, reputation, and funding. What these considerations miss is the drama of moments of discovery, the shared understanding by researchers from the most senior to the most junior about the direction they are taking, and the frustrations of blind alleys or false positives. Strategic thinking for its own sake, particularly about research, can lead to a rather bloodless account of what in practice is a primary reason for academics' continuing commitment to their university careers. Those few of their number who do not feel the imperative to explore and

---

[1] Grateful acknowledgement is made to Professor Trevor McMillan for discussions prior to the writing of this chapter. Errors and misapprehensions remain the author's.

test to destruction current knowledge, whether by scientific experiment or through dusty archive, are likely to feel out of place amongst peers who have that compulsion.

Many researchers are willing to sacrifice personal and family life, and to cover huge distances around the globe for collaborative work or international conferences. They dedicate themselves tirelessly to the unremitting cycle of research grant application, research grant implementation, and research findings dissemination. In what follows, therefore, the reader should bear in mind the excitement and huge personal satisfaction for researchers, whether working individually or in teams, of constructing and testing a hypothesis, designing fieldwork or study, and following through where the evidence leads – but also the many obstacles to progress. Funding sources may not deliver, referees can be fickle or quixotic, appropriate research staff or research students may not be forthcoming, or may fall ill, prove to be incompetent, or seek other employment. Valuable equipment may be lost or broken, particularly in hostile terrain, data may go up in flames or be discarded in error, and misunderstandings and feuds, sometimes lasting for years, may break out. The institutional infrastructure may be perceived as a hindrance, particularly when issues around health and safety, copyright, intellectual property, and research ethics all have to be separately negotiated. Other professional activities, including commenting on or refereeing others' work, or examining doctoral theses, must be accommodated, and the sometimes heartbreaking effort of securing publication in key international journals must be steadily pursued. It is no surprise that at times even the most committed staff lose motivation and question whether their lives might be better spent, and whether the rewards of research are proportionate to its cost.

Behind the necessary rhetoric of vice-chancellors' annual reports, selecting research plums from an assembly of recent successes, therefore, lie concealed the effort, fatigue, and tedium that sit behind even the most enthralling results. In the period when the creation of Lancaster and its sister institutions was in contemplation, however, there was public and governmental support for research as an assumed national good. The University Grants Committee, allowing that while "research and teaching must inevitably compete for the time of every university teacher, they should be regarded not as conflicting but as complementary activities", had quoted the Advisory Council on Scientific Policy as having reached the firm conclusion that

> There are circumstances in which research can best be pursued in research institutions. But there is no doubt that, in general, the universities provide a very stimulating environment for the successful pursuit of basic research: that many of the most original and fertile minds are to be found there; and that teaching and research have favourable reactions on each other. It is of vital national importance that the small proportion of people in each generation who are gifted in research should have full opportunity to pursue their natural bent.[2]

The Robbins Report picked up and reinforced the same theme, while indicating that the stages at which the most original work was likely varied markedly between the disciplines, and also, particularly for the humanities, saw a role for "persons of first class ability … whose breadth of culture, ripeness of judgement and wide-ranging intellectual curiosity are priceless assets".[3] Furthermore, the principle of a dual funding regime between the UGC and the research councils was securely in place when Lancaster was taking its first steps in research:

> The relationship between the Committee and the Research Councils is thus one of partnership. We [i.e. the UGC] provide general grants for teaching and research, each university deciding, by its own free choice, how much and what kinds of research should be developed from these grants. The Research Councils provide earmarked grants for research, the particular projects or lines of research being inspired or conditioned to a greater or smaller extent by requirements which are, at any rate for the time being, beyond a university's financial capabilities or outside its own priority choices.[4]

---

[2] University Grants Committee, *University Development 1957–1962*, Cmnd. 2267 (London: HMSO, 1964), paras. 159 and 62.

[3] Committee on Higher Education, *Higher Education: Report of the Committee Appointed by the Prime Minister under the Chairmanship of Lord Robbins 1961–63*, Cmnd. 2154 (London: HMSO, 1963)), paras. 53 to 63, and especially para. 60.

[4] University Grants Committee, *University Development 1962–67*, Cmnd. 3820 (London: HMSO, 1968), paras. 447–9, drawing on the recommendations of the Trend Committee (Committee of Enquiry into the Organisation of Civil Science, *[Report]*, Cmnd. 2171 (London: HMSO, 1963)).

Reference has already been made to the dominance of Oxford and Cambridge in the backgrounds of members of the Academic Planning Board (see Chapter 1). The academic pedigree of the founding members of staff, a vital element in establishing research quality, was of paramount significance in setting the tenor of the new institution. It thus comes as no surprise that, of the initial heads of department, six had first degrees from Cambridge, four from Oxford, three from London, and one each from Glasgow, Manchester, and Adelaide; or that their higher degrees showed a similar profile. They, in turn, drew on the significant pool available at the time[5] of high-quality academic and research staff when appointing to their own departments. The Academic Advisory Committee monitored the quality of the early appointments and, at its final meeting in October 1969, once again received information on all recent academic appointees and "resolved to report [to the Privy Council] that it was satisfied with the academic standard of the persons appointed".[6] Of the 53 staff listed for that meeting as having been newly appointed, 13 had first degrees from London, 7 from Oxford, 3 from Manchester, 2 each from Cambridge, Durham, Edinburgh, Liverpool, Southampton, and Wales, 1 each from Lancaster and East Anglia, and a handful from eminent overseas universities. In the science subjects, staff invariably came with doctoral degrees on appointment, even for junior posts, while the pattern in other subject areas was more varied, reflecting a time when fewer entrants to the profession of university teacher in non-science subjects undertook doctoral research.

Besides appointing staff of high calibre, the foundations of a strong research environment were quickly laid. All academic staff were given contractual rights to generous sabbatical leave provision, and a series of inaugural lectures was held that laid out the basis of different subject areas for staff, colleagues, and the general public.[7] Research students quickly appeared in subjects such as Chemistry and Environmental Studies, and there was a generous ratio of highly skilled technical staff to academic staff (1:1 in the early years) that meant equipment could be designed and made on site, ready for installation as soon as buildings were ready to receive it. Indeed, Roland Dobbs in Physics set up such well-founded laboratories, with such excellent research infrastructure, that they have stood the test of over 40 years' continuous use. He also encouraged all staff, including research associates, to use their own initiative in applying for research grants.[8] Another example of forward

---

[5] The author, a student and junior administrator at the time when Sussex, Essex, East Anglia, and York were recruiting, remembers the palpable sense of zest about the new horizons available to younger academic staff within higher education, including those already in established posts at excellent universities, and their openness to becoming involved with the plateglass institutions as a matter of choice.

[6] Minute 5.3 of the "Notes on the Proceedings of the Academic Advisory Committee", held on 16 October 1969 (UA.1/15/2/6) (hereafter: AAC, October 1969).

[7] The University of Lancaster, *Inaugural Lectures, 1965–67* (Lancaster, 1967), included the text of twelve inaugural lectures of founding professors.

[8] The variety of outside finance attributable to Physics was particularly noted by the Vice-Chancellor in October 1968: see minute 5.5 of AAC, October 1969.

thinking was shown by Terry Mansfield in Biological Sciences, when he began the controlled planting regime[9] that evolved into the construction of the solar domes at the Biological Sciences Field Station and the study of physiological stress on plants that later became a strand in major research initiatives for LEC.

Nor was practical experimentation confined to the sciences. The Nuffield Theatre, the brainchild of Professor Tom Lawrenson, is an example of the innovative research and teaching initiatives that could be achieved in a non-science subject when the institutional mould was not yet set. The studio was and still is an inspiration in enabling research into theatre history and contemporary experimental theatre in a practical laboratory setting: a simple shed-like design with no windows, a gridded ceiling, mobile electrical services, and flexible flooring and seating.[10] Integral to the concept was a long studio area for viewing of perspective theatre, so that a Parisian public theatre of the seventeenth century could be built to life-size proportions and the staging difficulties worked out from the authentic text. The Nuffield Foundation was persuaded to contribute £80,000 to a theatre design, in close proximity to the Great Hall, that was intended to "enliven the drama and above all bring the play back to life, off the page [and] on to the stage, at the most important point, that of its birth".[11]

Staff in all departments were strongly encouraged to have their work published, and the Academic Advisory Committee noted with pleasure both the large number of publications in process and the ease of finding publishing outlets.[12] There was a rapid growth in taught masters' courses and in doctoral research students: by October 1969 456 were registered, of whom 112 were full-time research students. They were funded in a variety of ways: by relevant research councils, especially the Science Research Council,[13] or by secondment on salary from another educational institution, or by state studentships from the Department of Education and Science; or, alternatively, they were self-funded.[14]

The particular strengths of the university in management and business subjects were also apparent at an early stage. The University Grants Committee took particular pride in the steps that had been taken from the late 1950s to encourage management studies, and in

---

[9] An aerial photograph of 1970 already shows the neat arrangement of small, separately planted plots on the site of the future Field Station. I am grateful to Maureen Harrison for this information.

[10] Professor Lawrenson, on one occasion staging a play that required boisterous interaction between players and audience, is said to have ensured that some students were bussed in and plyed with alcohol for the desired effect.

[11] See: T. E. Lawrenson, "The Place of the Theatre in the Modern Humanities", *Inaugural Lectures 1965–67* (Lancaster, 1967), pp. 63–79; and McClintock, *Quest*, pp. 79–81.

[12] Minute 10.53 of AAC, October 1969.

[13] At this time the research councils, including the SRC, were prepared to fund masters level courses that did not necessarily lead to doctoral research. Departments such as Operational Research particularly benefited from this regime in the early years.

[14] Minute 9.1, AAC, October 1969, and related statistical tables.

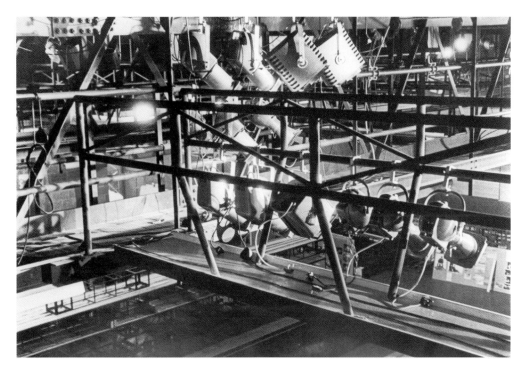

The original lighting rig for the Nuffield Theatre Studio, showing the scope it offered for experimentation and training

the universities' enthusiastic response to the national need that had been identified in this area.[15] Lancaster had embraced this opportunity and by the end of the 1960s had a School of Business and Organizational Studies that, through five subject areas, had "brought together one of the most experienced groups of business teachers and consultants in any University in the United Kingdom".[16] The university, in common with Bath, City, Loughborough, UMIST, and Warwick, had also been given a special allocation for management education[17] and, rather than providing a general, broad training, was concentrating on the development of expertise "in an important function or management technique, and gaining the necessary breadth of understanding as the trained mind reacts to actual situations", since "real expertise is gained by tackling real problems".[18] Two disciplines in particular led the problem-based approach. The first was Operational Research, defined as the study "of the consequences of decisions in complex situations in business, industry and defence, [and]

---

[15] University Grants Committee, *University Development 1962–67*, paras. 370–89.
[16] University of Lancaster, *School of Business and Organizational Studies Graduate Studies Prospectus*, 1970–71 (Lancaster, 1970), p. 19.
[17] University Grants Committee, *University Development 1962–67*, para. 388.
[18] University of Lancaster, *School of Business and Organizational Studies Graduate Studies Prospectus*, 1970–71 (Lancaster, 1970), p. 19.

designed to identify the most effective courses of action",[19] and the other was Systems Engineering, where problem-solving of real-world problems "meant the interacting human activity which makes up the business of living, as opposed to the 'artificial' world of the laboratory experiment in which the researcher is free to decide what to vary and what to keep constant".[20]

Despite what was, by comparison with the early twenty-first century, a benign environment for research, and the strong encouragement given to it, there were nevertheless obstacles to immediate success. The recruitment of a critical mass of staff for each subject area was a gradual process, the new buildings at Bailrigg each had to be designed, financed, built, and fitted out in a climate of frequent cuts in government capital expenditure, and there was not yet an expectation of universities seeking capital from the private sector. Moreover the Library, despite receiving a higher percentage of the university's recurrent grant than any other university outside Oxford and Cambridge,[21] was inevitably at a substantial initial disadvantage compared to more established institutions. The greatest limitation, however, was the pressures on staff time at a place where every practice, procedure and course offering had to be designed *ab initio*. Nevertheless, the Academic Advisory Committee was content to note:

> that neither the demands of the collegiate system nor the administrative demands of a
> new and rapidly expanding university reduced unduly the time available to the academic
> staff to pursue their research, although these demands, which were essential to the pioneer
> work being done, were substantial,

and was particularly pleased to see both the volume of research grants and the range of research being undertaken for industry.[22]

Thus, within ten years of the university's opening, and with over 3000 undergraduate and postgraduate students in place, the university had established some 40 disciplinary areas, with the expectation that all of them would undertake substantial research activity. These disciplines, spread across natural sciences, technology, humanities and social sciences, and business and management, were immensely variable in terms of their size and mode of operation, and the resources required to sustain their full teaching and research potential

---

[19] University of Lancaster, *School of Business and Organizational Studies Graduate Studies Prospectus*, 1970–71 (Lancaster, 1970), p. 22.

[20] Peter Checkland, *Systems Thinking, Systems Practice* (Chichester: Wiley, 1981), p. xii: the two departments later combined into the single department of Management Science.

[21] Minute 5.4 of the Academic Advisory Committee, 11 October 1968.

[22] Minutes 10.21 and 10.23 of the Academic Advisory Committee, 11 October 1968. A similar concern had been faced by the Vice-Chancellor in December 1966: "When I review the research projects in progress, the books being written, and the papers which appear, it seems to me that many must have found the secret of putting more than twenty-four hours into the day" (University of Lancaster, *Second Annual Report*, p. 3).

were, with the benefit of hindsight, hugely ambitious. Indeed, Charles Carter in 1971 had voiced his concern to the Court about the inefficiencies of small departments:

> that is, costly in relation to the teaching done, but also (in many cases) intellectually inefficient because there is not enough interplay between scholars in the same subjects. My impression of the results of studies in this area is that major science and technology departments (uniting within themselves several sub-disciplines) ought to have 30–40 staff, and departments in the humanities ought to have at least 15 staff.[23]

This issue of size was a theme to which he was to return in successive annual reports.

Notwithstanding the freedom of research activity already available to staff, or perhaps because of the scope for innovation at Lancaster, research centres also began to emerge. In the early days these usually consisted of small clusters of like-minded colleagues with ideas for research directions that they wished to pursue, in addition to or as an alternative to their work within a particular department. Over time the centres were increasingly used for interdisciplinary or thematic research, and were progressively codified by the university, especially when they took on quasi-departmental responsibilities for staff, research grants, or research students. While some might argue that they are a distraction, and carry some of the same risks and inefficiencies as small departments, a close acquaintance with their contributions indicates that they have been a source of strength for Lancaster. They have allowed new initiatives to develop quickly, and have enriched the ability of Lancaster staff to create alliances with each other and with external participants in ways that would not otherwise have been likely to take place.

The first formally recognised centre was the International Centre for Research in Accounting (ICRA), constituted with a trust deed in 1971 "to promote theoretical and empirical research in accounting and finance and to provide a focal point for co-operation on research between academics, professional practitioners of accounting and finance, industry, financial institutions, and local and central government".[24] Another was the Centre for North-West Regional Studies, established to study regional problems, both contemporary and historical, and spanning geography, archaeology, biology, agriculture, economics, and town planning.[25] A third was the Richardson Institute for Conflict and Peace Research. The university had early appointed a reader in peace and conflict research, Dr Paul Smoker. In 1969 the Lancaster-based Peace Research Centre and the Conflict Research Society agreed to amalgamate with the peace and conflict work, and the new, merged entity became part

---

[23] University of Lancaster, "Seventh Annual Report presented by the Vice-Chancellor to the Meeting of the Court on December 11th 1971", pp. 3–4.

[24] *Staff Handbook, 2006–07* (Lancaster, September 2006), p. 87.

[25] Marion E. McClintock and David C. A. Shotter, *Serving the Region: A History of the Centre for North-West Regional Studies at Lanacster University 1970–2006* (Lancaster: Centre for North-West Regional Studies, 2006), pp. 1–46.

of the university. The centre, externally funded from sources such as Cadbury, Rowntree, and Gillett, was to cover a broad range of research:

> Its predominant concern has been with violent or potentially violent conflict, and research has ranged from discussions of particular situations to highly abstract theory ... These have included the transmission of peace symbols to children, conflict in Northern Ireland, the application of mathematical and statistical techniques, the use of all kinds of simulation, and more generally the study of alternative futures.[26]

This was an example of a centre that had its own staff, conducted its own programme of research, and made provision for research, and taught students. In approving the set of rules governing it, the Senate required reassurance that the control of its teaching would be in the hands of the Department of Politics, of which it was a section.[27]

The developing research quality was an element of the everyday life of the university. Staff appointments, with their qualifications, were reported to each Senate meeting, as were the latest research grants received. From 1971 onwards there was an annual listing of publications by members of staff,[28] which gives an exceptional insight into the areas of research output and the growing international scope of Lancaster's research activity. Furthermore, when *Fulcrum* began publication in 1974, generous coverage was given to research topics.[29]

Each year the Vice-Chancellor, reflecting on recent academic developments, made sure that research and scholarship were a priority for report, but also tied these developments to wider moral issues too which he saw as inextricably related. In 1971, for example, he reported on the selection of projects from a long list for funding by the university that had been supplied by local authorities: problems of the Lake District economy; interdepartmental environmental improvement; control of odours from the processing of animal by-products; planning of nursing services in Westmorland; and the effects of open-plan offices.[30] In 1973 he spoke of the plans by Conflict Research to set up an experimental community in Chile; of exploration of caves in Venezuela; of the study of the Moon and Mars by the Lunar and Planetary Research Unit; and of links with the International Federation for Theatre Research. He also drrew attention to the editorship of at least six learned journals, and office holders

---

[26] "Proposal for the Richardson Institute to move to Lancaster University", Senate, 16 November 1977 (GM/77/424).

[27] Minute S.77/162, Senate meeting on 16 November 1977.

[28] University of Lancaster, *Publications by Members of Staff, 1963–71* (Lancaster, December 1972): this annual listing continued in an unbroken sequence up to the calendar year 2005, by which time over 1400 items per year were being listed.

[29] *Fulcrum* was published about three times a term by the Information Office from 1974 to 1990.

[30] University of Lancaster, "Seventh Annual Report Presented by the Vice-Chancellor to the Meeting of the University Court on December 11th 1971", p. 9: a sum of money had been set aside for this purpose, as an example of the university's wish to benefit its hinterland.

for a range of learned societies and national policy groups by staff of the university.[31] In 1974, at a time of economic entrenchment and political disarray, he spoke powerfully of "this dark age of failure [where] the quality of civilisation is at risk", and of the enduring values of education for "the development of values, the maintenance of intellectual quality, the increase of wisdom". He saw universities as more essential than ever, for their intellectual effort, their business of maintaining standards of civilisation, and

the means by which successive generations can reach an understanding of human achievements which is profound and not superficial. They provide the scholars who, working at the boundaries of knowledge, can push forward to conquer that which is still unknown,

and uphold "an appreciation of standards of scholarship and a sense of joy in discovery and wonder at achievement" that matters most.[32] In 1975 he celebrated the Department of Accounting and of ICRA, especially for its contribution to setting accounting standards, but expressed some concern that not enough work was being undertaken on the impact of government on the economy, while welcoming the contributions of the university to "quality of life and to a right sense of values" through music, visual arts, the Nuffield Theatre Studio, the provision of the Great Hall as venue for a brass band summer school, and work on archaeological sites in Cumbria.[33] Yet again he pointed to the need for:

direct study of the nature of the human predicament as continued growth presses on the resources of the planet and creates new social problems ... [the need for] strengthening the sense of caring, lessening the impersonal hardness of larger organisations, making technical or social change enjoyable instead of frightening and disruptive. And finally, there is still an inconsistency between the hard and systematic study devoted to (say) physical problems in the sciences and the relative neglect of moral dilemmas. It can well be said of universities in Britain and throughout the world that they have helped many men to be knowledgeable but fewer to be wise.

His reports in 1977 and 1978 were also accompanied by a selection of departmental reports that reflected on the current strengths and weaknesses of their separate research positions.

Charles Carter's final verdict on the university's research profile, as he prepared for a year's sabbatical leave in 1978–79 before retirement, was, however, significantly downbeat:

I note that Senate received reports during the year of 86 external research grants, on varied and relevant matters such as "Pressures on women engaged in factory work", "The breakdown of superfluidity in liquid helium-4" and "Open-plan schools". The record of attraction of outside funds is good, but not yet good enough ... Research funds tend to

[31] University of Lancaster, "Ninth Annual Report", 15 December 1973, pp. 12–14.
[32] University of Lancaster, "Tenth Annual Report", 14 December 1974, pp. 7–9.
[33] University of Lancaster, "Eleventh Annual Report", 20 December 1975, pp. 5–7.

be strongly concentrated in particular departments, but this year ... [some staff] have benefitted from the University's own new fund for small research grants. The experience of administering this fund does not suggest that there are many well-developed ideas for research which are failing to find support; but that, of course, leaves open the question as to why some individuals appear to have difficulty in producing sound research proposals, or even have no desire to produce any at all.[34]

The questions about relative performance between colleagues with the same opportunities remain pertinent to this day, but the note of hesitation about Lancaster's research performance was new, and relevant to the condition in which Lancaster entered the financial crisis of 1980–81.[35] There seems to have been a temporary loss of research momentum in some parts of the university,[36] and it is interesting to speculate why. Probably no one cause was dominant, and the reasons include the wide disciplinary scope and small departments to which reference has been made, a second generation of heads of departments who at the time were perhaps less established in their respective fields than the founding heads, the increasing load of teaching as staff:student ratios approached the norm for other institutions, or the soaring cost of equipment in a period of high inflation; and all these factors were compounded by the financial difficulties of 1980–81, leading to premature retirements, unpaid leave of absence, threats to the future of some departments, and retrenchment for others (see Chapter 6).

However, it was not just at Lancaster that a problem was perceived, as is demonstrated by two contemporary reports on national policy. In 1979 the Advisory Board for Research Councils (ABRC)had asked Sir Peter Swinnerton-Dyer to consider postgraduate education in the areas covered by the research councils. His report[37] covered terrain that was to become very familiar: training for postgraduate students, preference for work in groups, the quality of doctoral supervision, review of performance at the end of the first year, and completion rates. In parallel, in 1982 the ABRC and the UGC published a joint report on research in universities[38] that commended the dual support system of funding between the UGC and the research councils, urged universities to channel proportionately more of their funding

---

[34] University of Lancaster, "Fourteenth Annual Report", 16 December 1978, p. 3.

[35] See: M. E. McClintock, "The University of Lancaster: The First Thirty Years" (lecture delivered on 27 July 1994), pp. 6–7.

[36] There is a curious absence of any comment on Lancaster's research profile or the contribution of its research in a key document, "A Strategy for the 1980s", produced by the Development Committee in the spring of 1980, when efforts were being made to anticipate the cuts that were expected from the UGC: see *Fulcrum*, No. 55, May 1980, p. 2.

[37] Advisory Board for the Research Councils, *Report of the Working Party on Postgraduate Education*, Cmnd. 8537 (London: HMSO, 1982). See also GM/82/206, Agendum SB.3 of Senate, 17 November 1982.

[38] Advisory Board for the Research Councils and University Grants Committee, *Report of a Joint Working Party on the Support of University Scientific Research*, Cmnd. 8567 (London: HMSO, 1982).

into research, to concentrate and select their research ares, use centralised university committees to determine research concentration, encourage collaborative research between departments or between universities, and reward research related to industrial contacts. There were also to be government-funded new blood posts to replenish the ranks of the staff (see Chapter 6).

The Senate's response, whilst welcoming the recognition of the centrality of research but apparently not appreciating that the underlying messages of the ABRC report were the first signs of major change in research management across the sector, was negative about most aspects of it. Members reacted adversely to the suggestion that large departments had advantages in research, replied that the nature of research varied so much between departments that generalisations were not helpful, stated that it would be "iniquitous" to impose sanctions for inadequate completion rates based on small samples, and observed that the "research councils operated very differently in awarding quotas and that some kept an undesirably close control on the direction of research in what were fundamentally independent institutions".[39] Nevertheless, the Research Committee was encouraged to send out a questionnaire to departments and centres about impediments to research and stimuli that staff would find helpful: the unexpectedly high response rate again emphasised the variety of research and scholarship between subject areas.[40] Some departments or centres were able to make what the Research Committee accepted as convincing claims to be national leaders in their fields; half of the rest were shown to have vigorous and productive research programmes. The importance of the Library having funds available to purchase special collections was emphasised,[41] the practice of using graduate students to share the undergraduate teaching load was extended to non-science subjects for the first time, and the proposition was put forward that some research assistants and post-doctoral fellows might be internally funded. News that Lancaster was in the bottom three of institutions for the first round of new blood posts, achieving only one from the long list it had submitted,[42] sharpened the sense that action by the university to intensify its research effort was imperative, set against an external context of increasing national calls for the separation of funding for teaching and research.[43]

Fortunately for Lancaster's future as a research-led institution, the Development Committee took decisive action to remedy the downward spiral. A report to the Senate

---

[39] Minute S.82/166, Senate meeting on 17 November 1982.

[40] "Report on replies from departments and centres ...", GM/82/377 (amended), Senate meeting of 19 January 1983.

[41] The Library was at the same time facing significant cuts across the board: see *Report of the Librarian, 1981–82* (CQ/83/1).

[42] "Increased Assistance for Research", GM/83/17, for the Senate meeting of 1 August 1983

[43] See minute S.83/115, Senate meeting on 1 June 1983. A variety of devices to manage national research funding were under discussion, with a growing emphasis on selectivity, discrimination and differential funding.

from a working party set up a year earlier[44] was explicit in recognising that the percentage of income received from research grants and contracts, low in 1980–81, was 44th out of 48 institutions for 1981–82, above only Bradford, St Andrews, Stirling, and Ulster, with 6.2% for Lancaster as against 19% for Sussex and 13.7% for York. Furthermore, even in the eight departments that accounted for 89% of research income over the past three years, 74 of the 138 staff had made no bids. The report's authors could also see a clear separation across all departments between frequent, occasional and non-publishers. If Lancaster, said the working party, was "not to be (or to continue to be?) among the sinking universities (in Parkes' formulation)"[45] it must substantially improve its research reputation in general, but especially in science and technology which influence its funding levels most directly". The Development Committee was therefore recommending, in line with the ABRC, that £750,000 over three years be allocated for research, to be managed on a competitive basis by four area research committees, with a particular emphasis on projects that would assist subsequent external research grant bids, be innovatory, and free staff temporarily from teaching. There should be encouragement for considering additional research centres and institutes, on the clear understanding that such entities might be terminated as well as established. Research training and supervision and research student completion rates were to be addressed, and an institution-wide listing of sources of research funding should be issued.[46]

Several interesting points emerge from the report and its consequences. First, it was framed in the light of an unexpectedly favourable financial outturn for the 1981–82 financial year, in which, after several years of breakeven or small deficits, a surplus of £1.3 million had been achieved,[47] coupled with the view (prevalent at the time) that such accumulated balances should be reduced, particularly if directed towards longer-term strengthening of the university's academic position.[48] Secondly, there was a determination that all areas of the university should have an equal chance to compete; not just those in science and technology, nor those who were already successful. Thirdly, the significance of research students' contributions both to research success and research risk were placed at centre stage, where they remain to this day. And, fourthly, the level of response and interest

---

[44] "Postgraduate work and research", GM/83/290, with three appendices, for the Senate meeting of 13 November 1983.

[45] Sir Edward Parkes, retiring chairman of the UGC, was said to have commented about this time to university information officers that, while some of the new universities were nudging Oxford and Cambridge for elite research, others were sinking below institutions that were the poorest at the time of their foundation.

[46] "The Select List of Sources of Research Grants and Fellowships for Academic Staff" was published annually from 1984 to 2006.

[47] This favourable result, achieved partly as the result of extra income and partly from savings, was to be an exception in the financial profile of the rest of the decade (see Chapter 6), but its consequences for policy were profound.

[48] Para. 7 of Report of the Development Committee to Senate, 23 November 1983 (GM/83/310).

across the university was high, and engendered a spirit of optimism and a fresh start. The four research committees, all of which were personally and jointly serviced by the Registrar and Deputy Registrar, were kept busy in formulating exact terms and conditions for the grants, having proposals refereed and ranked, and managing both the awards to the successful and feedback to those who were not. By March 1984 the committee for business and computational studies had been awarded £46,171, engineering and sciences £85,888, humanities £51,424, and social sciences £41,088. The largest grant (£16,841) was for work on isotopic purification of ⁴He; the smallest (£1000) for a study of the law and economics of health and safety legislation.[49] The sums spent, despite their modesty and even though their effects were not immediate, probably represented the most significant investments, as a catalyst, in the history of the university.

Concurrently with these actions, and in common with all other institutions, Lancaster was required to respond to 29 Questions posed in November 1983 by the UGC, whose new chairman, Sir Peter Swinnerton-Dyer, preferred a more open and consultative approach to higher education policy than some of his predecessors. Each category was contextualised by a brief statement, and for research it was posited that:

> In the natural sciences (in the widest sense) there is a reasonably clear distinction between scholarship and research … It is harder to draw this distinction in the social sciences, and harder still in the arts. It is axiomatic that scholarship is part of the duty of every teacher in higher education … But research in some subjects requires facilities additional to those needed for scholarship, and in some subjects those facilities are expensive. In all subjects the largest component of university research is the thinking time of staff, which is extremely difficult to quantify.
>
> It is widely believed that the cuts of the last few years have fallen more heavily on research (and in particular on scientific research) than on teaching. This appears not to be what the Government would have wished, …[50]

followed by questions on cuts, dual support, selectivity, and investment.

Lancaster's response, formulated after much hard thought and widespread discussion, neatly encapsulates current institutional thinking about research at the time:

> We recognise that some staff are better at teaching than research, and vice-versa, and that while at the university level all should engage in both, some might spend a greater proportion of time on one rather than the other. This implies some internal selectivity in research funding. We do not however favour any earmarking by the UGC, because in our view selection can be conducted far more constructively by universities themselves.

---

[49] *Fulcrum*, No. 91, 15 March 1984, p. 2.

[50] University Grants Committee, *A Strategy for Higher Education into the 1990s* (London: HMSO, 1984), paras. 17 and 18.

Three reasons were given for this assertion: first, that selectivity might apply at localised level, even between subsections of particular departments; secondly, that growth points might lie at the interface between disciplines, "and the subject-directed organisation of policy at the centre – Research Council as well as UGC – responds uneasily to unorthodox patterns"; and, thirdly, that centralised data would be historical rather than topical:

> It follows of course from this argument that maintenance of the dual support system is essential, and that selectivity should be within, not between universities, because there are points of excellence in all.[51]

As we have already seen, the 1980s were proving to be a highly formative period for British higher education policy, with government, research councils, and the UGC all moving forward rapidly.[52] While this chapter properly focuses on developments at Lancaster, they should be interpreted against a wider background of fundamental national change. When the Vice-Chancellor indicated in November 1984[53] that a further basic review of university finances by the UGC was not expected to be as traumatic as its 1981 predecessor, adding that the theme of increased selectivity and centralised research planning was on the way, he was prefiguring a Green Paper of May 1985 that put the position more starkly:

> Both quality and economy argue for some concentration of research activity – particularly where expensive equipment is needed – and concentration implies selectivity. There is a debate about whether research and teaching need to be carried out together ... The UGC has said (UGC.5.14) that it will be more selective in its allocation of research support; that each university should know what resources it devotes to research and should plan their distribution carefully; and UGC allocation and university planning should be interactive. The Committee is considering with the CVCP, the ABRC and the research councils the idea of university research plans. The Government hopes that new selective planning and allocation arrangements can be formulated and begin to operate by the academic year 1986–87 ... Greater concentration and selectivity may mean that some departments or even whole universities will lose research funding from the UGC. Universities will still have discretion over the funds at their disposal, and be able to seek research funds from other sources. Research will be a consideration in the necessary process of rationalisation.[54]

And thus the process of research assessment exercises came into being.

---

[51] Para. 15 of Lancaster's reply to the UGC, published in *Fulcrum*, No. 93, 10 May 1984, p. 2.

[52] There is, perhaps surprisingly, no single published account of progressive government intervention in university research from the time of Sir Keith Joseph's period as secretary of state onwards.

[53] Minute S.84/216, Senate meeting on 21 November 1984.

[54] *The Development of Higher Education into the 1990s*, Cmnd. 9524 (London: HMSO, 1985), paras. 5.3 to 5.7.

The UGC issued guidance about this new planning exercise,[55] with a deadline of 30 November 1985 for completed responses. Each submission was to include: present research expenditure, under 37 departmental cost centres, including both research-directed expenditure and external research income; research planning machinery and practice; overall research plans and priorities; and research profile by individual subject areas, including numbers of research staff and research students, justification of priorities, and "titles of not more than five recent books or articles, or other comparable examples of research activities, produced since 1980, which the university would regard as typical of the best of its research in the subject area".[56] As the preparations for the submission proceeded, involving much disaggregation of information held for other purposes, the new Vice-Chancellor suggested to Senate that:

> The [British] universities believed comfortably that they had done a good job since 1981. The government, however, thought that the universities … the UGC and the department of education and science had shown themselves to be incompetent.[57]

Material for the submissions was presented to the Senate on two occasions, in October and November 1985, at the first of which there was agreement

> to affirm the view that the departments of practitioner arts in the university had a special part to play in providing a service to the community outside as well as inside the institution,[58]

while at the second tribute was paid "to the hard work done by departments and cost centres and particularly to the registrar on whom a heavy burden had fallen".[59] A general meeting of staff was held to consider drafts submitted beforehand, and there was also time for the Council to look at the submission before despatch.[60]

The results, trumpeted in the *Times Higher Education Supplement*,[61] brought little comfort to Lancaster, not helped by an error in the information issued by the UGC,[62] and neither did the concurrent announcement of the financial outcome, which

---

[55] University Grants Committee, Circular Letter 12/85 of 9 May 1985.

[56] Annex 1 to UGC Circular Letter 12/85.

[57] Minute S.85/183 of Senate, meeting on 12 October 1985: the speaker (for the minute gives an almost verbatim account of what was said) was Professor H. J. Hanham, who was passionate about raising Lancaster's research profile.

[58] Minute S.85/156, Senate meeting on 26 October 1985.

[59] Minute S.85/187, Senate meeting on 20 November 1985.

[60] For the content of the submission, see UA.1/2/3/2 and UA.1/2/1/1.

[61] Ngaio Crequer, "The strengths and weaknesses", *The Times Higher Education Supplement*, 30 May 1986.

[62] Business and Management had been incorrectly listed as below average, rather than average.

directly reflects [the UGC's] assessment of the research effectiveness of the Lancaster departments. The funding model is science-driven and particularly reflects two things, research volume and research council evaluations. By all accounts we were hard-hit by the relatively low volume of research in certain areas ... We were also damaged by the fact that our science departments, apart from Psychology, were not rated above average.

The UGC has reiterated the view it expressed last May[63] that Lancaster University is spread too thin, in that we try to do too much for a university of our size. We are one of the few universities singled out for advice of this sort.[64]

In his comments to the Senate, under a heading of "The message conveyed and intended", the Vice-Chancellor indicated that Lancaster was "roughly in the middle of the league table, but a bit further down than it expected to be".[65] He further predicted that, because the UGC was recovering from the exhaustion brought on by an exercise for which it was not fully prepared, there was unlikely to be another for five or even ten years.

In summary, 14 departments were deemed to be outstanding or above average, 13 average, and 10 below average. The 3 departments that had been starred as outstanding were Psychology (work on recognition processes), Sociology (economic sociology and social theory), and Educational Research (including its research centres). Above average were Accounting and Finance (corporate financial disclosure), Systems (soft systems methodology), Linguistics and Modern English Language (applied linguistics and natural language processing by computer), History (social history, and history of science), Philosophy (individuals' research), and Religious Studies (Eastern religions, and modern religious thought and methodologies). Biological Sciences, Physics, Environmental Science, Computing, and Engineering were all rated as average, but Chemistry as below average. The university, said the Vice-Chancellor, must ask every department to review its current plans, showing how it would build on its strengths; how the rigidity of departmental boundaries could be softened, especially in the engineering/environmental science/geography spectrum; and how weaknesses were to be eliminated. Chairs must be filled in Chemistry, to recognise the strength of polymer chemistry, and in Accounting and Finance.[66]

One immediate step taken was to replace the four functional research committees of 1983 into a single policy body, with terms of reference[67] that included advice to the Senate

---

[63] The UGC had held its final visitation at Lancaster in May 1985, before Professor Hanham took up his post.

[64] "Comments by the Vice-Chancellor on the UGC Letter" (GM/86/174), Senate meeting of 4 June 1986.

[65] Minute S.86/107, Senate meeting on 4 June 1986.

[66] The chair in Accounting and Finance was to replace Professor Edward Stamp, Director of ICRA, who had died in January 1986 and who, as the Vice-Chancellor told the Court, had been the person who persuaded Harry and Ruth Hanham that they might move from Massachusetts to Lancaster: see University of Lancaster, "Twenty-Second Annual Report", 1985–86, p. 5.

[67] Appendix 1 of a Report on Graduate Studies (GM/86/202), considered at an extraordinary meeting of the Senate held on 21 June 1986.

and the Development Committee, biennial meetings between the departments and the committee, special investigations *ad hoc*, and informal encouragement and support for research. Obligations about research students were also laid on the committee, including their regulations, the quality of their supervision, and their completion rates. The chairman of the committee, a direct appointment by the Vice-Chancellor, was Professor Philip Levy, the founding professor of the Department of Psychology, and already a member of several influential national bodies. He became effectively the first dean for research,[68] and a few months after his appointment set out some key issues in a *Fulcrum* article: the financial and reputational significance of research, the need for access to larger single sums of money, especially in the sciences, the value of interdisciplinary collaboration, and the relative strengths of particular areas. He went on:

> While there are many opportunities for new lines and new strengths, we probably have limited human capacity let along money. Choices will have to be made. But many academics will defend to the death their right to attempt a personal line of research that others may regard as somewhat ordinary. How diverse can we afford to get? How much capacity is left? …
>
> New research is a risky business. Significant personal time and often money too, is committed without any guarantee of success. In this sense I see the university research fund as a resource for risk investment with growing possibilities, where costs and risks are shared … The goal of the investment is to produce a payback in greater reputation or money, and preferably both.[69]

Another important approach, under guidance from the UGC,[70] was the consolidation of areas of strength. The School of Management and Organisational Sciences was the first to change its structure, building on moves it had made a decade earlier to achieve more organisational cohesion than other clusters of subjects, and as the only non-science part of the university to have its own building.[71] While its members recognised the wish on the part of the new vice-chancellor to accelerate this trend, there was a wariness of closer integration:

> Professor Checkland emphasized that his stance as chairman has consistently been not to represent the School as more of an organisational entity that it is, for it is essentially a semantic creation. The reality of power for subsidised institutions such as a university is

---

[68] The term dean for research was later officially used for the role, before it became a portfolio for a pro-vice-chancellor. Professor Levy's successors were Professor John Urry (Sociology), and Professor Peter Diggle (Mathematics and Statistics, and subsequently the School of Health and Medicine).

[69] Philip Levy, "Establishing research priorities", *Fulcrum*, No. 115, 5 February 1987, p. 2.

[70] Sir Peter Swinnerton-Dyer, "Monitoring Research Selectivity", Circular Letter 9/87 of 10 March 1987; see also the university's reply (GM/87/243).

[71] Gillow House opened in 1975; it is now much enlarged by the addition of two further phases, and the name of the building and its function are now co-terminous.

that it is in the hands of those who can allocate resources. Here they are principally in the control of departments, and it is difficult to cajole autonomous departments to act together … [The School] is perceived as potentially a source of strength for the university (and not simply for its money-gaining potential) but its lack of external impact is a frustration to the university, and something which very much concerns the Vice-Chancellor … His message to the university is that at present it does not have a management school: if it wants one, it must face the structural issues and decide what to do about them; and the message to the School is that the members of it must face the issues outlined and come to a corporate response about the pressures being exerted before a solution is imposed from the School from outside.[72]

The SPARC, as part of the formulation of the Academic Plan, commissioned a series of discussion papers, and the fourth of these, about the School, proposed closer integration.[73] In short order a not unfavourable response came back, noting that after a series of internal meetings the School was able to report:

There is agreement that the School needs to adopt a new strategy for the future, and that the evolution of the structure should be determined in the context of that strategic development. The School wishes to create an organisation which is operationally effective for consortial activities, and to have resources which at least in part are allocated from a central core …

The momentum of the School's research activity has considerably increased over the past five years and considerable efforts are being made to achieve further success in obtaining research funding from the research councils, industry and public sector bodies. Centres for such research activities will be set up as appropriate. The School has not taken a view on whether the increased research effort should be at the expense of outside consultancies.[74]

The Vice-Chancellor acted swiftly to create the post of dean for the School, and to fill it with an external appointee, Professor David Ashton, with a brief to reform the School's academic structure, its research, and its reputation.[75] The core departments at the time were Accounting and Finance, Behaviour in Organisations, Management Learning, Marketing, Operational Research and Operations Management, and Systems, with Economics and

---

[72] Note of a report by the chairman of SMOS to Board of Studies F, 26 November 1986, transmitted to SPARC for its meeting on 17 December 1986.

[73] "School of Management", SPARC Discussion Paper No. 4, presented to the Senate on 25 March 1987.

[74] "Future development of SMOS", draft paper to the SPARC, February 1987. The external consultancies, as part of the School's mainstream activity, were dissolved over the next few years.

[75] See Kwon, "Reputational Objects: A Critical Re-Evaluation of Corporate Brand Management", especially pages 108–10, 212–29.

Law as associate members of the School, and the reorganisation was intended to create a Management School "aimed at making Lancaster a leading European Centre for management education", coupled with arrangements for promoting research in the School with due regard to research selectivity, including interdepartmental research and some new research centres.[76]

Biological Sciences and Environmental Science also came under pressure to rationalise. A UGC report[77] proposed that earth sciences should be supported nationally at one of three levels, with the intention that the same model be applied to other sciences – Level 1 conprised well-found centres for substantial research and teaching; Level 2 well-found centres for honours teaching; and Level 3 general earth science centres – and suggested that there should be a series of regional committees to manage the process. The SPARC quickly moved to encourage the two departments to bring forward a proposal for Level 1 status, within the definition of the earth sciences review, and to form an institute that would:

> allow for greater efficiency in research expenditure and an eventual rationalisation of resources in the environmental and biological activities of the university ... In particular, the definition of a research topic, environmental pollution, which will utilise the talents of no less than 24 of the existing staff in the two parent departments ... the Institute will seek actively to develop existing links with local NERC Research Institutes and with industry; links which will result in more efficient use of national resources and an improvement in multidisciplinary research quality.[78]

An initial target date of October 1987 was given for the new institute, although the Academic Plan indicated that the process of merger into a single interdisciplinary department had begun, with Professor Terry Mansfield, FRS, as the first director, and with strengthened links to the Institute of Terrestrial Ecology at Merlewood, the Proudman Oceanographic Laboratory at Bidston, and the Freshwater Biological Association at Windermere.[79] Within the broad theme of environmental pollution there would be a focus on terrestrial, aquatic, and atmospheric systems, environmental systems and control technology, and also ecology, physiology, pathology, biochemistry, and biophysics.

No sooner had these moves been made, however, than the Vice-Chancellor warned the Senate that the next stage of the institutions' stated plans would form the basis of the universities' revised research ratings, and "that a significant share of the UGC's resources for research would become even more concentrated in a few main centres, and also move

---

[76] Section 5.2.1 of the draft Academic Plan (GM/87/227), presented to Senate on 13 May 1987. The move was confirmed in minute S.88/78, meeting of the Senate on 1 and 28 June 1988.

[77] "Strengthening University Earth Sciences" (the Oxbrough Report), a summary of which (GM/87/231) was circulated to the Senate as part of a series of extraordinary meetings on 13 and 30 May, and 3 and 17 June, 1987.

[78] Paper (no date, no author, no reference number) considered by SPARC on 2 June 1987.

[79] Minute S.87/135, Senate meeting on 30 June 1987, accompanied by document GM/87/129.

away from basic to applied research".[80] He was alluding to an ABRC discussion document that, postulating the concentration of research activity in areas of strategic national importance, suggested that the "lack of purposeful direction, nationally, in the redeployment of university research effort, both between and within institutions", meant that the required degree of concentration would not happen quickly enough. The ABRC therefore proposed differentiation between three types of department: Type R, with undergraduate and postgraduate teaching and substantial research activity across the range of fields; Type T, with teaching and scholarship but without advanced research facilities; and Type X, the hybrid between T and R, involving collaboration between institutions. This separation of departments would be accompanied by the research councils' development of interdisciplinary research centres that would account for a large part of their support for research. Each would have a "positively managed coherent programme of work, undertaken by a small number of core staff and visiting teams of researchers".[81] Such an explicit, radical and rapid dismantling of the dual support system and the shift of policy-making from the UGC to the ABRC would, if it had been implemented, have swiftly reshaped many universities' destinies, and there was swift and immediate indignation, not to say outrage, from many institutions.[82] And while the Vice-Chancellor was able to reassure Senate in January 1988 that the R, T, and X proposals had been dropped, he nevertheless indicated that the idea of university research centres (URCs) would continue. They were to be established across the system, initially in the sciences, with a proportion of each university's revenue earmarked for their funding.[83] Moreover, funding for teaching and research would be separated, and a more elaborate method than the diary exercise of the 1960s[84] to determine the use of academic staff time would be undertaken.

Unsurprisingly, the ABRC move was followed by an announcement from the UGC about a further research selectivity exercise, accompanied by a request for comments on a revised procedure and methodology.[85] The accompanying proposals were far removed from the tentative measures of 1986, and foreshadowed the shape of the research assessment exercises for the rest of the cycle to 2008. Units of assessment rather than departments were to be used, the role of outside experts was hotly debated, professional institutes and learned bodies were to be closely involved, the grading criteria were more closely defined, including

---

[80] Minute S.87/137, Senate meeting on 18 November 1987.

[81] "Summary of main conclusions and recommendations for "A Strategy for the Science Base", ABRC, 1987: see especially paras. 1–3 and 12.

[82] See paras. 33–6, Secretary of State's Speech to the CVCP, 30 October 1987 (GM/87/414, Senate meeting on 18 November 1987).

[83] Senate minute S.88/2 (iii) of 20 January 1988: in practice, however, the R, T, and X notion proved to be a powerful shorthand tool for future policy-making, while most of the few URCs set up were not a success and were dispersed by the end of their first decade of operation.

[84] See paras. 159–61, University Grants Committee, *University Development 1957–1962*, estimating that about half of academic staff time was spent on research.

[85] Sir Peter Swinnerton-Dyer, "UGC Circular Letter" 15/88 of 9 March 1988.

publications, research grant income, and external recognition (or esteem), and a common rating scale was to be put in place for all disciplines. Lancaster's response was low-key but emphasised the crucial nature of

> the quality of the peer judgement made on [the submissions]. We therefore urge that wide and differentiated peer groups be used in determining the research rankings, and we should also much prefer that they perform their tasks openly ... We believe that individuals involved in this kind of appraisal should expect to be called upon to justify that evaluation.[86]

The letter also encouraged as wide a range of evaluator measures as possible, since "Our departments, schools and institutes operate in diverse ways according to the circumstances appropriate to their disciplines and the external environment against which they operate."

The university was also required to report on its arrangements for monitoring research selectivity. In addition to the establishment of the Management School and the Institute for Environmental and Biological Sciences, it was also able to report on the setting up of a School of Engineering, Computing and Mathematical Sciences, the merger of its modern languages into a single department, and of its creative arts into a school[87] as evidence of increasing concentration of effort in selected areas. Already there was a mood of increasing confidence, and the year's report to the Court took research as its theme. The Vice-Chancellor was able to refer to earth sciences at Lancaster as being one of only seven top-ranking institutes in the country,[88] and the report also celebrated the emphasis on interdisciplinarity, the surge in research grant income, successes in cardiovascular pharmacology, the achievement of the coldest place on earth, and developments in mechatronics and machine-readable language corpora, as well as research on the local region, face perception, and public understanding of science.[89]

An issue of concern, however, was the future of Chemistry. The principal area of research strength was in polymers, a field in which the sole URC had been awarded to Manchester, and where the UGC sub-committee on equipment was suggesting to Lancaster that polymer chemistry might be subsumed into Physics – at a time when student recruitment to both subjects was declining nationally at a rapid pace. Not surprisingly, Senate members "expressed considerable disquiet at the prospect of any science department at Lancaster being relinquished",[90] but the subsequent UGC reviews of both subjects threw up the same

---

[86] M. E. McClintock to P. K. Jones of the UGC, 20 July 1988 (UA.1/2/3/4).

[87] H. J. Hanham to Sir Peter Swinnerton-Dyer, 3 June 1988 (UA.1/2/1/3): see also sections 7.12, 7.1.4, 7.2.1, 7.4.3, and 7.4.7 of the Review of the Academic Plan (GM/88/164), 1 June 1988.

[88] The official designation was that Lancaster was included in Group 1, Type I (a spectrum of medium to large departments that contributed to interdisciplinary as well as mainstream earth sciences; equivalent in academic status to Type M) (UGC Circular Letter 23/88, 11 May 1988).

[89] University of Lancaster, "Twenty Fourth Annual Report" 1987–88 to the Court (December 1988).

[90] Minute S.88/75 (7.1), Senate meeting on 1 and 25 June 1988: see also S.88/113(f) (12 October 1988) and S.88/144 (16 November 1988).

issues of size related to the resource base.[91] It was at this rather uncomfortable juncture that Lancaster was finalising its entries into the 1989 research selectivity exercise.

The 1989 submission, delivered by hand in London on 22 March 1989, went in under 30 categories[92] that were graded on a five-point scale, with 5 equating to international excellence in some sub-areas and national excellence in virtually all others and 1 equating to national excellence in none or virtually none of the sub-areas. This time explicit league tables were published, and Lancaster found itself listed as 16th in *The Times*,[93] a result that the Vice-Chancellor declared "did not look disadvantageous despite some problem areas: the performance of the university had enabled it to keep up with the competition".[94] The recent excellent result in earth sciences was not included: other areas of excellence (5) were religious studies, sociology, and accounting, with strength (4) in history, statistics, psychology, educational research, and linguistics.[95] The big disappointment was a 1 for Chemistry, and proposals were soon formulated for the department to be divided up between a School of Physics and Chemistry and the Institute of Environmental and Biological Sciences.[96] The resources of the department, it was said, were being used "to strengthen interdisciplinary research in physics and materials, biochemistry, and environmental chemistry, where there are already strong research groupings at Lancaster".[97] The subsequent loss, in 2000, of a mainstream science department and its accreditation with the Royal Society of Chemistry, was to be a major blow for Lancaster.[98]

The 1989 outcome overall, however, gave a significant boost to morale and to UFC income to Lancaster.[99] Additional research centres were proposed and approved by the Senate,[100] and there was a renewed determination to maximise research grant income; a *Research Bulletin*, issued quarterly, gave current information on funding sources to all staff.[101] A

---

[91] Minute S.89/34(b), Senate meeting on 15 March 1989.

[92] See RAE 1989 submission (UA.1/2/3/3). All the modern languages and creative arts were separately entered, and there were three entries under mathematics. Business and management studies, however, also included economics and systems, but accountancy was separate.

[93] Sam Kiley, "Low research rating could force college departments to close", *The Times*, 26 August 1989: see also *The Daily Telegraph* for 26 August 1989.

[94] UGC Circular 27/89 of 23 August 1989.

[95] The units of assessment did not necessarily equate to the departments of a similar name, and the use of the lower case therefore signifies a research area rather than an organisational unit.

[96] Minute S.89/128(f), Senate meeting on 11 October 1989: see also S.90/29 (21 March 1990) and S.90/63 (6 June 1990).

[97] Lancaster University, "Planning Statement to the UFC", 22 June 1990.

[98] The decision remains controversial and there continue to be senior members of the university who would like to revive provision of the subject in its full form.

[99] See UFC Letter of 9 March 1992, showing £7.77 million of UFC R funding for 1991–92, and £8.6 million for 1992–93.

[100] For example, centres in advanced learning technology, education and training, and environmental change: see *Staff Handbook* 2006–07, pp. 83–6 (UA.1/29/1/1).

[101] *Research Bulletin*, Nos. 1 to 58 (October 1987 to January 1999) (UA.1/2/5/11).

continuing area of concern, however, was the recruitment of research students, where the improved research position was hampered by

> our relative weakness in attracting postgraduate students in many areas of the university. Only one or two of our departments are safely above national norms for research student numbers ... The proportion of postgraduates of all kinds is a major index of the quality of our growth. The danger is that we might increase our undergraduate teaching and other basic training activities to the detriment of research.[102]

Colleagues were reminded about the reputational value of strong postgraduate numbers and the importance of the "intellectual impertinence and energies of youthful minds, and their enhancement of Lancaster's community life", their presence giving "a significant signal to the world about the vitality of the university and its claim to be a research university", and the announcement was made that a working group under the joint aegis of the Dean of Graduate Studies and the Chairman of the Committee for Research would meet and make recommendations to appropriate bodies.[103]

The UFC undertook consultation about the 1989 exercise and issued its requirements for the next one to be held early[104] in 1992, with a deadline of 30 June for submissions. The ratings achieved were intended to be used by the forthcoming Higher Education Funding Council for England, Scotland, and Wales,[105] and to be arrived at on the basis of peer review by specialist panels. Significant changes included the opportunity to enter only those staff actively engaged in research (although with summary information required for those omitted), a prior announcement that no research funding would be allocated to the lowest point of the five ratings available, and more detailed instructions on how to submit interdisciplinary research. The scale of the exercise, now including all the former polytechnics, was much enlarged, with 172 institutions assessed instead of the 55 in 1989. The Vice-Chancellor was quick to alert colleagues to the importance of exercising the option of selection

> and asked that individual cost centres should discuss the relative advantages of specific exclusion, inclusion and movement [between units of assessment] ... in the light of the overall advantage to the university: while there was an incentive to leave people out to ensure a high ranking, the need for a high number with which to multiply that rating was also of critical importance.[106]

---

[102] Philip Levy and Richard Dutton, "We Need More Postgraduate Students", *Research Bulletin* No. 11, November 1989 (UA.1/2/3/11).

[103] See: "Research Student Recruitment, 1989–90" (UA.1/2/3/6).

[104] UFC *Circular Letter* 5/92, February 1992.

[105] Northern Ireland was also included, and all the remaining exercises thus covered all regions of Great Britain.

[106] Minute S.92/31(b), Senate meeting on 18 March 1992.

Lancaster submitted under 27 units of assessment, omitting applied mathematics, and including both economics and accounting with business management, thus totalling 433 academic staff, with 21 omitted.[107] The debate about how to present the Management School, and especially about the inclusion of accounting with the School, had been hotly contested by staff and senior officers.[108]

The results, published in December 1992,[109] proved to be outstanding news for Lancaster, since the institution was now listed amongst the top ten institutions overall, with 95.4% of its eligible staff included. Units of assessment that achieved a 5 rating were environmental studies, statistics and operational research, sociology, business and management studies, linguistics, theology, divinity and religious studies, and education. No unit was rated as 1, and the polymer chemists, entered under metallurgy and materials, achieved a 3. Amidst the general jubilation, the Pro-Chancellor wrote to express his pleasure and admiration:

> By coming ninth amongst the research universities, Lancaster has demonstrated a remarkable improvement of its research efforts, and turned in a performance which is truly impressive … It so happens that I have been in contact with many of the lay members of the Council in the last few days. I found that all shared my very positive appreciation of the research review outcome.[110]

By comparison with its position a decade earlier, Lancaster had thus made a powerful change to its research standing, and it is worth reflecting on the causes of that success over a relatively brief period. Several factors were at play: the underlying quality of the academic staff, especially those appointed in the surge of 1967–72, who had spent a further ten years advancing their research careers; a second round of new blood posts that had been more plentiful for Lancaster; the internal investment in heightened research activity that had borne fruit; and the impact of strategic groupings, especially for environmental studies and business and management, but also by the inclusion of women's studies, computer-supported cooperative work, and science and the environment within sociology. There had also been stronger leadership in research policy and implementation since the first and second exercises, and a rising research culture and expectation of success. No researcher, for example, ever quite knew when the Vice-Chancellor might appear at his or her elbow to demand an explanation of current research activity. Although his terse response to the Senate about the 1992 result was to encourage "everyone to consider how

---

[107] RAE 1992 submission (UA.1/2/3/7).

[108] See Kwon, "Reputational Objects: A Critical Re-Evaluation of Corporate Brand Management", pp. 218–20. The opposition was spirited, and persisted to the moment of the opening of a university forum at which the Vice-Chancellor announced this decision (personal recollection of the author).

[109] UFC, *RAE 1992: The Outcome* (Circular 26/92).

[110] Sir Christopher Audland, Pro-Chancellor, letter of 21 December 1992 to the Vice-Chancellor: the 1992 exercise was the third and last with Philip Levy as chairman of the Committee for Research.

Professor Harry Hanham, Vice-Chancellor, 1985 to 1995

the university might perform even better on the next occasion",[111] it was made by a person who of all people knew how dangerous it would be to lessen institutional research effort. Instead, consideration was to be given to a university-wide graduate school to increase postgraduate activity, especially for research students.[112]

Nationally, the 1992 RAE proved to be something of a watershed for higher education. The exercises had consistently been seen as controversial: their consequences had a significant impact for institutions' funding and reputation, and the procedures adopted were open to fundamental criticism: peer review because of its subjectivity; publications because weightings may be applied that work against full recognition of some types of research, particularly on subject boundaries; citations because they can be rigged; and research income because it is primarily an input rather than an output.[113] After the 1992 RAE, however, a judicial review of the refusal by the HEFCE of the downgrading of the result for the Institute of Dental Surgery highlighted the lack of stated criteria on which panels could make their judgement and the absence of accountable feedback to units of assessment

[111] Minute S.93/2(a), Senate meeting on 20 January 1993.

[112] Report to the Senate of a meeting of the Committee for Research held on 5 February 1993 (SASA/93/411).

[113] "The evaluation of research outputs in higher education", in Johnes and Taylor, *Performance Indicators*, pp. 146–72.

and their institutions.[114] The solution advocated by Professor Jim Taylor, of direct funding by research topic and hence the implicit abolition of dual funding, contrasted with another study of the time that proposed more reliance on quantitative indicators, such as citations and impact factors, combined with a more selective approach to data collection to improve efficiency.[115] While a funding council review of the exercise expressed broad satisfaction with the process, if sufficient time for data collection was allowed,[116] a subsequent analysis based on a study by Professor Ian McNay was more critical. He suggested that while there had been the benefit of more explicit attention given to research activity and its management, the effects on staff in terms of stress, pressure to be accepted as research-active and the consequences of failure, the possible negative effects on teaching, and some equality issues were significant disbenefits.[117] Indeed, the leading research universities began to pull away from peer institutions in order to differentiate themselves as institutions that set the research agenda. First the Russell Group[118] was set up early in 1994, initially to represent members' interests to government, and that was closely followed by the 94 Group.[119]

At the same time there was some encouragement to be gleaned from a White Paper stating that the Government "accepts its role as the main funder of basic research. It wishes to sustain within the United Kingdom expertise across the core disciplines of biology, chemistry, mathematics and physics and to provide the climate where centres of international excellence can develop and flourish. It recognises the importance of providing a framework in which science can progress, as the President of the Royal Society said, through the ideas, inspiration and dedication of individual scientists."[120]

The university felt confident to proclaim itself as a research-led institution,[121] and to develop the research infrastructure and support services that would match that identification. One project gaining support was an initiative to make Lancaster an international centre

---

[114] John Griffith, *Research Assessment: As Strange a Maze as E'er Men Trod* (London: Council for Academic Freedom and Academic Standards, 1995).

[115] Jim Taylor, "Measuring research performance in business and management studies in the UK; the 1992 RAE", March 1994, pp. 1–8 and appendices (unpublished MS).

[116] HEFCE, CP. 6/93 (June 1993), pp. 1–6.

[117] Higher Education Funding Council for England, "The Impact of the 1992 Research Assessment Exercise on Higher Education Institutions in England", M 6/97 (Bristol: HEFCE, 1997), http://www.hefce.ac.uk/pubs/hefce/1997/m6_97.htm.

[118] The Russell Group was named after the Russell Hotel, Russell Square, London, where the first informal meetings took place. In 2010 it had 20 member institutions that between them accounted for two-thirds of UK research grant and contract income.

[119] The 94 Group, named after the year of its establishment, had in 2010 19 member institutions of smaller but research-intensive universities, including Lancaster and others founded in the 1960s, with a primary aim to promote excellence in research and research-led teaching. Professor Paul Wellings was appointed as the chair of the board for the period 2009–12.

[120] *Realising Our Potential: A Strategy for Science, Engineering and Technology*, Cm. 2250 (London: HMSO, 1993), para. 3.4.

[121] Minute S.93/72, Senate meeting on 2 June 1993.

for studies of John Ruskin and his circle[122] through a foundation that was intended to bring the Whitehouse Collection to a custom-built library at Bailrigg. Shortly afterwards the Centre for the Study of Environmental Change secured substantial three-year funding from the ESRC, and there was some discussion about the use of internal funding for some medical and health research in selected areas.[123] A move towards the devolution of research policy to the five faculty boards took place, and within the science grouping to the three separate institutes and schools for Environmental and Biological Sciences, for Engineering, Computing and Mathematical Sciences, and for Physics and Materials.[124] The Management School was taking a pro-active stance to research that included a controversial evaluation of individual members of staff linked to a rating of the journals in which they were publishing. Overall, the university had the stated intention of maintaining its position as a research-led institution that would seek RAE ratings of at least 4 in most units of assessment, that would promote strong research groups and new areas that could attract external funding, that would account for its research project costs, and that would identify thematic research programmes between faculty-based graduate schools.[125] The Vice-Chancellor urged that the university

> look to Stockholm, home of the Nobel Prize, rather than to Bristol, home of the Funding Council … He stressed the need to develop major new areas of study that responded to national needs (health, rather than medicine, and new small-scale technologies). Partnerships were needed to encourage a flexibility of response, including closer links with significant European institutions, as well as with regional partners and the Open University. International research centres must be developed, and landmark facilities. Postgraduates, especially research students, must grow significantly in number to become as numerous as undergraduates.[126]

The hint about health research referred to a series of strenuous efforts, led *inter alia* by Professor Nick Abercrombie, to establish an institutional research presence in health-related research that would consolidate and develop a range of initiatives, already involving some 60 staff, in medical statistics, work with the health service (including a joint masters degree with S. Martin's College), public health research and practitioner support, as well as the Lancashire and Cumbria Medical Research Foundation and a range of departmental activities. Thus the Senate, despite the great uncertainties facing the university, felt able

---

[122] Minute S.93/71, Senate meeting on 2 June 1993; and document SASA/93/733.

[123] Minute 1 of an untitled report to Senate from the Committee for Research (4 February 1994); and document SASA/94/366.

[124] Report from the Committee for Research to the Senate (1 June 1994) (SASA/94/633).

[125] Section C.1 of Planning Statement to 1997–98 (University of Lancaster, July 1994). Total research income had increased in 1993–94 from £4.9 million to £5.9 million.

[126] Minute 8.2 of the meeting of the Court held on 17 December 1994.

in March 1996 to approve the setting up of the Institute for Health Research, initially for three years.[127]

The period when universities felt able to turn their attention away from the research assessment exercises between each one became progressively shorter, and preparations for RAE 1996 began almost two years ahead of the submission date of 30 April 1996. Each of the six exercises proved to have its own distinctive style: RAE 1996, the first under the new funding councils, also marked the first, and problematic, electronic submission, with many software problems.[128] Furthermore, as institutions increasingly vied with each other for every morsel of tactical advantage, so the instructions for submission became ever more detailed and elaborate. Detailed criteria for judgements in each of 60 panels were issued, and the ratings scale was stretched to include a 5* that would mark international excellence in a majority of sub-areas, as well as a division of 3 into 3(a) and 3(b). The exercise, it was stated, would rely on the judgement of panels and was not to be mechanistic. Four output items were required for each member of staff, accompanied by an instruction that all the material referred to should be made available for the panels on request, and the deposit of all Lancaster's outputs in a temporary central location was arranged. This move proved to be sensible for retrieval and verification purposes, but was one that put further strain on the goodwill of the staff involved.[129]

Submissions for the 1996 RAE, the fourth such exercise and the last for which preparations took place during the vice-chancellorship of Harry Hanham, were made under 26 units of assessment, involving 464 staff and with a 92% inclusion rate.[130] The results, published on 19 December 1996, again showed Lancaster in the top ten institutions. Ivor Crewe, looking around the 94 Group institutions, felt compelled to comment on the strong performance of the smaller research-orientated universities and to note that in his view there was no case for a small super league of research-based universities.[131] The results, however, brought to the fore the stark differences of view between those who argued that research quality should be rewarded wherever it was located, irrespective of institutional standing, and those who were adamant that investment should be in already excellent institutions.[132] The Russell

---

[127] Minute S.96/35, Senate meeting on 20 March 1996; see also AR/96/1623 (November 1996), together with document AR/96/504.

[128] See Higher Education Funding Council for England, "RAE 1996: Conduct of the Exercise: RAE Manager's Report." RAE 96 1/97 (Bristol: HEFCE, 1997), http://www.rae.ac.uk/1996/c1_97.html.

[129] See paras. 71–2 Higher Education Funding Council for England, "RAE 1996: Conduct of the Exercise: RAE Manager's Report", for a discussion of the difficulties faced by panels in relation to some institutions' output.

[130] RAE 1996, submission to the HEFCE (April 1996) (UA.1/2/3/9).

[131] John O'Leary and David Chanter, "Cambridge disputes Oxford's supremacy in research ratings", The Times, 20 December 1996: Professor Ivor Crewe, as chairman of the CVCP as well as vice-chancellor at Essex, was, of course, making both a general and a particular judgement in this statement.

[132] See The Independent, The Daily Telegraph, and The Guardian (all 20 December 1996), and The Observer (22 December 1996) for the development of these arguments.

Group and the 94 Group took increasingly strongly stated positions to government about the research significance of their respective institutions.

Three of the Lancaster units – management, religious studies, and sociology – achieved the coveted 5* in 1996, supported by five more with a 5 rating, and none with a 2 or a 1. Yet the mood amongst senior officers

> was rather one of caution and soul-searching about how best to build upon our success. I recall a similar down-beat atmosphere after the 1992 RAE when many forecast gloomily that we would never be able to maintain our high standard … In 1992 there was a sense of near incredulity at our achievement whereas by 1996 everybody accepted that ninth in the premier league was a perfectly fitting place for Lancaster to occupy.[133]

These carefully chosen words were written in the context of an institution just commencing the implementation of a four-year Recovery Plan (see Chapter 6), which made both additional investment in areas of success and support for those that were faltering more problematic. In Lancaster's case the absence of a tail of low-performing units had been an important component of its success, so the balancing act for the next four years was particularly difficult. Overall the university made its economies during 1997–2000 in areas other than academic staff, thus enabling the number submitted in the 2001 exercise to be on a level with 1996.[134] This underlying stability was of course less apparent to those departments with relative losses of staff numbers: the Management School was perpetually wary of being regarded as a source of cross-subsidy, while Environmental Science drew attention to the reduction of its staff from 26 to 17 in the space of three years.[135] The most unwelcome and unexpected result was a 3a for Physics, and the possibility of an appeal was mooted. In the meantime the Senate was assured that "Physics had an important role to play and drastic action should not be taken prematurely without understanding more fully the extent of its problems and the reasons for them".[136] Linguistics had not achieved the rating it had expected, and the humanities overall were apprehensive for the future, while the Senate was also asked to consider a merger of Politics and Philosophy and the establishment of a single School of European Languages and Cultures.[137] Although the merger did not take place, and the school made sense for pedagogical and resource purposes as well as for research

---

[133] Joe Shennan [Deputy Vice-Chancellor], "And a Happy New Year – surely?", Bulletin 11, 7 January 1997.

[134] The numbers of staff available for submission at Lancaster were 506 in 1996 and 518 in 2001: see Higher Education Funding Council for England, "1996 Research Assessment Exercise: The Outcome", RAE 96 1/96 (Bristol: HEFCE, 1996), http://www.rae.ac.uk/1996/c1_96.html. and Higher Education Funding Council for England, "2001 Research Assessment Exercise: The Outcome", RAE 4/01 (Bristol: HEFCE, 2001), http://www.rae.ac.uk/2001/Pubs/4_01/. These figures include all A Category staff, including excluded staff.

[135] Minutes S.97/20.3 and S.97/20.15, Senate meeting on 19 March 1997.

[136] Minute S.97/4.22, Senate meeting on 22 January 1997.

[137] Minute S.97/2.1, Senate meeting on 19 March 1997.

reputation, these examples illustrate the extent to which academic policy was being shaped by the requirements of the university's research profile. It would also be fair to add that in the period from 1997 to 2008, covering the final two exercises, the university seemed to many of its staff to be continuously in research assessment mode, even if it did not carry out the dummy exercises undertaken at some other institutions.

A review of Physics, which included the involvement of external advisers, was rapidly put in hand and weaknesses, such as they were, were found not to be fundamental, for, "despite its recent 3a ranking, its reputation ranks favourably with Physics departments in the bulk of UK universities, most of which have a grade 4. It has elements of international excellence that give it a higher grade potential";[138] this judgement was coupled with a view that more industrial links should be forged. The department was required to undertake a series of actions to return to full teaching and research viability, and was shortly thereafter judged to be no longer a targeted area.[139] It reverted in 2000 to being a free-standing department rather than a school, and its staff undertook a sustained effort for a different outcome at the next exercise.

The university was also able to take advantage of restructuring funds on offer from the HEFCE. After a generalised approach by Lancaster that did not find favour with the council, personal discussions between the Vice-Chancellor and the Chief Executive of the HEFCE led to specific bids for two projects: Environment Lancaster and Communications Lancaster. A grant of £1.856 million over three years was approved for use on staff appointments and physical remodelling.[140] The benefits of this funding were not only the opportunity for additional student load in the sciences, some building work, and some additional staff but also:

> further significant benefits made possible by the HEFCE injection of facilitating resources. The development reported in December [1998] of the recognition by NERC that the developing strengths of Environment Lancaster were such as to merit the conduct of an appraisal of the possible relocation of some of their research institute laboratories to ... Bailrigg has occupied a great deal of resource and planning time over seven months.[141]

The proposed moves involved liaison between the Institute for Environmental and Biological Sciences, the Institute for Terrestial Ecology (ITE) at Merlewood, Grange-over-Sands, and the Institute of Freshwater Ecology at Ambleside to discuss collaboration over a range of research areas. There was also to be a combined proposal, under the banner of the Lancaster Environment Centre, to the Joint Infrastructure Fund (JIF) for the relocation

---

[138] "Review of Physics at Lancaster", report to the Academic Planning Board on 3 June 1997 (PO/97/106).

[139] Minutes APB/97/32 of 11 June 1997, and APC/97/16 of 31 October 1997.

[140] Letter of 17 February 1998 from Wendy Rigby, HEFCE Regional Officer, to Professor W. Ritchie.

[141] "HEFCE Restructuring Support: Progress Report to 31 July 1999: Overview and Environment Lancaster" (VC/99/315 A and B), and minute APC/99/54 (16 July 1999).

of the Biological Sciences Field Station to a new building. Within the Communications grouping a JIF proposal was to be prepared for additional research space for informatics, involving Psychology, Statistics, Computing, and the Communications Research Centre.[142] The bids fell at their respective final hurdles. In the case of Environment Lancaster, however, sufficient momentum had been created to proceed further, drawing on investment by NERC and funding available from an HEFCE Poor Estates initiative for the costs of relocating the field station, as well as obtaining funding by the university. An extended discussion by the Senate, following resolutions by the Council, led to a conclusion that the project, provided that it did not exceed £12 million in total, could proceed.[143] The ITE at Merlewood, part of the NERC Centre for Ecology and Hydrology, had complementary research skills in land use, soil ecology, environmental change, radioecology, and environmental chemistry. Up to 70 NERC staff were expected to transfer, and the benefits to Lancaster were to include additional well-founded laboratory space, additional shared facilities, and scope for ease of research collaboration.[144] At the same time the Centre for the Study of Environmental Change was merged with Philosophy to become a new department, called the Institute for Environment, Philosophy and Public Policy (IEPPP), so drawing together research areas with shared interests in public knowledge of and response to environmental (and climatic) change.[145] In the meantime the very different but equally welcome Ruskin project had come to fruition, and on 9 May 1998 HRH Princess Alexandra formally opened the custom-built library and welcomed the arrival of the Whitehouse Collection to Lancaster (see Chapter 7). The Ruskin-related material is held on a 25-year bailment from the Educational Trust Limited, and makes Lancaster a world-class leader for Ruskinian studies. In addition, the landmark building won a range of architectural awards.[146]

All the time, in the background, work was continuing to increase the capacity of the university to extend its range of funding sources, including from Europe, and to have a closer engagement with industry and commerce.[147] The LU Graduate School was established, with a particular focus on doctoral research, and seedcorn funding was invested, via the Committee for Research, in projects that were judged to have the potential to develop, as well as in early career research. A scheme of slightly larger grants made by the committee, known as Enterprise Zone, gave scope to staff to apply for funding over three years for projects that came with viable business plans and a clear specification of their research direction. Policies on intellectual property and copyright were further developed, and there was growing and explicit attention given to issues of research ethics.

Preparations for RAE 2001 were launched in late 1997, with regional seminars and a

---

[142] "HEFCE Restructuring Support: Progress Report to 31 July 1999: Communications Lancaster" (VC/99/315C).

[143] Minute S.2000/2(g), Senate meeting on 19 January 2000.

[144] Minute S.2000/15(d), Senate meeting on 23 February 2000.

[145] Minute S.2000/40, Senate meeting on 23 February 2000.

[146] See UA.1/27/3/9 for information about the reception of the Ruskin Library.

[147] See Appendix A.

national consultation exercise. Lancaster, in its reply to the latter,[148] emphasised the primacy of research quality based on peer review, the centrality of single disciplines combined with full assessment of interdisciplinary research, a focus on the rating of units rather than individuals, the advantages of summary feedback, the use of explicit and clear criteria, and an insistence on the proportion of staff entered at unit level being published. The subsequent published statement of assessment panels' criteria and working methods[149] attempted to give comprehensive definitions of the sub-disciplines to be covered by each panel, and in practice demonstrated the extent to which disciplines were diverging from each other in their detailed methodology. Thus it could be easier to compare staff assessed under, say, units in accounting from Aberdeen to Exeter than it was to compare staff in accounting with those in economics at any particular institution.

At Lancaster a central working group set up mentoring arrangements for each unit under which Lancaster was likely to submit, using for each one colleagues who were both related to and distant from the coverage of the unit involved. Close attention to and discussion with individual members of academic staff who were unlikely to be included took place, and the list continued to be refined up to the point of submission. Draft submissions were prepared and each was critically assessed by two reviewers; and careful thought was given, as Lancaster left behind its Recovery Plan period, about making highly selective investments in staff for key units. Advice on policy was sought from the 9 members of Lancaster staff who had been appointed to one of the 69 panels, and in certain cases additional external advice was obtained for units where strategic choices about the mode of submission were required. The university expected there to be heightened levels of external verification, in addition the requirement for the despatch of publications to relevant panel members proved onerous, both in their collection and their return.

Lancaster submitted 447 full-time equivalent staff under 25 units of assessment at the end of April 2001.[150] The results, published in December 2001, gave a national showing of 55% of staff in a 5 or 5* unit of assessment, up from 23 % in 1992 and 31% in 1996, and thus the funding councils had the *post hoc* task of apportioning an unchanged QR resource over more high-ranking units. The *Times Higher Education Supplement* hailed the results as a triumph – evidence of new growth, good management, and high productivity – but also as a disaster – the successes had overwhelmed the system and potentially set universities to fight each other for funding.[151] There were questions about whether the improvements were

---

[148] Letter of 6 March 1998 from M. E. McClintock to David Pilsbury, HEFCE; and HEFCE response of April 1998.

[149] Higher Education Funding Council for England, "Assessment Panels' Criteria and Working Methods." RAE Circular 5/99 (Bristol: HEFCE, 1999), http://www.rae.ac.uk/2001/Pubs/5_99/.

[150] RAE 2001: submission to the HEFCE, April 2001 (UA.1/2/3).

[151] "Researchers rise to the challenge of excellence", *Times Higher Education Supplement*, 14 December 2001, p. 26: the proportion of researchers in 1 or 2 rated units had fallen from 24% in 1996 to 6% in 2001.

Professor George Pickett, FRS, at work in his physics laboratory

real or tactical, and whether a process that showed constant improvement on the scale of 2001 was sustainable.

League tables in the national press showed contradictory outcomes drawn from the same data, depending on their method of analysis. Lancaster appeared in the top ten institutions in *The Times* and *The Guardian*,[152] with 5* once again for management and sociology, and a step from 5 to 5* for statistics. Gratifyingly, the rating for physics was 5*, accompanied by a 90% submission rate, an unprecedented increase from the previous 3a and fully vindicating the university's decision to continue its support of the department. The School of Law and the new Department of European Languages and Cultures had both improved their ratings from 3a to 5. The two disappointments were the Institute for the Environment, Philosophy and Public Policy, and Art, both of which were rated 3a: there was particular disquiet about the application of the RAE criteria in the case of the former, whose staff had achieved groundbreaking work with colleagues in the natural sciences on environmental issues.

A spate of highly diverse research centres were established after the RAE 2001 results, including the Literacy Research Centre,[153] the Centre for the Economic and Social Aspects of

---

[152] *LUNews* for December 2001.

[153] Minute S.2002/48, Senate meeting on 29 May 2002.

Genomics,[154] the Institute for Entrepreneurship and Enterprise Development,[155] the Centre for Mobilities Research,[156] the Centre for Research in Human Development,[157] the Centre for Collaborative Provision in the Public Sector,[158] and the Centre for Nanoscale Dynamics and Mathematical Physics,[159] all of which contributed to a widening and deepening of the research base. More collaboration within the region was encouraged; for example, with Liverpool, where Professor Sir Drummond Bone was vice-chancellor; on the Cockcroft Institute with both Liverpool and Manchester; and as part of the N8 consortium (see below). Success bred success in the formula-based allocation of £9 million SRIF funds to Lancaster in February 2003,[160] and Lancaster was noted in *Research Fortnightly* as coming top amongst institutions in terms of its success rate for research funding.[161]

For the Department of Art, however, there were proposals for closure as part of a strategy for creative arts that was intended to give room for investment in Music and Theatre Studies. The head of Art, Mr Davies, told the Senate that the department had "been acting purposefully to prepare itself for the next research assessment exercise",[162] and argued for a reversal of the proposal. It became apparent, after intensive work over the summer of 2004, that a larger grouping of the creative arts, including the related public arts providers, was likely to be the preferred institutional solution. The continuing debate about how the creative arts might be structured at Lancaster was therefore to be finally resolved in the form of a proposal for a Lancaster Institute for the Contemporary Arts that would be set up from 1 August 2005. Not all the proposed partners were equally happy, and members of the Department of Music were particularly uneasy about their universal absorption in an entity labelled as contemporary.[163] A quieter alteration was made to the IEPPP a few months later, which became the Institute for Philosophy and Public Policy.[164]

Other strategic and research-related groupings were also developed. One was InfoLab21, where a new building (see Chapter 7) and the nature of its planned activities were co-terminous, in order to link

> the international research in Computing and Communications Systems, and the delivery experience and training capabilities of ISS, to companies based in the Knowledge Business Centre within the InfoLab21 building ... It has challenging targets to meet in creating jobs, helping business, and delivering training, as well as in academic development. It will also

---

[154] Minute S.2003/23, Senate meeting on 26 February 2003.
[155] Minute S.2003/46, Senate meeting on 28 May 2003; now a department of the university.
[156] Minute S.2003/47, Senate meeting on 28 May 2003.
[157] Minute S.2004/47, Senate meeting on 26 May 2004.
[158] Minute S.2004/74, Senate meeting on 6 October 2004.
[159] Minute S.2006/18, Senate meeting on 22 February 2006.
[160] DTI Press Release, 12 February 2003.
[161] Minute S.2007/58, Senate meeting on 10 October 2007.
[162] Minute S.2004/33, Senate meeting on 23 May 2004.
[163] Minute S.2005/22, Senate meeting on 23 February 2005.
[164] Minute S.2006/06, Senate meeting on 18 January 2006.

act as a focus for the development of research in ICT in the northwest. It is therefore a hybrid structure ...[165]

and one that would help Lancaster to meet the increasing emphasis on the relevance and economic impact of universities' research.

Reference has been made to the increasingly important alliance, for strategic and reputational reasons, of the N8 group of universities, which had emerged as the result of a new venture by Deputy Prime Minister John Prescott in 2004. He had initiated the Northern Way, which was intended to establish the north of England as an area of exceptional opportunity that combined a world class economy with a superb quality of life; it was led by the three northern regional development agencies, in the case of Lancaster the NWDA. A growth fund of £100 million was to be invested over the five years 2005–10 to fund ten priority workstreams, including £6 million for "Strengthening the North's Knowledge Base", albeit with capital rather than revenue sums. The eight research-intensive universities involved – Durham, Lancaster, Leeds, Liverpool, Manchester, Newcastle, Sheffield, and York – were to bid into the funds.[166] The most significant N8 result for Lancaster was its lead role in developing networks for sustainable water use, with a view to making a bid to the next Comprehensive Spending Review[167] for this work; an outcome that also reflected the growing significance of the Lancaster Environment Centre and the university's involvement in bringing NERC staff into the heart of the university. The LEC building that would accommodate the newcomers and combine them with Lancaster colleagues was started in March 2002 (see Chapter 7) and was jointly opened by the Vice-Chancellor and Professor John Lawton two years later. In addition, the adjacent Gordon Manley Building, housing Geography and the third of the university's knowledge business centres, was officially opened in 2007, completing an environment-related complex that extended from the south spine to the western perimeter road. Furthermore, rather than consolidate around a research institute encompassing only the NERC staff and the research activities of Environmental Science, Biological Sciences, and Geography, the decision was made later in 2007 to form a single academic unit from the three departments (and the NERC staff) in order to

> break down disciplinary boundaries and bring together research and teaching, and other activities, in the fields of environmental, geographical and biological sciences ... and exploit opportunities for new developments across a range of areas, including climate change, sustainable development, biodiversity and ecosystems.[168]

By the beginning of the 2009–10 academic year the departments were fully integrated into a single entity that continued to use the umbrella term of the Lancaster Environment Centre.

---

[165] Preamble to the constitution of InfoLab21 (AR/2005/427, Senate meeting of 25 May 2005).
[166] "N8, Senior Management Briefing Note, May 2006": paper to UMAG, 5 June 2006.
[167] Minute UMAG/06/272 of 23 October 2006.
[168] Minute S.2007/62, Senate meeting on 10 October 2007.

InfoLab21, with the accommodation for the School of Computing and Communications to the left, and the Knowledge Business Centre to the right

During the period 2001–08 the university returned to its long-held ambitions for research and teaching in health and medicine. As already noted, the Institute for Health Research had drawn together a number of themes on health-related research across the university, with particular emphasis on end-of-life care. These included an agreement to introduce the degree of DClinPsy, which brought with it a direct involvement with the NHS across the region and placements for cohorts of doctoral students. There was also exceptional statistical strength in a Unit of Medical Epidemiology within Mathematics and Statistics that made it ripe for inclusion within health and medicine. As part of the continuing collaboration with the University of Liverpool, and with the primary focus on teaching, the Centre for Medical Education was set up in late 2004[169] and became a department in 2006. A year later the Senate agreed to approve a School of Health and Medicine from October 2008,[170] incorporating the department, the Institute for Health Research, and related entities. In addition, staff who had early in 2006 formed the Biomedical Sciences Unit – out of the non-environmental elements of the broad church that had made up Biological Sciences since the university was founded – also joined the School, with the intention of making a separate submission into RAE 2008.[171] Lancaster was thus for the first time able to demonstrate medical and health expertise across a wide field.

Since the period between the final two research assessments was seven years, university staff might have anticipated a spell of relative calm and purposeful activity leading to

[169] Minute S.2004/97, Senate meeting on 17 November 2004.
[170] Minute S.2007/61, Senate meeting on 10 October 2007.
[171] Minute S.2006/51, Senate meeting on 18 January 2006.

the next RAE submission. Instead, there was considerable turbulence in both policy and procedure. Soon after the results of RAE 2001 had been absorbed a joint review was set up by the UK funding councils, overseen by Sir Gareth Roberts,[172] as a first stage of consultation with stakeholders. The intention was to draw up a series of models for discussion, based around the form of expert review (peers or others), the algorithm of objective data (including the use of metrics), the extent to which self-assessment by institutions could be used (subject to validation), a debate around the use of historical data in relation to research performance, and so-called cross-cutting themes that would include a definition of excellence in research, the distribution of funds between subjects as well as institutions, and the uniformity and equality of the process.[173] Lancaster's reply, drawing also on the 94 Group's response, was consistent with its previous views: an expression of strong support for peer review, for quantitative data as supporting information, and for a close relationship between teaching and research in the arts and humanities. There was scepticism about self-assessment and over-reliance on historical data, but support for institutional discretion in the preparation of submissions and advocacy of priority for transparency of process and equity of outcome.[174] A few months later replies to a second round of questions were despatched, again endorsing reliance on expert peer review, a six-year assessment cycle, and the option of a less burdensome approach for less research-intensive institutions, and including the statement of a strong preference for a total return of all eligible staff in order to reduce games-playing. Overall, however, Lancaster was more concerned about how the relationship between quality profiles for institutions and the ratings for individuals might work, and about a lack of clarity overall regarding how the revised procedures, including the new quality profile for members of staff, would function.[175]

By February 2004 the HEFCE felt confident to announce a census date for RAE 2008 of 31 October 2007, with completed submissions to be made a month later, and with the period for research outputs defined as 1 January 2001 to 31 July 2007 (later revised to 31 December 2007). Assessment would be undertaken by 15 main panels and 67 sub-panels,[176] and the results were to be published on a continuously graded quality profile for each submission. At this stage there was still a clear intention to repeat the exercise in the form set out at six-yearly intervals.[177] An addition to the requirements for submission, however, was an instruction that each institution should draw up an internal equality code of practice to include the structures within which RAE-related decisions were to be made and

---

[172] President of Wolfson College, Oxford.

[173] "RAE: review by the joint funding bodies: memorandum to staff" (AR/2002/1264 of 14 October 2002).

[174] "Response to the review by the joint funding bodies", 28 November 2002 (AR/2002/1589).

[175] Ray Macdonald, "Review of research assessment: response form", 30 September 2003.

[176] Professor David Otley was appointed as head of main panel I, and Professor Michael Pidd of sub-panel 36.

[177] See Higher Education Funding Council for England et al., "Initial Decisions by the UK Funding Bodies." RAE 01/2004 (Bristol: HEFCE, 2004), http://www.rae.ac.uk/pubs/2004/01/rae0401.pdf.

the mechanism for appeals – for example, about non-inclusion – against them. Lancaster, drawing on its newly minted faculties for much of the work, nevertheless agreed that a central steering group, chaired by the pro-vice-chancellor for research (Professor Trevor McMillan) and reporting to the Vice-Chancellor, should take final responsibility at institutional level for the management of the code.[178] Guidance on submissions was published by the HEFCE that sought to elucidate how the quality profiles would work in order to judge individuals who ranged from four-star quality and world-leading to the producers of unclassified items that fell below the national standard or did not meet the research definitions for the unit concerned. The three elements that would contribute to each quality profile were to be research outputs, research environment, and indicators of esteem, and the published criteria and working methods of the main and sub-panels demonstrated how widely these were to differ between disciplines – in some cases, even cognate ones.[179]

There was, however, growing dissonance between the RAE process and the national political scene, which was related partly to the growing influence of the post-1997 Labour government regional development agencies, and partly to the determination of the Chancellor of the Exchequer that there should be increased investment in the sciences. That investment was intended to have a direct impact on the growth of the knowledge economy, and was to emphasize the increasing importance of knowledge transfer between university research and business. In parallel with this science-directed funding, Richard Lambert[180] was commissioned by HM Treasury, the Department for Education and Skills, and the Department for Trade and Industry to review the health of the process. The 33 recommendations of his wide-ranging report[181] proposed a much higher profile and more structured procedures to galvanise the intended two-way process between universities and businesses. Academics with relevant qualifications, it was suggested, might become non-executive directors on company boards, while business people might be exempted from training in order to lecture in universities. Universities would use their alumni networks to build closer links with their graduates who were employed in the business economy, model research collaboration contracts between the sectors would be drawn up, and the government would be encouraged to invest in permanent and substantial third stream funding, allocated by means of approved business plans from universities, and drawing on metrics – anything from working with SMEs to consultancy, contract and collaborative research or licence agreements – that could provide a predictable way of allocating funds by

---

[178] "RAE 2008: Lancaster's code of practice" (AR/2005/628), approved by the Senate on 12 October 2005 (S.2005/77).

[179] Higher Education Funding Council for England et al., "Guidance on Submissions." RAE 03/2005 (Bristol: HEFCE, 2005), http://www.rae.ac.uk/pubs/2005/03/rae0305.pdf. Higher Education Funding Council for England et al., "RAE 2008 Panel Criteria and Working Methods: Panel A." RAE 01/2006 (Bristol: HECFE, 2006), http://www.rae.ac.uk/pubs/2006/01/docs/aall.pdf.

[180] Subsequently Sir Richard Lambert, Director-General of the CBI.

[181] *Lambert Review of Business-University Cooperation: Final Report* (London: HM Treasury, 2003). The first regional launch of the report took place at Lancaster on 29 January 2004.

formula. The government, Lambert urged, should take into account world-class excellence in research, while at the same time treating excellent research undertaken with industry as being of equal value. In addition, research funding relevant to business should support university departments that demonstrated strong support from business, using the regional development agencies as the vehicle for allocation. He also, more controversially, included sections on proposals for the management, governance, and leadership of universities that were intended to make them more industry-facing.

This highly influential report was the background to a further report from HM Treasury,[182] later in 2004, covering investment in science and innovation. That report in turn led, in March 2006, when plans for RAE 2008 at universities were well advanced, to a move by HM Treasury to implement the generic policies published two years earlier, drawing attention to the Government's "firm presumption that after the 2008 RAE the system for assessing research quality and allocating 'quality-related' (QR) research funding to universities from the Department for Education and Skills will be mainly metrics-based".[183] The document continued by saying that a shadow metrics system would be run by the Government alongside RAE 2008, and launched an immediate consultation on how the metrics system would work. While acknowledging that the Government knew preparations were well under way,

> If an alternative system is agreed and widely supported, and a clear majority of UK universities were to favour an earlier move to a simpler system, the Government would be willing to consider that.[184]

Lancaster at once publicly confirmed its commitment to proceeding with RAE 2008 as already planned. During the subsequent uproar amongst institutions, Bill Rammell, Minister of State for Higher Education, reassured institutions in June:

> As I said, the income-based models we are preparing are for STEM subjects. For other subjects, we recognise that a more complex process may be required, and this might mean an element of separate peer review ... we are suggesting using peer review to select and quality assure metrics ... The 'new system' will begin to be phased in and feature in funding allocations from 2009–10 in England.[185]

In addition to trenchant methodological objections raised about metrics and the political pressures generated by the intervention of HM Treasury, an analysis by Lancaster colleagues

---

[182] *Science and Innovation Investment Framework 2004–2014* (London: HM Treasury, 2004).

[183] *Science and Innovation Investment Framework 2004–2014: Next Steps* (London: HM Treasury, 2006), Executive Summary.

[184] *Science and Innovation Investment Framework 2004–2014: Next Steps*, paras. 4.17, 4.18.

[185] Bill Rammell, "Research funding beyond 2008", speech to the HEPI Conference, 21 June 2006.

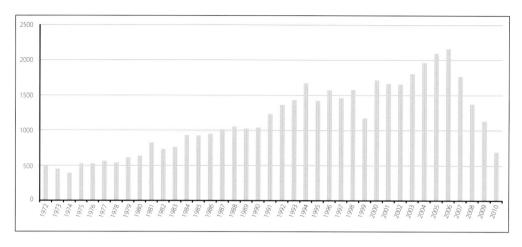

Figure 6: Publications by members of staff 1972–2010. Data for the years 2007–10 are in the process of collection.

also revealed the poor performance of modelled allocations under the proposed metrics system when compared with the actual QR allocations from 2001.[186]

After such upheavals, the detailed preparation of RAE 2008 submissions came almost as a relief, and followed the familiar pattern of discussion of strategic groupings within the choices presented by published criteria and a critical examination of draft documents that left nothing to chance. Lancaster submitted in 22 units of assessment, covering over 90% of eligible staff, and entered the work of 611 full-time equivalent people.[187] Work by the RAE panels was undertaken over a full 12 months, but finally, on 17 December 2008, the results were published, showing Lancaster to be in the top 20 institutions overall. Of Lancaster's research activity, 19% was judged to be of 4* quality, 42% of 3*, 31% of 2*, and 7% of 1*. For the second time physics came first in the UK, and other outstanding results were recorded for allied health professions and studies (for biomedicine), computing, earth systems and environmental sciences, business and management studies, sociology, and art and design. The outcome for biomedicine, entered by Lancaster for the first time, was an important signal about the quality already achieved within the School of Health and Medicine. The unit for art and design, used to cover the full range of the work in the Lancaster Institute for the Contemporary Arts, and hence the former departments of art, music, and theatre studies, gave those areas for the first time the accolade they deserved. While the benefits to institutional reputation of RAE 2008 remained outstanding, the HEFCE decision shortly after the announcement of the results to enhance the funding of some subject areas at the expense of others, however, meant that the outcome was not fully reflected in the funding received.

[186] Peter Diggle and Amanda Chetwynd, "On the relationship between actual and modelled QR allocations", 27 September 2006 (p.diggle@lancaster.ac.uk).
[187] See: "RAE 2008: submission to the HEFCE" (UA.1/2/3/1).

The medal for The Queen's Anniversary Prize, introduced to mark the 40th anniversary of Elizabeth II to the throne and awarded to Lancaster on three occasions

A year after the release of the RAE 2008 results the consultative process about the replacement process, the Research Excellence Framework,[188] continued to be negotiated between the many parties deemed to have an interest in how UK university research should be shaped in the future. The discussions that had taken place late in the RAE 2008 process were refined into a document that included a politicised definition of research as "a process of investigation leading to new insights effectively shared". Briefly summarised, the future assessment structure was intended to lead to a selection of staff regarded as substantial researchers and chosen for entry within submitted units. The first criterion by which their work would be judged would be output quality (60%), using citation information for pre-identified areas of science and permitting the inclusion of so-called grey literature, including such items as licences and patents, with a reliance on peer review for the remaining subjects. The second criterion would be the impact of the research (25%) in terms of demonstrable benefits to the wider economy and society,[189] and the third the research environment within the submitted unit and its institutional environment (15%), including research grant income and the volume of research student success. A four-star rating system for the overall profile was planned, but separately starred judgements, each with its own sub-strands, were to be used for each of the three criteria listed above.

The discussion moved on in subsequent months, particularly as the reliability of impact

---

[188] Higher Education Funding Council for England, "Research Excellence Framework: Second Consultation on the Assessment and Funding of Research", 2009/38 (Bristol: HEFCE, 2009), http://www.hefce.ac.uk/pubs/hefce/2009/09_38/09_38.pdf.

[189] The HEFCE planned to undertake a pilot study of annual impact statements by each institution, as proposed by Professor Paul Wellings (REF: second consultation, Footnote 6). Early in 2011 the percentage attributable to research impact was reduced to 20%.

criteria were strongly criticised by institutions, and gradually the definition of impact was broadened and the timescale over which its effects were to be measured was extended. By the end of 2010 the REF exercise had been slowed down, with submission deferred to 2013 and the funding implications to 2015. Lancaster took part in two pilot submissions[190] to test the methodology, and inevitably the need for further refinement of the process was indicated, much as the former RAE exercises had built up their practices over successive exercises. At Lancaster there was an emphasis on the need to ensure that research impact across all disciplines was demonstrated, together with more energy put into trans-faculty research funding bids, combined with an expectation that more resources would be required for staff who would be taking part in competitive bidding.[191] The research infrastructure was also being enhanced by work on the institutional EPrints repository built to include bibliographic entries with full-text attachments wherever possible. By September 2010 Lancaster's repository was the seventh largest in the UK, and provided a firm foundation for open access to research through self-archiving.[192]

The debate about research profile and status continued rather noisily at national level, ranging from the Russell Group once more advocating research concentration at a limited number of institutions to a more widely felt concern that vital curiosity-led research could be endangered, for "Nothing good ever got invented by accident, apart from some silly fun stuff like the slinky, post-it notes, penicillin, warfarin, and X-rays".[193] Meanwhile, much energy was being invested in the necessarily never-ending renewal of Lancaster's research. To take an example from Lancaster's earliest research endeavour: the Lancaster Environment Centre, under its director Graham Harris,[194] was driving forward a set of themes based around environmental change and pollution, chemical organisms and the environment, water catchment and aquatic processes, informatics, and agriculture, starting with fundamental research but in each instance delivering specific benefits. An example was the prize-winning work by Professor Bill Davies[195] on chemical signalling in plants that helps the plant regulate the rate of growth of new shoots and thus cope with drought; this work has obvious applications in the arid conditions of mainland China and in Australia, but

---

[190] Lancaster made pilot submissions for English language and literature, to which was added linguistics because they would lack a panel of their own in REF 2014, and for physics: see SEC/2010/2/1280, paper to Senate on 14 November 2010.

[191] Trevor McMillan, "Improving our research performance and getting ready for REF" (SEC/2010/2/1280); paper to Senate on 14 November 2010.

[192] Information supplied by Michael Dunne, 1 September 2010.

[193] See, for example, "V-c: focus research cash or 'mediocrity' awaits", *Times Higher Education* (No. 1919, 22–28 October 2009), p. 6; and David Mitchell, "Pointless studies are the key to evolution", *The Observer*, 27 September 2009, p. 42. The latter article in particular resonated with many people at the time, and gained wide support.

[194] I gratefully acknowledge a discussion with Professor Harris on 6 August 2009.

[195] "Research project award of the Year", THE Awards 2009, Winners' Supplement, *Times Higher Education*, 15 October 2009: the university also won its third 2009 Queen's Anniversary Prize for this work.

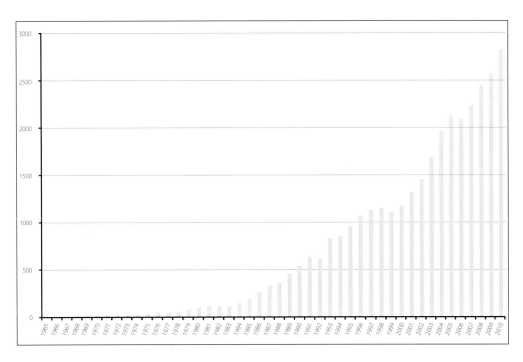

Figure 7: Research income by financial year, 1965–2010

also in parts of the USA. The Waitrose Centre for the environmentally sound production of fresh produce from a global supply base is another research centre within LEC that contributes to solutions for world-wide problems. The large research student cohort in LEC, including 33 new recruits for 2009–10, is coupled with an intention that the research should increasingly inform masters degrees and, in time, the undergraduate curriculum. Another shared collaboration, the Cockcroft Institute, has been awarded £16 million by the Science and Technology Facilities Council[196] to undertake further research into the next generation of particle accelerators that will produce more energised and intense particle beams, work that has applications in energy, security, health, and environment. The School of Health and Medicine continues to build up its research staff base and its research reputation within the region and nationally. Three doctoral training centres have been awarded to Lancaster that facilitate four doctoral years – an MRes followed by a PhD – for students in selected areas. HighWire,[197] for example, "seeks a creative fusion between three key disciplines, namely computer science, management and design", and is funded under the EPSRC Digital Economy programme with the support of both large companies and small regional

[196] LU News, 16 October 2009.
[197] http://www.highwire.lancs.ac.uk/, as at 3 December 2010.

The Lancaster Institute for the Contemporary Arts in the snow, built of European larch and officially opened in 2011

businesses. The STOR-i DTC[198] in the Management School proclaims its "ground-breaking approach to statistics and operational research", and has the funding to recruit 40 students a year. A third centre is a joint collaboration between Lancaster's Physics department and its peer department at the University of Manchester.

The Lancaster Institute for the Contemporary Arts, a participant in HighWire, has also benefited from a £10 million investment in a new building, completed late in 2010, and designed to provide performance space for art, design, music, and theatre studies.[199] The building houses the research group ImaginationLancaster, including the collaborative research project VivaCity 2020, which investigates future urban sustainability and how

[198] http://www.stor-i.lancs.ac.uk/, as at 3 December 2010.
[199] LU News, 2 October 2009.

urban dwellers and developers reach decisions that lead to such a condition, as well as how such decisions can best be influenced. A further cluster has incorporated Philosophy, Politics and International Relations, and Religious Studies into a single entity from August 2010, as an element of a wider Resilience research project in the Faculty of Arts and Social Sciences.[200]

There are many contradictory forces for any research-intensive institution to resolve, and Lancaster has its share. Established areas of strength, of which there are generous numbers within the institution, rightly expect appropriate resourcing. On the other hand, new initiatives and a new generation of researchers seek seedcorn investment, and the underlying research environment (previously the concept of a well-founded laboratory) is essential if research output is to be sustained. A recent downturn in research council grants, with plummeting rates of success for funding applications, coincided with a commercial sector that from late 2009 was retracting previous tentative overtures to universities, making the Lambert path more difficult to negotiate.

At Lancaster the strongest performers for research grant income continue to be in science and technology, a situation that in turn raises questions of how far other areas of the university can increase their rates of return and how researchers can diversify their sources of funding, especially away from reliance on the research councils and charities and towards industry and commerce. The recruitment and sound supervision of research students is a strategic priority, for they bring tactical and strategic benefits to the research groups within which they work: yet their funding and support are difficult at a time when new graduates feel impelled to work off their indebtedness rather than move to study for higher degrees, and when the threat of currency volatility worldwide and government measures to combat illicit immigration make overseas recruitment more precarious. There are more external bureaucratic impediments to research, including employment legislation, and the management of research ethics and copyright require increasing effort by principal investigators; all these constraints have to be managed without becoming insuperable obstacles to success. Nevertheless, harmonious relationships between research groups, faculties, and the centre can maximise opportunities for new initiatives at subject boundaries and contribute to a research profile of which Lancaster, exceptionally fortunate in the calibre and commitment of its researchers, can take much pride.

---

[200] Minute S.2009/48, Senate meeting on 7 October 2009; the new department was to be named Philosophy, Politics and Religion.

Finance

THIS CHAPTER WILL briefly examine the financing of the university from 1961 to the present day. It is a narrative that is by no means a smooth account of steadily rising revenues and expectations, and one in which at least five phases can be identified. First, there was the initial funding of the university and the creation of policies and procedures that were to be used for the management of the university's financial affairs from 1961 to 1978; secondly, there were the Thatcher years, with particular reference to 1979 to 1983, when Lancaster, in common with most of the sector, underwent swinging cuts and was required to move forward from them; thirdly, there was a period of prudence and growing university reputation that led to new growth in size, scale and ambition from 1984 to 1995; fourthly, there was a severe cash flow problem and recovery from this, from 1995 to 2000; and, finally, there was a decade of renewed financial vigour and confidence at the start of the new millennium, until the recession of late 2008 once again placed at hazard the finances of all universities.

The new University of Lancaster assumed responsibility for its own financial affairs on 15 December 1964, three months after the award of its Charter. For the previous three years the fledgling institution had been reliant on Lancashire County Council's infrastructure and staff for the procurement and administration of all the necessary income and expenditure, the management of capital grants, and the establishment of the foundation Appeal. The County Treasurer, Mr N. Doodson, acted as Honorary Treasurer to the Executive Council for the Establishment of a University at Lancaster, a company limited by guarantee with

the authority to receive funds and disburse them on behalf of the institution they were in the process of setting up. Indeed, early staff of the university took pride in receiving two contracts of employment: one from the county council, and one on behalf of the new university.

In acting as the banker for the Executive Council, the county council was in turn drawing on both its own funds to the tune of £50,000 per annum, together with more modest annual contributions from Westmorland County Council and the county boroughs of Barrow-in-Furness, Blackburn, Blackpool, Burnley, and Preston.[1] These sums were not treated as part of the first Appeal (see below). All external funding from the UGC and other bodies was routed through Lancashire County Council. In January 1964, however, a separate account was set up and regularly replenished by the county council, and the newly appointed Finance Officer of the university had direct access to this during the rest of the 1964 calendar year. In practice the growing band of people who were appointed to the staff of the university, starting with Charles Carter in April 1963, were closely engaged in leading and implementing the necessary planning and coordination of the university's financial affairs. It is a tribute to all concerned, given the complexity and speed of the process of establishment, that the areas of friction between county and university officers remained so

---

[1]   Para. 24, "Final Report, The University of Lancaster Appeal" (Hooker Craigmyle and Co. August 1965) (UA.1/13/1/4/1).

minor. In addition, the pre-1974 county council officers were generous in their support in kind, especially in terms of time and hospitality. They acted with impressive promptness at a senior level to deal with the numerous different categories of financial business involved, from the conversion of the Waring and Gillow factory at St Leonardsgate for temporary accommodation (£230,000) to the fee for an external assessor for the appointment of the founding professor of physics (40 guineas).

Once the university was established under its Charter it was eligible to receive recurrent grants from the UGC and to acquire the assets and liabilities from the Executive Council, including a welcome surplus of £56,000 on trading to date. In addition to recurrent and non-recurrent funds from the UGC, the university was already benefiting from the early proceeds of the Appeal, led by Lord Derby, and intended to fund aspects of the university's operation not covered by UGC funds. The ability to draw down money from this source at an early stage was important, since even such basic items as a telephone exchange or the landscaping of the Bailrigg site were not allowed for in UGC (and hence Treasury) funding.[2] On the other hand, parliamentary grants for agreed salary supplementation, rates, and other earmarked sums were made, and in addition there were student fees from the relevant local education authorities, grants from local authorities and other donations, and some small-scale research funding, of £24,000 in 1964–65, rising to £267,000 in 1972–73.[3] Nevertheless, the importance of the UGC recurrent grant in the early years of the university was paramount: in 1972–73, for example, that source represented £2.869 million from a total annual turnover of £3.855 million, and was to remain in a similar proportion until the cuts of the Thatcher years. The Finance Officer, Mr Robert Boumphrey, came into post from the University of Durham on 1 October 1963, and he was joined by an assistant finance officer and a senior clerk in January 1964, with four other junior posts added during the year. The staff of the office, which included salaries, wages, and pensions, then remained constant until 1970. At that point Mr Boumphrey became the Establishment Officer and Mr Harold White, appointed to run the management accounting function, became the Finance Officer, a post he occupied until 1992. Given the amount of manual record-keeping in the early years of the university, and the rapid growth of the institution, the determination of Charles Carter to keep his financial administration lean and mean is evident.

The vagaries of the revenue account were often politically driven, as, for example, when universities' enthusiasm for expansion in the light of the Robbins Report exceeded the government's ability to fund additional places[4] or the ability of universities to acquire other sources of funding, determining in part their ability to manage their own futures. The Appeal was thus fundamental for the provision of discretionary funding, and Lancaster's total of

---

[2] "The uses of the Appeal Fund, 1964–71", Appendix (ix) of McClintock, *Quest*, p. 419.

[3] "Selected financial information, 1964–73", Appendix (viii) of "Selected financial information, 1964–73", Appendix (viii) of McClintock, *Quest*, p. 418.

[4] Statement by Charles Carter to the Executive Council, meeting of 26 November 1963.

£2.2 million, achieved by January 1967, was the second-highest of the seven new universities.[5] Lord Derby was involved throughout. The process had begun in the spring of 1961, when county council officers wrote to numerous organisations for support in principle to back up their assertion of a regional desire for a new university, and asked them demonstrate their essential financial support. Early in 1962, however, Sir Frank Bower, CBE, who was personally known to the Lancashire County Council chairman Sir Alfred Bates, volunteered to help with the fundraising. He was co-opted onto the Executive Council, and thence onto an informal sub-committee, to work on an appeal. The files of correspondence[6] reveal his tireless efforts to identify facilities or services that would not be eligible for government funding, as well as his stream of suggestions about who might be approached and how; for, in his view, an appeal should have been launched concurrently with the other earliest moves of the Academic Planning Board and the Executive Council. He was persuaded to wait until the first vice-chancellor had taken up his post, but then renewed his calls for rapid action.

In the meantime, Sir Frank sought to obtain clarity from the UGC about its position on what supplementary funds a university might add, from its own discretionary funds, to a grant-aided building. As he noted, the reply from Sir Cecil Syers re-expounded the problem rather than suggested solutions, and hence did not provide the necessary guidance: "We are thrown back on our imagination – which is rather a shaky foundation for a prospectus."[7] Sir Cecil had indeed identified three types of building project: entirely publicly funded; entirely privately funded; and those combining both types. While acknowledging that all three types might attract grants for furnishing, equipment and/or fees, he indicated that the UGC

> can and do recommend grants for such things as playing fields, sports pavilions, reasonable recreation facilities (e.g. gymnasia). But they cannot do everything, and it rests with each university to make a list of its own priorities ... Private benefaction comes in to supplement this and to speed up the attainment of things which cannot be provided for in what I may call the programme from public funds. The most obvious case, in relation particularly to the new universities (although it also applies to existing universities) is halls of residence. As you know, the Committee have had to take the line in relation to the new universities that they must do first things first and assist those universities to obtain the essential nucleus of academic buildings (lecture theatres, laboratories, student and staff amenity buildings, etc.) and cannot in the initial stages provide money for halls of residence – if only in fairness to those existing universities which still have so low a percentage of students in residence.[8]

Sir Frank also undertook a survey of other universities' contemporaneous appeals. Their targets seem modest – £400,000 at Southampton and £500,000 at both Nottingham and

---

[5] Michael Sanderson, *The History of the University of East Anglia, Norwich* (London: Hambledon and London, 2002), p. 55. The final total was £2.579 million.
[6] See UA.1/13/1/5/2.
[7] F. Bower to C. P. H. McCall, 7 January 1963 (UA.1/13/1/5/2).
[8] Sir Cecil Syer to F. Bower, 2 January 1963 (UA.1/13/1/5/2).

Birmingham – and their results show varying levels of success in attaining even these levels. Occasionally appeals exceeded the target, as at Sussex, for example, where professional fundraisers were not used and where the bulk of the work was undertaken by the vice-chancellor and the chairman of his Council, John (later Sir John) Fulton commented:

> We aimed at £500,000 and in fact have got quite close to the million mark. We regard this as being a good result in a County that has no great industrial wealth, though as you know there are many wealthy residents.[9]

Sussex had also benefited from being the first of the seven new universities, with all the attendant publicity that brought, for, by contrast, potential donors approached to support Lancaster commented that they could not fund all the new institutions and did not know how to choose between them. One positive result of the survey, however, was that Sir Frank conceded the need for a six-month preparation period, as well as acknowledging that he could not run an appeal in Lancashire while living in Essex.

Gradually an appeal brochure was assembled and approved.[10] In March 1964 Hooker Craigmyle and Company were appointed as fundraisers, and Colonel W. B. Shine came to Lancaster to lead the Appeal for the next eighteen months. At first he had a shared office in Bailrigg Mansion, but after a couple of months the lodge at the entrance from the A.6 (later demolished) was given over to his work. A target of £2 million was announced, of which £1.5 million was to be for capital works and £0.5 million for endowment, but at the last moment the Vice-Chancellor had the target increased to £2.5 million. A total of 25 regional groups was identified, stretching in pre-1974 Lancashire as far south as Wigan, Widnes, Rochdale, and St Helens, and north to Westmorland (although not to Cumberland);[11] only Accrington, Burnley and Liverpool failed to appoint to their groups. In his final report Colonel Shine paid tribute to all the regional chairmen, whom he described as "in most cases, of a high order. It was on these key men that the main task of organising and maintaining the enthusiasm of their local group of Stewards depended … Stewards were recruited by the Regional Chairmen and, although some fell by the wayside and were replaced, it is certain that not all Chairmen were as well served by their Stewards as the Chairmen served the Appeal Organisers."[12] Indeed, while 62% of chairmen themselves subscribed, only 30% of stewards did so. The local authorities, who had already contributed generously to the setting up costs, were prevailed upon also to contribute to the Appeal, although the Lancashire County Council gift of £0.5 million for The County College set a special example.

Other significant gifts included £70,000 from the British Institute of Marketing for a

---

9   J. S. Fulton to F. Bower, 14 November 1963 (UA.1/13/1/5/2).

10 "The University of Lancaster 1966 The First Seven Year Plan 1971" (November 1964).

11 Cumberland County Council did, however, contribute £1000 per annum: see W. B. Shine, "Final Report, the University of Lancaster Appeal" (Hooker Craigmyle, August 1965), para. 98(g).

12 W. B. Shine, "Final Report, the University of Lancaster Appeal" (Hooker Craigmyle, August 1965), paras. 82–3.

chair in that subject, the cost of building the Chaplaincy Centre from the churches, a grant from the Nuffield Foundation for the Nuffield Theatre Studio and Workshop, and funding from Turner and Newall for a travel fund for academic staff research. Notwithstanding the UGC explanation to Sir Frank Bower, the university still had to find £188,844 for indoor and outdoor recreational facilities, and in practice the Nuffield Theatre has been used as a laboratory just as much as any science facility. On the other hand, despite denying that halls of residence could be funded, the UGC was prepared to assist with the first Lancaster college, to be named Bowland,[13] showing the extent to which the committee was able at the 1960s scale of university development to act flexibly and use discretion. And of the £12 million building programme of 1964–74, £1.6 million came from the Appeal[14] rather than the £2 million originally suggested, leaving the university able to use the rest on the establishment of chairs and other valuable facilities.[15]

A Finance Committee established by the Council met for the first time on 8 January 1965, with Mr P. F. Scott as chairman,[16] and held seven scheduled meetings in 1964–65. Besides the formal business, including the reappointment of Barnett, Crewdson and Company of Manchester as the external auditors, the policy-setting included an agreement that the Department of Operational Research, because of its revenue-generating capabilities from commercial contracts, be allowed to keep its own accounts.[17] A report from the Vice-Chancellor laid out the position on non-recurrent expenditure at each meeting, and the capital works programme was consistently a major agenda item, closely followed by issues relating to staffing, from procedures for redundancy for short-term contracts to payments for staff training and education. Sometimes less weighty matters found their way into the business: for example, a payment of £11 15 shillings for moving the car of a new member of staff from Belfast to Heysham.[18] By June 1966 the Hazelrigg site of 152 acres had been purchased for £37,462[19] and tenancy agreements for the land and properties settled. A request by Professor Bevington of Chemistry that Lansil donations of £11,000 should be allocated exclusively to fund chemistry research students, rather than contribute to the shared chemistry and physics building complex, was not approved, but permission was given for the Students' Council to receive part of the £8 per student per annum fee from

---

[13] The UGC contributed £580,000 to Bowland College, and the Appeal Fund put in £48,000: see Building Programme 2A, Appendix V, Finance Committee agenda of 13 June 1966.

[14] McClintock, *Quest*, Appendices (vii) and (ix).

[15] A notable early individual donor was John Welch, after whom a room is named in University House, who had served on the Lancashire County Council and been its chairman for a period; two of his children also followed his example.

[16] Mr Scott (1917–2010), made CBE in 1982, served as chairman of the committee until July 1983. He was also a generous donor to the university.

[17] The separate accounts for Operational Research, Marketing and Systems Engineering came to an end in 1971, when university companies were established. They in turn were laid down in the 1980s.

[18] Minute 11 of Finance Committee, 8 January 1965.

[19] Some adjacent woodland was later purchased at a further cost of £1850.

local education authorities. Fee levies were often under discussion: for lodgings, for external examiners, for external examination invigilators, or for higher degree awards, as well as their remission to certain categories of graduate students. Subcommittees were set up for assistant staff, and separately for technical staff, but the Finance Committee was itself expected to pronounce on maternity leave provision, holidays and overtime pay, and Saturday work for Library staff, and approval was given for a Staff Association and for a grant of £100 for the first year of a university publication, *Continuum*.[20]

The accounts for the first year (1964–65) retrospectively took in part of the period for which the Executive Council had held responsibility, i.e. 1 August to 14 December 1964, and showed a turnover of £334,000. A particular difficulty related to the sole computer, for which the university had received a UGC grant of £100,000[21] as well as a building to house it. The choice of machine was a 16K ICT 1909, but it fell to the professor of mathematics to point out that the word computer referred to

> a complex of electronic and mechanical equipment which performs logical and arithmetic operations on suitably coded information. It does not include the equipment ... which translates instructions and data into patterns of punched holes on card or tape [that] are examples of what are known as 'peripherals',[22]

and which would cost the university a further £14,000.

The balance sheet total at the end of the first full year of the university's operation, on 31 July 1966, was £2.753 million. The most expensive department to run was Physics, at a cost of £48,452: on the other hand, the department had brought in a third of the year's research grants for the university, a proportion that rose to over half during 1967–68. There were growing unexpended balances of departmental allocations, as well as a practice of carrying funds forward to which departments clung tenaciously over the years, and which persisted to the early years of the twenty-first century. Salaries of teaching staff totalled £189,578; those of technicians, clerks, "and other subordinate staff" came to £32,939. There was an agreement in principle to establish a post office at Bailrigg: initially this was housed close to Bowland Tower, before a move close to the Library, where it continues to give invaluable service to the whole university community, and especially overseas students.

During 1966–67 more of the material on staffing policies and their implementation was contained in subcommittee minutes that came as reports to the Finance Committee, although there were still occasions on which such items as non-standard promotions or an individual's removal expenses appeared on the main agenda. Non-recurrent grants continued to be a major preoccupation, and the terms on which shops and other commercial

---

[20] See UA.1/14.

[21] To gauge the relative cost of the computer, a comparison may be made with Phase 1 of the Library, at a building cost of £152,000. Once established, of course, computers then became a constant budgetary item, growing ever more powerful, more indispensable, and more expensive.

[22] E. H. Lloyd to the Finance Committee, 1 May 1966.

The east end of the newly refurbished Alexandra Square, May 2011.

premises would occupy prime space around Alexandra Square were discussed and refined at each meeting. There was pessimism about how the anticipated recurrent grant for 1967–68, £200,000 short of the anticipated sum,[23] would limit the size of the student intake, and a concern that if there were to be only 1550 students by the end of the first decade, rather than the 3000 anticipated, negative consequences would result both for the staff–student ratio and the level of non-recurrent grant. The Vice-Chancellor, correctly, was consistently concerned about the university reaching a certain critical physical size, even if it meant some over-capacity for a while, on a site where there was no choice but to build new any space that was needed. The staff–student ratio was negotiable, in his view, provided that some favour was shown to the sciences while they achieved subject coverage: the loss of whole buildings would not have been.

In the event the university achieved the 3000 target before the ten years were up, but not before there was heightened concern over the furniture and equipment allocation. It is necessary to remember that, in the 1960s, the UGC was allocating funds against detailed schedules that it had earlier appraised, and that allowances for furniture and fittings in new

---

[23] CFC, "Recurrent grant 1967–68" (S/66/156, December 1966), paper to the Finance Committee, meeting on 13 March 1967.

buildings appeared under the same budget line as pieces of specialised scientific equipment. The problem came to light early in 1967, when the Vice-Chancellor informed the Senate that the UGC proposed to "implement, with immediate effect, a system of rationing of money for equipment and furniture, which will be superimposed on (and will in effect supersede) the present arrangements for equipment grants. This is in preparation for the introduction in 1968 of a block grant for equipment related to student numbers, and not to ascertained needs",[24] and he made a request for information that would substantiate a claim for a supplementary ration. The tenor of the replies he received from senior colleagues can be gauged from his letter to the chairman of the UGC, pointing out that the university would receive £422,000 for a 15-month period, instead of the estimated expenditure of over £900,000, to cover furniture for new buildings and scientific equipment for departments about to teach third-year students for the first time, as well as carrying out their research. He went on:

> I cannot exaggerate the anger and bitterness of science staff who find, after being advised by the UGC itself not to hurry purchases of equipment, that money is no longer available to meet purchases from lists which your Committee has already approved on the advice of assessors … Nor do we, on the administrative side of the university, find it easy to understand how the UGC can claim that it still recognises an obligation to furnish new buildings, if its grants are so far short of the sum required to do this.
>
> I am at my wits end to know what we can do about this problem, unless your reserve for special needs proves to be of exceptionally generous size.[25]

A partial supplementary grant was received later in the year, and budgets adjusted accordingly, but the episode demonstrated the level of uncertainty that the new institution had to contend with. On the other hand, the UGC could be swift and effective in its *ad hoc* support: for example, in July 1967 the Finance Committee was told that a non-recurrent grant of £18,920 had been made for the freehold purchase from Treasury funds of 88 acres at Barker House Farm for sports facilities, on which the Alexandra Park residences would later be built; probably one of the best value for money acquisitions ever made by the university.

Another issue that would become more significant as the years went by was the government's realisation that income from overseas students was growing in value, but was not consistently levied. The university was therefore informed that, from the beginning of the 1967–68 academic year, there must be a minimum charge of £250 a year for all newly admitted overseas students.[26] The Secretary of State promised the House of Commons further guidance on what was to become a contentious political issue, and this was released

---

[24] CFC, Memorandum to All Heads of Departments, 9 February 1967; paper to Finance Committee, meeting on 13 March 1967.

[25] C. F. Carter to Sir John Wolfenden, 6 April 1967; paper to Finance Committee, meeting on 10 April 1967.

[26] Minute FC.4/12, Finance Committee meeting of 9 January 1967.

in April, accompanied by some softening of additional payments by students already in the UK.[27] Not surprisingly, the government then had to set up a balancing fund, via the British Council, to cover the fees of students from developing countries,[28] while internally the university had to learn how to assess the financial status of overseas students in line with complex rules.

The management of the colleges was becoming an increasing issue. At the university's inception they had been given a degree of financial autonomy not granted to the departments, including their own bank accounts and audited annual accounts, as well as decision-making powers about clerical and portering staff.[29] The need for consistency of treatment across the university in charges levied and facilities offered became increasingly important, however, beginning with residence charges. When the university was arranging commercially sponsored residences for Cartmel and Furness colleges (see Chapter 7), the Vice-Chancellor became aware that students living in such blocks would have a self-service tenancy, by contrast to the services provided in accommodation funded by the UGC or the university. Again, three of the five colleges established by 1968 wished to have weekly cleaning of rooms but no compulsion to take meals in college, one had no views, while the fifth (County College) wished to insist on students taking breakfast and at least one other meal in college every day, and to have full room cleaning.[30] At first the intention had been to provide university catering in every college, but while physical provision was made at Bowland, Lonsdale, and Cartmel the space earmarked for catering in County was re-allocated before the building work began, and no such provision was made in subsequent colleges. Self-service facilities were being developed in parallel with large refectories, and snack bars also began opening around the campus for all users. Not surprisingly, the catering deficit began to grow and by July 1968, when it had reached £12,000, the Finance Committee decided to offer incoming students contracts whereby they would receive heavily subsidised meals if they undertook to enter the scheme for the whole academic year,[31] a scheme that was once again short-lived.

The Finance Committee was also invited to take an interest in two broader issues. The first was a summary by the UGC of its evolving funding policy:[32] broadly, that undergraduate numbers would run slightly ahead of Robbins figures (i.e. up to 225,000 places by 1971–72),

---

[27] Administrative Memorandum 14/67, Department of Education and Science; paper to Finance Committee, meeting on 9 May 1967.

[28] British Council, Overseas Students' Fees Award Scheme; paper of 3 January 1968 to the Finance Committee, meeting on 8 January 1968.

[29] The Exchequer and Audit report of 1968 noted that the annual turnover of each college would shortly rise to around £30,000 per annum, and this is borne out by extant County College accounts to 31 July 1973.

[30] Minute FC.8/5, Finance Committee meeting of 12 June 1967: readers should bear in mind for the rest of this chapter that a catering deficit was a regular feature of many of the annual accounts.

[31] CFC, "Catering Policy" (VC/68/261; paper to Finance Committee on 8 July 1968).

[32] J. F. Wolfenden, Letter to Vice-Chancellors of 13 November 1967; paper to Finance Committee on 11 December 1967.

but in arts-based rather than science-based subjects, in line with current Advanced Level trends; that undergraduate provision would take precedence at the relative expense of postgraduate courses; that more collaboration between universities and other sectors of higher education would be encouraged; that indicated rather than earmarked grants, e.g. for university libraries, would signal UGC areas of preference; and that, broadly speaking, the time had come to an end as far as the additional selection of academic areas was concerned, and universities should develop what they had rather than attempt to diversify. This demand-led emphasis on arts subjects would, of course, lay up problems for the future.

The second general issue was to be of great long-term importance to all universities, including Lancaster. The expansion of the universities, from a cost of £4 million per annum just after World War II to £200 million by 1967, meant that this head of HM Treasury expenditure had been signalled as substantial to the House of Commons and was ruled to fall properly under the inspection of the Comptroller and Auditor General, who was to be given access to the books and records of the UGC and the universities with effect from 1 August 1967.[33] As predicted, Lancaster was one of a half-dozen places visited and, not unsurprisingly, some issues were found,[34] including the level of external charges levied by Operational Research for services rendered, the lapse of departmental inventories and stock records, little sign of joint purchasing between departments, and the apparent absence of the provision of financial information from the centre to the colleges. Satisfactory answers to all these queries were supplied, and although the chairman of the UGC felt able to congratulate everyone on the mutual goodwill and usefulness of the exercise, the undermining of university autonomy – even if justified – was keenly felt in subsequent years, particularly when coupled with procedural guidance for universities to incorporate into their regulations.[35]

Fig 9 (see page 222) shows the annual turnover of Lancaster from 1964 onwards, and the progressive increases in volume. After the first five years of policy-making the work of the Finance Committee became more routine, although with the exercise of a general purposes function that was recognised briefly in its title during the 1980s and 1990s. In addition to regular business, the committee also had responsibility for initial consideration of quinquennial submissions to the UGC.

The explanatory memorandum[36] accompanying the figures for 1972–77 gives a useful snapshot, for by 1971 student numbers had reached 3000, an achievement assisted by the increasing proportion of graduate students on one-year courses, especially in business studies. The memorandum was nevertheless at pains to point out that the university had met and exceeded the undergraduate targets it had been set, including the new category

---

[33] CVCP, "University Accountability" (undated, unsigned); circulated to the Finance Committee on 11 December 1967.

[34] D. A. Dewar to A. S. Jeffreys, 10 May 1968 (FO.68/10/211); paper to Finance Committee on 10 June 1968.

[35] J. F. Wolfenden to Vice-Chancellors, 23 December 1968; paper to Finance Committee on 10 March 1969.

[36] Appendix to FO/71/165, Finance Committee meeting of 16 September 1971.

of 75 Junior Year Abroad students from the USA. Welcome was given by the committee to a suggestion by the UGC that student numbers should rise to 5400 by 1976–77, with an academic and related staff of 620, coupled with a request that the science-based students in the total should rise above 1900, "since our proportion of science and technology is so much below the national average". The increase in student numbers would, the UGC was assured, require no further site works, while commercially funded residences or a local reserve of lodgings would provide the necessary student residence provision. The university was, however, resistant to any further worsening of its staff–student ratio, since "Members of staff at a university like Lancaster work for long hours. We do not believe that it is possible, either by an increase of effort or by a better organisation of work, to achieve further economies. We cannot think it is the university's duty to plan to do its job less well." After a summary of current subject mix and expansion (see Chapter 3), the document summarised anticipated expenditure as 63% for academic departments, 11% for maintenance of premises, and 8% for the Library; a healthy balance. The annual cost per student in 1971–72 was approximately £870, and Lancaster was able to demonstrate that its costs were contained in line with other new universities. Non-recurrent funding for music and visual arts was requested – the Nuffield Theatre being already in place for Theatre Studies – as well as additional teaching accommodation for psychology and biochemistry.

The quinquennial settlement for 1972–77 did not, however, reach the university until January 1973. The accompanying letter to the Vice-Chancellor,[37] although described as a framework within which universities would run their own affairs with a minimum of detailed direction, nevertheless ran to fifteen closely spaced pages containing both general and institution-specific requirements. In particular, the UGC was not prepared to allow much increase in postgraduate numbers, and was particularly unwilling to offer them for science students, on the grounds that provision there had already grown rapidly, was expensive, and did not allow for what was seen as an urgent need for additional postgraduates in social sciences and business studies. The balanced growth that Lancaster was seeking became distorted by this outcome, a shift that contributed in later years to a perception that the sciences could not grow and might therefore be discounted in the overall profile of the university.[38]

The letter also made reference to further allowance for increased costs, for it was issued just as a period of sharp inflation, triggered by rapid increases in international oil prices, was taking off. The effects of the rapid inflation were destabilising. Costs rose sharply but unevenly across heads of expenditure, while supplementation lagged behind. Staff mortgages became relatively cheaper, but that effect depended on rapidly rising salaries against a volatile retail price index. Student costs, including rent, moved into double figures, and even into mid-year as well as annual increases, sparking rent disputes that affected

[37] Kenneth Berill to Vice-Chancellor, 15 January 1972 (UGC 24/44/04); paper to Finance Committee meeting of 22 February 1973.

[38] See the discussions of the Academic Planning Committee in the mid-1990s.

cash flow and brought unwelcome disciplinary action in their train (see Chapter 4). The Student Representative Council also suffered sharp increases in costs without compensating additional income and moved into deficit, particularly on salaries. The remaining financial autonomy of the colleges, already under pressure, became untenable as the costs of catering, the prices of and income from conferences, relative increases in salaries and wages, and problems with income from staff flats meant that special treatment for them was finally ruled to be out of order, and they were required to be fully integrated into standard university systems.[39] While the university had set about building up reserves which, under prevailing accounting practice, could be carried forward, any money not spent rapidly diminished in value, undermining the customary prudence of the institution. Finally, the quinquennial system of funding universities by the UGC was replaced by an annual cash-limited grant, with grant levels for the succeeding three years indicated rather than assured. All in all, the years of steep inflation were difficult for Lancaster, except for some relative decreases in the costs of the loan-financed residences.

These inflationary pressures and consequential instabilities paled into insignificance, however, in comparison with the government squeeze on universities under the premiership of Margaret Thatcher from May 1979 onwards. John Ashworth, a senior civil servant whom the University of Salford was fortunate enough to acquire as its vice-chancellor just as the severest of the cuts fell in July 1981, has repeatedly labelled this period as a time of opportunity and transformation for Salford, with the implication that it also was for others.[40] Salford's reduction, of 44% in a UGC recurrent grant that made up 84% of the university's income, was particularly savage, and puts into perspective the 15.5% of about 77% that Lancaster suffered. Nevertheless, the short-, medium- and long-term effects on Lancaster were profound and permanent, and the tenor of the university never quite recovered its earlier optimism and vitality. The period of principal difficulty, from 1979 to 1983, coincided with much of the vice-chancellorship of Professor Philip Reynolds, and his full and frank annual reports to the Court provide an excellent overview of a tense financial period for the university.

One early warning sign was pressure from the Students' Union for an increase of 20% in its share of the *per capita* annual fee that came to universities, in proportion to student numbers, for their general support. This request was coupled with concerns about the funding of *Scan*, as well as reluctance by the university to underwrite the leasing of the Sugar House in Lancaster as a nightclub and social venue or to support the Community Action Group.[41] The difficulties over funding of student-directed facilities was increased by a DES decision to move the financing of student unions from the student awards system to the

---

[39] The final independent college bank account, for Cartmel College, was closed in 1978. Two cottages in Galgate, purchased from Cartmel bar profits, were not sold by the university until the summer of 2003, however.

[40] John Ashworth, "How to take a financial crisis and turn it to your advantage", *Times Higher Education*, 26 November – 2 December 2009 (No. 1924), pp. 26–7.

[41] Finance Committee, meetings of 8 May 1979, 8 September 1979 and 8 November 1979.

general recurrent grant, with effect from 1981–82, for each institution to distribute as it saw fit.[42] Thus in future students' unions would be regarded as one amongst a range of student facilities to compete for funding, rather than as the recipients of sums that were to some extent earmarked.[43] The resistance of campus traders to the idea that a Students' Union shop be established, on the grounds that they were to be proof against further competitive outlets until the university population exceeded 10,000, was, however, not upheld.

By late 1979 some departments were overspending their annual allocations, technicians' pay rose by 13% to compensate for previous under-provision, and the unit of resource per student had began its inexorable decline. In June 1979 the new government reduced the total universities' grant, announced only the previous month, by £9 million, while at the same time raising overseas student fees by 22%, after places had been accepted and in addition to the 9% increase already applied to this income stream. The required increase in fees, however, then triggered a decrease in UGC allocation in anticipation of the additional income, while also requiring that any scheme of bursaries had to be funded from non-UGC sources. Moreover, these moves were followed in October by UGC advice to restrict 1980 student admissions to 94% of the 1979 total,[44] thus creating further unease.

Lancaster's approach to the impending storm was an attempt during 1980 to manage the position, with a forecast deficit of £0.5 million in 1983–84, by making anticipatory moves. These proposals included what the Vice-Chancellor described, perhaps rather euphemistically, as "a detailed survey of the work of all departments, services, and the administration and the colleges with a view to identifying changes in our arrangements or to our academic provision that could be made with least damage to fundamental purposes".[45] A touring inquisition by the Development Committee led to recommendations for the phasing out of certain programmes, moves that were hotly resisted and that received adverse national publicity.

The new calendar year of 1981 was marked by a letter from the UGC warning universities that there would be a further £30 million reduction in the grant to universities for 1981–82, thus compounding the difficulties arising from the overseas student fee changes and leading the UGC to observe that "the orderly development of the system is now threatened by a rapid reductions in resources of such a magnitude that the Committee's legitimate role and duty to offer guidance to universities based on its acquired knowledge of the system as a whole now assumes a new importance", and that, therefore,

> The Committee invites universities to undertake their planning for the 1981/82 academic year on the basis that the relevant grant allocations for many universities will not be sufficient to enable them to maintain all existing commitments … The Committee intends in its letters of grant allocation, to be issued next Spring, to give guidance to

---

[42] "New arrangements for Student Union financing", DES press release, 5 February 1980 (Finance Committee agenda for 12 February 1980).

[43] Minute FC.80/4, Finance Committee meeting on 12 February 1980.

[44] Fifteenth Annual Report of the Acting Vice-Chancellor to Court, meeting on 15 December 1979.

[45] Sixteenth Annual Report of the Vice-Chancellor to Court, 13 December 1980, pp. 1–2.

universities on home student numbers distributed between arts, science and technology, and medicine. These figures ... are likely to imply a total home university population in 1983–84 not very different from that in 1980–81 ... The Committee believes that it is of great importance that all members of your university should be made aware of the financial constraints under which universities will have to operate ...[46]

The forebodings of the UGC were realised in a White Paper of March 1981, leading to the notorious cuts across the sector in July. In Lancaster's case the cumulative effect of withdrawal of funding that was deemed to relate to overseas student fee increases, a general reduction in grant (presumed by government to be about 8.5% across the board), and reduction of home student numbers was to be £1.6 million per annum at 1981–82 prices by 1983–84 – i.e. some 15.5% of the UGC grant over three years. In addition, the UGC had overpaid recurrent grant for 1980–81, and Lancaster's £480,000 share of the overpayment was to be clawed back over three years. Most of the proposals for retrenchment that the Senate had put to one side a year earlier returned to the live agenda, coupled with plans for a teaching staff reduction of about 70, at an average cost of £16,000 each, in addition to the 21 posts already frozen.[47] Furthermore, the UGC was at last seeking to correct the implications of the declining numbers of science students,[48] so that staff reductions were to be felt most keenly where teaching loads were heaviest. The sole redeeming feature of the announcement was that some of the costs of voluntary severance and early retirement would be met by the UGC.

In addition to staff losses and other means of reducing the salary bill such as no-pay leave, heads of services around the university were asked to consider the effect on their provision if cuts of 8%, 12%, or 16% were made. The response from the Library was not atypical:

> The Library is central to the work of teaching and research in the university. It provides a range of services to suit the needs of all its users from the newest student to the most advanced research worker. It follows that that any level of cut on an already economical service will diminish the effort of every Library user.[49]

In practice, because services such as the Library had already been cut in the late 1970s, the main reductions in 1981–82 were in academic departments, and included closures of some (see Chapter 3) together with reductions in departmental resources of all kinds. Additionally, there was an almost complete absence of new appointments for several years, particularly because Lancaster's first bid for new blood posts was unsuccessful. Student numbers declined from 5017 in 1981–82 to 4706 in 1984–85, and only again passed the 5000 level in

---

[46] E. W. Parkes to the Vice-Chancellor, 30 December 1980.

[47] FO/81/63, Finance Committee agenda of 18 September 1981.

[48] Lancaster's projection for 1983–84 showed it as having the lowest proportion of science and technology of any university in the UK: see Development Committee report to the Senate (R/81/57), p. 4.

[49] A. I. MacBean and Arthur Davies (LD/81/27a) to the Finance Committee, 12 January 1982.

Waiting for the bus, early 1970s: the underpass below Alexandra Square, specifically designed to accommodate double-decker buses (copyright, John Donat/RIBA Photographs Collection)

1987–88.[50] The building programme came to a dead stop, in part because staff and student numbers and the overall volume of activity were not increasing, and little maintenance was undertaken. By September 1982, however, the Vice-Chancellor was able to report on a "significant and unexpected surplus" for 1981–82, and a year later to:

> a firm foundation upon which to build anew, if further financial shocks are not around the corner. The chairman of the Finance Committee will report how the anticipation of a deficit before the year began was by the middle of the year turned round to expectation of a surplus, partly because of the speed and effectiveness of our economies programme, partly because our overseas student numbers held up very much better than we expected, and partly because the generous endorsement by the John Fisher Foundation of a chair in electronic engineering helped us to persuade the UGC that our science and engineering target should be increased by 40, an increase that brought with it a significant increase in grant.[51]

The next few years were not so financially dramatic. The university felt able to invest

[50] Fig. 9 of McClintock, "The University of Lancaster: the First Thirty Years" (Lecture of 27 July 1994).
[51] Nineteenth Annual Report of the Vice-Chancellor to Court, 17 December 1983.

some of its own funds in the development of research for a limited period (see Chapter 5), and efforts were made to generate additional income by, for example, the establishment of a Commercial and Industrial Development Bureau,[52] increases in prices to research funders where possible, conference and holiday lettings of college accommodation, and the continual revisiting of fees and other charges that the university could make. There were also negotiations in 1983–84 on the feasibility of establishing a business park on university land although, perhaps fortunately for the university, the scheme foundered on technical difficulties and did not go ahead.[53]

Nevertheless, the financial pressures persisted. In June 1985 the Vice-Chancellor reported that all but two academic vacancies had been frozen and non-academic budget heads had been cut back to the point where the prudent maintenance of the estate and compliance with legislation were under contention. The university would therefore enter the 1985 86 financial year with a deficit budget on the general revenue account,[54] along with a plan to reduce expenditure by about £0.5 million a year, starting in 1986–87, by a saving of between 60 to 80 posts a year. Such a declaration is less alarming, however, when it is understood that the figures relate to the year's general revenue turnover, and leave out of account the general revenue reserve of £1.69 million, built up between 1981 and 1984.[55] Furthermore, the stated accounting policy of the university in each year from 1980 to 1988 was that the university was a non-profit-making institution whose financial reporting was to demonstrate the proper use of the resources received and used, rather than the determination of net income.[56] In other words, the acquisition of annual surpluses was not part of the planning process in the 1980s, and a breakeven position was acceptable. When consideration of the preliminary 1986–87 estimates took place, however, there "was some debate about the level of deficit that would be acceptable as a planning target" and a view "that the only prudent course was to aim at reducing the deficit to about £0.5 million as indicated by Council".[57] At the end of the year an improvement led to what was essentially a breakeven position on general revenue, although the reserve was raided for equipment funding for both teaching and research.[58]

Matters had not improved when the budget assumptions for 1987–88 resulted in an initial projected deficiency of £1.9 million, including increases in USS contributions and a possible 7% pay award. The Finance Committee, declaring that assumption to be unacceptable, agreed to require SPARC to reduce the £1.9 million to £600,000, principally from academic departments and services. A process of voluntary premature retirements was put in place, together with a so-called cash economy that devolved more responsibility to departments and required them to live within their means, using solutions appropriate for their particular

---

[52] Minute FC.84/43, Finance Committee meeting of 8 May 1984.

[53] Minute FC.84/75, Finance Committee meeting of 25 September 1984.

[54] Minute FC.85/50 and FC.85/71, Finance Committee meeting of 19 June 1985.

[55] Report of the Chairman of the Finance Committee, Annual Accounts for 1984–85, p. 1.

[56] See the introductory material to the Annual Accounts of 1980 to 1988.

[57] Minute FC.86/45, Finance Committee meeting on 17 June 1986.

[58] Report of the Chairman of the Finance Committee, *Annual Accounts for 1986–87*, p. 1.

circumstances, but with an eye to cuts in academic salaries.[59] The draft Academic Plan captured the tone of the discussions:

The financial outlook is very serious:

(a) In 1986–87 the deficit on revenue account is expected to be about £276,000;
(b) In 1987–88 the revenue account deficit at current levels of activity would be £1.9 million, effectively exhausting our free reserves by April/May 1988.

This is unacceptable to Finance Committee and Council …

(c) Financial projections beyond 1987–88 are necessarily more speculative but the estimated annual deficits are:
  – In 1988–89 £2.2 million
  – In 1989–90 £2.9 million

On these figures, the accumulated overall deficit by July 1990 would be about £5.3 million.

Our present estimate is that, if the University is to balance its books by the end of the present planning period [i.e. up to July 1990], we need by then to reduce academic staff costs by the equivalent of about 55 posts as well as to reduce annual expenditure under other heads by some £0.9 million, or to generate equivalent amounts of new income.[60]

The measures taken to reduce the deficit, however, particularly the early departure of staff, did not match the predictions and by February 1988 the Finance Committee was declaring itself "very concerned" about expenditure levels and "the real possibility of a 1988–89 deficit that will more than exhaust our accumulated revenue balance", and repeating its view that most of the savings must now be made by the academic departments.[61] Career consultants were hired, there was talk of possible Council action on compulsory redundancy, and the Deputy Vice-Chancellor (Professor J. H. Shennan) was asked to head a Committee on Departmental Staffing – popularly known as "Joe's Destaffing Committee" – to review all departments with potential deficits. At the end of the financial year, however, the Treasurer[62] was able to announce a net deficit of £164,000 before transfers to reserves, or £626,000 after transfers against a forecast to the UGC of £938,000, while predicting two further years of

[59] "Cash economy" (FO/87/16 (revised)) and "Notes on points … of the cash economy system", Finance Committee of 16 June 1987.
[60] Paras. 3.1 to 3.3, University of Lancaster, Academic Plan (GM/87/307, revised June 1987), Finance Committee agenda of 16 June 1987.
[61] Minute FC.88/2, Finance Committee, meeting on 19 February 1988.
[62] The term Treasurer was briefly used for the chairmen of the Finance Committee from 1987 to 1996.

deficits and a break-even position in the third year. The college accounts were now in credit, and there was some modest capital expenditure to provide for residential rooms for second year Charlotte Mason students who were to be taught at Bailrigg[63] (see Chapter 7).

The high level of concern continued unabated during 1988–89 and, despite substantial increases in research funding and success with a further round of new blood posts, the year ended with a net deficit of £800,000, leaving only £0.2 million in the general revenue reserves but no less than £1.48 million across certain departmental reserves. For the first time the suggestion was made that departmental reserves should be redistributed around all academic areas, which elicited the predictable response: instead, departmental allocations were reduced all round in order to make some contribution to a fund for capital expenditure.[64] The Treasurer noted that Council was determined to keep the 1989–90 deficit as low as possible, despite the discomfort that this would cause, and he also drew attention to the "need for capital spending from revenue on building … if the University is to meet the objectives of the Strategic Plan",[65] an acknowledgement that new building could no longer be deferred. The Vice-Chancellor also warned the Council that the UFC had expressed some anxiety about Lancaster's financial forecasts, and that the institution was one of 13 universities causing them some concern.[66]

The 1988–89 financial year was also important for two external changes. The first was a move towards satisfying a new SORP that would, after a transitional period, require institutions to operate a single income and expenditure account, rather than the separate accounts for general revenue, equipment and furniture, colleges, and appeal fund that Lancaster had been used to operating. Thereafter, despite the stated misgivings of the Treasurer, an annual depreciation figure was to be included in the accounts. The second was the discussion around a Financial Memorandum that would, from 1 June 1989, constitute a financial contract between the university and the UFC and determine the conditions under which payments would be made by the latter to the former.[67] In the years to come the document would be refined and enlarged, and would become fundamental to the relationship between the university and its funding council.

The accounts for 1989–90 showed a small but gratifying surplus of £88,000, after setting aside £100,000 for future building projects, thus bringing the accumulated balance to £301,000[68] on a turnover of just over £40 million. Research income was also reported to have grown by a further 20%. This was the moment at which the university first ventured into private sector funding for capital building projects, with a scheme for the original

---

[63] Treasurer's Report, *Annual Accounts for 1987–88* (December 1988), p. 1.

[64] Minute FC.89/57(a), Finance Committee meeting of 19 September 1989: see also FO/89/44 for a schedule of departmental reserves and deficits, showing sharp differences in relative financial health, and the comparative strength of both the sciences and management.

[65] Treasurer's Report, Annual Accounts for 1988–89 (December 1989), p. 1.

[66] Minute CO.89/91.5, Council meeting on 1 December 1989.

[67] N. T. Hardyman to the CVCP, UFC Circular letter 11/89 (May 1989).

[68] Treasurer's Report, *Annual Accounts for 1989–90* (December 1990), p. 1.

Graduate College, to be built north of The County College, under a business expansion scheme (BESRES) on terms approved by central government. Once the building was complete, at a cost of around £3 million, it was to be sold to Sun Life for £5 million and repurchased five years later at a price of about £6.5 million, covered by a loan from RBS. In the meantime the premium of £1.824 million was invested and shown in the annual accounts as a debtor under current assets, while LANCORD, an existing university company, was deployed to manage the building on behalf of the business expansion company, for which it received a management fee.[69] The university also embarked on a Development Campaign, with a fully staffed office and a portfolio of high profile projects.[70]

This moment of breakeven, at the quarter century of the university's existence but preceding the fire-storm of the mid-90s, offers a useful watershed to reflect on Lancaster's overall financial position, at a time when the funding of universities progressively moved to more of a business model but before the post-1992 institutions doubled the size of the sector. Lancaster shared many of its constraints with institutions of a similar age and size; others, especially its deliberate location in north Lancashire, brought additional pressures to bear, particularly in the generation of additional discretionary income. The Vice-Chancellor, in his 1988–89 Annual Report, had referred to the "problem of success",[71] by which he meant the range and scale of current operations, the need to redistribute staff numbers to areas of particular strength, and the increasing shortage of space, whether for research laboratories, postgraduate expansion, extra staff, or conference and hotel accommodation. But he also identified the need to grow student numbers, especially in the sciences and at postgraduate level, since "we have not yet reached a sufficient size to secure our future in terms of long-term growth and funding"; in other words, the university had to run faster in this Looking Glass world in order not to fall behind. In principle, Lancaster was taking all the right steps: its financial policies were prudent and carefully monitored, its research reputation was climbing steeply and was to reach a pinnacle in 1992, overseas recruitment was being actively pursued, the work of the CIDB was gradually being assimilated into the departments, and a new development campaign was being launched. Yet the reality was that each of these successes also brought additional costs; the CIDB activity, while an essential precursor of later contract income, was slow to bring significant returns; and the sole long-term outcome of the Development Campaign was the establishment of the Ruskin Library. Externally the funding council changes, from UGC to UFC, and UFC to HEFCE, appear in retrospect to have hampered the institutions for which they had responsibility and brought about discontinuities in policy and advice, and certainly of personnel with long-accumulated knowledge of the sector. Internally as well, the first

---

[69] Minute CO.90/4(c), Council meeting of 16 March 1990; and Note 19, Annual Accounts for 1989–90 (December 1990): in fact, the transaction was rescheduled for completion on 29 September 1995, using £350,000 from RBS and £150,000 of university funding.

[70] Minute CO.89/82, Council meeting of 29 September 1989; and CO.90/6, Council meeting of 16 March 1990.

[71] Vice-Chancellor's introduction, Twenty Fifth Annual Report 1988–89, p. 3: see also minute S.88/27, Senate meeting on 10 March 1988.

generation of key senior officers retired in quick succession during 1990–93 – Donald Smith (building development), Michael Forster (registrar), Harold White (finance officer), George Cockburn (university secretary), and Walter Fairbairn (pro-vice-chancellor) – removing both continuity and deep knowledge of the institution.

The search for funding of capital building works was reflected in the Treasurer's allusion, in presenting the 1991–92 accounts to the Court,[72] to the need to borrow against the university's assets for teaching buildings, while anticipating that residences might be funded from rental income. However, the 1992–93 financial year brought other obligations to the university when Charlotte Mason College at Ambleside was fully integrated into the university. Significant costs came with it, including the drastic improvement of the Ambleside telephone system at a cost of £115,000 and urgent work to obtain fire safety certificates, as well as work on a master plan to bring the campus up to standard.[73] Moreover, a change of external auditor for the accounts of the college's junior common room revealed significant deficiencies to be addressed.[74] The university's capital building programme was steadily accelerating and, as the Treasurer reminded the Council in March 1993, it had recently approved major capital projects to the value of £15 million. Hence the most significant development was the launch by the university of three more business expansion schemes in order to raise funds for two more projects: the new Pendle College and Chancellor's Wharf. Lancaster Residences (LUR) I and II were launched on 11 March 1993, to raise £7.5 million, and LUR III in July for a further £3.5 million.[75] The scheme was sponsored by Noble and Company, the exit arrangements were made with RBS, a holding company (Northmount Estates Ltd.) was set up, and all three transactions were put in place by 31 December 1993, when the relevant tax provision came to an end for new schemes.[76] It is interesting to note that these financial arrangements were being put in place concurrently with the commencement of the building works, rather than in advance, and this sense of accelerating pace is to some extent reflected in the proceedings of the Council: for example, at the March 1993 meeting concerns were expressed by members about "the request being made for a decision on a complex matter at very short notice and with a minimum of documentation".[77]

---

[72] "University accounts", minutes of Court, meeting on 12 December 1992.

[73] Minute CO.92/69, Council meeting of 2 October 1992; minute FC.93/46, Finance Committee meeting of 11 June 1993; and minute BC/93/18, Buildings Committee meeting of 2 March 1993.

[74] Minutes FC.93/47 and 48, Finance Committee meeting of 11 June 1993; and minute CO.93/43(b) of Council, meeting on 30 June 1993.

[75] Document FO/93/68 and minute CO.94/4(b), Council meeting on 5 March 1993; document FO/93/130 and minute CO.93/24(a), Council meeting on 21 May 1993; minute CO.93/43(d), Council meeting on 30 June 1993.

[76] As notes to the 1992–93 annual accounts reveal, the considerations payable were £2.748 million and £5.900 million for new Pendle, and £4.200 million for Chancellor's Wharf. The initial loan arrangements with the RBS were for three loans totalling £8.6 million, but in order to obtain RBS agreement to the debenture issue, the three were replaced by one of £7.5 million, the balance to come from rental income (Finance Committee, 17 February 1995).

[77] Minute CO.93/4(b), Council meeting of 5 March 1993.

The accounts for 1992–93 showed an increase in total income from £53.3 million to £64 million, including an extra £2 million from research and contracts and £1 million from catering and residences, with the balance relating to the inclusion of Charlotte Mason College, a factor that also increased the fixed assets by £10 million. The value of the capital building assets had been professionally revalued and stood at £103.6 million, while external borrowing from all sources now totalled £10.5 million.[78] The new Treasurer, Mr Peter Browning, was able to report that, with a surplus of £145,000 for 1992–93, the accumulated surplus was now £397,000, of which £350,000 had been committed by the Council to the George Fox Building.[79] The sums now owed or committed by the university put into perspective the inadequacy of an announcement by the HEFCE that it would be distributing £21.9 million of capital funding for the entire, enlarged sector for 1993–94, of which none was for new estates projects, and from which Lancaster would receive a weighted formulaic contribution of £163,328.[80] It therefore comes as little surprise that the Council agreed at this point to set up a working party that would consider future policy on capital funding, and in particular whether variable or fixed rate funding was the most advantageous.[81] The working party had to hand an influential report by Professor Andrew Bain to the HEFCE, in which he assessed the options for capital development and advocated that universities should use the long-term capital market, probably within consortia of institutions, with the potential for raising up to £300 million per annum in private capital.[82]

Meanwhile, the Vice-Chancellor had been pressing for the university to purchase the freehold of the Bailrigg site from the City of Lancaster, to replace the 999-year lease of 1963. Whether his concern that local authorities would be obliged to sell off their land to purchasers who might not respect the conditions of the current lease would have later been vindicated is not clear, but there were certainly many advantages for the university's long-term future if it held the title to its own land. The Pro-Chancellor, Vice-Chancellor, and Treasurer were therefore commissioned by the Council to take this objective forward and, by the use of anticipated VAT refunds,[83] made the purchase in December 1994, with £300,000 paid forthwith and a further £200,000 to pay by 1 August 1995.[84]

By May 1994 the Director of Finance, Chris Savory, reported to the Council that, in the

---

[78] Report by the Director of Finance, Annual Accounts for the year ending 31 July 1993 (3 November 1993), p. 3; and minutes of Court, 11 December 1993.

[79] Minute CO.93/65(a), Council meeting of 1 October 1993.

[80] Capital Allocation Policy and Estate Formula Funds, HEFCE Circular 36/93 (September 1993).

[81] Document FO/93/244; Council minute CO.93/65(c), Council meeting on 1 October 1993.

[82] Andrew Bain, "Private Sector Funding in Higher Education," (Bristol: Higher Education Funding Council for England, 1993).

[83] The level of VAT recovery, back to 1973, was such that it was worth a full-time member of the Finance Office having this task as his sole occupation for some months. £1.15 million and rising had been achieved by December 1995 (FO/95/394).

[84] Minute CO.93/81(e), Council meeting on 10 December 1993; report from the Director of Finance to Council, 18 February 1994; minute CO.94/4(a), Council meeting on 4 March 1994.

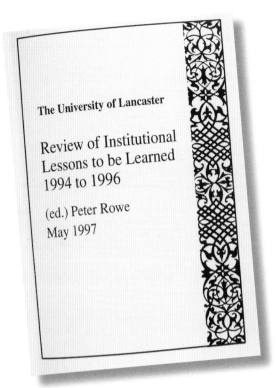

The CRILL report of May 1997, written to examine lessons to be learned by the university in the wake of the 1996 cash flow problems

The University of Lancaster

Review of Institutional Lessons to be Learned 1994 to 1996

(ed.) Peter Rowe
May 1997

light of the Bain report, the Council's working group was "convinced of the benefits to financing at least part of the University's capital funding needs by directly accessing the long term capital markets".[85] Presentations had been made by five firms of potential advisers on 18 March, and the unanimous decision had been that Barclays de Zoette Wedd Limited should be appointed, a choice then ratified by the Council. The advisers made a presentation to the Finance and General Purposes Committee on 10 June 1994,[86] and in July the Council was asked to agree that there should be a launch of £55 million of long-term debenture stock, if possible by 31 July, to be quoted on the London International Stock Exchange. Preliminary versions of an offering circular from BZW, a placing agreement from Allen & Overy, and a trust deed from Berg and Company were also included in the agenda, along with an extended list of further capital building projects. The Director of Finance explained that the university had by now taken on £15 million of loan finance, and he anticipated that another £35 million of new capital was needed, thus reaching the base line of £50 million that Andrew Bain had suggested as a minimum figure for such a launch. He noted that the stock would be tradable and that a vehicle company would be needed to sit between the university on the one hand and the trustees of the stock on the other, and went on to explain

---

[85] Document FO/94/181 and minute CO.94/21(a), Council meeting on 20 May 1994.
[86] "The advantages of the long sterling market", presentation by BZW, 10 June 1994.

the legal obligations of Council members to satisfy Stock Exchange requirements, as well as the insurance cover that would be provided for them.[87] And so the Council resolved, on a show of hands, to "approve the launch of up to £50 million of long term debenture stock (for a period of up to thirty years), to be quoted on the London International Stock Exchange, to be issued in two tranches of £40 and £10 million as market conditions permitted". Members also approved the formation of a new company, wholly owned by the university and to be called Pinecrest Developments Limited, through which a legal charge would be provided over those university properties pledged as security. These low-key decisions, combined with approval given under the same agenda to the Tower Avenue development, an additional 900 residential places at South-West Campus, and tenders for the Library Extension and the Ruskin Library, effectively cast the dice for the events of the next two years, documented in publications written in 1996–97 (the CRILL report[88]) and in 2002.[89] Readers interested in the fine detail can find it in these accounts, and the narrative below concentrates on headline events as they were experienced at the time.

The objective of placing debenture stock by July 1994 was not realistic, for there were many due diligence processes to be carried out, principally under the chairmanship of the Pro-Chancellor, Sir Christopher Audland. There was also an extensive verification exercise, involving all members of the Council other than the Chancellor, HRH Princess Alexandra.[90] Time dragged on, and interest rates edged inconveniently higher. Approval from the HEFCE for entry into the transaction finally reached the university on 23 December 1994, too late to move before the Christmas and new year period, and the letter set out eight conditions, including a maximum effective interest rate of 9.75% gross, funding council approval of the covenants required by the lender, the ring-fencing of the cash raised for specified purposes, the underwriting of the issue, and the setting aside of even amounts of funds by the university in each of the 30 years for repayment at the end.[91] A Signing Meeting was held on 20 January 1995, but the external financial markets were not in a state to meet the funding council's conditions.[92] In the meantime, in a decision that seemed quixotic even at the time, the university changed its banker from Barclays, with whom it had had a long relationship and an arm of which was working on the bond issue, to National Westminster.

---

[87] Minute CO.94/42(a)(2), Council meeting on 1 July 1994.

[88] P. J. Rowe, *Review of Institutional Lessons to Be Learned, 1994 to 1996 [the Crill Report]* (Lancaster: Lancaster University, 1997): summaries of the evidence for the review are held at UA.1/16/4/10.

[89] Ritchie and McClintock, "Capital Building and Cash Flow at the University of Lancaster".

[90] Rowe, *Crill Report*, pp. 150–5 and UA.1/20/1/7/3: hard copy signatures had to be collected from all Council members in the late autumn, two of whom were respectively at an internet café in San Francisco and en route to New Zealand at the relevant time.

[91] Letter from Graeme Davies, Chief Executive of the HEFCE, to Harry Hanham of 23 December 1994.

[92] Minute FGP.95/3(a), Finance and General Purposes Committee meeting on 17 February 1995: the estimated costs associated with the issue were also rising, from £476,000 in July 1994 to £800,000 in February 1995. The final cost was almost exactly £1 million.

The short-term financial competitiveness offered by the latter was to be outweighed a year later when the university needed to seek immediate support from its banker, with which it had at the time no long-term relationship. There were also signs, for those wishing to examine them, that some of Lancaster's indicators of financial health were uncomfortably distant from the sector mean in terms of short-term solvency and retention of reserves, although they were positive on diversity of funding sources where overseas student fees and research grant income were shown.[93]

The stock finally went on sale on 30 March 1995 and the transaction was complete by 5 April. The Offering Circular,[94] issued by perhaps the only university that will ever feature on the Official List of the London Stock Exchange,[95] is therefore a document of some historic interest. In addition to the financial information and the auditors' report, the properties at Bailrigg and Ambleside used as security were separately identified, covering academic, residential, and social and communal buildings, with a certified open market value of £61.45 million for Bailrigg and £4.52 million for Ambleside.[96] Information was included about the governance structure of the university, about its academic reputation, and about each and every Council member who was accepting responsibility for the validity of the contents, including the students.[97] Under the Placing Agreement BZW was to acquire any surplus stock, and dealings in it became available as soon as the issue was complete. There was provision for issue of further stock up to a total of £50 million, and the university had the option to redeem the stock if it was prepared to take the whole £35 million. The principal undertaking by the university was onerous: "The Stock will be a direct, unconditional, and secured obligation of the University", with the Royal Exchange Trust Company as the named trustee.[98]

Widespread media coverage of the issue[99] commented on the potential wider application of the approach used by Lancaster for other institutions, and a smiling Director of Finance told *Newsview* that "There is absolutely no gamble factor".[100] *Inkytext* was somewhat more sceptical:

As the money is spent over the years, some of the decline in earned interest will be replaced by the rental income produced by some of the buildings we spend it on. The major

---

[93] FO/95/032 and letter of 30 November 1994 from the HEFCE.

[94] See UA.1/20/1/7/5 for the Offering Circular.

[95] The University of Cambridge in January 2010 announced its intention to raise £400 million from a bond issue, but it was not clear that it needed to involve the London Stock Exchange ("Cambridge goes to market to raise £400m", *The Times*, 5 January 2010).

[96] Valuation by Gerald Eve, chartered surveyors, on 30 March 1995 (p. 13 of Offering Circular).

[97] The responsibility entered into by these individuals was reckoned to be current for up to six years, and continued even if during that time they were no longer members of the Council.

[98] Clause 2(1) of the Offering Circular.

[99] For example, in the *Financial Times*, *The Daily Mail* and *The Times* on 25 March 1995, and the *Asian Wall Street Journal* on 27 March 1995.

[100] "Bond secures stable future for university", *Newsview* No. 41 (April 1995).

problem will always be servicing the capital borrowing related to buildings that produce no distinct and immediate income e.g. the library extension. Don't forget that our current building programme is not particularly intended to cater for more students, but initially to help us keep our market share. Whatever we do with the cash it must be used to help increase and ensure our future income. To squander it like the North Sea oil money would be ruinous. But at least it might keep us out of overdraft for a month or two.[101]

And so the final Council meeting of 1994–95 on 7 July brought the year to a quiet close, with a service in the Chaplaincy Centre for Council members, a forecast surplus of £90,000 on the annual outturn,[102] and the congratulations of the Audit Committee to the Director of Finance on his success in placing the debenture stock.[103] Yet over the summer the outgoing Vice-Chancellor, during the annual leave of the Director of Finance in France, commissioned KPMG to undertake a special investigation. The purpose of this exercise was to examine the 1995–96 revenue and capital budgets and test the assumptions on which they were based, to review the cash flow forecasts in order to identify peak borrowing requirements and the potential for non-compliance with external covenants, to check the 1995–96 revenue budget, capital programme, and cash flow forecast to test their assumptions and their consistency with each other, to review the adequacy of the financial management reports and the manner in which variances were reported, and to review an apparent over-spend on the premature retirement compensation scheme that the university had set up in 1994–95.[104] In his final report before his retirement to the Academic Planning Board in September the Vice-Chancellor explained that during August he had become aware of travel claims and suppliers' bills not being paid, a Finance Office forecast that showed a net cash flow problem by the year end of over £5 million (well in excess of the £3 million permitted under the Financial Memorandum without HEFCE approval), an excess of premature retirement commitments, and the generation of the £90,000 surplus by the inclusion in the general revenue accounts of both funds and balances that had not been shown in the previous month's accounts. He had also received a request from the HEFCE for a revised submission of the financial appraisal for the South-West Campus project.[105]

The incoming Vice-Chancellor had to respond quickly to a complex web of inter-related issues. His efforts to communicate them were not assisted by the Council being told in October that members could not, under the terms of engagement, be shown the KPMG report, but only a summary of the issues raised, to which the University Secretary added the news that the HEFCE would be keeping Lancaster under particularly tight scrutiny for

[101] *Inkytext* 75, 29 March 1995 (UA.1/9/3/2).
[102] "Financial position as at 31/7/95 from Director of Finance" (PO/95/72).
[103] Minute IA/95/32, Audit Committee meeting on 20 June 1995.
[104] Letter of 18 September 1995 from KPMG to S. Lamley, University Secretary; paper to Council, meeting on 6 October 1995.
[105] Minute APB/95/131, Academic Planning Board meeting of 20 September 1995.

some months to come. Members naturally expressed concern that a cash flow issue had been identified so soon after they had accepted personal liability for the debenture stock, one noting acerbically that "while welcoming the frankness with which the university had treated the HEFCE, [he] asked that similar treatment be given to members of Council".[106] In November the Vice-Chancellor asserted to the Senate that, while the problems revealed to him were serious, they "lay far short of anything to be described as a general crisis",[107] adding that action had already been taken in :

> The establishment of a capital expenditure project group; some refusals on future expenditure, pending more clarity ... a robust revision of the premature retirement arrangements ... some strengthening of the financial management in the area of estates ... robust scrutiny of the monthly management accounting reports; and reviews of certain financial projects.

To the Finance and General Purposes Committee two days later, however, he was rather less upbeat:

> The executive summary of the [KPMG special investigation] had drawn particular attention to:
>
> (a) a transfer from the revaluation reserve that was included in the 1995–96 budget but was not an item of revenue;
> (b) a shortfall of £450,000 on premature retirement provision;
> (c) a shortfall of £400,000 on provision for depreciation.
>
> A deficit on the 1995–96 out-turn was now more likely unless corrective action was taken ... There had also been a significant adjustment of £1.3 million in respect of the cash flow projection for the financial year 1998–99 because of an error in forecasting the arrangements for the buyback of the university's business expansion scheme properties.[108]

The Council thus received in December 1995 converging and unpalatable news from Finance and General Purposes, Audit, the premature retirements group,[109] and the capital expenditure project group. There was particular disquiet about the movement of ring-fenced funds into the revenue account in order to achieve a small surplus; not so much because of the size of the amount involved (£320,000), but because of the principle of appropriating

---

[106] Minute CO.95/72, Council meeting of 6 October 1995.
[107] Minute S.95/98, Senate meeting of 15 November 1995.
[108] Minute FGP.95/79, Finance and General Purposes meeting of 17 November 1995.
[109] The sum set aside for 1995–96 was £600,000; the expenditure £998,000 and the forward commitments, and hence the external auditors' advice for the annual accounts, was £1.4 million; minute CO.95/81(a), Council meeting of 8 December 1995.

earmarked funds, and of doing so without consultation. A contested vote gave short-term approval for this move, with the intention that the funds subsequently be reinstated.[110] The Vice-Chancellor also reported on cuts in the academic budget that were being implemented, and at the Academic Planning Board in January 1996 he warned members about impending cash flow problems for the next three years unless significant cuts in departmental and capital building expenditure were made.[111] To the Finance and General Purposes Committee he further noted that a second KPMG report:

> had made grim reading and indicated a worse position than revealed in November and December 1995 when initial corrective action had been take. The external auditors [KPMG] had in the light of their January report indicated a reluctance to sign off the university accounts for 1994–95, without adding a qualification that as of January 1996 the university did not appear to be a going concern, and that assurance was needed to prove substantial corrective action was in place,

coupled with a projected deficit of £9 million for July 1996.[112]

The opening months of 1996 were a time when the institution was under intense pressure from its Audit Committee, its external auditors, the HEFCE, and potentially the Trustee for the debenture issue, to which problems were now added the grave matters of whether the university was a going concern, the possible transfer of Charlotte Mason College to S. Martin's, and the management of staff disengagements.[113] The university was reaching the stage when each problem amplified the impact of every other one, but although the documents of the time show an institution under stress, each issue was separately and calmly addressed. In February the external auditors declared themselves reassured, and in March the Council (at a meeting ironically long arranged to be held at Charlotte Mason College) agreed a suite of measures to keep the institution under control, including the decision in principle to sell land and property at Hazelrigg.[114] In May, when some unintended staff and student observers were present for part of the

---

[110] Minute CO.95/8/1(c), Council meeting of 8 December 1995. Other priorities took over, and the exercise to reinstate the funds was never carried out.

[111] Minute APB/96/008, Academic Planning Board meeting of 17 January 1996: the projection at this stage was of a negative cash flow of £4 million during February, with an upper level projection of £16 million by June 1999.

[112] Minute FGP.96/4, Finance and General Purposes meeting of 14 February 1996: the Council was assured that the special investigations and the external audit function, both being carried out by KPMG, were being kept appropriately separate within the company.

[113] The net savings from staff disengagements were intended to be £1.4 million in 1996–97, £1.8 million in 1997–98, and £2.3 million in 1998–99; draft letter of 4 March from the Vice-Chancellor to Professor Brian Fender, Chief Executive of the HEFCE.

[114] Minute CO.96/3(v), Council meeting of 8 March 1996.

Council's discussion,[115] members were prepared to endorse a process of formal negotiation with S. Martin's College about the future of Charlotte Mason College, to receive a staff and student petition, to proceed with staff reductions (without a compulsory redundancy policy), to accept an updated financial forecast up to 1998–99 that revealed the cash flow problems, and to agree an action plan for implementation during the financial year 1995–96.[116]

What happened next is succinctly narrated in *Managing Crisis*:

On 5 July 1996 the council was, however, unable to agree the budget for 1996–7 as presented to it, and the university secretary, while reporting that a short-term borrowing facility of £4.8 million had been agreed with NatWest and the HEFCE for the period to 31 July 1996, also told the council that further borrowing, to a sum unspecified, would be required until mid-October. By the time the council reassembled on 24 July, following a meeting of the finance and general purposes committee earlier the same day, members were told that a request had been made to the HEFCE for short-term borrowing of up to £9.5 million for the two months of August and September 1996. By now NatWest was requiring more detailed analysis of the university's request for a secured loan of up to £7 million, in addition to an unsecured loan of £2 million or more; and the day after the council had met, the local manager wrote to Coopers and Lybrand, seeking a financial and structural analysis of the university's position ... In the meantime, the disposal of the South-West Campus, proposed in order to reinject cash into the university, had run into significant logistical and legal difficulties. The proposal was subsequently terminated.

The summer of 1996 was a distressing period for Lancaster since, as the pro-chancellor reported to the council that October:

Early in August ... the bank told the University it was not willing underpin all of its needs for short- and medium-term finance unless the institution committed itself to a radical recovery plan that would clear the core overdraft problem by 1999–2000: a similar message also came from the HEFCE.[117]

VCSAG was in almost continuous session, and there were *ad hoc* meetings between senior staff and representatives of Coopers and Lybrand culminating in a critical discussion on 26 September in London when the Vice-Chancellor had personally to face the "bitter realism personified in the senior bankers, bondholders and men in grey suits who had told [them]

---

[115] A group of staff and students who entered the Senate Chamber during the meeting were, after an adjournment, invited by the Pro-Chancellor to be present for the discussion of a policy of staff reductions.

[116] Minutes CO.96/30, CO.96/31, and CO.96/32, Council meeting of 24 May 1996.

[117] Ritchie and McClintock, "Capital Building and Cash Flow at the University of Lancaster," pp. 39–40.

Professor Bill Ritchie, Vice-Chancellor, 1995
to 2002

... .that the University was autonomous and should make its own way".[118] The tribute the Pro-Chancellor paid to Professor Ritchie that autumn, referring to his tough first year in office as vice-chancellor, was well deserved: "he had in a calm, courageous and sustained manner ... tackled all the problems that he had encountered and had carried the university community with him",[119] for it was his strength and credibility as a fellow academic that was fundamental to his ability to keep the university moving forward. And, as in the early 1980s, staff of the university were prepared to give their personal support, for 122 of them agreed to lend 5% of their annual salary to the university for a period of one year from August 1996.[120] Not only did this contribution make some small addition to the cash flow, it was one of the features that impressed the "grey suits" in deciding whether to give their acquiescence to the measures requested by Lancaster.[121]

By the time the Council reassembled in October the University Secretary was able to supply the terms of reference for the development of an action plan that would be acceptable externally and from which decisions and their implementation would flow internally,

---

[118] Minutes of the meeting of the Court, 9 February 2002, p. 5.
[119] Minute CO.96/69, Council meeting of 5 July 1996.
[120] *News Update*, No 38 (25 June 1996).
[121] W. Ritchie to M. E. McClintock, private communication.

with benchmarks, milestones, and monitoring dates.[122] Mr Quentin Thompson, an early operational research graduate of Lancaster, was representing Coopers and Lybrand, and the appointment of an acting director of finance (Mr Charles Gordon) was announced. The meeting was protracted, and rehearsed again much of the ground already familiar to Council members. The view of the Audit Committee was that the university was continuing to trade while insolvent, calling into question whether the external auditors might qualify the annual accounts for 1995–96: the support of the bank and the HEFCE, however, gave all concerned a way forward.[123] As the Deputy Vice-Chancellor reported to staff,

> Our University continues to be a going concern. We have succeeded in persuading all the key players ... that we have developed a Recovery Plan which, if fully implemented, will help to restore us to full financial health and allow us to protect the high reputation for research and teaching which they wish us to sustain.
>
> It must also be acknowledged, however, that the improvement in our situation remains provisional. The Plan requires us to take a number of difficult decisions over the next three months of a kind which most people, and particularly those of us who lived through the academic restructuring of the mid-eighties, would have preferred to avoid.[124]

The difficult decisions to which he alluded particularly centred around the academic restructuring. The Senate meeting of October 1996 was told that the HEFCE was prepared to rephrase the timings of payments of its recurrent grant to the university, and the overdraft was secure until the end of November, but the Vice-Chancellor's acknowledgement of a dearth of democratic processes was echoed by Senate members' perception that "far-reaching decisions were being made without Senate members being confident of the processes involved, or knowing who was making the decisions, how they were being discussed, or what means would be used to feed them into the university's structures".[125] Or, as *Inkytext* put it,

> Lift up your hearts ...
> PRAYER. Bless our SLUMP [Special LU Management Posse, aka VCSAG], O Lord, and guide their SLURP [Strategic LU Recovery Plan]. Grant them wisdom, understanding and righteous vision, for not all are as well endowed therewith as some might wish. Give them courage, stamina and thick skins, for they shall have need of them. Endow them with the insight that they may be wrong. Remind them, should ever they think TINA [There is No Alternative] that there are always myriad alternatives. Above all give them mirrors that they may see themselves therein.
> Bless also those who shortly discover they are teaching lovingly prepared courses for the

---

[122] S. A. C. Lamley, report to Finance and General Purposes on 4 September 1996 (SU/96/38), presented to Council on 4 October 1996.

[123] Minutes CO.96/80 and CO.96/81, Council meeting of 4 October 1996.

[124] Joe Shennan, Lancaster's Recovery Plan, *Bulletin 1* (2 October 1996) (UA.1/9/3/8).

[125] Paras. 94.4 and 94.13 of minute S.96/94, Senate meeting on 9 October 1996.

last time. And even more to those they have the gall to ask to do it twice before quietly leaving.[126]

The proposed academic restructuring framework from VCSAG was issued to heads of departments in late October,[127] and by the time Senate met in October the recommendations it contained had been rehearsed, digested, and repudiated in plentiful supplementary papers. The aim was to achieve a gross reduction in academic area costs of £1.4 million (£0.8 million net after reinvestment), the allocation of 415 FTE undergraduate numbers from weaker to stronger areas, the loss of 35 academic posts, and streamlined faculty and administrative structures. The Senate was told that it

> had the power ... to reject the proposals placed before it, in which case the senior officers would be obliged to act on that basis in relation to external agencies ... [and] that the HEFCE was likely to make the acceptance and implementation of a plan a condition of grant, and the absence of a plan was therefore not an option.[128]

And so "An earnest, concerned and subdued Senate broke up after four and a half hours of often inconclusive discussion ... [and] VCSAG and Restructuring Committee members were left in no doubt about the widespread hostility towards their proposals".[129] Much detailed negotiation took place, and by the time Senate next met in January 1997 a process of academic restructuring was essentially in place. In the meantime, the Council had approved a Recovery Plan to cover 48 months of rehabilitation,[130] with an emphasis on early savings and with the objective of ensuring that the university retained a surplus of income over expenditure of at least 5% over the four years and built sufficient reserves to reduce the bank funding requirement as quickly as possible and to make selective reinvestment. The plan included information about the historical deficit of £8.086 million for restructuring costs and the transfer of Charlotte Mason College,[131] together with a bank overdraft of £4.60 million and an accumulated surplus of £4.17 million. There would be efficiency savings of 3% p.a. over the period, and £1.3 million of staff savings from the 240 people prepared to leave the payroll at specified dates. Gap savings would come from unfilled vacancies, and the loss of some 40 posts would be balanced by reinvestment of £600,000. A further premature retirement and voluntary severance scheme was to be put in place, but this time it would

---

[126] *Inkytext* No. 172(a), Sunday 6 October 1996. Readers who want the flavour of this period should particularly look at *Inkytext* Nos. 170 to 185 (October and November 1996) (UA.1/9/3/2).

[127] Document PO/96/278, 24 October 1996.

[128] Minute S.96/106.3, Senate meeting of 13 November 1996.

[129] "Senate barks but does not bite", *Inkytext* No. 181(a), 14 November 1996.

[130] "Lancaster University Recovery Plan August 1996 – July 2000", document at Council on 6 December 1996.

[131] The formal transfer of Charlotte Mason College to S. Martin's College took place in March 1997, and at the same time additional properties at Bailrigg were substituted for those at Ambleside for the purposes of security for the debenture.

be selective, the savings would have to be realised by 2000, and staff would not be replaced other than as part of reinvestment.

Although the university worked in an atmosphere of continual high alert during the Recovery Plan period, the dramas of 1996 were fortunately not to be repeated. A new Director of Finance, Mr Euan McGregor, came into post on 3 February 1997, and naturally spent his first few weeks re-examining every assumption, forecast, and calculation that he had inherited, both positive and negative. By the time of the March 1997 Council meeting he was able to report[132] that NatWest had confirmed an overdraft facility of £4.4 million, the HEFCE would again reprofile their grant payments for 1997–98 and 1998–99, KPMG had signalled their intention to sign the certificate for the 1995–96 annual accounts, and Coopers and Lybrand had issued a letter of comfort following their latest review of the cash flow projections.

In the months that followed, as the academic and administrative restructuring took effect, the capital building programme was steadied and confined to the completion of projects already in the pipeline, and staff learnt to work within the frugality of the new regime efforts were made to exceed the targets set and achieve normality more quickly. While the HEFCE and Coopers and Lybrand continued to monitor the university's performance on a regular basis, with Professor Nick Abercrombie as the project manager for recovery, most staff and students became increasingly unaware of this background to the university's annual round. An HEFCE evaluation of internal control arrangements[133] following a visit to Lancaster in August 1996 had been broadly positive, as was a review of the finance function by Robson Rhodes.[134] By May 1997 Professor Abercrombie, now elected as deputy vice-chancellor, was able to present three sets of restructuring documents to the Council, the first two being on the academic and administrative reshaping that had been agreed by the Senate. The third, reporting on a Committee on Committees at a meeting where the CRILL report was also debated and fresh in Council members' minds, was the most comprehensive review of the university's committee structure and intentions ever undertaken, starting as it did from first principles and building an integrated structure with clear accountability and reporting lines.[135] At the same time a more tightly controlled series of severances and retirements was under negotiation.

By July 1997 the Director of Finance had proposed and had accepted a tax-efficient pay scheme that yielded cash benefits to staff who entered it and released discretionary funds for university use. By now 350 staff disengagements had been agreed, but the open-ended

---

[132] Document FO/97/016, report to the Council on 7 March 2007.

[133] "Evaluation of internal control arrangements", HEFCE Audit Service (August 1996); and minute CO.96/79, Council meeting of 4 October 1996: a senior auditor from the NAO had also been at Lancaster during the same period and had indicated that "the NAO was not in a position to say the launch of the debenture stock was a bad idea, although there was some criticism of the HEFCE and the university relating to the processes of the launch" (CO.96/74(c)).

[134] Minute CO.97/7 and related documents, Council meeting of 7 March 1997.

[135] N. Abercrombie, "Review of the committee structure" (AR/97/677), May 1997.

nature of the 1996 offer under which they had been negotiated meant that the departures were orientated towards the part-time and more junior members of staff,[136] while the more focused scheme of 1997 concentrated on full-time and more senior academic and administrative staff, and was a more gradual process with savings that would be gained further down the line. The Director of Finance also indicated that the debenture issue had been set up under procedures that were not benign for the university, and carried hidden costs and risks to the institution.[137] Finally, he drew attention to some aspects of the capital building programme that were continuing to cause concern, especially the Library Extension and the Ruskin Library.

The annual accounts for 1996–97 show some dramatic shifts by comparison with the year before, particularly under expenditure, effects that were amplified by the disposal of Charlotte Mason College:

	1996/97	1995/96
	£000	£000
Income	73,941	78,537
Expenditure (including taxation)	73,218	89,315
Surplus/(Deficit) for the year after depreciation of assets at valuation	723	(10,778)
Difference Between a Historical Cost Depreciation Charge and the revalued depreciation charge	1,040	1,670
Historical Cost Surplus/(Deficit) after Tax	1,763	(9,108)

Figure 8: Relative financial position of the university for the financial years ending 31 July 1996 and 31 July 1997

In sum, the university's senior officers could sign up to an

> Improvement in the historical cost balance on the Income and Expenditure Account from a deficit of £9.1 million to a surplus of £1.8 million [that] is testimony to progress in implementing the Recovery Plan agreed during 1996/97. The focus on tight cashflow management ensured that the University operated within the revised facilities agreed with NatWest and the HEFCE ... tight budgetary and cashflow controls will be essential in managing peak requirements during [1997–98]. In summary, the University has stabilised its financial position and is on track to achieve sustainable recovery.[138]

Or, in the words of the chairman of the Finance Committee to the Court:

---

[136] Minute AUD/97/26, Audit Committee meeting of 25 April 1997: cleaning staff, for example, left in such numbers that some of them had to be replaced almost straightaway.

[137] Minute CO.97/59(c)(D), Council meeting on 4 July 1997.

[138] W. Ritchie and E. T. McGregor, Annual Accounts 1997, p. 3.

Mr Cann described Lancaster as a highly geared university, which owed a great deal of money, and needed to earn a great deal to pay the interest. It was a finely-tuned engine which, though successful, required a lot of preventative maintenance. The university was required to do well in all areas of its activities, and to complement its academic excellence in order to move forward to greater success.[139]

A substantial change of student funding methodology was about to be introduced in 1998, when the long-standing system of mandatory fee awards for undergraduates was changed to a fee structure of individual payments by students or on their behalf, initially at £1000 per annum,[140] but with no flexibility to charge either less or more. It is a measure of how finely-tuned the sector was that the HEFCE felt obliged to rephase the recurrent grants for 1998–99 for all institutions.[141] Lancaster therefore had to make preparations for individual assessment of students' financial circumstances and the efficient collection of their fees. Since for 1996–97 the HEFCE recurrent grant had fallen to only 37.4% of budgeted income, student fees of 18.2% (including overseas students) were of great importance.[142] By the end of the calendar year the Council had approved a proposal from the Finance and General Purposes Committee that N. M. Rothschild be appointed as advisers on the financial structure of the university,[143] including the impending repayment of the business expansion schemes. This move was necessary given the university's overall performance at a time of considerable pressures from HM Treasury, which were transmitted by the HEFCE in the form of a requirement for especially close adherence to the Financial Memorandum.[144]

Budget-setting began early in 1998 and, building on an *ad hoc* procedure the previous year, the Director of Finance initiated it by setting out the parameters within which the exercise would take place, including constraints, permissible virements, incentive structures that included the carrying forward of faculty funds to the next financial year, internal charges and transfers, and a timetable of an outturn review by February to approved budgets at Council by May. While the process of negotiation and iteration in practice took longer than three months, some elasticity in the extent to which the detail of annual budgets is settled by the final Council meeting of each academic year meant that the procedures laid out for 1998–99 have served the university well ever since.

---

[139] Minute 6, Court meeting on 11 December 1997.

[140] "New funding arrangements for higher education … in 1998–99", DfEE letter to vice-chancellors and principals, 18 November 1997.

[141] HEFCE *Circular Letter 33/97*, 23 December 1997.

[142] Student-related residence and catering income was 14.2% of the total, and research grants 15.3%. The university was carrying £44.47 million of external borrowing, compared with the £12.45 million that was the sector mean: see document FO/98/018, Report to the Finance and General Purposes Committee, 5 February 1998.

[143] Minute CO.97/102(a), Council meeting on 5 December 1997: see also minute FGP.97/65, Finance and General Purposes meeting on 17 November 1997.

[144] Minute CO.98/5(d), Council meeting on 6 March 1998.

The first draft of a financing review from N. M. Rothschild reached a group set up by the Finance and General Purposes Committee in February 1998 to consider medium- and long-term financing strategy; its contents examined the university's overall financial position and compliance with the Financial Memorandum, the possibility of revising the terms of the debenture issue, and the replacement of the three business expansion companies with a single loan arrangement over a longer period. It was the debenture stock that was the more difficult issue to unpick. In late 1996 the university, at the insistence of the HEFCE, had gone to current bondholders to ask for some amelioration of terms, but had been rebuffed,[145] for to investors the original issue was an attractive long-term investment, while to the university the drawbacks were becoming ever more apparent.[146] The fixed interest rate of 9.75% was some 2% above what could now have been obtained in March 1998, £70 million of property was tied up as security for a bond of £35 million, and the sinking fund was an expensive and inefficient means of repayment that would require topping up by the university as 2025 approached. In addition, as specific named properties depreciated over time, or if the university's overall financial position diminished the value of its estates, the university was potentially liable to have more and more of its estate sucked in as additional security to a bond whose price remained unchanged until the day of redemption. Nevertheless, whatever solution was proposed would have to appeal to whichever bondholders held the stock at the time that the university made its overtures for change. The solution favoured by N. M. Rothschild was the insertion of a specialist insurer with a high credit rating who would be inserted between the university and the bondholders, coupled with regular, periodic payments that would pay the interest and reduce the capital sum involved.[147] And thus the exercise with the code-name Project LIMA came into being, code-named in this way to secure the necessary confidentiality for tradable stock under LSE conditions.

The first task undertaken by the LIMA working group was the reconsideration of the buyback arrangements and subsequent funding of the loans obtained through the business expansion schemes. Because of the university's weak balance sheet the Royal Bank of Scotland was only prepared to improve on terms of the existing agreement that were causing difficulty by forcing the university into a more expensive lending facility. The Director of Finance therefore entered into negotiations with other providers, including Bradford and Bingley, who were prepared both to offer better terms and to enter into a facility agreement of £7.5 million for 25 years. By the RBS deadline of 30 September 1998, under powers delegated by the Council, a small group of officers took up the Bradford and Bingley offer and reported accordingly to Council at its next meeting.[148]

---

[145] The University Secretary, Mr Stephen Lamley, carried out this negotiation.

[146] Document AR/98/341, 23 February 1998.

[147] Section 5 of Financing Review (N. M. Rothschild and Sons Ltd., 1998).

[148] The resolution of the three LUR companies was to be a buyback of £12.8 million, met by £3.9 million on deposit, a 20-year loan from RBS of £7.5 million, and £1.5 million from the university's current funds. The variation on these arrangements was the replacement of the RBS loan with the Bradford and Bingley facility: see FGP.98/74 of 13 November 1998.

N. M. Rothschild undertook preliminary work in parallel on the restructuring of the bond and, by September 1998, were able to report on negotiations with MBIA-Ambac International about a process that would give bondholders the benefit of the Ambac AAA credit rating to the bond.[149] At the same time the university would seek credit ratings from Moody's and Standard & Poor's, and these would provide the basis of approval by the Ambac board of cover for Lancaster, coupled with discussions involving the HEFCE for the necessary approval of such an arrangement.

The annual accounts for 1997–98 showed a steadily improving situation. The HEFCE intervals in its monitoring of the university's progress were increasing, the overdraft facility was being reduced to £3 million, income showed a small increase and expenditure a further decrease, and there was an historical cost surplus of £4.2 million. Staff numbers had fallen from 2371 to 2291 (of whom 316 were part-time and 230 honorary), gap savings between appointments were made for as long as reasonably possible (and, inevitably, for rather longer than reasonable in the view of some), and a much enhanced maintenance programme was put in place. The accounts were fully in line with the Recovery Plan targets.[150]

The safe passage of the bond restructuring was far from a foregone conclusion, however, especially when the detailed negotiations around the drafting of the necessary documents began. In March 1999 the Director of Finance made a presentation to the Council in which he

Outlined the onerous conditions of the existing stock debenture, the relationship of the university with the stockholders via the trustee, and the status of the stock as an illiquid investment without a formal credit rating ... Four options for change had been considered: redemption by a formula set out in the Trust Deed, which would have cost around £27 to £28 million at current prices; repurchasing of the Stock, which would be almost as costly; restructuring ... and the do-nothing option ... there had been seven stages to the process. The first was the appointment of N. M. Rothschild [and the refinancing of the BES companies] ... The second stage, the intensive analysis of the university's finances and management structure by the monocline insurer, MBIA-AMBAC, had been the most difficult and extended. The crisis period had still been relatively recent, and there had also been a perception, totally incorrect but prevalent, that the university had defaulted on its obligations under the stock, so that negotiations between London and the New York credit committee [of Ambac] about why this apparently weak financial institution should be supported had not been straightforward. During this process and in the subsequent stages the academic reputation of the university had been a crucial element in establishing Lancaster's credentials.[151]

---

[149] Minute 3, Medium and Long-Term Financing Strategy Working Group, meeting on 10 September 1998, FGP.98/61 of 11 September 1998, and CO.98/68, Council meeting on 2 October 1998.

[150] Lancaster University, *Accounts 1998*, pp. 2–3; see also FO/98/1297, report to Finance and General Purposes of 13 November 1998, and minute 5.1, Court meeting of 6 February 1999.

[151] Minute CO.99/1, special meeting of Council on 19 March 1999.

The key features of the arrangement were the annual repayment of both capital and interest, improved risk management, especially the removal of the loan-to-value covenant, the establishment of a relationship with a single negotiator, and the replacement of the redemption fund by a debt service reserve. There were also improved terms for the security cover, including the phased release of properties to a value of up to £13.8 million over two years and a net present value benefit of about £3.6 million. The financial covenants included a required ratio of current assets to current liabilities of at least 1.2:1, the maintenance of minimum cash and reserves, and a premium to Ambac in the event of any breaches. There were useful advantages both for the stockholders as well as to the university, and it was this balance between the parties that eventually carried the day.

The initial intention had been to complete the restructuring by April 1999, but it was not until August that the Council could be told that the March proposals had, with the addition of a £0.5 million fee to current stockholders, been approved, that a special emergency general meeting for the stakeholders would take place in London on 22 September, and that the whole transaction had been codified in the Fourth Supplementary Trust Deed.[152] Since approval had been given in advance for 87% of the stockholdings, the outcome was not in doubt and the new arrangements came into force the following day.

The annual accounts for 1997–98 contained another surplus in excess of 5% and a cleared cash balance of £4 million. Income showed a modest increase from £74 to £76 million, despite an atypical fall in research grant income, while expenditure was stable, especially since the absorption of a salary increase had been assisted by a small decline in staff numbers. As the Vice-Chancellor noted, the time had come to generate new net income, since "Cost-cutting is not enough. If we are to move forward in line with our competitors, we need to develop new and additional areas of business in all areas of the university."[153] Although the nominal conclusion of the Recovery Plan period still lay a year ahead, the 1998–99 year-end position effectively brought it to a close, enabling normal business to crowd in again. The millennium year, once national excitement about whether all computer-directed processes would collapse was demonstrated to be unfounded, marked a point of further stability: there was an increase in income of £6.7 million (to £84 million), a further surplus in excess of 5%, and the achievement of the 1.2:1 ratio between net assets and net liabilities required under the restructured bond. Standard & Poor's, publicly confirming a BBB rating for Lancaster, stated that it reflected "the impressive recovery from the financial problems of a year ago".[154] As the underlying position stabilised, however, so the capital building programme began once more to take priority. For a year and more officers had been working on an estates strategy involving both internal and external consultation, and had reached the provisional conclusion that potential capital expenditure of £127 million over ten years might be needed;

Assuming that the University is capable of continuing to deliver annual surpluses at the

[152] Memorandum to Council members, 20 August 1999 (AR/99/866).
[153] Vice-Chancellor's Foreword, *Report and Accounts* (1999), p. 2.
[154] Standard & Poor's press release, 27 June 2000.

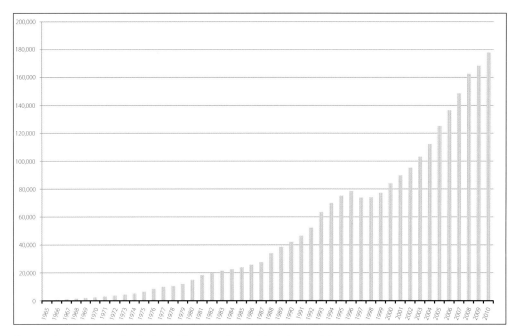

Figure 9: Annual turnover for the financial years ending 31 July 1965 to 31 July 2010

levels that have been achieved in recent years, then it is reasonable to assume that the institution will be able to generate sufficient cash to support an annual spend in the range £3 to 5.5 million i.e. a quarter to a third of the total programme.

As the University is not in a position to increase its balance sheet borrowing, the remainder of the funding will have to be derived from external sources or off balance sheet funding. This target is achievable but will necessitate innovative approaches and careful assessment of the implications and, in particular, the degree of risk transfer and future income forgone. The two key areas where this will apply will be in the refurbishment and upgrading of the utility infrastructure and in the provision of new and refurbished residence accommodation.[155]

The building programme that grew out of the estates strategy is described in Chapter 7, as are the financial structures that supported the residences project in Appendix B, although the intensive negotiations surrounding the latter should be held in the reader's mind as a backdrop to the next decade.

The annual accounts for 2000–01, despite a shortfall in recruitment that led to a loss of income of £1.47 million from reduced tuition fee income and HEFCE clawback, again

---

[155] University of Lancaster, "Estate Strategy to 2010, Version 3" (May 2000); see also CO.2000/26, Council meeting on 23 June 2000.

achieved a surplus close to 5%.[156] The outgoing vice-chancellor was able to reflect on a healthy balance sheet, secure long-term funding, and a cash balance of £19.4 million at 31 October 2001, by contrast with the £9 million shortfall only five years earlier. Yet he also warned of pressures from substantial increases in staff costs that, after the years of tight constraint, were again becoming evident.[157]

The financial years 2002–03 to 2007–08 were a period of relative prosperity for the university sector, including Lancaster, thus enabling the incoming vice-chancellor to focus on the university's strategic direction and external reputation. The university's income grew from £95.4 million in 2001–02 to £162.4 million in 2007–08, while the year-end accounts regularly showed an underlying surplus in excess of 4%.[158] The effects of the increase of the tuition fee from £1000 to £3000, adjusted for inflation, contributed to growth: the substantial pay settlement of 2006, however, at a time of exceptionally low inflation, was an appropriate corrective for the sector but a drag on university finances. During the period there was an increasing emphasis on devolution of responsibility to the faculties, particularly from 2005, and their infrastructure staffing inevitably contributed to an increase in overheads, particularly when coupled with ever-increasing external legislation with which the university has to be compliant. There is a heavy responsibility on academic staff, who are the people most directly involved in earning the university's teaching and research funding streams, but who make up only about a third of the university's total staffing complement.

The debt ratio continued to fall during the period, and in 2005 the university was able to make a further adjustment to its borrowings, when it replaced the fixed loan from Bradford and Bingley with a revolving credit facility from Lloyds TSB, thus increasing its flexibility and reducing interest costs. At the same time a substantial capital programme commenced, and the level of maintenance was progressively increased in an attempt to bring the whole of the university's physical plant up to a satisfactory minimum level. While the customary cautionary statements were made at Council and Court about the need for efficiency, effectiveness, and strong financial discipline, the setting and management of annual budgets across the university was, by comparison with the mid-1990s, not too painful. Another sign of institutional confidence was the decision in 2006 to purchase two parcels of land, totalling 63 acres, part of which was Hazelrigg land that had been sold in 1996.[159]

During 2008–09 the university took the major step of redeeming the debenture stock, thus enabling the university to restructure its borrowing arrangements and to secure up to £80 million of borrowing facilities with RBS, to cover the redemption of the

---

[156] See: Lancaster University, *Report and Accounts 2001*, p. 31.

[157] Vice-Chancellor's Foreword, *Lancaster University Report and Accounts 2001*, p. 3.

[158] The surpluses, adjusted for permitted exceptional items, were: 2001–02: 5.8%; 2002–03: 6.2%; 2003–04: 4.9%; 2004–05: 4.2%; 2005–06: 4.1%; 2006–07: 3.8%; 2007–08: 4.9%; 2008–09: 4.2%.

[159] See document AR/2006/657 and attachments, issued to the Finance Committee in September 2006.

bond, to discharge the consequential exceptional charges, and to create a variable rate revolving credit facility.[160] Amongst other schemes in the pipeline, this move enabled the Sports Centre project to be undertaken (see Chapter 7). The Standard & Poor's rating for the institution at the year end was A stable,[161] and there was another strong outturn performance.

The international and national recession of 2008, however, inevitably brought this more sanguine position to an abrupt close. The Vice-Chancellor warned the Court in his 2008 annual report[162] that investment in higher education was slowing, government policies such as the Equivalent or Lower Qualifications were altering funding patterns, and international economic conditions were deteriorating, meaning that there would be substantial financial pressures on payroll, pensions, infrastructure, and energy costs. All these fears were subsequently realised, and Lord Mandelson's cuts to higher education budgets late in 2009 proved to be a tiny precursor of the swathe of reductions by the new coalition government of 2010. Lord Browne's review of undergraduate tuition fees (see Chapter 3), and the new government's uncertain response to it, led early in 2011 to universities having to contemplate charging undergraduate fees of up to £9000 per annum from October 2012. Reductions in recurrent grant for teaching began, however, in April 2011, leaving a period of 15 months before the commencement of the new fee regime, with all its implications for student recruitment and indebtedness. Uncertainty about the position on postgraduate funding and fees, a potential cap on overseas student recruitment,[163] and the growing pressure on government if too many institutions opt for the highest fee levels added additional unwelcome volatility to the sector. In this context it was to be expected that the Vice-Chancellor's message in his written report to Court in late 2010 would be bleak, for he suggested that the cuts facing the universities could far outstrip even those of the Thatcher government[164] at a time when a quarter of the university sector is already in deficit[165] and cuts of £915 million between 2010 and 2013 are forecast.[166] While Lancaster's operating and financial review for the year ended 31 July 2010 displayed a strong financial position across all performance indicators, it was coupled with an analysis of key risks and a warning that

> From 2010/11 the HE sector faces greater uncertainties, from which it has remained somewhat sheltered so far. Significant pressures on government expenditure, the approach

---

[160] Lancaster University, *2010 Report and Accounts*, p. 49.

[161] As at early 2011 the rating stands at A+ with a stable outlook.

[162] Lancaster University, *Report and Accounts 08*, p. 3.

[163] "Universities hit out over £5bn threat to courses", *The Observer*, 6 March 2011, pp. 1, 7.

[164] Lancaster University, *2010 Report and Accounts*, p. 3.

[165] Pricewaterhouse Coopers, "Weathering the storm: Coping with financial challenge in the higher education sector", quoted in *Times Higher Education*, No. 1931 (21–27 January 2010).

[166] "Universities push for rise in tuition fees as funding chiefs plot £315m budget cut", *The Times*, 28 January 2010.

taken by the new coalition government and an uncertain outlook for the world economy
will result in real volatility in some sector funding streams ...[167]

In the early months of 2011 those words of warning have been realised and indeed amplified,
and the financial perils of the current period for UK universities are all too evident. Against
that backdrop, the success of the university's finance staff as the Outstanding Finance Team
in the 2010 Times Higher Education Leadership and Management Awards[168] was a pleasing
accolade for a cohesive and talented group of colleagues.

The university will therefore expect to manage its expenditure ever more prudently in
the years to come, and to develop and diversify its funding streams. As its 50th anniversary
approaches in 2014, preparations are also being made for the launch of a Jubilee Campaign,
2011–16,[169] which is intended to raise £40 million in philanthropic income, as well as increase
the alumni with whom the university has contact from 65% to 80% of its graduates. The
funding will assist Jubilee bursaries and scholarships, and research on food security, ageing,
shaping the future workforce, religion and social action, and building cultural capital.
Appropriately, the slogan for the campaign will be "supporting the university's *work*, not the
university – the future is in our hands".

---

[167] P. W. Wellings and S. J. Randall-Paley, statement of 19 November 2010, Lancaster University,
2010 Report and Accounts, p. 57.

[168] Lancaster University, *2010 Report and Accounts*, p. 27.

[169] "Lancaster University: Celebrating 50 Years of Excellence" (presentations by Nick Fragel,
Director of Alumni and Development, to the Council and to the Faculty of Arts and Social
Sciences), January 2011.

CHAPTER SEVEN

The physical domain

P ROBABLY LANCASTER CITY'S most important gift to the university was the 999-year lease
of 200 acres of farmland two miles south of Scotforth,[1] a site bounded on the west by
the A6, the London–Glasgow railway line, the Lancaster Canal, and the Lune estuary, to
the east by the M6 and the ascent to Clougha, and to the south by the former industrial
village of Galgate. This site, carved out from the edges of Lancaster Rural District, Ellel and
Scotforth, has, of course, a long history of its own. The first material evidence is the traces of
two roundhouses at Barker House Farm which are contemporary with the Roman fort three
miles to the north, but were built and used in a style similar to their Iron Age forbears, rather
than the new material culture imported by the Romans.[2] Ellel, immediately to the south, is
one of the few places in the wastes of north Lancashire to be named in the Domesday Book,
but no physical evidence of its early history or the immediate surroundings has come down
to us. The hamlet of Bailrigg occupies the northern edge of the university site and gave its
name to the mansion there:[3] Professor John Rodwell has uncovered evidence of the use of
an area near the mansion as a gentleman's hunting ground, which explains the plentiful

---

[1] McClintock, *Quest*, pp. 12–13, 20–1, 47.
[2] D. C. A. Shotter, "The Thirty-Fifth Archaeology Forum," *CeNtre WoRds* New Series No. 7 (2008):
pp. 90–1. Peter Iles and D. C. A. Shotter, *Lancaster's Roman Cemeteries* (Lancaster: Centre for
North-West Regional Studies, 2009), p. 7.
[3] The term "Bailrigg" is used throughout the chapter as a shorthand for the whole university site.

supply of mature trees. Most of the land, which is mainly clay with pockets of black silt,[4] was used as pasture for small dairy farming at Bigforth, Barker House, and Brandeth, all of which are incorporated into the university, including the stone buildings, cobbled yards and adjacent shippons where extant. Bailrigg Mansion, built for Herbert Lushington Storey by Woodfall & Eccles (1899–1902), is constructed in neo-Elizabethan style and has a garden designed by Ernest Milner and extended by Thomas Mawson in 1907.[5] The former stables, which are contemporary with the mansion, were later converted into a house which is now the vice-chancellor's residence.

The particular circumstances within which the seven new universities were founded meant that there was considerable interest in them as a group, and their building programmes, leading to some useful comparative literature. Birks' *Building the New Universities*[6] has stood the test of time well, posing questions evident at the time but still critically important today about the decisions made on behalf of the new universities

---

[4] This substance was referred to from time to time at the Buildings Committee as "cow-gut".

[5] Thomas Hayton Mawson, *The Life and Work of an English Landscape Architect: An Autobiography* (London: Richards Press, 1927), pp. 139–40. Elizabeth Kissack, *The Life of Thomas Hayton Mawson: Landscape Architect: 1861–1933* (Windermere: privately published, 2006), pp. 39, 79. Janet Waymark, *Thomas Mawson: Life, Gardens and Landscapes* (London: Frances Lincoln, 2009).

[6] Tony Birks, *Building the New Universities* (Newton Abbot: David and Charles, 1972).

Bailrigg Mansion from the air, taken before the coming of the university and showing the formal Milner/Mawson gardens

relating to their physical form and location. The definitive work of Muthesius, *The Postwar University*,[7] puts all readers in his debt, while a pan-European study, *Campus and Study Environment* (2009), published in Denmark, quotes more recent student views, and Hartwell and Pevsner give a useful thumbnail sketch of the Bailrigg site as at 2008.[8] More locally, *Quest* (1974) has a chapter devoted to the building programme[9] that covers in detail the activity about and on-site prior to the 1964 opening of the university, and the first decade of the building programme.

Lancaster's development comes well out of these volumes. Tony Birks confesses to a personal preference for the new environment created at Lancaster amongst the Seven, in the context of the logical "structuring of a system about a line, usually that of the main means of movement, open at both ends for further addition, and with activities attached to this line and growing outwards from it at right angles",[10] using an urban concept based on a linear structure that makes Lancaster "a model for university plans in the future". Muthesius develops this theme and adds praise for the humanity, the balance, the pedestrian liveliness, and the "characteristic Lancaster dialectic of the 'ordinary' which seemed to ensure the greatest approximation to the utopian aims [of the postwar universities]",[11] while Hartwell and Pevsner comment on "the outstanding educational initiative of the mid-1960s", where

[7]   Stefan Muthesius, *The Postwar University: Utopianist Campus and College* (New Haven: Yale University Press for Paul Mellon Centre for Studies in British Art, 2000).
[8]   Clare Hartwell and Nikolaus Pevsner, *Lancashire: North*, The Buildings of England (New Haven: Yale University Press, 2009), pp. 413–18.
[9]   McClintock, *Quest*, pp. 45–59.
[10]   Birks, *Building the New Universities*, pp. 19, 127.
[11]   Muthesius, *Postwar University*, p. 170.

The architects were Bridgewater, Shepheard and Epstein, the buildings of traditional (rather than modular, prefabricated CLASP) construction in brick and concrete, the palette brown and cream. Traffic and pedestrians are carefully separated, and the place has an accessible, friendly atmosphere with the principal axial route given variety by courtyards and green spaces.[12]

The area of the main buildings, on their plateau 300 feet above sea level, can be seen from miles around, encircled by open land, and with the irregular skyline of flats and various roof types clustered into the form of a distinctive small town. The local community of the 1960s took a keen interest in what was taking shape on the steep hill south of Lancaster, and to this day there are, for example, taxi drivers eager to relate how they were involved, even while at school, in helping out in junior capacities at Bailrigg.

The scope of this chapter, in part because of the wealth of existing documentation, will briefly recapitulate the first decade of the university's physical development and then focus on the question of what happened next, and what became of the early vision described so eloquently. Because the City of Lancaster was able to provide accommodation at St Leonardsgate and elsewhere in the city for teaching, research, and initial student services, and because lodgings in Morecambe and Lancaster were readily available, the site at Bailrigg could be developed according to a master plan that looked forward to the future. The first step had been to appoint a site development architect; after experience at the other greenfield universities, there was a well-tested procedure available for Lancaster. Architectural practices, including local firms at the insistence of the Vice-Chancellor Elect, were short-listed with the help of the Royal Institute of Architects. The brief prepared by Mr Carter[13] described the main features of the site and the buildings currently on it, the university's plans for growth, and a timetable that set the autumn of 1966 as the target for the first buildings to be ready for use. He indicated that there might be up to 10,000 students by the end of the century,[14] that teaching buildings should be concentrated so that students crossing boundaries between arts and sciences could move easily from one to another by the hour; that a third of the students were to be resident initially, rising to at least one half as soon as possible;[15] that there should initially be six colleges for 3000 students, who would be able to return to them for meals; that married members of staff would live on site only if they were either the vice-chancellor or a college principal; that the plan should emphasise the relationship between university and city; that playing fields would probably have to be provided on other, flatter land; that there should be facilities for non-resident students to work and socialise; that there should be some communal services and a place for the

[12] Hartwell and Pevsner, *Lancashire: North*, p. 60.

[13] C. F. Carter, "Notes for architects on the planning of the university site" (21 May 1963) (UA.1/27/8/1).

[14] His estimate was close: the number of full-time students in 2000 was about 10,600.

[15] The current proportion of students in residence is now maintained at about two-thirds of the total.

Jan Thorn, "The Battle" (1969), a timber construction in the Anglican and Free Church Chapel, Chaplaincy Centre

chaplaincy work of the main religious denominations; that the adaptability of buildings was of key importance; and that the building stock should as far as possible be kept working throughout the year. Finally, he noted that the UGC did not regard the appointment of consultant architects as necessarily implying that they should be employed on the design of individual buildings.

Architects from eight short-listed architectural practices were interviewed in London on 17 and 18 June 1963, and on 2 July a press statement announced the appointment by the Executive Council of Messrs Bridgewater, Shepheard and Epstein of 42 Bruton Place, Berkeley Square, London to prepare an outline development plan for the university site.[16] By the end of the calendar year Tom Mellor & Partners of 23 Park Street, Lytham, who had also been interviewed, had been appointed to work on the first science building, to which was then added the first phase of the Library. As Muthesius notes, the Lancaster commission "became, and remained, far and away Epstein's most important work".[17] Born in 1918 in the Rhineland, Gabriel Epstein was educated in Germany, Belgium, Israel, and England, and was apprenticed to Eric Mendlesohn when he started his studies at the Architectural Association School of Architecture in London. Certainly he has frequently referred to Lancaster as the "favourite child",[18] and the practice was still being consulted about the

---

[16] C. P. H. McCall, Press Statement, 2 July 1963.

[17] Muthesius, *Postwar University*, p. 162.

[18] Gabriel Epstein, "An architect gives his verdict", *The Lancaster Graduate* (No. 7, Autumn 1989), pp. 19–21.

Peter Brook, oil painting of Galgate Mill, c. 1969 (copyright, Peter Brook Estate)

master plan as recently as 1991. It is also to his credit that, when Warwick finally admitted that its site design was dehumanising and impractical, it was to Bridgewater, Shepheard and Epstein that they turned for help.[19] Peter Shepheard,[20] the senior partner in 1964, was a distinguished landscape architect and a particular advocate of imaginative tree planting on a large scale. In an interview with *John O'Gauntlet*[21] he described how there were to be closed spaces within the buildings, for shelter from the wind, but:

> Every time you walk out of the buildings you can see all these marvellous views over the whole countryside, as we are leaving all the rest of the site free. The initial necessity of building on this high ground [the platform on which the perimeter road encircles the key buildings] was one which guided many of our later actions. When you look at the plan you can see that the site, which is 200 odd acres, has a very steep slope down to the road ... one in ten, one in fifteen – and in addition rather marshy. It's clay land, so the rain that soaks in at the top of the hill oozes out on the slope in the form of springs. It's rather badly drained, and we, at one time, considered the possibility of forming this system of

---

[19] Muthesius, *Postwar University*, p. 122.

[20] Mr (later Sir) Peter Shepheard, 1913–2002, town planner and landscape architect, was *inter alia* president of the Institute of Landscape Architects 1965–66, and of RIBA, 1969–71. He joined Bridgewater in the shared practice in 1943.

[21] "John O'Gauntlet interview with Peter Shepheard", *John O'Gauntlet*, No. 4, March 1965, unpaginated.

squares by stepping them up the hill, but isn't really a good idea ... There's a dense wood on top of the hill which stands like a ring, and cuts out wind and traffic noises from the M6. We felt we had to incorporate this in our plans.

He then, however, goes on to explain that the site is not suitable for sports fields because, once the buildings were placed on the top of the hill, there would be very little flat land left. The practice took on a new partner, Peter Hunter,[22] in 1966, and he too played a major role in the design and execution of the early buildings.

The account of how Gabriel Epstein's intervention at the interview about the core design of the built-up area made such a strong impression that the contract was theirs has often been told,[23] but it is also the case that the intentions stated by the practice well fitted the brief prepared in advance by Charles Carter. Planning work began quickly, although not all the ideas developed could be put into practice. The Third Policy Memorandum,[24] for example, suggested that each college would have guest flats, a principal's residence, flats for vice-principals and male and female tutors, domestic bursars' and cooks' flats, and ten resident domestic staff and a porter. There would be music and utility rooms, kitchenettes as well as a dining hall and associated kitchens, a senior common room with its own dining room, sports rooms for table tennis, quiet games, and billiards, a sewing room, two darkrooms, and sick bay facilities. It is much to be regretted that so many of these proposed facilities were discarded, presumably on financial grounds.

However, there were also tensions. The Vice-Chancellor Elect was driving along the rapid development of all aspects of the university, and this included the building programme. Early in 1964 he wrote to Peter Shepheard,[25] saying how delighted everyone had been "at the speed with which you appreciated the broad characteristics of the site and produced for us an acceptable outline plan", and how he and his colleagues "greatly admire your work as architects", but expressing deep concern about "progress in filling in the details of this plan, which (we think) requires work on the spot in Lancaster which you have not proved able to undertake ... and about the prospects of getting the building design work done within the very tight time limits of the U.G.C.'s accelerated plans". For example, no agreement had yet been reached on the heating and other services. By comparison with York, he believed that there should be an immediate design team of 10, rising to 25 a year hence. In fact, the early phases all kept to schedule, with the design work shared out between five architects: Gabriel Epstein, Tom Mellor, Haydn W. Smith of Taylor Young and Partners (Manchester), Roger Booth of Lancashire County Council (Preston), and G. W. G. Cassidy of Cassidy and Ashton Partnership (Preston), who combined to add variety and life to might have otherwise

---

[22] Peter Hunter, an urban planner and architect, set up his own London office in 1990, and is particularly known for his work at Salford Quays and in Belfast.

[23] McClintock, *Quest*, p. 48–9. Muthesius, *Postwar University*, p. 162.

[24] University of Lancaster, Policy Memorandum No. 3 dated 30 October 1963.

[25] C. F. Carter to P. Shepheard, Esq., 18 February 1964 (UA.1/27/8/1).

been dull uniformity.[26] There was, of course, also a huge array of main and sub-contractors, engineers, stonework consultants, furnishing designers, and recreation ground contractors involved,[27] all under the day-to-day supervision of the indefatigable Donald Smith, who from October 1963 to 1991 was the university's Building Development Officer. Not only did Mr Smith cheerfully carry an enormous work load, like the Finance Officer with only a small team behind him, but he was forever anticipating what might come next. A particular talent was his ability to have outline plans in his drawer for highly desirable items that he was able to produce with a flourish whenever the UGC found it had some funds, for example at the end of a financial year, that would benefit from immediate application.[28]

From early 1965 the Council set up a Buildings Committee, a high profile body within the university attended by the Pro-Chancellor and the Vice-Chancellor.[29] Sir Stanley Bell[30] was the inaugural chairman, and he was succeeded by Mr Percy Stephenson.[31] Long-standing members included Lady Clitheroe of Downham, who was succeeded by Mrs Fitzherbert-Brockholes of Claughton Hall. Meetings of the committee would begin at 10.00 a.m. and must have lasted much of the day, for in the early months up to five sets of architects would be present as well as senior academics and relevant university officers, and from 1969 one or more student representatives. User groups and shadow syndicates for new colleges were formed, and their members included in informal discussions with architects and officers from time to time. The span of work of the committee was also wide: as well as broad development issues, there could be up to 15 pre-contract items and 25 pieces of work in progress,[32] and these would include issues of infrastructure, such as the detailing of the Underpass or the routing of traffic at the entrance from the A6, that recurred on successive agendas.

In the early years there was a Committee for the Embellishment of the University.[33] Money was set aside from the Appeal Fund for the external and internal adornment of the public spaces in the university, which, given the functional character of the architecture, introduced some welcome variety. Mr Michael Argles, the founding Assistant Librarian, took a particular interest in this rather open-ended activity, and external bodies and artists were generous in helping the university to acquire pictures and sculptures. The single most

---

[26] C. F. Carter to the Academic Advisory Committee, September 1969 (UA.1/29/7/12).

[27] See, for example, the supporting advertisements published in the *Lancaster Guardian*, 19 July 1967, pp. 6–8.

[28] Personal recollection of the author, supported by references in the papers of the Buildings Committee.

[29] Charles Carter was made chairman of the CVCP Buildings Sub-Committee in 1970.

[30] Sir Stanley Bell died on 23 July 1972.

[31] Mr (later Sir) Percy Stephenson died on 22 February 1979. For a time a room in the original Lonsdale College was named after him.

[32] See, for example, the minutes of the Buildings Committee held on 3 May 1967 (G.67/285).

[33] UA.1/27/2/5.

Anna Hirsch-Henecka, sculptor of 'Daphne' (now in County South), 1973

'Dual Form' by Barbara Hepworth, in Alexandra Square, 2009

important purchase was of Barbara Hepworth's 'Dual Form',[34] but contemporary paintings were also bought and proved to be complementary to those collected by Professor Irene Manton (see Chapter 5). Dr Hirsh-Henecka's 'Daphne' was assembled on site within the first courtyard of Cartmel College and, similarly, John Hoskin's 1975 abstract sculpture was made on site and placed against the corner of the Physics Building. Benches were purchased and others donated, the woodland beside Lake Carter was improved, a memorial was set up within Grizedale College to mark the 1866 murder of Elizabeth Nelson on Green Lane, and small fountains were installed in the courtyards of Furness College and the Library. Inevitably the money ran out before the ideas about how to use it dried up, and not all the embellishments proved to be permanent, but a pattern of interest in the public arts was set. Indeed, in recent years some thought was given to having a sculpture park on the rising ground behind Bigforth Farm buildings, a matter to which the university may later return.

Meanwhile, in the early summer of 1963 Mr Barton Townley left Bailrigg Mansion and his father vacated the lodge by the entrance from the A6, enabling the Vice-Chancellor Elect and his immediate staff to occupy the office and living space in the mansion and use the lodge for the Appeal. After an intensive planning period the first contractors came on site in November 1964. A fine sequence of photographs, taken from the same spot from 1964 to early 1967,[35] shows the building of the Underpass, Alexandra Square, and the buildings immediately surrounding the square, starting with a line of posts standing in pasture, through the waterlogged conditions of the excavation work to the completed buildings that we see today. By October 1966 the Vice-Chancellor and the initial administrative staff were able to move into the first phase of University House. The Vice Chancellor's office looked out on views that included a sweep of land from Blackpool Tower to the hills of the Furness peninsula. He was able to tell new students that:

> For some years to come, the activities of the university will be divided between its permanent site at Bailrigg and its temporary home at St Leonard Gate. All undergraduates entering in 1966 should spend some part of their time at Bailrigg ... This division of the university into two places is a great nuisance, but it is worth remembering that Aberdeen has been similarly divided for many years, without any disastrous results for its educational efficiency. In 1966 only one college, Bowland, is ready for use (and even this has to have added to it a residential annex, due for completion in 1968). Consequently members of Lonsdale and Cartmel colleges who are working at Bailrigg will enjoy the hospitality of Bowland college while their own buildings (due for completion in 1967 and 1968 respectively) are being erected.
>
> ... In two years, Alexandra Square will be surrounded by shops, and by then three dining halls ... and two coffee bars will be available – perhaps also a public house. Facilities like

---

[34] For many years the sculpture was positioned outside the Great Hall and often formed the backdrop to graduation photographs: more recently it has been relocated to Alexandra Square.

[35] See UA.1/9/1 for photographs of construction of the Underpass.

the Centre for Music and the Arts and the Religious Centre will be completed or well under way, the Sports Hall should be ready in 1967, and the new grass playing fields in 1968. (A hard playing area and one or two temporary pitches are available now: otherwise sports clubs will have to borrow from other clubs in the vicinity …) The immediately surrounding area will mostly be 'out of bounds' because building work is going on, there will be a great deal of mess and mud (for the first buildings were only just finished in time), and the wide open spaces of the site consist of rough pasture and woods full of brambles.[36]

Photographs of the time show vehicles parked immediately next to half-completed buildings, and alumni from early days recall walking on duckboards in wellington boots to get to their lectures.

By 1968 the balance between city and campus had shifted the other way, with the majority of staff and students permanently located at Bailrigg. The late summer of 1968, when the shops, banks, and post office opened in Alexandra Square, and students moved into residence in Bowland, Lonsdale, and Cartmel colleges, marked the moment when the Bailrigg community came together. An aerial photograph of the time[37] shows the network of roads around the perimeter and between buildings in the area northwards from Alexandra Square. Bowland Tower, the Chaplaincy Centre, County College, and Cartmel Lecture Theatre are under construction, while the first phases of the Library and University House, the Computer Building, Bowland and Lonsdale Colleges, the Faraday complex (including the wings for Physics and Chemistry), and the garages where the LEC workshop now stands are all in place. Apart from the emerging County College, all the buildings to date were clad in a facing Stamford brick from Lincolnshire, and this unifying material successfully bound together the disparate forms and functions juxtaposed with each other.

The UGC funded the teaching accommodation, including staff offices that were sufficiently large to hold seminar groups, as well as lecture theatres and laboratories for practicals, the Library, the Computer Building, and all the public spaces of squares, roads, driveways, and the north spine. Below ground was a six-foot-high duct running north–south along which all the main services were channelled. Buildings that were financed from appeal funds, such as the shops, the Chaplaincy Centre, County College, were intermingled with those financed by the UGC. Thus Lonsdale and Bowland colleges were designed to be mirror images of each other, with dining and refectory space linking the two (now the Conference Centre), but Bowland was financed by the UGC while Lonsdale drew on Appeal funds. The space norms were more generous than they were to become later: 240 sq. ft for teaching staff and 120 sq. ft for study bedrooms, with care taken to achieve good sound insulation between them.

---

[36] C. F. Carter, text for Student Council booklet for new students, 1966. For a more systematic listing of anticipated completions from 1966 to 1970, see document G.66/546(B), Buildings Committee papers of 1 June 1966.

[37] Undated, but a postcard version of it is postmarked 23 November 1968.

An aerial view of the university in late 1968, showing County College, the Chaplaincy Centre, and Bowland Tower under construction (copyright, *Lancashire Evening Post*)

Because it was expected that students would eat communally, little or no kitchen space within the residential areas was provided to begin with, and toilets and bathrooms were shared, an aspect of student life that inevitably brought to the fore the issue of the extent to which men and women would be housed separately. The colleges at Lancaster were planned to be for both men and women: Cartmel College syndicate, however, agreed early in 1968 that there could be mixed corridors, as at any hotel. The national press picked up on this debate[38] and a fierce exchange of views took place in the correspondence columns. Charles Carter had already made his personal views known in 1963:

> In a non-collegiate university much of the social life of students centres on a large students' union, normally mixed. At Lancaster we propose to have smaller social units, which we call 'colleges', and which will serve the needs of non-resident as well as resident students. We would like each college to be a cross-section of the whole university, and this sets us the planning problem of finding ways in which resident men and women

---

[38] The issue of mixed corridors became conflated with the privately expressed view of Dr David Craig, Dean-Elect of Cartmel College, that it was acceptable for unmarried students to have sexual relations with each other; the so-called mixed bedrooms furore. At the time the university opened, the legal age at which students became adults was still 21.

students can have sensible privacy from each other, and still come together to create the social structure of the college,[39]

and these views had been supported in published letters from wardens from halls of residence at other universities. In 1968, however, the issue had become more explosive, and the Senate, warned by the Vice-Chancellor that there was a prospect of donations to the university being withdrawn, declared that:

> arrangements for student residences must have regard to the proper interests of parents and the wider community, along with the wishes of men and women students. No arrangements would be made which might in any way be interpreted as an invitation to sexual licence. Consequently rooms for men and women would be arranged in separate blocks, floors or sections of buildings ... the proposals of Cartmel College for mixed corridors should be rejected.[40]

The college duly came back to the Senate at its next meeting with amended proposals and, although the issue slowly faded, it left a memory that would reinforce publicity over student activism at Lancaster in the 1970s.

Initial planning for County College, which was to be funded by Lancashire County Council, took place under the aegis of Bowland College, but a separate shadow syndicate was formed late in 1966. While the first three colleges had combined residential with academic space County was intended to be both wholly residential, to provide for 310 students and associated staff, and immediately recognisable and permanently identified with Lancashire County Council, as a traditional university college with blocks grouped around an open cloister.[41] The method of construction was based on a nucleus of ten pre-cast concrete components, using arching to combine the panel and the frame, and was intended to be maintenance-free externally. Internally there was extensive use of timber and ply veneers. The project architect was Dennis B. (Ben) Stephenson, described as a man of outstanding ability, with legendary attention to all aspects of design.[42] To achieve the maximum potential of the study bedrooms he had an internal, full-sized mock-up of a student room set up on the floor of a mill weaving shed in Preston, and many adjustments were made to achieve the practical objectives of a comparatively small living area. The datum plate was set by County Alderman Henry Lumby on 4 May 1967, the topping out ceremony took place on 10 October 1968, and the official opening, with a formal ball at which County Council officers were present, was held on the evening of 9 December 1969. The college took on a distinctive identity from the day of its opening,

---

[39] "Mixed hostels", C. F. Carter to *The Guardian*, May 1963.

[40] Minute S.68/202, Senate meeting on 15 May 1968: see also *Lancaster Guardian* of 17 May 1968, and a Committee of Council minute of 22 May 1968.

[41] See UA.1/27/7/6, from which this paraphrase and the following material are drawn.

[42] David Prowse, Lancashire County Council, letter to M. E. McClintock, 8 August 2003.

not least because of its striking courtyard with an oak tree at its heart,[43] its large corner kitchens, and the absence of a hurried changeover on the hour that accompanies academic teaching.[44] Fortunately, despite many later changes to the college (see below), the original core building has been retained, in part as a testament to the County Council and to a particular form of student life early in the university's existence.

The year 1969 proved to be the moment of the greatest number of completed buildings for some years, for in addition to County College, Furness main college and residences for Lonsdale, Furness, and Fylde colleges were completed. The Great Hall, the Learning Aids Building, and the Assistant Staff House opened at the northern end of the site, as did the first phase of the complex of buildings for Biological Sciences and Environmental Science, at the southern edge of the built-up area, and central workshops and a service station on the eastern edge of the central site. The Chaplaincy was dedicated in April, and Phase 3 of the Library opened a few weeks later. The Vice-Chancellor moved to the newly purchased Emmanuel House at Haverbreaks, and Bailrigg House became the Medical Centre, including the provision of a small number of beds for sick students.

Much time and attention was given throughout these early years to student residence within the college structure. Birks regards the provision of student living accommodation within university premises as axiomatic,[45] but the UGC and the HEFCE (with HM Treasury in the background) have been more equivocal about what priority to give to this aspect of university activity. On the one hand, universities such as Lancaster have been deliberately sited away from large centres of population and do not draw on large numbers of students living at home, while, on the other, the funding bodies have been reluctant or unable to make financial provision for this purpose (see Chapter 6). While it can be argued that acting as a hotel is not part of a university's core function, Lancaster's Academic Planning Board regarded the colleges as being at the heart of the student experience, while the educational and recruitment value of having students living at the university, especially in the context of expanding international student numbers, is clear. The twists and turns of Lancaster's approach to student residence have been significantly influenced by these larger external debates and the search for a viable way through them that would fulfil its strategic aspirations.

Thus, the UGC in the mid-1960s had made it plain that it was unable to provide wholesale funding for residences, even at collegiate universities such as York, Lancaster, or Kent, and other solutions had to be found. At Sussex, East Anglia, and Lancaster loans were used for this purpose. As Birks notes,

---

[43] The oak tree was the subject of a Tree Preservation Order in 2002.

[44] An unsuccessful attempt was made as early as 1973 that an academic department might move into the college: see memorandum by Michael Mullett (CY/73/119, 4 June 1973). In 2010, following refurbishment, some limited teaching accommodation was created on the first floor of the original building.

[45] Birks, *Building the New Universities*, pp. 25–6.

The second generation [of residential accommodation] did not emerge until the funds ran dry. Based on borrowed capital, the second type is widely known as the 'Lancaster Scheme' after the university which pioneered it in 1967. It is loan-financed student housing consisting essentially of new residences which must generate enough income to pay back the original capital loan and interest ... Such a system is circumscribed by the prevailing rates of interest, the cost of building to minimum acceptable standards, and the amount the student can reasonably be expected to pay from his grant. Normal market forces should keep all three in balance, but in 1971 they became so far out of line that loan-financed student housing schemes had to be temporarily shelved,[46]

particularly because of the difference between a letting period covering the 33 weeks of standard residence and the 52 weeks of the year.

In fact the genesis of the idea at Lancaster had come even earlier, for a letter of 1963[47] from the UGC is headed "Student Residence in a Period of Emergency", and talks about alternative approaches to student residence were held by the UGC with government education departments and the Ministry of Public Buildings and Works with an expectation that these might lead to collaborative action between universities for "cheaper and more rapid residential provision". The idea, although attractive to Charles Carter, proved to be complex in practice. A memorandum of September 1966[48] to the UGC showed how a scheme could be made viable, but only if there was some financial support for furniture and equipment, professional fees, and general rates. It also indicated the pressure that was being placed on the Vice-Chancellor by the chairmen of both the Finance and Buildings committees to progress the scheme. There were legalities to be considered: whether the university might be taxed on a commercial source of income, whether a ministry licence would be required,[49] how the leasehold nature of the university's tenure might make difficulties for lenders, and whether a limited liability company structure was an appropriate mechanism. Meanwhile, the Ratepayers' Association expressed concern that its members might be unreasonably disadvantaged by the perceived competition.

Much time was spent at the Buildings and Finance committees, and at the Council, on preliminary discussion of the potential consequences of having private student accommodation on campus, while in the background the UGC was urging Lancaster to take a lead. Consultations took place not only with Lancaster students but also with student groups at Manchester, Liverpool, and Leeds, and included consideration of what level of rent would be acceptable (if anything, somewhat higher than for ordinary residences because of the perceived level of greater autonomy) and the balance between single and double rooms

---

[46] Birks, *Building the New Universities*, pp. 27–8.

[47] J. F. Wolfenden, chairman of the UGC, letter to the Vice-Chancellor, University of Lancaster, of 22 November 1963 (UA.1/27/3/18).

[48] University of Lancaster, "A Proposed Scheme for Student Residence", 23 September 1966 (UA.1/27/3/18).

[49] Some restrictions on building from World War II still lingered into the 1960s.

(showing an increasing preference for single occupation). Beginning with Cartmel and Furness colleges, the intention was to build small square units based on a common kitchen/dining room area that would be assembled in different combinations so that the result would provide residential flatlets in a variety of irregularly shaped buildings three to four storeys in height, with a staircase in the middle, and using university brick.[50] Mr Haydn Smith, later to be described by Charles Carter as having "the rare ability to build down to a price, and yet to ensure that his client is not allowed to sacrifice essential quality",[51] was involved in the scheme from the outset, and was appointed as its architect in October 1967. Despite some delays in the provision of the loan arrangements, blocks of flatlets were built behind Cartmel, Furness and Fylde colleges between 1968 and 1977; County West, of 1977, represented the end of the loan-financed provision. All these blocks have subsequently been demolished and replaced by UPP residences (see below), but, despite their perhaps extravagant use of land and the maintenance problems they increasingly presented, their domestic scale, size, and location – separate from but closely aligned to the parent college – were much favoured by the students who lived in them. Birks, in particular, regarded the Lancaster scheme as attractive, noting that it provided

> several different options within its economical plan, and at the same time by means of its irregular ground plan a series of small and intimate facades which help to give the individual student confidence in the individuality of his own corner of the university. This design provides one of the major touchstones for future development.[52]

The wisdom of making this student accommodation available on campus became increasingly clear when the local authority on several occasions proved unable to help the university to house students. In June 1974[53] the Buildings Committee was told that a proposal to buy a row of terrace houses in the city for conversion to student accommodation was likely to lead to a definition of their use as multiple occupancy, for which compliance with complex legislation would be necessary. The Vice-Chancellor noted that a radical solution, and one that would not be welcomed, would be for the City to treat students like any other young persons seeking accommodation at a time when government targets for additional student numbers might be reduced and a national programme of additional residences was unlikely. By October it appeared that multiple occupancy requirements would be even more onerous than expected and "could seriously affect the viability of converting property in the City for student occupation".[54] The arguments dragged on, and indeed worsened in succeeding months, for by June 1979[55] the waiting list for council-owned housing had grown

---

[50] Minute 6, meeting of Council on 22 March 1967.
[51] Confidential report of CFC to the Academic Advisory Committee, October 1969.
[52] Birks, *Building the New Universities*, p. 33. See also Muthesius, *Postwar University*, pp. 168–9.
[53] Minute BC/74/41(ii), meeting of the Buildings Committee on 18 June 1974.
[54] Minute BC/74/63, meeting of the Buildings Committee on 29 October 1974.
[55] Minute BC/79/24(ii), meeting of the Buildings Committee on 19 June 1979.

to around 2,500 and newcomers to the list could wait for up to two years for a flat. Against that background, the university was in a cleft stick: student numbers were increasing, finance was not forthcoming for further residences at Bailrigg, and no further provision was available in Lancaster. There was even discussion about building some terraced housing at Bailrigg, but no obvious site was available and the suggestion went no further. In practice, although senior officers could not have foretold this turn of events, student numbers were to fall in the mid-1980s (see Chapter 6) and by the time they rose again the external funding environment had changed considerably.

Not all projects that were started came to fruition. One interesting initiative, later aborted, was the Umbrella Project, begun in late 1969 as a proposal for a student theatre to be used two or three times a week by the Theatre Group and let out at other times for student activities. Issues of funding, noise, and location were raised, but students were warmly encouraged in the course of a UGC visit in 2 December to continue with their plans for a reinforced circular fibreglass dome that it was hoped could be placed near the Pavilion.[56] Advice on the structure was provided free of charge by an expert at the University of Surrey, the scheme was included in the university plans for the 1972–77 quinquennium at a notional cost of £75,000, and outline drawings were produced.[57] Over the next 12 months, however, the issue of cost and the relationship of the proposal to the arts complex around the Great Hall led to the proposed site moving from place to place, including locations near the Mound[58] and even at the former County Cinema in Dalton Square, Lancaster. Increasing uncertainty about whether it was a viable scheme meant that it reached an impasse and was eventually quietly dropped.

Another scheme was ideas for additional colleges. Once Colleges 7/8 had taken shape as the future Pendle/Grizedale complex, a shadow syndicate was set up for Colleges 9/10, to be built at the northern end of the site beyond the County College. Although the group that was established held regular meetings[59] and made significant progress, including a decision about a name for College 9 (Rossendale), the UGC's cap on student numbers in the early 1970s meant that there was sufficient college capacity already available. The gaps between the group's meetings increased, and the scheme came to a halt. It was to be nearly 15 years before the ninth and last Bailrigg college, The Graduate College, came into being.[60]

Increasing cost pressures were experienced in the early 1970s, and questions about the possibility of two-year degrees, longer undergraduate teaching years of up to 45

---

[56] The Pavilion previously stood where the new Sports Centre is placed.

[57] See UA.1/27/9/12.

[58] The Mound was a spoil heap at the far south-east corner of the site that, attractively planted with small trees and shrubs, was a familiar landmark until its removal to make way for InfoLab 21.

[59] See UA.1/4/1/10.

[60] Although Charlotte Mason was for a brief period in the 1990s designated as a college of the university, it was of course located at Ambleside (see below).

weeks, or restrictions on overseas student numbers were heard.[61] While in June 1970 the Vice-Chancellor envisaged a building for Engineering, a possible extension to the Library, a tentative suggestion of a swimming pool, and four more colleges (7/8 and 9/10), he discouraged consideration of more science teaching space, anticipated that arts teaching would take place in Fylde College, and foresaw a case for the business school departments to have their own building.[62] By November he was clear that all the university's immediate requirements would not be met: the expected national increase in student numbers had been reduced by 20,000. He was prepared to concentrate on Gillow House for business subjects and add Visual Arts to colleges 7/8 from within existing university revenue, at the expense of a further phase of University House, work on environmental conservation, provision for music, or Colleges 9/10.[63] It is against this background that the cost-cutting apparent in the buildings of the early 1970s became so prevalent.

The initial discussions about the Engineering Building are a helpful starting point for an understanding of this more uncertain period. In 1969 the Vice-Chancellor had pressed strongly for a simple box design that could be fitted out as need arose and added to in phases. There is a sense of increasing tension in successive Building Committee discussions of this topic, with the Vice-Chancellor pushing for low costs and a "break away from conventional, orthodox habits of thought involving e.g. heavy steel frame, etc. Only an envelope was required at this stage", while Professor D. R. Harper, the external adviser to the Buildings Committee from 1963 to 1975, argued for a building of "good standards, good control-led environment, and something more than just an ordinary factory. He was uneasy about a shed type of building and considered that much more will be required."[64] Mr Hadyn Smith, appointed as architect for this project, suggested that the best site would be south of Fylde College, on the east side of the Spine, with office accommodation fronting onto the Spine and practical laboratories at the rear, to be built on two stories, with ceiling heights of 12 ft at ground floor and 10 ft at mezzanine level. Time pressures for submission to the UGC meant that further discussion in principle had to be curtailed if the building was to be fully designed by April 1970 and completed by July 1972.[65] Despite the low building height, however, site inspections revealed that the foundations would have to be dug to 10 ft instead of the intended 5 ft because of the prevailing ground conditions,[66] and other additional costs crept in.

---

61 See Committee of Vice-Chancellors and Principals of the Universities of the United Kingdom, *University Development in the 1970s: A Statement of Views by the Committee* (s.l.: CVCP, 1970), paras. 21 ff.

62 CFC, "Building Programme 1972–4" (G.70/580): paper to Council on 30 June 1970.

63 CFC, "Building Programme", memorandum to Council on 21 November 1972.

64 Minute BC/69/41(i), Buildings Committee meeting on 4 June 1969.

65 Phases 1A and 1B were handed over in August 1972.

66 Minute BC/69/78, Buildings Committee meeting on 19 November 1969: increasing problems about ground conditions led in 1975 to a more systematic appraisal of the site than had been possible under the time pressures of the mid-1960s.

The development of the Engineering Building was, however, simplicity itself by comparison with Gillow House (now the Management School). Discussion of this project first surfaced at the Buildings Committee in October 1970, when Mr Hunt of Tom Mellor and Partners proposed that a project intended to provide teaching space for 400 students, with a second phase of another 170, might be reduced to a single Phase 1A of 290 only.[67] Over the next few weeks ideas were put forward and discarded, including for a library/publications room, a records room, a graduate common room, a grand entrance, and a director's suite, while the departmental representatives argued in vain for the use of high quality finishes on prestige areas.[68] There was a funding stalemate until February 1972, when an allocation of £350,000 for Phase 1A was made for 1973–74, with the intention of asking for £256,000 for Phase 1B.[69] The division of the job into phases necessarily led to some inefficiencies in items such as engineering services and the provision of offices, as opposed to lecture theatres or computer terminal space. As the first arts teaching provision at Lancaster that would be separate from a college, there was also uncertainty about how the building would function outside normal office hours. The site was eventually handed over for a Phase 1A contract on 2 April 1973 at a contract price of £470,000 and a planned completion date of 1 July 1974. By October 1973, however, delays in steel deliveries and a shortage of labour were leading to considerable frustration[70] even before Phase 1B began in December at a contract price of £354,000. More delays on Phase 1A and a slow start to 1B brought anticipated completion dates to January and June 1975 respectively, and it was decided to collapse the two phases together and move the departments in during July and August 1975. In the event Phase 1A was progressively handed over in March and April, and 1B in June, so that, five years after initial planning, the building was finally ready for use.[71] It proved, with its three floors grouped around an irregular inner grassed courtyard, staircases at each corner, and spurs for lecture theatres and computing facilities, to be practical and flexible in terms of ease of movement, and capable of ready transfer of space between departments.

Colleges 5 and 6, to be named as Furness and Fylde respectively, were intended to be opened in stages from 1969 onwards. Both were to be clad in the university brick; both were to contain teaching accommodation, although the Fylde office space was more restricted than that of Furness and thus less suitable for seminar groups; and both had their own bars, junior and senior common rooms, staff flats on the roof, and student residence space in the main college building and in loan-financed residence. The provision of snack bars rather than refectory space, however, marked the conclusion of large-scale catering, and henceforward the bars and junior common rooms were to be the hub of college life. Furness,

---

[67] Minute BC/70/54(vii), Buildings Committee meeting on 13 October 1970.
[68] Minutes BC/70/66(vi), BC/71/8, and BC/71/27(vi), of meetings of the Buildings Committee held between November 1970 and April 1971.
[69] Minute BC/72/4, Buildings Committee meeting on 8 February 1972.
[70] Minute BC/73/55, Buildings Committee meeting on 30 October 1973.
[71] Minute BC/75/19(ii), Buildings Committee meeting on 13 May 1975: in fact, the empty building was used in the spring of 1975 for hearings of the Appeals and Equity Committee.

with its exceptionally long and generous foyer space, has become a welcome gathering point for a range of activities, but the fountain in the courtyard was subsequently planted over. Fylde, built on a significant slope, has a porters' lodge placed at the bottom of a wide flight of stairs, distinctive bay windows to the offices, and, for a period, had an observatory on its roof. Their building histories were, however, different. Furness was begun before the delays in supplies of materials and shortages of labour that became prevalent while Fylde was under construction, and these obstacles proved to be a mere prelude to the difficulties faced by colleges 7/8 (Pendle and Grizedale).

The first six colleges had stayed true to the principle that study accommodation should be provided for non-resident students, who would feel entitled during the day to enjoy college amenities and ambience as much as their resident colleagues. By 1970, however, when thought was being given to Colleges 7/8, this policy had run into difficulties: first, there was an over-supply of Library study space in a university of less than 4500 students; and, secondly, the UGC was under strong government pressure to reduce the overall cost of the universities' building programme.[72] At Lancaster the Vice-Chancellor suggested that either study space be converted to teaching space in existing colleges, or that some academic activities, such as the Comenius Centre, should move into the Library. In either case he intended that there should be communal reading rooms for non-resident students in the colleges. In addition, because Gillow House was in preparation, Colleges 7/8 would not need to include arts teaching accommodation. Thus when Dr Alan Wellburn, convenor for College 8 (Grizedale College), presented a planning paper to the Senate conference of September 1970 he anticipated no teaching accommodation but emphasised the inclusion of reading rooms and locker space for non-residents. Since the site provisionally allocated was north of Lonsdale Annexe, and heavily wooded, he suggested that the college be named after Grizedale Forest and have as its focus the study, use, preservation, and protection of the countryside.[73]

The Senate accepted the new policy on study space, and the shadow syndicates for Pendle (College 7) and Grizedale met together, with Gabriel Epstein appointed as the architect, to discuss the possibility of sharing communal facilities. The proposed site was moved from the north of the site to south of the business school,[74] and discussions about a twinned college took place. The intention was to move away from the large shared kitchens, such as those provided for 16 students at the County College, to smaller social groupings. The smaller study bedrooms – now reduced to 90 sq. ft – and the absence of teaching accommodation also led to a more compact set of buildings, and there was concern that internal courtyards would be too small and constrained. On the other hand, there was a growing sense that more variation should be encouraged in the positioning, size, and variety of texture of the university's building stock, and the experiment of twinned colleges was therefore welcomed

[72] "Building programme", CFC to all FSSU staff, August 1970 (VC/70/77).
[73] A. R. Wellburn, "College 8" (undated, but September 1970).
[74] Minute BC/71/16, Buildings Committee meeting on 23 February 1971.

as an efficient and innovative way forward, albeit with concern about the paucity of catering facilities south of Alexandra Square.[75] The capital cost per student place was estimated to be around £1500 for a complex involving two colleges of 250 students each, and the scheme, other than the colleges' shared communal areas, for which £200,000 of Treasury funds would be forthcoming, was to be financed by a bank loan. Flats for married students and staff, and guest rooms, would be additional.

Recurrent costs were also a growing consideration. Separate loan arrangements had been made for each of the loan-financed schemes and, by 1971–72, 800 of the 1686 resident students were in loan-financed accommodation. The extent to which the different rental levels could be averaged out was becoming a political as well as a financial issue for students. Moreover, the costs of administration, portering, cleaning, and laundry were outpacing income and their impact on student rent levels was increasingly contentious. Discussion of the twinned colleges edged forward. A sample study bedroom was tested by students, who took it in turn to live in it for several days at a time, and modifications were made in the light of their comments.

Despite the previous decision not to include any teaching accommodation, the UGC's refusal to fund the next stage of the fine arts led to a proposal that Visual Arts should occupy office space and a long, roof-lit gallery on an additional floor at an additional cost of £80,000,[76] and the Finance Committee approved an overall loan of £750,000 from the National Westminster Bank.[77] The intention was that work would start in April 1973, for completion between July and November 1974 for both colleges and Visual Arts. The scheme, however, met with almost every conceivable problem. The tenders came in 20% over the intended price and further trimming was made in finishes, fittings, and furnishings, leading both to a loss of quality and the resignation of Dr Wellburn as Grizedale convenor. Although a tried and tested contractor was used he was unable to supply the numbers or quality of bricklayers or joiners necessary for the work, while quarries were operating on a three-day week, strike action stopped delivery of components such as doors and windows, persistent rain and high winds meant that extra bracing had to be used, and the schedules slipped ever further behind. At meeting after meeting of the Buildings Committee there were reports about shortages of qualified labour and, despite Sir Percy Stephenson's personal efforts to intervene with the main contractor, the project entered a second winter season in 1974[78] with 80% of Pendle now watertight, but the rest of the site open to the weather. Pendle College was given priority and, after great exertions by the sub-contractors, students were able to come out of lodgings and into Pendle residence for the Lent Term 1975. The cost of this haste was, however, a great number of defects and overall loss of quality.[79] Once

---

[75] Minute BC/71/27, Buildings Committee meeting on 27 April 1971.

[76] Minute BC/71/73(ii), Buildings Committee meeting of 2 November 1971.

[77] Document SU/72/54 and minute FC.72/7, Finance Committee meeting of 30 May 1972.

[78] Minute BC/74/54, Buildings Committee meeting of 24 September 1974.

[79] There were persistent rumours of gaps in the walls between rooms sufficient to see light through, and noise insulation was poor.

Pendle was occupied work on Grizedale accelerated, and students were able to move in for the Michaelmas Term 1975, with Art and the Environment and the Scott Gallery occupying the top floor space.

The completion of Fylde, Pendle, and Grizedale colleges in 1975, painful though those experiences were, in retrospect marked the end of the initial development of the university's built environment. In a summary written for the Council in October 1974 the Building Development Officer had noted that a recent capacity return to the UGC had assumed a 1:8 staff–student ratio for arts and social sciences. This capacity survey was the UGC's response to its inability to support the building programme for the country's burgeoning student numbers: to achieve some parity of treatment, institutions' capacity records were to serve as a baseline on which judgements could be made about future development. Residential accommodation, for which loan finance would be assumed, would, however, be excluded.

Lancaster's return to the UGC[80] was the first attempt since the university opened to take a systematic look at its total land holdings and their current and potential use. It is no surprise that the capacity and the match of the existing building stock in relation to student numbers proved to be uneven, although in general it demonstrated that, unless student numbers were increased, there was sufficient or excess capacity in most areas. Moreover, the UGC moved the staff–student ratio to 1:10, meaning that, with the new space coming on stream in Gillow House, Lancaster's teaching capacity would already be assessed as 5400 students and sketch designs for extensions to University House and the workshops could therefore not proceed until further UGC approval had been given. Furthermore, the UGC had ruled that any further subsidy for residential places would not be included in the financial year 1974–75, although

> As there is always a possibility that at the eleventh hour some university may be unable to take up their allocation of funds we are preparing drawings and likely costings for County West, a four-storey annexe sited north of the Languages Services building for 131 students planned in groups of about 12.[81]

The report also indicated that the maximum potential of the site, including Barker House Farm and Hazelrigg, might be in excess of 20,000, numbers that a small town such as Lancaster might have some difficulty absorbing. Barker House Farm, initially purchased for sports fields, was deemed to be suitable for either arts teaching or student residences, and small parcels of land north of the current site might be purchased to give a capacity of

---

[80] "The University of Lancaster, Development Capacity of the University Site: A Report" (February 1974), pp. 1–84 (no date, no reference number).

[81] D. B. Smith, Report of the meeting of the Buildings Committee held on 24 September 1974 (GM/74/582 (A)). An estimate of available residential space made a few months later suggested that there were 2236 single rooms, 142 double rooms, and 47 flats for married students, while 1700 students were living off campus and there were 82 staff flats (BC/75/40(iii)(a) of 30 September 1975).

12,500. Hazelrigg, the only other alternative for significant expansion, would involve high siteworks costs, including a bridge or bridges over the M6, and was probably viable only if it were to be used for an additional 4000 students or more. Thus a strategic decision for Lancaster might have to be either to remain at 11,000 or move to 15,000: not surprisingly, the university stated the maximum figure.

County West was eventually approved, once again on the basis of loan finance, although not before delays and cost reductions had slowed down the process. It was eventually opened in October 1977 and, despite cockroaches, damp, and the rather crowded accommodation, was remembered with affection by most students who lived there. It was also particularly useful for housing international students and junior research workers on short-term visits. There was a domestic feel to the lower elevation of two stories and the planted and grassed courtyard that the building fronted, opposite the Round House and next to County Main on one side and the office space for Theatre Studies on the other.[82]

Thereafter the building programme for major developments essentially stood still for over a decade. In that time some additional residence rooms for Fylde College opened in 1979, an extension for Environmental Science and Biological Sciences became available in January 1980, the swimming pool opened in December 1980, the west wing of University House was completed in June 1981, Geography moved to a new annexe behind Physics in 1985, and Computing then moved to the Engineering Building. In addition, some allotments at the south end of the site briefly became available, Bowland Tower was altered, the Boat House at Halton purchased, the Sugar House opened as a student nightclub, and the Joint Refectories between Bowland and Lonsdale Colleges were thrown together so that larger-scale functions could be accommodated. A business park situated on the campus was discussed but failed to make progress, and Gillow House was partially upgraded in 1987 to make a suitably prestigious suite for the appointment of a dean and his immediate staff. But that was all.

A dominant theme during this period of unintended cessation was a pre-occupation with how the existing building stock could and should be used, and Long Vacation outbreaks of minor conversions and alterations became a perennial feature of the weeks after the July degree congregations were over. There was increasing emphasis on energy saving and the efficient use of buildings, while health and safety issues, including the tighter management and replacement of fume cupboards[83] and more attention to fire precautions, rose up the agenda. The maintenance of the first buildings on site, which all too soon showed signs of wear from use and exposure to the prevailing south-west winds, had to be faced, and involved especially an urgent programme of external and internal painting.

Indications that the university was running out of space came in 1986, when the Space Allocation Committee had exhausted their ingenious solutions to fit additional functions and people into existing areas, and the repeated device of taking in rooms from residential

---

[82] County West was demolished in 2007: see below.
[83] An explosion in a fume cupboard in December 1990, in which, fortunately, no one was injured, heightened the focus on remodelling the cupboards, particularly their venting, and increasing the training for their use: see CO.91/8(a) of 8 March 1991.

Spring blossom in the square by the Jack Hylton Music Rooms, named after the music impresario who died in 1965

areas for teaching space simply put too much pressure on residential requirements.[84] By now Lancaster was leaving behind the financial problems of the late 1970s and early 1980s, student numbers had levelled out and begun to rise once more, additional staff were being appointed, and the university, raising its aspirations to become a research-intensive institution with an international reputation, was in an *ad hoc* way increasing the proportion of space dedicated to research teams. Expedient solutions were no longer sufficient, and the university had to face what proved to be a sustained programme of building over the next 20 years that brought exceptional challenges in terms of finance; of the management of building operations; of the harmonisation of building works with the rhythm of the academic year; and of the increasing significance of an active maintenance programme concurrent with new building. There were, moreover, significant changes in personnel, including, between 1990 and 2003, four directors of estates – Donald Clark, Michael Haslam, Ernest Phillips, and Stephen Lunn – each of whom necessarily brought his own perspective to bear on priorities and design. The national context had also profoundly altered as the paternalism of the UGC gave way to the hands-off approach of the UFC and as the sector prepared for a doubling of size in 1992.

One early decision by the Senate during the vice-chancellorship of Professor Harry Hanham was to draw together the creative arts subjects. From 1987 the university was required, under an agreement with the DES, to bring students from Charlotte Mason

---

[84] Some 500 rooms were reallocated in this way: see BC/89/30(ii) of 6 June 1989.

College to Lancaster for their second year of study. The funding for an additional 58 student residence places gave the university an opportunity to convert the Visual Arts and Peter Scott Gallery space within Pendle College to student rooms and to fund Lonsdale Hall, close to Lonsdale Annexe, for Visual Arts, with academic space on the two first floors and student rooms above. The Scott Gallery also moved, from Pendle into a refloored and roofed-over external courtyard originally built to mirror the shape and size of its nearest neighbour, the Jack Hylton Music Room. Success in the Earth Sciences review led to further work on the shared space for Environmental Science and Biological Sciences,[85] and in 1989 a mezzanine floor was added to the Engineering Building, making more efficient use of the space there. More prosaically, a detached reception building was added to the north-west of University House, including space for the telephone exchange, and for Careers above, linked by a footbridge to University House.

For the time being the problem of additional residence was addressed on a piecemeal basis. The most significant development was the decision in 1989 to approve the building of 120 new residence rooms[86] for what would become the Graduate College. Initially postgraduate students had been allocated across all colleges of the university but, as at other institutions, their distinctive needs led to suggestions that an additional, ninth college be created for both one-year masters degree students and research students. Unlike other colleges, however, which came into being with a shadow syndicate, the decision to build preceded the appointment of the founding principal, Dr Christopher Park, and the formal inauguration of the college, by some months. The four-storey block was to consist of 28 groups of four *en suite* study bedrooms that would share a joint kitchen. This complex was novel for several reasons: the cost of building was to be supported in part from the pooling of rents and income from Long Vacation conferences and holiday lettings; the tenancies were to be let for a full year; and it was the first of the Business Expansion Scheme developments at Bailrigg. More starkly, it was the first college not to open with communal facilities.[87] Despite its height in comparison with lower structures nearby, the building fitted into the landscape well, and the front door of each block opened onto an attractive inner courtyard. The first students came into residence in October 1990 and, as predicted, the absence of any dedicated college space made for difficulties, despite the support given by Lonsdale College. There was relief when, by 1993, it proved possible to add a further block of 55 *en suite* rooms together with a porter's lodge and office accommodation that would complete the square, with finance being provided by borrowed money on a sale and lease-back basis.[88]

---

[85] Minute BC/89/30(ii), Buildings Committee meeting on 6 June 1989.

[86] *Fulcrum*, 16 March 1989, No. 134, p. 1.

[87] Colin Adams, "Sloping roof not only new slant", *Fulcrum*, 3 May 1990, No. 142, p. 1.

[88] "Residences project group: report to PARC" (PO/92/46), February 1992. The Graduate College was relocated to the South-West Campus (later Alexandra Park) in 1996 (see below), and the original northern blocks were at first retained as Graduate Hall. From 2003 they became part of Bowland College, for use by undergraduates and some academic visitors.

Even before the Graduate College blocks were complete a feasibility study had been undertaken to assess a site to the east of Cartmel College, still within the perimeter road but behind the commercially sponsored residences, for a further 130 residence spaces.[89] Cartmel College Syndicate unanimously proposed that the new building should be named after the founding principal of the college, and first Provost of Colleges, John Creed.[90] The impetus for the building came from a perceived urgency to recruit more students while maintaining a 50% level of students in residence, and PARC had agreed to proceed with a scheme costing £2.8 million, to be funded by the same BES route that had been used for the Graduate College. For the first time, undergraduate rooms were to be built with *en suite* facilities, since it was believed that students would increasingly come to expect that standard of accommodation and that it would increase the attractiveness of the additional rooms for income generation during vacations. Students were angered, however, by the lack of consultation and by the provision of apparently elite accommodation that they saw as divisive and as highlighting the existing dilapidation of nearby rooms.[91] The building went ahead but, being positioned close to the existing residences, also met strong student objections on grounds of noise and vibration, especially from auger boring.[92] The question of how to manage building operations in close proximity to students working and living at Bailrigg, especially during the Quiet Period in the Summer Term, was to become a recurring theme thereafter.

The block, which for the first time also included dedicated accommodation for disabled students, was built by Laing North West Limited. All seven houses were handed over in stages during September 1991 and, in total, provided 176 study bedrooms that, with some shared rooms, could accommodate 208 students. The four-storey building, arranged, like the Graduate College, with a curtain wall to the perimeter road and with the front doors of the houses looking inward to a semi-courtyard, was officially opened by Mrs Jean Creed on 6 January 1992.[93] Later in the same year five more blocks of four storeys each, totalling 192 rooms, were added to Furness College at a cost of £2 million.[94] In that instance consultation had been extensive and students had decided that they would like flats of five to seven single study bedrooms that shared communal facilities. While the rents at the John Creed Building were £40 a week, those in the new Furness blocks were £29 a week. Thus increasing differentiation in the styles and prices of student accommodation evolved, a move that found favour with their occupants.

Meanwhile, at the other end of the site, the first incursion into the South-West Campus took the form of a combined hotel and university training suite. The provision of an hotel

---

[89] Minute BC/90/48(ii), Buildings Committee meeting on 5 June 1990.
[90] John Leslie Creed, a Latin scholar and a founding member of the Department of Classics, died on 5 May 1990, aged 61.
[91] Minute CO.90/103, Council meeting on 30 November 1990, together with document SU/90/39 and a letter of 26 November 1990 from LUSU to the clerk of Council.
[92] Minute COC.91/02, Committee of Colleges meeting on 6 February 1991.
[93] *NewsView*, No. 9, January 1992, p. 4.
[94] *NewsView*, No. 23, October 1992, p. 6.

on or near the university had been an aspiration of Stephen Jeffreys from the early 1970s, and he had made repeated efforts to interest external companies in financing and building an hotel that would match the university's growing needs for superior accommodation for short courses, visitors and special university occasions.[95] His efforts were unavailing, but the topic re-emerged in the late 1980s. By then the Management School had acquired a higher national profile and the needs of its post-experience teaching provision for senior managers meant that high quality facilities were essential for recruitment, while the Commercial and Industrial Development Bureau was also bringing in business partners to the university. Fortunately Mr Michael Berry, managing director and chairman of English Lakes Hotels (ELH),[96] and the Vice-Chancellor were equally enthusiastic about forming a collaborative partnership for the creation of a complex that would be run cooperatively to the benefit of all parties, and with a particular emphasis on links with the Management School, for whom it was of "paramount importance".[97] The land would be leased to ELH for 150 years, who would initially build 80 rooms with enough communal space, including generous car parks, to allow for later expansion.[98] The university would build an attached management training centre of three training suites, each with one plenary space and three adjoining syndicate rooms, together with associated office space, for £1.7 million. The intention was

---

[95] See UA.1/27/4/1.

[96] Michael Berry, Reid Yuen, and Roderick Braithwaite, *A Sunlit, Intimate Gift ... Low Wood on Windermere: A Tribute to the Tri-Centenary of the "Low Wood Hotel" 1702–2002* (Low Wood, Windermere: English Lakes Hotels Ltd, 2002).

[97] *Fulcrum*, 3 May 1990, No. 142, pp. 2 and 4.

[98] Minute CO.90/4, Council meeting on 16 March 1990, and document CWS.90/6.

that the courses centre would break even by September 1993, or earlier if internal funding could be identified. There would be a joint building contract and a single design process, and shared publicity and booking procedures to maximise business.

The first sod was turned by Mr Berry and the Vice-Chancellor in May 1990 and, despite a contractor's bankruptcy *en route*, the hotel and management centre both opened their doors ahead of schedule, on 13 July 1991, with an official opening by HRH Princess Alexandra in December. No additional funding was forthcoming, however, and both parts of the scheme initially struggled to generate a sufficient volume of business. Indeed, in 1995 KPMG was commissioned to undertake an investigation of whether the university should increase its stage from 20% to 50% of the whole. The idea went no further, and over time both parties have learned to work together for their mutual benefit. The hotel built an additional 40 rooms in 2005, and ELH now have a further stake in the district with the acquisition of the modernist Midland Hotel at Morecambe from Urban Splash in 2009, and of additional properties in the Lake District.

The early 1990s marked a reawakening of estates-related activity in the university. There was a growing interest by staff and students in the campus environment and when, in 1992, numerous trees were marked for felling, there were many protests. A second opinion was sought and, although the previous consultants' views were upheld, in practice only 12 trees were cut down. The episode marked a greater focus on the landscape as an integral part of the university, and led to the setting up of the Landscape Working Group that reported to the Buildings Committee.[99] Moves were also being made to create a dedicated cycle track between Bailrigg and the city centre, a project that required City Council approval. The concept was approved in principle late in 1991,[100] but months of discussion, including a public meeting, took place about whether cyclists should be routed along the A6 or through Bailrigg village and Collingham Park. Given the increase in traffic volume that has taken place in the subsequent 20 years the latter choice has proved to be wise, and the cycle track, opened in May 1993, is well used on a daily basis.

Further evidence that the university was becoming more environmentally aware was the increasing emphasis on economical and effective energy use. In part much could be accomplished with better controls, but the University Engineer also entered into prolonged negotiation with the Central Electricity Generation Board to review proposals for a combined heat and power (CHP) facility. A site near the main boiler house was available, as was a pipeline for high pressure gas, to the east of the M6. The scheme eventually agreed relied on National Power to provide £1.2 million, to which the university would add £300,000, on the basis of a ten-year contract for the sale of surplus electricity and the use of the project for demonstration and advertising purposes. Council approval in principle was given late

---

[99] Minute CO.92/47(a), Council meeting on 1 July 1992; and CO.92/70(d), Council meeting on 2 October 1992.
[100] Minute BC/91/121, Buildings Committee meeting on 18 November 1991.

in 1990[101] and the plant was officially opened in November 1992,[102] since when it has been reliably generating both heat and power.

A plan of a different kind that was not carried through was the building of a mosque by the university, discussed in 1990, about the inadequate provision for the increasing number of students coming from Islamic backgrounds. The Islamic Foundation had funds available, and the intention was that the university would hire a consultant architect – probably Cassidy and Ashton because of their proven work on the Chaplaincy Centre – for a new building that would be situated close to the centre, perhaps as part of a more formal entrance to the university. The estimated cost of the project steadily escalated, however, and there were concerns about the acquisition by the Islamic Foundation of freehold rights to university land. Discussions about an alternative site, near Green Lane, became desultory, and after further months of negotiation it also became clear that the necessary funding would not be forthcoming. Alternative arrangements were made within existing buildings to provide dedicated prayer space, but it is an issue for which a longer-term solution has yet to be found.[103]

The university was also looking outwards. A view gaining ground was that the original decision to locate the institution three miles south of the city centre should to some extent be reversed, while also relieving space problems at Bailrigg by the use of premises in or around Lancaster. The debate, well summed up by a 1991 meeting of the Council,[104] began in the context of a report by the Vice-Chancellor that control of the Storey Institute was reverting back to Lancaster City Council and that the university, as part of a debate about whether the university might use part of the premises, was working with the City on how to bring students to the centre and revitalise it. He could, he said, imagine a whole college being located in the City, and he was supported by a lay member who suggested that Lancaster Castle might be used for student accommodation, since "further expansion of the university solely at Bailrigg [was] detrimental to the city's future".[105] Student members wasted no time in suggesting a free bus service between Lancaster and Bailrigg, while an alumnus member of the Council, recalling earlier tensions between City and university, urged care on the integration of students into its life.

Discussions continued between the Town Hall and University House, and a cost-sharing exercise[106] enabled the LU Archaeological Unit and Adult Continuing Education in October 1992 to leave "their campus bunkers last week to begin a new life in the Storey Institute in

---

[101] Minute CO.85(d), Council meeting on 5 October 1990, and document SU/90/32.

[102] *NewsView* No. 25, October 1992, p. 1; and *NewsView* No. 26, November 1992, p. 3.

[103] Luka Vujicic, "University's priorities questioned over faith space delays", *Scan*, Week 9, Lent Term, 10 March 2010, p. 10.

[104] Minute CO.91/53(d), Council meeting on 2 July 1991.

[105] With closure in early 2011 of HM Prison at Lancaster Castle, this is a debate that has re-opened.

[106] For an expenditure of £135,000, the university obtained rent-free accommodation for ten years: minute BC/92/89, Building Committee meeting on 6 October 1992.

Lancaster's historic centre".[107] A lease was briefly taken out with the Alexandra Hotel for student accommodation, and sites such as the former County Hotel[108] and buildings along the North Road also came under consideration. In addition, serious thought was given to moving some academic departments to the complex formerly used as the Royal Albert Hospital (see below). The Students' Union had been using the Sugar House as a social centre from 1982, and in 1994 the lease was bought out in favour of freehold possession. The university was also heavily committed from 1992 onwards to the upgrading of the former Charlotte Mason College as its Lake District Campus.[109]

In the meantime there had been growing problems related to teaching accommodation, and especially the availability of lecture theatres at a time when class sizes were growing. Early in 1992 it was decided to create a teaching block[110] that would consist almost solely of lecture theatres and seminar rooms, at a total gross cost of £3.5 million, and would be positioned where the users could still fulfil the ten-minute turn-around time on the hour. The accommodation was to include tiered lecture theatres for 500 and 150 places respectively, another flat-floored lecture theatre for 150, and several seminar or workshop rooms for 50 each that would be capable of being thrown together for larger numbers. Acoustics, visual aids, and blackout were to be of a high standard, with flexibility for conferences and other public occasions, including a concourse for exhibitions and social gatherings. The plans drawn up by Shepheard and Epstein for Council in March 1992 show the building much as it was finally laid out, although the largest lecture theatre was later excised on grounds of cost. University brick was still available for cladding, and the building was designed to be in sympathy with the Engineering Building immediately to the north and the new Pendle College to the west. The intention was to have the new building ready for the academic year 1993–94. The lowest tender, after negotiation and including fees, was £3.228 million from Laing North West Limited, but just as the Council was about to accept, the Provost of Colleges (Mr Vernon Pratt) suggested that an additional two floors of 178 *en suite* student rooms, at a cost of £13,900 each, might be incorporated.[111] Despite the complexities that arose from the finally agreed addition of one extra floor, the George Fox Building was completed on time[112] and the annual meeting of the Court in December 1993 was one of the first formal events to exploit the new space.

At the same time the pressure to increase residential provision led to a proposal by the Provost of Colleges and the University Secretary that a further 200 places be provided by October 1993, by means of a new Pendle College.[113] The rationale was that undergraduate

---

[107] *NewsView* No. 23, October 1992, p. 1.

[108] The County Hotel, a large rambling building opposite Lancaster Castle Station, had been empty for some years and was subsequently demolished.

[109] This commitment ended in 1996: see Chapter 3.

[110] Minute CO.92/7, Council meeting on 6 March 1992, and documents SU/92/5 and PO/91/137.

[111] Minute CO.92/86(c), Council meeting of 4 December 1992.

[112] Lancaster University, *Annual Report 1993*, pp. 14–15.

[113] Minute CO.91/12, Council meeting on 4 October 1991; and document SASA/91/451.

admissions were buoyant and the costs of building operating at the time were advantageous to the client. The rather surprising decision to re-form Pendle College from its Siamese twin relation with Grizedale seems not to have caused controversy, and by November a figure of up to 500 additional spaces was mentioned.[114] There was also an insistence, based on experience of problems at the Graduate College, that communal space must be provided from the outset. The proposed method of funding was the increase of pooled college rent levels well above the rate of inflation, although it was recognised that this was the last time for some years that the device was feasible.[115] Other schemes, including an outline for an Amounderness College at Barker House Farm, would have to be self-financing. By October 1992 the tenders were received, the lowest being from Fairclough Building,[116] and the contract was let for £5 million, plus VAT and fees, for the construction of 474 rooms.

The implementation of the Pendle scheme, however, proved problematic. A combination of building trades problems and exceptionally wet weather meant that the planned occupation for the beginning of the Michaelmas Term 1993 turned into near-chaos, exacerbated by the deferment of contingency plans in the hope that completion on time could be achieved. New first year students, arriving with their parents, were put into temporary accommodation, only to be told they would have to move once the new space was ready, while returning final year and postgraduate students were temporarily displaced. A vigorous exchange in Council[117] led to apologies, sympathetic treatment of second moves, and the promise of further investigations. The inconveniences were, in truth, short-term, and the rooms, when occupied by their rightful tenants, were found to be fully acceptable, but the episode was a further warning to the university that the exigencies of the building trades and the welfare of students must be reconciled.

Further residential space, but this time away from Bailrigg, was obtained by means of a lease of 125 years from British Waterways on a stretch of derelict land beside the canal at Aldcliffe Road in Lancaster.[118] The plan was for 246 study bedrooms, a bursar's flat, and a management office in three blocks of two and three storeys, with four to eight students in each flatlet and associated car parking. The budget was up to £3.5 million including furniture.[119] Lancaster City Council approved the plans in February 1993, but lengthy discussions ensued with British Waterways and the city about a footbridge, public access over the site, and mooring arrangements, thus delaying the start of work until August

---

[114] The final decision was 432 rooms at £13,000 each (PO/92/54; report to Council on 6 March 1992).

[115] The estimated annual increases above inflation were respectively 7%, 6.5% and 6%: see PO/92/46 of February 1992.

[116] Subsequently AMEC Building Limited.

[117] Minute CO.93/66.2, Council meeting on 1 October 1993; report by Jenny Henley (LUSU) to Council; *NewsView* No. 41, October 1993, p. 1.

[118] Minute BC/92/57, Buildings Committee meeting on 14 May 1992.

[119] Minute BC/93/8, Buildings Committee meeting on 2 February 1993.

1993.[120] The three blocks opened on 1 October 1994 and the rooms were immediately taken up, mainly by second year undergraduates from a range of colleges.[121] By agreement with the Chancellor's office the complex was named Chancellor's Wharf. Despite suggestions that the blocks might be sold off during the cash flow problems of 1996, and again when the large-scale Jarvis scheme for residences was initiated in 2001, the buildings have been consistently popular since they combine access to central Lancaster with the standards of security and maintenance provided by the university.

As part of the process of planning for the future, Shepheard and Epstein were invited to revisit their original plans for the university and update them to take account of an immediate expansion to 7500 students and a possible further expansion in the range of 10,000–15,000 by 2005. Their consultative exercise took place during 1991 and their report,[122] while endorsing most of the design principles articulated in the 1960s, nevertheless introduced some crucial variations. The suggestion that some development might take place in Lancaster has already been discussed, but there was also presumed to be a greater reliance on public transport and more effort expended on making internal campus spaces lively and increasing their landscape interest. Probably the most radical departure was the move, already being pursued pragmatically, away from the original salad bowl mixture of academic and residential space:

> ... for sites within the perimeter road, buildings for academic use ... should take priority over residential buildings. This is vital to ensure quick, convenient journeys between teaching buildings. The bulk of future residences on campus must, therefore, be sited outside the perimeter road, and are shown in a new area of development to the south west as an extension of the pedestrian spine. The plan also envisages some development on the university's site at Hazelrigg ...[123]

At the same time national policy was shifting towards private sector investment in universities. Sir Idris Pearce chaired a UFC working party which saw the higher education estate as requiring positive and active management, and recommended that institutional managers should be free to act "untrammelled by unnecessary constraints", while being offered the help of financial intermediaries to raise money from commercial sources, with the balance to be provided by HM Treasury.[124] This radical shift in the relationship between the universities and the funding councils nevertheless included provision for much more

---

[120] Minute BC/93/34.2, Buildings Committee meeting on 20 May 1993.

[121] *NewsView* No. 55, October 1994, p. 3.

[122] "Lancaster University: Draft Development Plan Report, revised October 1991", which contains brief summaries of meetings with groups of staff and students held in May 1991.

[123] "Lancaster University Development Plan 1991–2005" (November 1991), a four-page leaflet widely circulated within the university.

[124] Polytechnics and Colleges Funding Council and Universities Funding Council, *Capital Funding and Estate Management in Higher Education* (Bristol: PCFC, 1992), paras. 1–4.

intensive data collection and retention about university estate strategies, including explicit reports on space utilisation, coupled with minimal intervention in major projects by the funding councils. The councils, it was said,[125] should supplement commercial resources for the construction of residential accommodation, but would also provide funding for selected major capital projects. It was recognised, however, that the improved space utilisation could not take place without commensurate expenditure on library, catering and social facilities and equipment, and hence "Very substantial sums of Exchequer grant should be provided for capital expenditure over the next five years", and "Government-imposed constraints on institutions using part or wholly Exchequer-funded assets to raise funds should be lifted."[126] Moreover, the private sector should be given assurances about the continuity of government support for higher education.

These messages, on which Lancaster would base its future residential policy, were reinforced by an HEFCE circular a few months later, emphasising the rolling and longer-term perspective:

> Any strategy, and particularly an estate strategy involving proposals which may need a long development period ... must be capable of periodic review and amendment ... if it becomes out of date, the strategy itself should be re-evaluated in the new circumstances ... It should however take as long term a view as possible to reflect the permanent nature of property investment and the lead time for implementing proposals.[127]

Expanded advice was given on a strategic approach to the upkeep or replacement of the existing building stock, and the tone was more downbeat than that of its UFC predecessor, pointing out that the HEFCE budget would be selectively applied, meaning that some good value projects might receive no funding, or at least not the full cost. In August the Bain Report,[128] giving more specific guidance about how private sector funding should be applied, was published and was further reinforced by the HEFCE in March 1995,[129] when Lancaster was within days of launching its debenture stock for precisely the objectives set out by the funding council.

Thus there was an accelerating pace of building activity in 1993–94. In late 1993 the Music Building and the George Fox Building were opened, Lancaster City Council gave outline planning permission for building development on the South-West Campus, and the university purchased the freehold of the Bailrigg site. The Vice-Chancellor had been pursuing discussions about the university's possible future use of the Royal Albert Hospital,

[125] Polytechnics and Colleges Funding Council and Universities Funding Council, *Capital Funding*, section X.

[126] Polytechnics and Colleges Funding Council and Universities Funding Council, *Capital Funding*, paras. 208–13.

[127] HEFCE, "Strategic Estate Management" (Circular 7/93), January 1993, para. 7.

[128] Bain, "Private Sector Funding in Higher Education".

[129] HEFCE Circular Letter 16/95 (21 March 1995).

initially for academic space but then, in line with the planning schedule of Lancaster City, as a site for potential student housing.[130] The listed building and land had already played a part in the university's history, for it was the site originally considered for submission to the UGC in 1961, before the more appropriate idea of Bailrigg occurred to Mr Waddell.[131] The NHS had operated it as a residential hospital for the mentally handicapped, but when national policy changed in the 1990s places such as the Royal Albert became redundant and expensive heirlooms. The NHS and the City were keen to sell the building, and in Harry Hanham they found a vice-chancellor whose visions of occupying it matched their willingness to dispose of it. A paper tabled at the Council in March 1994 set out the case for the university to take it on and indicated that a plan had been prepared "for the use of the main listed building and certain other buildings as a hall of residence. This indicates that a satisfactory layout could be achieved giving a high quality of residential accommodation for about 500 students. It is believed students could be attracted to such a development because of the poor quality of lodgings in the city, provided that rentals were set at roughly the same levels as prevail on the campus for *en suite* accommodation."[132] In practice the costs of conversion and the distance from Bailrigg were insurmountable, and the building complex was later sold for use as a residential school for Muslim girls.

By 1994 the Graduate College social space was under way, and a new Pre-School Centre opened in March.[133] Work continued on urgent maintenance at Charlotte Mason College and on an extension to their Sports Hall, a tender had been accepted for the Graduate Management School, and the university purchased The Downings, a house close to the university's northern boundary, for use by postgraduate students. The Buildings Committee was transmuted into the wider-ranging Estates Committee, and individual groups were spawned to take care of named projects in a programme where concurrent projects became the norm. In that year four major capital projects came to the centre of attention: Tower Avenue, South-West Campus, Library Extension, and the Ruskin Library. All were to prove controversial in different ways; all feature in the CRILL report of 1997,[134] and all were seen as part of the reason for the cash flow crisis of 1995–96.

---

[130] Minute CO.91/71(a), Council meeting on 4 October 1991, and document SASA/91/444: see also Appendix 7(c) of Lancaster University, Estate Strategy to 2005/06 (completed March 1995).

[131] McClintock, *Quest*, pp. 12–13.

[132] H. J. Hanham, "The Royal Albert Hospital, 18 February 1994", and minute CO.94/3(c), Council meeting on 4 March 1994.

[133] The Pre-School Centre had originally been a private enterprise activity, organised by a group of parents (see UA.1/4/4). Charles Carter had brought it under the umbrella of the university and dedicated space near the Pavilion had been provided. A further extension was added in 2003 and the centre, which constantly achieves excellent OFSTED reports, is currently licensed for 154 users per session.

[134] Rowe, *Crill Report*: see Bibliography. The report was published close to the events it describes. The factual information in it was checked with relevant officers before publication, and will therefore be relied upon in the accounts below.

The Tower Avenue project[135] had multiple objectives: to bring an unlovely and underused part of the Bailrigg site into more active use; to give the Students' Union and its officers more and improved space; to manage the steep change in levels between the east end of Alexandra Square and the eastern perimeter road; to provide more commercial accommodation than could be catered for in Alexandra Square; and to open up access to a second south spine that would run parallel to the congested main route. The funding was to come from university revenue and the cost was to be held below the £3 million threshold at which HEFCE approval was necessary. It was intended that income would be forthcoming from residence rooms placed at the top of Slaidburn House, above the Students' Union, and from the additional shops and banks. Because it was an infill project that was constrained by neighbouring buildings and sharp differences in levels, pedestrians were to be offered a choice of a circular ramp from the south spine or a rather precipitous metal staircase from the lower courtyard to the level of the Square. A further problem was that most of the commercial premises were shallow in room depth, making them unattractive to many potential tenants.

The contract was awarded to Pochin for £2.97 million in February 1995, but a month later the cost had risen to £3.975 million and by October a further £0.1 million had been added. The final cost settled at £3.186 million, which was technically in breach of the HEFCE Financial Memorandum. Unfortunately, in anticipation of the work commencing quickly, Furness College and members of the JCR were persuaded that 32 rooms in the Dalton residence block should be demolished over the summer of 1994, not only leading to a loss of income from the lettings but also leaving a hole about which many adverse comments were made.[136] The project achieved some notoriety around the university and so named coordinators were appointed, who declared:

> For a university campus, it's quite unique. We are building for so many different purposes – shops, banks, residences. It means the contractors can't tackle everything in one go. There has to be a lot of close coordination.[137]

There were also concerns about the levels of noise for students in Bowland and Furness colleges, and financial compensation was eventually negotiated for those most affected. The complex was handed over in phases: July for the Spar shop and the shells of the banks, September for the LUSU shop and the completion of the ramp, and December for final completion and the move of the Students' Union from the East Wing of Bowland College, enabling *Scan* finally to use a new masthead, "The New Den, Slaidburn House",[138] in the first issue of the new calendar year. The tradition of drawing on local names was broken

[135] Rowe, *Crill Report*, pp. 40, 52, 58–64, 109, 50, 208.
[136] *NewsView* No. 58, January 1995, p. 4.
[137] *NewsView* No. 62, May 1995, pp. 4–5.
[138] *Scan*, Issue 7, 26 January 1996, p. 3.

for the courtyard outside Slaidburn House in favour of naming it after Edward Roberts, an American pioneer of provision for disabled students.[139]

The South West Campus project[140] marked the first development on what is now called Alexandra Park as a residences-only area of the university. Although the land had originally been purchased for additional playing fields, the pressure on the area inside the perimeter road meant that building to the south-west became increasingly attractive. The Academic Planning Board (APB) had been told in May 1994 that another 500 residential places were needed in eighteen months' time, and a dedicated project group was set up. An options appraisal commissioned from KPMG was produced only in February 1995,[141] however, and four choices were presented: do nothing, develop the South-West Campus, convert the Royal Albert Hospital, or develop in Lancaster City Centre. Although the running costs, at around £7.5 million, were similar to those for the Royal Albert, the South-West Campus was favoured over the other three by the Estates Committee in April, a decision endorsed by the Council in May 1995. The idea was to move the Graduate College, which had already outgrown the small area allocated to it at the northern end of the university, to the new location. An upbeat article quoted John Thacker of Shepheard Epstein Hunter describing a

> development [that] will eventually surround and incorporate the listed buildings of Barker House Farm and provides the opportunity to create a new character for this part of campus ... time was spent looking at the scale and proportion of the residential buildings and the urban spaces in the surrounding area and within Lancaster. These influences were drawn upon when developing both the design of residences and the streetscape.[142]

Although the underlying design was on a strict grid, the arrangement of the residences in terraces of three and four storeys, the slate roofs and external render, and the irregular contours of the internal courtyards, softened their severity and gave them a more domestic feel. There were to be 452 rooms, 311 of them *en suite* on 50-week leases, and communal and social facilities were included from the outset. Although the £8.25 million was to come from the proceeds of the debenture stock, the intention was that the development would be self-financing by 2001. The contract was awarded, as a letter of intent, to NorwestHolst Construction Limited in July 1995: formal approval for the project by the HEFCE was not received until July 1996, however, when the building work had reached its final stages, constituting a further technical breach of the Financial Memorandum. Work proceeded on time and to budget, and the new space was occupied for the first time in October 1996, the sole immediate complaint being the absence of laundrette facilities within the college. During the summer of 1996, in order to ease the cash flow problems being experienced by

---

[139] See UA.1/27/7/4.

[140] Rowe, *Crill Report*, pp. 44, 49, 52, 53, 65–8, 107–8.

[141] KPMG, "Appraisal of Options for the Development of New Student Accommodation for Lancaster University" (February 1995).

[142] *NewsView* No. 64, June 1995, pp. 6–7.

Lintel of 1691 at Barker House Farm: the initials refer to Richard (1643–1711) and Jennet (–1713) Barker

the university, efforts were made to put in place a sale and leaseback arrangement over a period of 55 years, but BZW Property Services were not able to identify a funder who would offer reasonable terms and the proposal went no further. In the meantime the university had acquired a college for graduate students, both resident and non-resident, that was particularly helpful to the growing international contingent at Bailrigg.

The complexities of the Tower Avenue and South West Campus projects, however, paled into insignificance by comparison with the Library Extension of 1993–97.[143] Although space in the Library had been intensively used, including through the changes made in 1988, it was clear by 1992 that more radical treatment was needed. The Library had been included with Information Systems Services in the July 1993 Planning Statement as areas to be brought together, and a way forward appeared with an HEFCE invitation to bid for "projects which reduce serious accommodation shortfalls in central facilities with priority being given to library and other learning resource facilities".[144] The Planning Officer worked hard with colleagues over the Christmas of 1993–94 to put together a document that would

---

[143] Rowe, *Crill Report*, pp. 36, 41, 52, 55, 58, 75–6, 110–47, 195–204, 209.
[144] Document PO/93/191, pp. 1–11; report to Council on 4 March 1994.

demonstrate increasing integration of the two services and help the university to take advantage of advances in information technology. The offer of an estimated 20% of the total cost (£1.114 million), was subsequently increased to 25% (£1.39 million), leaving £4 million to be borrowed from external sources. Building was to start early in 1993 and be completed that October. At a public meeting the Vice-Chancellor explained that the extension would run westwards onto an open green area, and would include a two-storey reading area, a central mall with shops and service areas, a balconied reading area, and an IT training suite on the top floor.[145] There was, however, a condition that the university must spend £400,000 of the HEFCE funds by the end of March 1995, and some problems relating to foundations and trees were touched upon.[146]

There was indeed unhappiness about the removal of a copse acknowledged to be a century or more old and harbouring rare species of blackberry.[147] More seriously, there were essentially two clients – the Library and ISS – and their combined total of required square feet far outstripped anything that could be accommodated within the constraints imposed on the scheme. The architects already appointed for the Ruskin Library (MacCormac, Jamieson, Prichard) were also invited to take on the Library, but this was a small practice working from London and the scale and complexity of the project meant this was a challenging undertaking for them. The design, which along the way was altered to include provision for an additional archive area underneath the Reading Room, mushroomed in scale and was then severely scaled back, losing reader and service space, and to this day the weather-boarded southern aspect of the extension shows where the Phase III space should have been.[148] The Librarian, Arthur Davies, retired in the summer of 1994, and his place was taken by Jacqueline Whiteside,[149] who found herself having to manage an exceptionally challenging project still in the process of detailed design. Extensive enabling works were found to be necessary to shore up the foundations of the site and create a platform on which the extension could be built. This contract was awarded to Pochin Limited, at additional cost, and work began in atrocious January weather. Spectators in nearby offices watched with fascination as it became clear that miscalculations with the positioning of vertical rods inserted in the platform meant that much of the work had to be scrapped and restarted. In the background discussions still continued about the precise alignment of the old and new levels, about furniture and equipment, and about cabling and specialist installations. Consignments of some 60,000 books were taken to White Cross in Lancaster for temporary storage, and some *ad hoc* remodelling and reduction of stock also took place.

The main contract was awarded by means of a letter of intent to John Laing Construction Limited on 23 June 1995 for £4.011 million and a completion date of 4 August 1996, with

---

[145] *NewsView* No. 51, June 1994, p. 1.

[146] Minute CO.94/3(g), Council meeting on 4 March 1994.

[147] *NewsView* No. 53, August 1994, p. 1; *NewsView* No. 54, October 1994, p. 7.

[148] In addition to loss of new space, existing basement storage would now be used for resited plant machinery.

[149] *NewsView* No. 55, December 1994.

a total project cost now calculated to be £5.82 million. The university was fortunate that other costs for furniture and equipment could be absorbed by the approved recovery of VAT, using a wholly owned subsidiary company (Lancaster University Library Services Limited), and the pursuit of savings continued, including a change in the design of the west window to the Reading Room, creating fixed rather than moveable louvers. Because of the university's cash flow problems and the scale of the project a further public meeting was held, chaired by the deputy vice-chancellor. This confirmed that work on the Library should continue,[150] but nevertheless the APB was forced to approve another £600,000, to be found from savings and deferrals elsewhere in the capital programme, and there was a distinct shortfall in shelving and furniture when the new space was initially occupied. Nor was that the end of the problems, for in May 1996 a bituminous liquid for waterproofing caught fire on the ground floor of the extension, in turn igniting a propane gas cylinder.[151] The fire was quickly extinguished without injury to anyone, but extensive smoke damage meant there was now no prospect of the extension being ready for the beginning of the 1996–97 academic year. Once the Christmas vacation began, however, ISS staff were able to move on 23 December, with the Library staff following on 4/5 January, so that, thanks to the heroic efforts of all concerned, the new premises were ready for student use by the beginning of the Lent Term.[152] The less welcome news was that the total project cost had now risen to £6.944 million.

The Library Extension and the Sir Alastair Pilkington Reading Room were officially opened by HRH Princess Alexandra on 8 July 1997, and over the succeeding months much effort was made to improve the functionality of what had been delivered to the university. The relationship with John Laing, however, which had proved difficult throughout the building period, culminated in a claim against the university of £2.9 million, "including retention and insurance claims relating to the Library capital expenditure programme ... the University refutes the basis of this claim".[153] A negotiated settlement was eventually reached, but this sour footnote to the project seemed to some to sum up the whole difficult experience.

The fourth and final project, the Ruskin Library,[154] at a building cost of £3.088 million, was formally opened by HRH Princess Alexandra on 9 May 1998[155] after a decade of hard work by many Bailrigg colleagues. The Whitehouse Collection of the works of John Ruskin (1819–1900), containing books, manuscripts, paintings, and drawings, had been held in the Ruskin galleries at Bembridge School, Isle of Wight, since the 1930s. The school was

---

[150] *News Update* No. 11, 14 February 1996.
[151] *News Update* No, 28, 16 May 1996.
[152] The Library was closed to users for only one day in the entire building and fitting out operation.
[153] Note 30, Lancaster University Accounts 1998, p. 32.
[154] Rowe, *Crill Report*, pp. 18, 37–8, 50–1, 52, 73–5, 113.
[155] Lancaster University, Annual Report 1998, p. 8.

known not to be able to continue housing the collection,[156] and Lord Lloyd of Kilgerran, the chairman of the Ruskin Education Trust Limited, had given his support to a proposal that the collection could come to Bailrigg, closer to Brantwood on Lake Coniston, where Ruskin had lived for his last three decades, in a building specially designed and built for the purpose.

The project first reached the Buildings Committee in October 1990, and was adopted as one of the main strands in a newly launched Development Campaign. The interconnections with the Library Extension project can readily be imagined, but a consistent theme was a plan for a free-standing building close to but separate from the Library. Richard MacCormac of MJP was appointed as architect in 1992, and he and the director of the Ruskin Programme, Michael Wheeler, spent much time discussing the concepts that would underpin the building. The outcome was the concept of a treasure box held at the core of a building around which would be wrapped a reading room, public gallery space, and offices. The ultra-modern building materials and techniques belie the symbolism: a raised causeway leading to heavy doors that, when opened, reveal a great bound box of Venetian plaster containing 1700 works of art by Ruskin and his circle, as well as his diaries, letters, manuscripts, books, and photographs. Curving stairs on either side lead to the two galleries, which are linked at the centre by a walkway that also gives onto a meeting room, and look down on a reading room. At the west end a basement entrance enables vehicles to unload direct into the building. The prominent site at the front of the university draws the eye to the ovoid form, the white façade and horizontal banding of which fit well against the backdrop of the Library's west window.

Funding for the project came in several stages. Smaller sums were accumulated by Professor Wheeler, and in 1993 the university, following a private donation of £0.5 million, agreed to contribute £600,000 over three years. The project then seemed likely to stall, and the APB in 1994 again considered whether the collection might be placed in the archive area of the Library Extension as an interim measure. Professor Wheeler, however, led the preparation of a bid to the newly-created National Heritage Memorial Fund that, after months of negotiation, resulted in the award in October 1995 of £2.314 million.[157] The contract was let forthwith to John Laing Construction Limited for £3.088 million. The building work, which included the installation of the passive ventilation system and the Venetian detailing, inside and out, as well as earthshaping work, proved complex. The Whitehouse Collection made its way from the Isle of Wight to Lancaster in the early days of 1998 and the opening exhibition[158] appropriately celebrated the local connections. Perhaps unsurprisingly, given that the building materials used had been pushed to their technical limits, there were initial problems with the air conditioning and with water ingress into the basement and through the roof into the reading room. These problems were eventually

---

[156] Michael Wheeler, "Lancaster and the Ruskin Collection", *Fulcrum*, No. 140, 18 January 1990, p. 3.

[157] *NewsView* No. 68, October 1995, pp. 1, 3.

[158] "Ruskin and the Lake District: an exhibition to celebrate the opening of the Ruskin Library at Lancaster University", 29 April–27 September 1998.

resolved with some minor modifications to the roof design, and a recent visit by Sir Richard MacCormac underlined his affection for and pride in the building.[159]

During the Recovery Plan period (see Chapter 6), notionally from 1996 to 2000, existing projects were taken to completion but inevitably there was considerable reluctance to contemplate further capital expenditure commitments. Indeed, the university withdrew from the Lake District Campus in September 1996 and responsibility for that part of the estate passed to S. Martin's College. The university also sold off most of the Hazelrigg land and property for £372,000 net as part of the efforts to ease the cash flow position, thereby foregoing a small annual income, but retaining ownership of a field station and access to woodlands for fieldwork.[160] The halt in new building persisted: the sole item approved for 1998–99, for example, was £1 million to cover a rolling programme of information technology maintenance across all areas of the university, although this decision was accompanied by hints about future investments in environment and communications and improvements in the Sports Centre.[161]

Gradually, however, there was a return to confidence and, as the Planning Statement for 2001–02 expressed it, while the major building programme initiated in 1987 was complete,

> Academic restructuring accompanied by changes in research and teaching direction has inevitably highlighted the dysfunctionality of ageing buildings. The benefits of the science restructuring will be accelerated by the investment of resources from HEFCE for the upgrading of laboratories, workshops and service areas, many of which were designed in the late sixties and early seventies for different research and teaching purposes. It is intended to seek HEFCE funding under the poor estates initiative in relation to conversion of areas to more effective teaching and research use, and provision is being made in the capital programme to supply matching funding.[162]

As part of a larger corporate plan that was intended to integrate all aspects of the university's planning processes into one unified corporate strategy document, an estates strategy was developed in 2000 and updated a few months later.[163] Planning work was reported as being well under way on what was to be InfoLab 21, on expansion of and extensions to the Management School, on additional sports pitches, on an enlarged Sports Centre that, it was expected, would also offer related student and catering facilities, and on a research facility that would house the NERC Centre for Ecology and Hydrology alongside the Institute of Environmental and Natural Sciences in a new complex to be called the

---

[159] *LU News*, No. 477 (7 May 2010).

[160] Report from the Director of Property Services, "Disposal of Land and Property at Hazelrigg" (document ps/96/06, 10 July 1996), (UA.1/27/4/6).

[161] Document AR/98/859: extract from minutes of Finance and General Purposes on 12 June 1998; report to Council on 3 July 1998.

[162] University of Lancaster, "Planning Statement 2001–02", report to Council on 3 July 1998 (document VC/98/R100).

[163] Document EST.2001/26: report to Council on 22 June 2001.

Professor Michael Wheeler and Mr Richard MacCormac with the model of the Ruskin Library, October 1995

Lancaster Environment Centre (see Chapter 5). A programme of modernisation of lecture theatres and meeting and seminar rooms, begun in 1999,[164] was to continue. There was also to be much improved and coordinated signage; the university was now so large and complex that verbal instructions about how to navigate around it were no longer sufficient. Less glamorously, however, a flood in September 2000 had demonstrated that the infrastructure of the university was in urgent need of upgrading and of an increase in its capacity.[165]

The university became increasingly accustomed to the production of estates strategies that looked forward over a period of up to a decade. A document prepared in March 1995 took the planning process to 2005–06; that in May 2000 to 2010. Although Shepheard and Epstein continued to design individual buildings, their role as site architects was replaced by FaulknerBrowns. Their master plan[166] included an expectation of the complete development of the South-West Campus for residence in a scheme that would incorporate

---

[164] "Lancaster University, Modernisation of Meeting Rooms, Seminar Rooms and Lecture Theatres", Mellor Associates, 1999.

[165] A thunderstorm on the evening of 26 September 2000 included a short bout of rain so intense that parts of the Great Hall, University House, Engineering, and the Management School Graduate School took in water from overflowing drains. Although the water quickly receded, the resulting damage to floor surfaces and coverings took months to sort out.

[166] FaulknerBrown master plan; undated, but from internal evidence dated early in 2003.

Barker House Farm and involve the demolition of the commercially sponsored residences at Fylde, Furness, and Cartmel colleges, as well as of Grizedale, County West, and County Main. Careful thought was given to sightlines, relative building heights and orientations, and to the relationship with the local planning authority.

In October 2003, however, after the appointment of Mark Swindlehurst as director of estates,[167] and as the new Vice-Chancellor, Paul Wellings, entered the second year of his appointment, there was a refocusing of the overall university strategy. As part of this review an estates strategy workshop in March 2004 brought together internal and external participants, taking the 2000 estates strategy statement as the baseline and enabling a free-flowing discussion to take place. It was not until 2007, however, that a new master plan was issued under the aegis of John McAslan and Partners,[168] at the same time as a landscape master plan by Ian White Associates[169] and an infrastructure master plan by ARUP[170] (see also below).

The first major post-Recovery Plan project was the realisation of the Lancaster Environment Centre. As so often at Bailrigg, a single plan was intended to fulfil several objectives.[171] It was intended, first, in collaboration with NERC, to relocate the Institute for Terrestial Ecology laboratories from Merlewood, Grange-over-Sands, to Bailrigg, alongside the refurbishment of accommodation for IENS; secondly, to develop the increasingly significant research capacity and standing of the Lancaster Environment Centre; and, thirdly, to replace the Biology Field Station.[172] The IEBS complex, begun in the 1960s, consisted by the 1990s of four rectangular blocks around a central courtyard, with smaller wings to west and south and with a prime and unused open space to the west. Although some of the original range was over 40 years old, the general condition of the buildings was good. The intention was to add, first, a three-storey block for the NERC staff from Merlewood, as well as a general circulation area that would include an internal courtyard under a canopy. There was also to be a university-managed block that would rehouse, on its southern aspect, the controlled experiments, then ongoing in the glasshouses at the Biology Field Station, in a highly controlled environment for laboratory work in hydrology, molecular ecology, soil microbiology, plant eco physiology, atmosphere and biosphere interaction, and soils. The whole scheme was, in the words of its project manager, the most technically complex building in the university,[173] with all the challenges which that represented, and it was also

---

[167] His current title is Director of Facilities.
[168] John McAslan + Partners, "Lancaster University Masterplan, 2007–2017" (undated but 2007). The firm also designed the Postgraduate Activities Centre (2008), the Learning Zone and Grizedale College (2009), and the Charles Carter Building (2011)
[169] Ian White Associates, "Landscape Masterplan 2007–2017" (2007).
[170] ARUP, "Lancaster University Infrastructure Masterplan 2007–2017" (2007).
[171] "Lancaster Environment Centre: Feasibility Study and Report, February 2000: prepared by the Bradshaw Gass and Hope Consortium for Lancaster University in partnership with NERC".
[172] University of Lancaster, "Estate Strategy to 2010" ((F)/00/34): report to Council on 23 June 2000.
[173] Comment made by Maarten van der Marel to the author, May 2010.

intended to form a landmark statement for the university as a prominent neighbour to the Library and the Ruskin Library and as the fulfilment of the complex and sophisticated research requirements of the institute's research teams. The NERC was to provide £6.6 million of funding for their area, which would consist of more general purpose laboratories and office space, while the university wing of £4.0 million would be funded by the HEFCE and the NWDA. Research alone, including research student supervision, was planned for the new space, and security, particularly for the NERC space and the controlled experimental laboratories, was intended to be tight.

The designs were further developed and then scaled back to fit within the budget.[174] When the tenders came in, in May 2001, however, they all exceeded the upper cost limits, in part because of the demanding specifications, and the dismal process of value engineering commenced, reducing the quality of finishes, fixtures, and flexibility of operation. The most serious of the reductions was the decision to locate the NERC workshop not in a basement area but at a separate site near the County College, where garages had formerly been provided. There were also extended negotiations regarding the terms on which the university would grant the 45-year lease to NERC for its building, the number of dedicated car parking spaces to be reserved for their staff, and detailed procedures for the operation of shared space. A limited letter of intent was issued to HBG in August 2001 for a budgeted contract sum not to exceed £8.089 million, which would include the building of the separate workshop. A decision by NERC to include further CEH staff from ITE at Windermere further increased their share of the cost, since immediate refurbishment to part of the existing IENS building became necessary. The original intention to complete the project in 2002 inevitably drifted, and it was not until July 2004 that the buildings were jointly and officially opened by the Vice-Chancellor and Professor John Lawton.

Broad-based research capacity in communications and informatics had been developing in tandem with work on the environment, and the 2000 Estate Strategy had identified the need for additional space in the Applied Sciences, especially for Communications Systems, Computing, and Psychology. Preparatory planning work led by Professor Ian Sommerville had resulted in a concept he christened InfoLab21, which was designed to combine all this work within a new building that, as with the LEC, would coincide with a new organisational structure. There was to be provision for staff, doctoral research, and masters level students, enlarged scope for undergraduate teaching, and a related knowledge business centre for corporate knowledge transfer. On the basis of targets to be agreed for the latter activity, the intention was to obtain £4.5 million from the NWDA and £3.45 million of the SRIF funds allocated to Lancaster,[175] and to make up the balance from the ERDF, the HEFCE, and the university's own revenue streams. The pro-vice-chancellor leading the project, Professor Richard Davies,[176] was keen to respond to the Government's knowledge-led agenda with a

---

[174] See UA.1/27/3/4.
[175] EST.2001/02: report to Council on 22 June 2001.
[176] Professor Davies subsequently became vice-chancellor at the University of Swansea.

Postgraduate Statistics Centre at night, 2010

The Management School, showing the successive phases of its development, including the Leadership Centre to the right

Looking north from the Postgraduate Statistics Centre, 2010, and showing the balance between buildings and open space at the heart of the university.

centre of excellence that would build on Lancaster's strengths, "provide showpiece facilities for the North-West business community, and be a catalyst for economic development", as well as to make the building a bold landmark feature. The site selected, off the southern perimeter road, is close to the M6 and is situated on a small plateau incorporating the Mound (see footnote 58), which makes it prominent from the motorway and from Ellel. The building, with academic space to the east, the knowledge business centre to the west, and circulation, meeting, and teaching space in the middle, is substantial in scale. The architecture is bold and modern, with extensive use of glass and a colour palette of weathered copper and orange. Internally, the building structures are exposed and a generous restaurant area on the top floor gives fine views across the surrounding countryside. It is, as many people have commented, an assertive building that you either love or hate.

Before building could commence, however, an extended period of negotiation took place with the NWDA,[177] since the agency was insistent that the university must enter into a binding contract on the generation of jobs and other measured outputs, with a financial penalty in the case of default up to the full level of their grant. In the meantime, the estimated total cost of the project rose to £15 million and the timescale for completion by October 2003 became increasingly unlikely. After much patient iteration, the contract was awarded to HBG in May 2003, but delays in the building process, in part because of difficult winter weather conditions, meant that academic staff and KBC tenants could only move into their respective spaces in the late summer of 2004. The formal opening was performed on 2 February 2005 by the Rt. Hon. Patricia Hewitt, MP, the then Secretary of State for Trade and Industry, and the building subsequently won the British Council for Offices best corporate work place award,[178] as well as a BREEAM rating of excellent.

Although the initial plans for InfoLab21 were intended to include Psychology, much of the research of that department, although technologically advanced, involved the study of human subjects, especially children, and thus required a different scale of facilities and a more informal working atmosphere. To meet these requirements, the novel decision was made to use a prefabricated building[179] with a 30-year life that, extended over two floors, would provide observation and test spaces as well as teaching and office accommodation. It would provide customised laboratory space

> Where research into infant visual and auditory perception will take place under sound-proofed conditions. The development of spatial abilities and those relating to motor control – for example reaching and grasping – will be studied using specialist equipment. ... Parents will be encouraged to be present during research involving their child and all studies will consist of activities that both infants and children enjoy doing.[180]

---

[177] See UA.1/27/3/10.
[178] *LU Text*, 2 February 2005.
[179] See UA.1/27/3/14.
[180] *LU News*, 7 January 2003.

The building was to be named after William Whewell, the nineteenth-century Lancastrian who became Master of Trinity College, Cambridge, and twice its vice-chancellor, and it swiftly took its place on Fylde Avenue, near the Engineering Building. Clad in university brick, it does not betray its origins to the casual observer, and was ready for inauguration by the Vice-Chancellor in January 2003, less than 12 months after its approval.

Despite the additional teaching space provided for the new Management School Graduate School in 1995, the School continued to be short of lecture theatres and breakout and group work spaces. Graduate student numbers were substantially increasing year on year, especially from overseas, attracted by the School's high 2001 RAE rating and by the impressive career trajectories of School alumni. At the same time there was heightened emphasis on peer learning, particularly at postgraduate level but also increasingly for undergraduates. The School needed space that, contrary to the functionality of its original plan, with its long, narrow corridors and lack of public space, would allow for students and staff to meet and intermingle throughout the day. More and higher quality accommodation was needed to match the high reputation of the School, although at the same time value for money had to be achieved. It was agreed that a rather grim east–west internal corridor would be closed off and replaced by a covered external walkway, the main entrance would move from the south Spine to the west side of the perimeter road, the catering facilities would be upgraded, and the Dean's suite would be moved to the top floor of the Management School Graduate School (MSGS). In addition, there would be dedicated space for a centre that would undertake research in leadership and develop and teach project management and entrepreneurship in the region. This proposal was facilitated by an announcement in January 2003 by Margaret Hodge, the then Minister of State for Lifelong Learning, Further and Higher Education, about a consortium that would bring Lancaster together with Ashridge Management College, the Open University, and the Learning and Skills Development Agency to supply leadership for the post-16 learning and skills sector.[181]

The outline of the Management School scheme was set out in the updated Estates Strategy of 2001, and during 2002 FaulknerBrowns assessed the options.[182] A generous area of green space remained open to the west of the School, on the same frontage as LEC and the Ruskin Library, and infill schemes were therefore put aside in favour of a three-storey extension to the west, resulting in a complex that runs from the Spine to the perimeter road. The university was prepared to invest £5 million from revenue, but that sum would have provided only half of what was required and the search was on to identify external sources of matching funding. The School's Dean, Professor Sue Cox, and the Vice-Chancellor met the Chief Executive of the NWDA in May 2003 and, while the project was viewed favourably, it was clear that "as with InfoLab 21, significant time and effort will be required by all concerned to turn high level interest into actual funding".[183] Negotiations crept forward

---

[181] "Management School: Proposed Development": report to the Finance and General Purposes Committee, 23 May 2003 (FO/03/45).

[182] FaulknerBrowns, LUMS, RIBA Stage C report, March 2003.

[183] Report to Finance and General Purposes Committee, May 2003, para. 4.2 (FO/03/45).

Students at work in the flexible spaces of the Learning Zone, Alexandra Square, 2010

slowly, but by October 2003 the NWDA had agreed to contribute £4.5 million that, together with the university's input, would fund the new facility. It would include two 50-seater and one 150-seater lecture theatres, be host to the Lancaster Leadership Centre, have several dedicated, high specification group work areas where executive teaching and events could take place, and provide a social space for students, staff, and visitors. The targets set for the Centre would include assistance to 10,000 SMEs over ten years, and it was committed to work with the region's businesses and to assist rural regeneration.[184]

Inevitable compromises were made in the detailed design to save money, and the external appearance of the new wing shows all too clearly the need to fuse together disparate functions. Internally, however, the spaces and the different levels work well to create an area that is at once welcoming, light, airy, and spacious. The building process, including the temporary displacement of large numbers of School staff to neighbouring buildings and the discomforts of noise and mess for those who remained, was trying for all concerned, and the diplomatic skills of Professor David Otley, Associate Dean of the School, were tested to their limit. Nevertheless, by January 2005 the contractors, HBG, were able to hand over a

---

[184] *LU Text*, 2 October 2003. The Institute for Entrepreneurship and Enterprise Development has been a major player in realising these objectives: see Appendix A.

Information Systems Services, 2010, the nerve centre for the research and administrative information technology of the university

ceremonial spade to the School to mark the completion of the extension, and the Leadership Centre was opened in exuberant style by Sir Digby Jones, the then Director General of the CBI, on 10 May 2005. The investment has demonstrably been a success. The open area was named the Hub, and the associated syndicate rooms and catering facilities are constantly busy and lively, while the space can also be used for special university occasions. The excellent lecture theatre space is used not only for the School but also for conferences and for the university's meetings of its Senate.[185] And, in addition to the postgraduate provision, undergraduates have gained work space adjoining the newly covered walkway, setting a trend that subsequently influenced the planning of the Learning Zone in Alexandra Square.

Not all building projects make such forceful statements as LEC, InfoLab21, or the Management School. The university's most significant academic innovation in the first decade of the twenty-first century was its success in moving to teach in the fields of health and medicine (see Chapter 3). Discussions involving regional partners, and Liverpool University in particular, led to the establishment of the Centre for Medical Education, and in October 2006 the first 50 students were admitted to the first year of a medical degree

---

[185] Senate formerly met on the top floor of University House, where the Vice-Chancellor's suite now is.

conferred by Liverpool but taught at Lancaster. Rather than build anew, particularly since after their first year the students are not taught at Bailrigg, the wing of the Faraday complex previously used for the Department of Chemistry was converted to become the Clinical Anatomy Learning Centre at a cost of £1.6 million. The new space was completed just in time for the mid-September arrival of the first cohort in 2006.

Another successful bid was for a centre of excellence in teaching and learning (a CETL) in postgraduate statistics, awarded by the HEFCE to the Department of Mathematics and Statistics in April 2005. This grant included an allowance of £4.85 million over five years for building costs. The university added some of its own funds in order to build out a streamlined two-storey extension at the back of Fylde College, close to the department, which was completed in December 2007. Its internal open space is light and airy, and it was the first building at Bailrigg to have a moat on one side.

In 2001 the university embarked on a major programme of student residential accommodation, a project that was extensive in time, in resources, and in ambition (see Appendix B). The programme included the transfer of Cartmel and Lonsdale colleges to Alexandra Park in the autumn of 2004.[186] The accommodation that formerly belonged to Cartmel College was added to County College and was named County South. For Lonsdale Bowland took most of the emptied space under its wing, and it was named Bowland North.[187] Not only were these student residences the oldest in the university, but the associated teaching accommodation had received little more than coats of paint and the infilling of mixing bays since the late 1960s. An extensive programme of refurbishment was therefore put in hand, led by Bowland North, which included replacement windows throughout. The staff rooms, which had previously been of sufficient size to allow the conducting of seminars, had, under pressure of student numbers, become less frequently used for that purpose. They were now to be subdivided, a move made feasible by the style of fenestration, while seminar rooms and small lecture theatres were upgraded and clustered on the ground floor, and no longer earmarked for particular departments. There was (and remains) much regret about these changes amongst some academic staff in the affected departments, although it is acknowledged that even more radical solutions have been implemented at some other institutions.[188] At least at Bailrigg students can still seek out staff when necessary, an important measure of student satisfaction.

The success of the new Management School teaching accommodation, especially for

---

[186] Lonsdale left nothing behind of its former existence; in the case of Cartmel, however, it proved impossible to move the Daphne sculpture by the lecture theatre or the mural in the former bar area. The block named after John Creed also retained that name.

[187] In and around Alexandra Square some of the space released, including the rooms above Slaidburn House, was placed with Furness College, which had lost residential space during the building of Tower Avenue.

[188] Full open-plan offices were, however, introduced into floors A to C of University House in the refurbishment of 2007–08, a process that involved decanting staff, a few sections at a time, to temporary accommodation in student residences that were empty because they themselves awaited refurbishment.

postgraduates, led to demands for similar provision elsewhere, so that students could work together on shared tasks in informal settings. At the same time, student study space in the Library was at a premium at certain times of year, and the hours of opening were more restricted than students were coming to expect. There appeared to be a single attractive solution to both problems, which was to convert the frontage of Bowland College at the top of the steps in Alexandra Square into a Student Learning Zone. This facility, at a cost of £2.5 million, was officially opened by Sir Alan Langland in January 2010. It is open around the clock throughout the year and includes PC access; students may eat and drink here while working. The styles of seating are varied across the main concourse, and even more variety is provided in the pods, or bays, on the inner side. It is proving popular with students, and finally remedies the loss in the late 1970s of dedicated college space for non-residential students.

Meanwhile, a further wing of the Lancaster Environment Centre was added, in which the former Geography department is now housed, together with a Knowledge Business Building that provides incubation units for start-up businesses. A postgraduate suite makes provision for masters and doctoral students, and the scheme also involved further refurbishment of the IENS building for research on environmental chemistry. The funding of £8.4 million for this scheme, which facilitated the incorporation of Geography into a unified academic and organisational structure with Environmental Science and Biological Sciences, was put together from SRIF2, HEIF2, ERDF, NWDA, and university cash reserves, and is a further example of a complex that now stretches from the south Spine to the perimeter road. The building, with its smart reflective finishes, is named after Professor Gordon Manley and was opened by Professor Martin Rees, FRS, on 22 May 2007.

Developments in some areas of the sciences inevitably led to increased demands for greater computing power, ever-larger data stores and faster and more powerful processing facilities, in addition to the ever-growing requirements of regular administrative and teaching use of websites, email and Internet services. While some staff of Information Systems Services had moved into the new Library extension in 1997, others had remained in the original Computing Building, and there were increasing calls for a dedicated building that would reunite the staff, and particularly one that would bring ISS closer to InfoLab21. After much negotiation over finance and many design stages, together with some value engineering that has meant space and facilities are more constrained than intended, a new building was approved for a site close to Pendle College. It has secure air- and water-cooled data and machine rooms at its core, and open-plan offices for some hundred staff clustered on three floors. The interior is functional, with grey as the predominant colour, relieved by vivid green, and the building is environmentally friendly, including a heat-resistant roof that uses the same technology as the Beijing Olympics stadium. The building was completed by September 2009, although it was Christmas before the shift of staff and services to the new premises was complete.[189] In May 2010 it won the same award as InfoLab21, that for the best corporate workplace in the region.

---

[189] Some computing capacity has been retained within the Faraday complex as an emergency backup.

The climbing wall at the new Sports Centre, June 2011

An external eye on familiar territory can be refreshing, and a new and thorough master plan by John McAslan-Partners for 2007–17[190] was welcomed. While its recommendations have in part been realised, many challenges remain. These include the need to

> reconsolidate the campus without the need for massively costly and disruptive interventions. Our masterplan establishes a detailed, rational strategy for sustainable long-term development.
>
> We believe that the core layout of the campus need not be significantly recast. However, there is no satisfactory sense of arrival at the campus. Its linear layout is not obvious, and it lacks cross-porosity [from west to east and vice versa]. The existing green spaces do little to alleviate a feeling of micro-urban compaction … [The] strengthening of the spine could be anchored by a number of key interventions, a new campus reception building of genuine gateway quality, landscaping, better access road, and improved public spaces, such as a new plaza at County College, and a redefined square in front of the George Fox Building.
>
> The architectural and spatial strategy would have the effect of opening the campus – unbuttoning it, as it were, releasing its sense of containment. It will become more convivial to study and live in. It will look better, and be easier to navigate; faculties will seem less separate.

Two allied reports were commissioned. The first, by ARUP,[191] about the infrastructure,

---

[190] John McAslan+Partners, "Lancaster University Masterplan, 2007–2017" (undated, but 2007).
[191] ARUP, Lancaster University Infrastructure Masterplan 2007–2017.

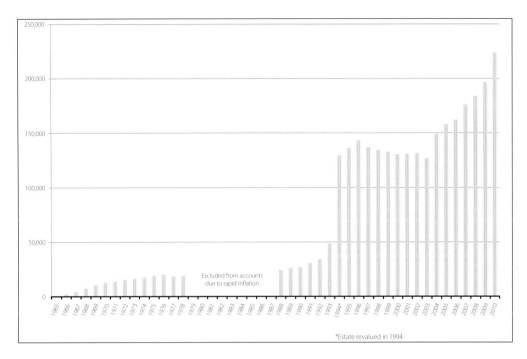

Figure 10. Value of estate; for the financial years ending 31 July 1965 to 31 July 2010

examined key practical issues ranging from energy use, water and gas installations, and fire alarms to the removal of asbestos and the upgrading of the original service duct underneath the Spine, and it culminated with recommendations that, taken together, would cost some £24 million at 2007 prices. It has the great advantage that the university can be confident that the sometimes concealed issues related to infrastructure are now fully acknowledged and their treatment can be brought into annual budget lines as expenditure is approved.

The second report was the landscape master plan from Ian White Associates, which gave a careful but sympathetic analysis of the strengths and weaknesses of the estate, acknowledged the development and maintenance demands placed on the university, and presented an action plan broken down into separately costed and discrete elements for prioritisation and implementation as funds become available. By the time of its publication in 2007 significant changes in the university's external appearance had recently taken place, including the building of a new entrance from the A6 to Alexandra Park and the demolition of the commercially-sponsored residences at Furness, Fylde, and County, which gave way to massed blocks rising above the perimeter road to the east. The familiar strengths were identified in the report, such as the attractiveness of the Bigforth entry from the A6, which passes through rising parklands, tree cover, and sports pitches, the intimate scale of the pedestrianised areas, and the variety of external spaces in and around buildings. The weaknesses were also evident: the damage caused by building work, the visual intrusion southwards of Alexandra Park and InfoLab21 on the southern ridge; the volume of cars and other vehicles; the constant changes in paved levels and surfaces, making walking hazardous and unattractive; and poorly drained sports pitches. The university was urged to thin and underplant its original 1850s woodlands with native broadleaves, to increase the spacing of the 1960s plantings, to develop a network of walking and running footpaths, to expand and deepen Lake Carter, to exploit the new pedestrian arc along a second and parallel south spine, and to upgrade and replenish hard and soft spaces everywhere. The report has proved a useful blueprint, and work towards achieving its recommendations includes the Halo project, which put pedestrian pavements and data cabling all round and under the perimeter road, the remodelling of Lake Carter, and extensive improvements to the sports pitches. There is, moreover, a dedicated member of the estates team whose sole task is to manage, upgrade, and maintain the public realm. Although much work on the estate will always remain to be done, the exceptional asset of the university's setting has been recognised and acted upon.

At the time of writing, the ambitious programme of building continues. The restoration of the original Bailrigg Mansion has commenced, with the intention of bringing the Milner/ Mawson gardens back to their original design as a second stage. To the west are the glass facades of the new steel-framed Sports Centre. After almost a decade of differing views and restricted funds, the decision was made to relocate the indoor sports facilities near Bigforth Farm, where members of the general public can readily visit, and to fund it from the proceeds of the debenture restructuring of late 2009 at a cost of up to £20 million. The complex, which will be 30% bigger than its predecessor, will include a 25-metre swimming pool with eight lanes, a climbing wall whose design has received input from Sir Christian Bonington, and provision for badminton, squash, fitness, and related facilities. A time capsule was buried by the Vice-Chancellor and the Athletics Union President in October 2009, and the intended completion is scheduled for mid-2011.

Within the perimeter road, and close to the newly-designated Lancaster Square that opens up the space between County College and its neighbours, is the timber-framed performance space for LICA. Theatrical work is staged there and social space and office accommodation is provided for the institute. This £10 million building, for which the ground was broken by Wayne Hemingway in January 2010, was opened for use in October 2010, with a formal opening held in March 2011. It is the first UK higher education project to be awarded a BREEAM outstanding rating.

At the centre of the university Alexandra Square is being rejuvenated, with a lift to an improved Underpass, a new design for the steps on the north side, including better disabled access, and new paving and planting. This iconic area, sitting at the heart of the university, is of particular sensitivity, and an extensive process of public consultation continued for months before the contract was awarded to Ian White Associates at a cost of £2.25 million, for completion during 2011. Further to the south, between the Management School and Grizedale College, is the Waterside Building, for which the budgeted figure was £10 million. It includes space for lecture theatres, seminar rooms, and offices, and the upper floors are available for Management School staff and postgraduate students. Approval was given in the summer of 2009, but the persistent freeze of the 2009–10 winter delayed the pouring of the concrete and the site was located at a busy crossroads in the university, making access difficult. In July 2010 the topping out and a naming ceremony after Charles Carter took place, and the official opening was held in April 2011 in the presence of HRH Princess Alexandra.

Once the County South refurbishment was complete approval for similar processes at Bowland College commenced in the autumn of 2010. In turn, space released in Furness College will be used as additional accommodation for the School of Health and Medicine in combination with the current provision in the Faraday Building and the continuing location of the biologists in their original building, for an overall budget of £12 million. The Physics and Library buildings, both in uninterrupted use since 1967, are also ready for renewal. Buildings that are vacated can be reused: the former Computer Building is to be fitted out for Human Resources and the existing Sports Centre will be converted for other activities. The retained residences, including Chancellor's Wharf, will be progressively updated, and the programme of maintenance is intended to increase in scale and as a percentage of annual turnover. A proposal for two wind turbines at Hazelrigg, for which HEFCE funding was available, was refused by Lancaster City Council in May 2010, but a reapplication for a single turbine was approved in April 2011. To the north of the university's land holdings an area for a science park has been purchased and vested in Lancaster City Council, but traffic flows at Galgate and the economic downturn probably means that the scheme will continue to wait.

Overall, it is likely that the emphasis on major capital projects will give way over the next few years to an upgrading of the existing building stock in order to make it work more efficiently and effectively, so that waste is reduced and space maximised within the context of a university site that is attractive, navigable, and safe.

Epilogue

N OVEMBER 23RD, 2011 will mark the 50th anniversary of the announcement in the House of Commons of the award of a new university to Lancaster. This brief thematic account of its history has covered the high and low points of its history so far, concluding with a year of particular strength in 2009–10, when the external indicators of success were outstanding nationally and internationally.[1] These were accompanied by an excellent financial out-turn and a seven-year capital programme that completed the stock of student residential accommodation for decades to come, as well as adding substantial additional teaching and staff space.

At the same time, however, a comparison of the relatively calmer days of this volume's commissioning in 2006 with the profound uncertainties of the time of its completion in 2011, underlines the volatility and vulnerability of UK higher education, despite its successes and its contribution to the national economy. As all institutions come to terms with what are generally agreed to be the most significant changes in the university sector for a generation, and as Lancaster seeks its sixth vice-chancellor, the institution will continue to need all the fleetness of foot and strong motivation that has characterised it so far. The challenges include but are far from being confined to the successful management of its strategic purposes, including the internationalisation of the university and the replication of equivalent student experience at institutions overseas whose students look to Lancaster for the quality of their degrees, the continued maintenance of excellence in both teaching and learning, the understanding and control of unpredictable impact of changes in information technology on working practices and potentially even the understanding of what the definition of learning will be, and the strategic positioning of Lancaster in the UK and the world. The single confident prediction is that the next fifty years will be at least as searching as the first five decades: whether they will also be as exhilarating and perennially fascinating as for our successors to judge. However, at the least Lancaster has laid down a fine geology of its first half century on which its staff and students can build for future generations.

---

[1] See: THE World Rankings at http://www.timeshighereducation.co.uk/world-university-rankings/2010-11/top-200.html; Guardian League Table at http://www.guardian.co.uk/education/table/2010/jun/04/university-league-table; Independent League Table at http://www.thecomplete-universityguide.co.uk/single.htm?ipg=8726; and Times Good University Guide at http://www.thetimes.co.uk/tto/public/gug/?CMP=KNGvccp1-times%20good%university%20guide%202011.

Commercial applications of the university's research

Fʀᴏᴍ ᴛʜᴇ ᴏᴜᴛsᴇᴛ the university intended that the benefits of its research should be applicable to contemporary issues and contribute to the economy.[1] Thus, Charles Carter told the Court in 1968[2] that in his view

> universities were able to make a direct contribution to national productivity by educating minds and providing training in special skills. The University of Lancaster had many resources which were of immediate value to the national economy. Its School of Business and Organisational Studies was already one of the biggest in the country. The School's constituent departments undertook much contract work for industry and commerce and for public bodies ... As reported at the previous annual meeting of the Court, the University was associated with the City of Lancaster in the project 'Enterprise Lancaster'.

This latter venture, established in 1967, was an early attempt to help Lancaster City to attract science-based developments to the locality, and was reinforced by both a Small Firms Club and an Advisory Panel for Local Organisations. The level of potential interest was shown when the Local Authorities' (Small Projects) Research Fund, set up by the university in 1972, was overwhelmed with proposals for financial support; it was possible to fund just 7 projects out of 130 applications received. Other contacts are documented in a brochure of 1981:[3] a computer-aided milling machine in Engineering was assisting a weaving machine manufacturer; work was under way with K Shoemakers Ltd at Kendal on microprocessor application; and departments in sciences and management were offering consultancy, short courses, and workshops to local companies.

In 1985 the university's investment in external links was strengthened by the setting up of the Commercial and Industrial Development Bureau, with a full-time director, Mr Geoffrey Yates. He and his staff worked hard to provide a single point of contact between the university and local businesses, in order to provide the latter with ready access to the increasing range of expertise within the university. Even if its slogans, "We have more to

---

[1] For the university's early contributions to the local economy, see McClintock, *Quest*, pp. 304–8.
[2] Minute 6 of the 5th Annual Meeting of the Court, 7 December 1968.
[3] The University of Lancaster, "Services to Industry and Commerce" (undated, but autumn 1981).

offer than you think", and "Did you ever think we did so much?", now seem endearingly tentative, the bureau's activities included successful short courses for industry, tailored to local needs; an exhibition at Bailrigg of university work applicable to the needs of local businesses; and plans for a business park that would have been situated close to where the George Fox Building and the Charles Carter Building now stand. Meanwhile, Lancashire County Council set up Enterprise PLC, which led economic regeneration across the county and provided funding for joint activities between the university and local companies.

A successor body in the 1990s, drawing on the lessons learned to date, was the unit for Marketing and Commercial Liaison within the External Affairs Division. Concerted efforts were made to secure funding under emerging European initiatives, and there was a growing recognition of a need, "in cooperation with the Research Office and the Committee for Research, to support faculties by identifying and bringing their attention to potential opportunities to create mutually acceptable and beneficial relationships with external organisations to enhance our research, training and consultancy activities".[4] As the new millennium approached the external incentives for this work increased, with earmarked investment funding made available from the EU and the British government. Professor Richard Davies, the pro-vice-chancellor responsible for links with industry, began the process of forming a cohesive team of people whose purpose was to develop working partnerships between the university and the local business world and to forge long-term relationships wherever possible while providing a range of customised support services particularly directed towards SMEs.

Although the university was unsuccessful in 1999 with a bid for HEROBAC[5] funds, partnership bids made in 2000–01, led by Manchester and working through the NWUA,[6] were successful in securing ERDF funds for action plans related to sectoral regeneration. This outcome led, in turn, to the establishment by the university of a Business Enterprise Centre, and sustained efforts were made to draw in academic input and current research activity and to base delivery teams in departments. This seemingly bland statement covers some exceptional efforts by professional staff to bring work labelled as "Third Mission" into the mainstream of academic departments, while not deflecting the fundamental research critical to the university's core objectives. The first of the HEIF[7] bidding rounds took place in 2001 and, although Lancaster did not receive funding from its submission, it was able to draw on its EU funding to enable students and graduates to work with SMEs in the region. Some 200 students were involved in teams set up in Computing, Engineering, Environmental Science, and the Management School. They became engaged in supervised projects that brought the immediate benefits of access to business advice for the companies involved and to employment experience that the students could draw upon for their own future careers; and, less quantitatively but of importance for the longer term, it was thereby demonstrated to small businesses that it was worth their while to invest in graduate level

---

[4]   C. D. Hannaford, notice of a MCL Group meeting on 13 October 1995.
[5]   Higher Education Reachout to Business and Community, funded by the HEFCE.
[6]   North West Universities' Association.
[7]   Higher Education Innovation Fund, funded by the HEFCE.

staff. In 2004 HEIF2 came on stream, and this time the university achieved funding of £2.4 million over two years, with matched funding from the NWDA of £2 million. The two main priorities were identified as the support of tourism and the development of environmental technologies and renewables, and:

> the launch of a range of new projects to provide assistance to Small and Medium Enterprises (SMEs) in the region. The projects will have a significant impact on regional competitiveness and growth, employee retention and employment generation ...
>
> The University has sometimes been seen locally as rather an ivory tower, but this is a wholly inappropriate label ... The problem is that we have not been funded to support local companies; the ERDF projects remove this funding obstacle.
>
> The projects support the government's agenda of bringing universities, businesses and communities together as part of what is known as "the third mission" ... Lancaster University is one of six major universities in the region, working together to deliver ERDF projects.[8]

The decade 2000–2010 marked an increased maturity of service as team members became leaders in their own right, and there were gradual shifts in perception when a growing proportion of academic staff participated in the new external links or formed their own. As ERDF funds continued to flow to the university it proved possible to match this resource from other sources and hence to create improved infrastructure in the form of dedicated building stock (see Chapter 7). The first such development was InfoLab21, where the first of three knowledge business centres was set up under the direction of Mr Steve Riches in a new and distinctive building that also housed Computing and Communications Systems.[9] This venture was closely followed at the Management School, where the Leadership Centre was located, and thirdly and finally by the Gordon Manley wing of the Lancaster Environment Centre. The change in approach was well captured in a brochure of 2005, indicating that:

> At Lancaster we turn ideas into action. The result is new policy, improved business processes and the development of novel technologies and services. We enhance the capacity of local businesses with support from European Development funds, and have a very wide range of commercial relationships with regional, national and multinational companies. These now form a core part of the mission of the University.[10]

HEIF3, which was allocated formulaically, based on institutional capacity, track record, and judgement, continued funding at 80% of the HEIF2 level for Lancaster, but despite this

---

[8] Richard Davies, Preface to LU Business Enterprise Centre, "Develop a Partnership with a World-Class University" (undated, but circa autumn 2002).

[9] The two departments were united in the School of Computing and Communications in August 2010.

[10] Vice-Chancellor's foreword to "Lancaster University: Business Interaction, Ideas, Knowledge and Wealth" (undated, but 2005).

relative setback, most of the core team remained in place. For HEIF4, however, Lancaster achieved the maximum funding possible, and a report of mid-2010[11] shows the diversity of activity benefiting from the scheme across the institution: Assure in Applied Social Science, the Centre for Knowledge Exchange in Health and Medicine, the Centre for Performance-led HR in the Management School, Creative IDEAS in LICA, the Investigative Expertise Unit and the Atypical Development Unit in Psychology, Leadership for Sustainability in Management Learning and Leadership, Lancaster Product Development Unit in Engineering, LUVU and Create in LUSU (see Chapter 4), and developments in Physics, including the Lancaster Quantum Technology Centre, are amongst those listed.

All three knowledge business centres remain dedicated to the interface between academic and external organisations. InfoLab21 is a centre of excellence for information and communication technologies, and its staff aim to raise the capability of digital industries in the region. Amongst its achievements are assistance to 585 SMEs in the North-West region over four years, leading to sales increases of £84 million and the safeguarding of a further £117 million of sales, as well as the creation of 718 new jobs created and the safeguarding of a further 1806.[12] The Lancaster Environment Centre, already internationally known for its work on increased crop production by selective irrigation methods (see Chapter 5), has many other strands relating to contemporary environmental issues. One example, building on long-term expertise in hydrology, is a study of the effect of land use on flood run-off generation and the mitigation of flood damage. Professor Philip Haygarth is leading a £6.5 million study over five years on the reduction of agricultural river pollution, using the River Eden as one of three test river catchments in England.[13] The Lancaster Environment Centre has also launched a free breakfast club for local environmental companies and businesses seeking innovative environmental solutions, to help researchers and owner-managers establish new contacts and set up collaboration with cognate academics in other institutions.

Generalisations are easy to make, and a specific example of one programme will exemplify the Lancaster approach across all three knowledge centres. This project, LEAD,[14] which directly addresses one of the original purposes of locating a university in North-West Lancashire – economic regeneration – was set up by the Institute of Entrepreneurship and Enterprise Development. Within Merseyside, Greater Manchester, Lancashire, and Cumbria there are both urban and rural areas for which economic growth is a problem, even in good times; places where economic activity starts from a low base, training and development are less accessible than in, for example, London and the South-East, and there is a particularly high concentration of small and medium enterprises, including micro SMEs of fewer than 20 employees each. LEAD, which has already been running for a decade and for which a clear need can be seen in the future, is precisely tailored to meet the demands

---

[11] Dion Williams, "HEIF 4 Programme Report, Q2 Apr-Jun 2010" (SEC/2010/2/1018).

[12] Lancaster and Morecambe, "Where Knowledge Leads" (undated, but September 2010).

[13] http://ltg-domino.lancs.ac.uk/info/lunews, 20 October 2010.

[14] LEAD stands for Leading Enterprise and Development. The author is grateful for access to LEAD files for the information given below.

of such an environment. The over-arching aim of the programme is to develop world-class leadership and management skills in order to grow and raise the productivity of businesses in the North-West, and it starts from the position of sharing in the world of the businesses concerned. Each cohort of clients attends a ten-month part-time course free to participants provided that they fulfil required levels of involvement. Funding has come principally from the NWDA, and the present £9.5 million programme will last until 2012.

Lancaster has two roles; first as a main provider of the courses, and secondly as the leader of a network of eight to ten providers, principally other institutions of higher education, across the North-West region. Rigorous targets are set in return for the funding, and usually exceeded, whether for the numbers of businesses assisted, jobs created or safeguarded, or productivity increased – and 90% of the businesses involved have obtained an average increase in turnover of £200,000. There is strong central project management under the LEAD director, Ms Sue Peters, both internal and external impact are measured, and there is systematic quality control. Furthermore, the programme itself is constantly subject to evaluation by senior academics, and has become increasingly robust and confident in the way it conducts the programme as it responds to client feedback.

The detail of the programme reveals the care with which it has been designed. The core requirements for the recruitment of the individual business leaders are that they should have between 4 and 20 employees, be the sole or major shareholders, have been established for at least four years, and have a clear market proposition they wish to test. After an overnight experiential gathering, the participants attend master classes that are both functional (the purposes and uses of cash, or constraints on businesses) or inspirational (for example, Sir Christian Bonington talking about leadership under severe conditions on Mount Everest). They join smaller and confidential action groups that focus on specific business issues, receive free face-to-face and telephone coaching, draw on tutors' expertise, and have mentors who come from similar backgrounds to their own. They are also able to invite fellow owner-managers to come into their businesses for a few days and comment on them. These combined measures are designed to break down owner-manager isolation and enable them to become more strategic, including in the development of their own staff. The ninth LEAD cohort graduated in January 2010, and included businesses from not only Lancaster and Preston but also Burton-in-Kendal, Carnforth, and Kirkby Lonsdale to the north, and Blackpool, Bury, Chorley, and Stockport to the south. Over 200 owner-managers have been through the programme, and the next step will be to devise a masters' programme designed specifically for their further development.

As the regional development agencies are phased out by March 2012 and the future of the HEIF initiative remains unknown, a 94 Group policy report[15] on how universities can use their research base to add value to business gives a balanced appraisal of how the relationships between the two might move forward in the future. This approach is

---

[15] Professor Trevor McMillan et al., *Enterprising Universities: Using the Research Base to Add Value to Business* (London: 1994 Group, 2010).

appropriate to universities on the scale of institutions included in the 94 Group, and gives the likely flavour of Lancaster's approach for the future. More work, it is noted in the report, is needed on support and incentives for academic staff who are able and equipped to engage in knowledge exchange and company creation at institutional and departmental levels, and who have the ability to present a coherent picture of what is feasible to external partners. A massive exploitation of intellectual property, or forays into venture capital partnerships, however, will probably continue to be the exception. Businesses, which are slowly gaining more confidence in their academic partners, need particularly to understand the long-term nature of academic research and the absence of quick fixes, and to accept that the partners with whom they are working have to sustain their core research base for business to utilise in the future. If the relevant government departments can raise their gaze above the immediate turmoil of an economic downturn, there is much that can be contributed by government to assist the process of economic regeneration, including the recognition and reward of excellence in the field so far, an improved recognition of the importance of universities' work with SMEs, and imaginative funding streams that map onto to the shared concerns within the regions. Lancaster's strategic approach[16] is to ensure that its research has appropriate and maximum impact, to make its expertise available to all organisations that can benefit from it, and to give its students the skills and knowledge that will enable them to make a substantial contribution to the workforce in the UK and beyond. Looking behind these objectives, the university will continue to work with familiar and new partners across the region, and to grow in wisdom and understanding of what is achievable and worthwhile for the external organisations, its graduates, and its own capabilities. It is an area of work that can only gain in significance in the future.

---

[16] http://www.lancs.ac.uk/researchenterprise/ke_statement/ (27 August 2010).

Funding and building of student residences, 2000–2010

T HE ESTATE STRATEGY TO 2010, approved by Council in May and June 2000, returned once again to the familiar theme of student residential accommodation,[1] noting that 60% of the existing stock had been built 25 to 35 years earlier and that substantial work was required to bring it up to current standards. A programme of refurbishment and upgrading within the perimeter road would, it was noted, result in a net reduction in the total number of rooms for existing colleges and, in order to maintain the current number or even increase it, there needed to be new development on the South-West Campus. A year later, a revised document made reference to consultations with N. M. Rothschild, financial advisers to the university,[2] and to a recommended strategic partnership, to start early in 2002 so that new premises could be completed by September 2003. The report also proposed the remodelling of the pre-1975 accommodation in a total exercise that could, it was anticipated, be completed within five years. The Council accordingly agreed to delegate to the Vice-Chancellor the establishment of a small steering group under his personal chairmanship,[3] and so commenced the single most large-scale and complex capital project ever undertaken at Lancaster, but one in which the detail would prove to be as significant as the concept.

The first meeting of the group, held on 8 August 2001, considered an options appraisal prepared by Rothschild.[4] The university's objectives were defined as the management of student accommodation without compromising the collegiate structure, the retention of legal title to properties within the perimeter road, approval for off-balance-sheet finance, and retention of certain service provision while transferring some risk. Four options were

---

[1] Document FO/00/31 (Version 3), submitted to Council on 23 June 2000.
[2] Document 2001/20, section 1 and para. 2.17: report to the Council on 22 June 2001.
[3] Minute CO.2001/33(e), Council meeting on 22 June 2001.
[4] N. M. Rothschild & Sons Limited for Lancaster University, "Options Appraisal for the New Building and Refurbishment/Remodelling of Residential Accommodation" (June 2001): Mr Stephen Dingle played a key role, particularly in the early negotiations.

considered: outright sale, sale and leaseback, securitisation,[5] and strategic partnerships. The group, as anticipated, agreed to proceed with the single option of partnership, by which the university would contract to receive student accommodation and associated services from a third party, typically for 25 years or longer, enabling the risk to be shared, the financing to be off-balance sheet and obtained from the private sector, and the legal title over the property to be retained by the university on expiry of the agreement. The private sector would be attracted by the income to be gained from new buildings, while the university would benefit by the addition of new residences and the integration of a refurbishment process into the new build programme. The logistics of the exercise were daunting, as was the need to keep a host of internal and external bodies appropriately consulted.[6] The group, after some hesitation, agreed to proceed straight to an OJEC notice and a memorandum of information.

By the third meeting the group had been given stated executive authority by the Council[7] and was in a position to appoint professional advisers as well as to seek expressions of interest. Of the 11 received, 8 were considered in more detail and 6 were placed on a long list of potential partners. By January 2002, after bids had been received against a detailed output specification and the four firms still interested had been interviewed, the executive group was able to propose the short-listing of two firms: Jarvis PLC and Norwest Holst Group PLC. Significant changes to the design had taken place, however, first, the initial larger-scale development would all take place on the South-West Campus; secondly, demolition and rebuilding, rather than refurbishment, would occur not only in the Cartmel, Furness, and Fylde commercially-sponsored residences but also at the County College main building and Grizedale College; thirdly, in order to obtain some share of the rental stream a partial share of risk would return to the university; and, fourthly, the partnership period might be extended to 30 years.[8]

Jarvis was declared to be the preferred bidder on 22 March 2002, and the way was open for the extensive documentation around the partnership to begin. In parallel, as the realisation of the scale of the project became known across the university, doubts were expressed about it: that the accommodation would be too expensive for students; that the letting periods were too long; that no adequate social facilities would be included; that there would be enormous disruption over an extended period; that students would suffer if their direct relationship with the university was lost over matters such as portering and cleaning (the soft facilities); that the university needed to attend to the anxieties of people living in

---

[5] Securitisation was used at the University of Keele, but was complex and not favoured by potential lenders: see *Education Guardian*, 27 May 2003, pp. 12–13.

[6] In the interests of clarity, the reader can assume throughout this section that the appropriate consultations were successfully completed unless otherwise stated.

[7] Minutes of Council Executive Group, 20 October 2001 (AR/2001/1176).

[8] Document AR/2002/92, 14 January 2002.

Ellel and Galgate about risks of flooding and the problems of extra traffic,[9] and that the university was moving into a large-scale venture that it did not wholly understand and perhaps could not control.[10] On 29 May[11] the Senate discussed at some length the proposal for one new college to be established on the South-West Campus, while being invited to accept that neighbouring blocks would (like Chancellor's Wharf) be extra-collegiate. The future of Bowland College also became a matter of increasing anxiety for its members, as the pressures for academic rather than residential space at the centre of the university became more explicit and appeared to undermine the viability of the college.

A special meeting of the Council, held on 19 July 2002 – the last for the retiring Vice-Chancellor, Professor Ritchie, and the first for the incoming President of the Students' Union, Mr Liam Danby – proved to be something of a watershed. Representatives of the external advisers[12] were present and the outline structure of the partnership was on the table. The university was invited to approve over 20 separate sub-agreements, either directly or through the actions of an Authorised Signatory Group to whom certain defined authority would be delegated. The intention[13] was that 2070 of the existing rooms would be transferred to a partnership, referred to as a Single Purpose Vehicle (SPV hereafter), and 880 rooms would be built on the South-West Campus, followed by a further 1440 on the main site – that is, 4390 rooms in the SPV, representing an increase of 1940 rooms across the university, plus 2200 rooms remaining in the university's direct ownership. County College (including County West), Cartmel, and parts of Furness, Fylde, and Grizedale would all be transferred, and all the commercially-sponsored residences would be demolished and rebuilt, except for County West, which was to be felled and not replaced. Bowland Tower, Bigland block at Cartmel, and Chancellor's Wharf were to be removed from the stock of residential accommodation. The development phase was to be completed by 2007, and the full term of the partnership was expected to be 34 years. Active maintenance and the supply of utilities to the South-West Campus would be the responsibility of the SPV; the university would provide the soft facilities for a fee, and would also receive a share of the ground rent, calculated on occupancy levels, and a share of upside profit. The rent was to be no more than £68 a week at 2003–04 prices.

The Vice-Chancellor, in urging the Council to move forward with the transaction, was prepared to stake his personal reputation on that recommendation. The President of the Students' Union, meanwhile, had four concerns: whether the cost of setting up new colleges had been included in the financial model; whether there had been sufficient consultation

---

[9] Letter from Hilton Dawson, MP, of 26 June 2002 to the Vice-Chancellor: see also the *Lancaster Guardian* of 21 June 2002 and *The Citizen*, 30 May 2002.

[10] Open letter of Professor Keith Soothill to Council members, 14 July 2002: some lay members also wrote in about their anxieties around this time.

[11] Minute S.2002/43, Senate meeting on 29 May 2002.

[12] The contributions throughout the project of Mr Anthony Burnett-Scott and Ashurst Morris Crisp were particularly outstanding.

[13] Commercial Termsheet as at 10 July 2002.

with the colleges; whether some of the existing residences might be kept available to students for longer than originally envisaged; and whether there should be breaks in the contract to create discrete phases, so that the university would be able to influence new and replacement residences within the perimeter road. He was unhappy with the proposed standardisation of internal layout and external appearance, and questioned whether it was necessary or appropriate to demolish County College. After a lengthy debate the Council agreed that the transaction should move forward and that the Council Executive Group should become a project executive once financial closure had been achieved. The President's first three recommendations were broadly agreed, and it was also accepted that the Council should be provided with information about the commercial consequences of discrete phases. This outcome was both positive and salutary, and the phasing of the project subsequently proved to be helpful to the university.

The post-Council negotiations were complex, shifting, and fluid. Applications for planning approval brought a flurry of local comments and protests,[14] and there was adverse criticism of the architecture for the space inside the perimeter road, which would be "flat, uninteresting and totally lacking inspiration ... The architectural outcome will not be of sufficient merit to warrant the disruption to staff and students, over several years, entailed in the demolition and construction."[15] Approval for detailed reserved matters was, however, received by late October,[16] subject to design details: other conditions included a transport assessment for the additional entry to the university from the A6, a green travel policy for the whole university, and the avoidance of damage to the Romano-British settlement at Barker House Farm. In order to maintain a dialogue with local residents a forum had been set up between the university and Ellel parish council.

The intention had been that the SPV would obtain the funding. As the Director of Finance and Resources reported,[17] however, Ambac found that its £35 million involvement with the university was dwarfed by the anticipated £120 million of the residences project, and that was not acceptable to Ambac. An invitation by Jarvis to Ambac, to insure the debt for the project, raised the prospect of obtaining investment ratings by both Standard and Poor's and Moody's for the residences project as well as agreement on a revised financial model that would involve drawing in both the new and retained accommodation. Since Ambac approval was reliant on its internal credit committee, the project was slowing. The university's need for new rooms by September 2003 was put at risk, and Jarvis needed to know in good time whether to order materials and supplies for a start on site. The agreed solution was to create a preparatory Phase 1A of 402 rooms that would form part of the

---

[14] See *Lancaster Guardian* for 2 August 2002, 9 August 2002, and 30 August 2002.

[15] Comments by Martin Widden and David Dawson quoted in the *Lancaster Guardian*, 2 August 2002, p. 9, and endorsed by CABE, to whom the project was referred by Lancaster Civic Society (19 June 2002).

[16] Insignia Richard Ellis Briefing Note (AR/2002/1300), 22 October 2002.

[17] Euan McGregor, Report to the Council on 22 November 2002 (FO/02/74): see Chapter 6 for an account of Ambac's relationship with the university.

Cartmel College bar at Alexandra Park, showing the adaptation of a barn at Barker House Farm

Graduate College and enable the final decanting of postgraduate students from the college's original northern location, with the work to be undertaken at Jarvis' own risk.[18] The letting period would be 51 weeks, and the university agreed to contribute £0.5 million towards the necessary infrastructure costs.

Meanwhile, there was a pressing need to face and resolve the issues confronting the colleges as the dynamic of a large new and replacement programme confronted the individual ethos, location, and style of all the colleges. As Alan Whitaker pointed out[19] in November 2002, the firm view of college members was that all student accommodation at Bailrigg should be collegiate, and that each college should have its own social space and should not exceed 600 rooms. To date the Graduate College, the sole college at the South-West Campus, had just one bar, a meeting room and a PC lab: if 2500 students were to be based at that location – a number almost equivalent to that reached for the whole university during the first ten years of its existence – there was a need at the minimum for a cash point, a laundrette, some catering, meeting rooms, a supermarket, and some

---

[18] A separate transaction was entered into for Phase 1A in March 2003 (see "Report on 402 Rooms Scheme"), and then merged into the main scheme in September 2003.

[19] Alan Whitaker (ProVice-Chancellor for Student, Staff and College Affairs), paper to the Student Accommodation Project Executive, 18 November 2002.

fitness facilities. Funding of £0.25 million had been included in the model to fit out two shells for social facilities, but against that there was the cost of bringing the listed Barker House Farm into use, at an estimated extra £3 million. A shadow syndicate for one new college had been meeting for some months: alternatively, however, two existing colleges might, given some incentives, be persuaded to transfer to the South-West Campus. A paper of January 2003[20] demonstrated how the latter arrangement might work: Lonsdale would transfer, and Bowland expand northwards into its space; Cartmel might also move, and County expand southwards; Furness and Fylde could stay in place, but with extensive decanting (particularly for Fylde) as demolition and rebuilding took place; and Pendle and Grizedale could remain as they were. The integration of the Barker House Farm complex – farmhouse, barns, outhouses, and a milking shed, grouped around a cobbled courtyard – was the subject of several hotly-debated options. Eventually a choice emerged[21] that would involve the university committing the complex to one of the two colleges expected to transfer and enhancing the allowance for social facilities of the second. The cost would be £4 million,[22] but Catering and Conferences would have a stake in the new arrangements, which it was hoped, would bring in additional trade. The farmhouse and outbuildings would be refurbished and converted for college use, and a glazed canopy would be placed over the courtyard area to form a central food court.

Work continued through 2003 between the 15 main parties involved in the transaction,[23] but financial closure was deferred from March to July, and again to September. Every contingency was evaluated and tested, and the parties were also interacting with each other as well as directly with the university. Ambac, for example, entered into a side agreement with Jarvis[24] involving a Fifth Supplemental Trust Deed to enable the project to continue to a financial close without an Ambac financial guarantee, while Jarvis and the university were required to enter jointly into an agreement with Lancashire County Council about the new link road from the A6 to the South-West Campus.[25] Despite the delays and the changes in transaction structure, N. M. Rothschild continued to take a positive view,[26] stating that the final transaction was in line with the original objectives and that the terms of the 38-year concession to the SPV represented the best that could be obtained, as were the arrangements

---

[20] Hilary Simmons, paper to Student Accommodation Project Executive, 31 January 2003 (AR/2003/104): the officers and current students of the two colleges concerned, together with their JCR constitutions and traditions, were to be transferred, leaving their former college buildings behind.

[21] Sarah Randall-Paley, "Barker's House Farm: appraisal of preferred option, May 2003" (FO/03/48).

[22] The final agreed budget was £4.6 million, and Norwest Holst was appointed as the contractor.

[23] Lancaster Student Accommodation, Main Project, Programme to Financial Close, issued 30 May 2003.

[24] Letter to Andrew Salter of Jarvis Accommodation Services, 26 September 2003.

[25] "Agreement ... relating to highway works at Preston Lancaster Road Galgate Lancaster in the County of Lancashire, 23 September 2003".

[26] Letter of 12 September 2003 from N. M. Rothschild to the Project Executive and the Authorised Signatory Group.

with the banks[27] and the terms of the agreement with Ambac. Finally, they noted that Phase 4 of the development was not committed,[28] and nor were the tests by which to judge it yet in place. Financial closure, documented in five hefty volumes,[29] was achieved at the end of September and work was immediately put in hand to ensure that compliance with the agreed terms would be dovetailed into the annual cycle of the university's business; a workshop ensured that the main officers involved were fully conversant with their additional responsibilities.

Perhaps unsurprisingly, the completion of Phase 1A proved problematic.[30] Of the 402 rooms, 42 were one week late and a further 72 late by 11 days: the university received compensation from UPP for the delays, all of which was passed on to students, and UPP also paid for temporary hotel accommodation. Even more worryingly, the rooms were not up to the agreed standard, and substantial remedial work was required. A residents' liaison committee was established and a workshop was held to consider lessons for future phases, so that Phase 2A rooms could be handed over from March 2004 onwards, while Phase 3 (within the perimeter road) was planned for 2004–05. Work continued on rectifying Phase 1, especially the landscaping and the quality of the masonry, and on building out Phase 2 within the South-West Campus. The university and the developer were working together on a shared understanding of the management of delays, of inspection of blocks prior to acceptance and on the improvement of room layout and finishes, and a baseline of an additional thousand rooms was agreed for October 2004. Barker House Farm was remodelled in the agreed form, and in September Cartmel College was transferred to its new location, while Lonsdale College moved into new accommodation a short distance away.[31]

As work commenced on the colleges within the perimeter ring road[32] the impact of the project on the university community at large became profound. Furness College blocks were soft-stripped and then demolished, under the fascinated close-quarters gaze of staff and students. A programme of renaming and re-signing buildings and roadways across Bailrigg was approved, including the formal designation of the South-West Campus as Alexandra Park. The pace of change, particularly as other parts of the capital programme took place,[33] combined with the need to sustain college identities and leave sufficient flexibility at each stage to allow for any further late completions of new space, tested the capabilities of

---

[27] The final funding requirement was £124 million, of which £117 million was to be provided by RBS and Barclays, and syndicated to NIB, Dexia, and the Bank of Ireland.

[28] Discussions in 2002–03 about Phase 4 included the expectation of demolition for Grizedale in July 2006 and the whole of County in July 2007 (AR/2003/1245 of 6 November 2003).

[29] Document titles, AR/2003/1376, November 2003.

[30] Andrew Neal, report to the Council Project Executive Group, 20 November 2003 (FO/03/107).

[31] The social facilities and bar for Lonsdale College were, however, not completed until 21 January 2005.

[32] Report and proposals from the College Relocation Group, December 2003 (CR/03/54 (revised)).

[33] At certain periods the university was able to boast of having seven tower cranes on site.

everyone involved and induced a growing sense of unfamiliarity amongst Bailrigg habitués as buildings disappeared and well-worn tracks were blocked or altered.

Jarvis' own position became a growing concern. Its share price had fallen steeply after the Potters Bar derailment of 10 May 2002 on rail track for which the firm had a maintenance contract. Now, in mid-2004, the firm was issuing warnings about its university construction arm[34] and senior staff were leaving in quick succession. Inevitably the confidence and morale of company employees plummeted, and increasingly sub-contractors at Bailrigg were not being paid and were vacating the site.[35] In late October Barclays exercised its call option on Jarvis' shares in UPP Lancaster Holdings Limited, and Jarvis moved to the sale of its university partnership business to the Alma Mater Fund Limited Partnership.[36] Norwest Holst, a contractor that already had a significant track record with the university, was invited to take over Phase 3, while Jarvis concentrated on the completion of Phase 2. The care that had been taken to draw up watertight agreements was thus vindicated at an early stage.

Out of 1600 rooms contracted for, 950 were made available at Alexandra Park by 25 September 2004, and a further 144 were soon completed and occupied. The deadline for the occupation of associated houses and flats was adjusted to November. A further 336 rooms were to be completed at the western side of Alexandra Park by Christmas 2004, although not intended for occupation until the following academic year. The university could then move to the full execution of Phase 3, for which the decision was made to use brick on the external facades to match the material of neighbouring buildings,[37] instead of the reconstituted stone of Alexandra Park. The old Cartmel blocks were to be demolished in the spring of 2005 and inner Fylde in the summer of 2006. Further efforts were made to improve the quality of room layout and finishes, including in essential detail such as the draining capacity of *en suite* pods. Increasingly there was dialogue with students and staff that assisted quality in Phase 3 and highlighted what additional remedial work was appropriate for the earlier phases. In May a presentation was given[38] about the realignment of Green Lane, which was to be stopped up so that in future what remained would serve only as a means of access to Lancaster House Hotel. The new road layout involved an anticlockwise one-way traffic system around Alexandra Park, designed so that pedestrians and cyclists could safely interface with vehicles at the entry and exit to Alexandra Park, and with provision for frequent bus stops.

A summary of the position at January 2005[39] had shown that 1368 Phase 2A rooms out of 1600 had been completed, with another 568 due to be handed over in March. The

---

[34] *Guardian*, 16 April 2004, p. 17.

[35] Minute 7 of the Student Residential Accommodation Council Project Executive Group, 2 November 2004 (AR/2004/1185).

[36] Andrew Neal, paper to UMAG, 9 November 2004, and *Financial Times*, 25 November 2004. The formal process of transfer was completed early in 2005.

[37] Minutes of the Council Executive Group, 1 March 2005.

[38] Minutes of the Council Executive Group, 3 May 2005.

[39] Estates Committee agenda, 3 February 2005.

Furness and Fylde residential blocks, built as part of the student residential accommodation project in 2004–05

1047 rooms of Phase 3 that had originally been scheduled for September 2005 would now be completed one year later. Inner and outer sections of Fylde, earmarked for demolition, were vacated and contingency space for County South students was provided at Alexandra Park. The 18 months from January 2005 to July 2006[40] were therefore dedicated to building the new blocks for Furness, Fylde, and County – colour-coded deep rust, dark blue, and cream respectively – and preparing for the time when the various parties would face the decision about whether to move to proceed with Phase 4. As Council was reminded,[41] this phase was expected to involve the demolition of both County and Grizedale colleges, and was to consist of 1047 *en suite* rooms, so that, at the completion of the phase, 80% of UPP accommodation would be *en suite*. A review group chaired by Mr Gary Middlebrook had established that there was student demand for more flexibility in terms of twin rooms, family accommodation, space for disabled students, and living areas associated with kitchens. Grizedale was judged to be beyond repair, since it would require new external facades, roof, windows, and insulation. County College, on the other hand, was found to be structurally sound, despite earlier concern about the extent of and danger posed by

---

[40] A topping out ceremony for Phase 3 took place on 24 March 2006.
[41] Report to Council, 2 December 2005 (FO/05/103).

The town houses, built in family accommodation style, at Grizedale College, 2010, replacing the earlier 1970s mansard roofline. Similar houses have been built at County College

high alumina cement, although a not inconsiderable programme of maintenance would be required. The occupancy levels across Phases 1 to 3 were good, and Phase 4 seemed increasingly likely to proceed, financed as before through UPP (Lancaster) Limited. In June 2006 Council authorised[42] the issue of a Phase 4 election notice, with the intention that 453 new Grizedale rooms, based on Accent House design, would be available by September 2007 in a mixture of town houses and flats. The existing Grizedale buildings were accordingly reduced to two neat mounds of blond rubble in the summer of 2006, although it was to be October 2008 before the new Grizedale residences were ready and October 2009 before the college took over its new social space and a bar.[43]

Once the decision had been made to retain the original County College buildings, discussions about their future use resulted in two floors being retained for 176 standard rooms, while the ground and first floors were to be remodelled for academic, college, and retail space. On the hitherto unused space to the north of County 346 new Accent House rooms were to be built in town house style, with shared living space on the ground floor

---

42 Minute CO.06/45(e), Council meeting of 16 June 2006.

43 The plaque in memory of Elizabeth Nelson, murdered on Green Lane in 1866, has been transferred from the original Grizedale courtyard to a retaining wall outside the new Grizedale bar.

and student rooms above. County West would be demolished in the summer of 2007, and the open space thus created between County College and the Great Hall would be turned into a piazza and a focal point for LICA.

As these final stages were carried out, the residences project became absorbed into the larger estates programme. While a possible Phase 5 was mooted, to refurbish the retained accommodation, at the time of writing the intention is that incremental improvements to the remaining residences will continue. Despite the many twists and turns of the project, overall it must be seen as a triumph for the university and for the senior managers most closely associated with its successive stages. There was disappointment that the poor quality of the Jarvis architectural forms in Phases 1 and 2 could not be reversed in time for Phase 3, but Phase 4 proved to be a turning point in producing a style of housing that students could mould to their needs, and which is more environmentally sustainable than earlier residences. Similarly, there is a painfully long wait for tree cover to become established on the southern slopes of Alexandra Park, but the Grizedale courtyards are havens of tranquillity, while the Lancaster Square at the extended County College is a sophisticated open space that lends itself to multiple uses for the future. There is admiration for the sustained contribution to the project by the colleges, whose staff and students faced major, albeit different, challenges to their identity and functions, with Grizedale being particularly disadvantaged for a significant period. The difficulties faced do not undermine the achievement of creating 6822 new rooms across the university without financial detriment while providing residence throughout the project to students to whom promises had been made. The university now has a stock of relatively new, flexible student accommodation that, under the terms of the transaction, must be maintained to appropriate standards over its 43 years, and that can support its burgeoning student population, particularly at postgraduate level.

Senior officers, 1963–2011

Chancellors

HRH Princess Alexandra, the Hon. Lady Ogilvy, KG, GCVO, Hon DMus

1964–2004

Sir Christian Bonington, CVO, CBE, DL, Hon DSc

2005–15

Pro-Chancellors

The Rt. Hon. The (18th) Earl of Derby, MC, Hon LLD

1964–71

The Rt. Hon. The Lord Greenwood of Rossendale, Hon LLD

1972–78

Mr W. D. Opher, Hon LLD

1978–80

Sir Alastair Pilkington, FRS, Hon LLD

1980–90

Sir Christopher J. Audland, KCMG

(Hon. Fellow of the University)

1990–97

Mr J. B. Heron, Hon LLD

1997–2003

Mr B. M. Gray, CBE, DL

2003–13

Vice-Chancellors

Sir Charles Frederick Carter (1917–2002), MA, Hon DSc

April 1963–September 1979

(Stanley Jevons professor at the University of Manchester, 1959–63)

Professor Philip Alan Reynolds (1920–2009), CBE, MA, FRHistS, Hon DLitt

(acting October 1978–December 1979)

January 1980–September 1985

(Professor of politics; Vice-Principal at Aberystwyth, 1961–63)

Professor Harold John Hanham, BA, MA, PhD, FRHistS, Hon DSc

October 1985–September 1995

(Professor of history at Harvard, 1968–72; of history and political science at MIT, and Dean of Humanities at MIT, 1973–85)

Professor William Ritchie, BSc, PhD, FRSGS, FRICS, FRS (Edin), OBE, Hon DSc.

October 1995–September 2002

(Professor of physical geography at Aberdeen, 1979–95; Senior Vice-Principal, 1992–95; joint editor, The Environmental Impact of the Wreck of the Braer (Scottish Office, 1994))

Professor Paul William Wellings, BSc, MSc, PhD, DL

October 2002–December 2011

(Deputy Chief Executive, CSIRO, 1999–2002; Chairman, 94 Group, 2009–)

Bibliography

University of Lancaster Archive

The main source of original documents from which information was drawn for this volume is the Archive, in which the material is arranged under the following broad JISC categories. Further information can be supplied on request

UA.1/1: Teaching
UA.1/2: Research
UA.1/3: Student administration
UA.1/4: Student support
UA.1/8: Public relations
UA.1/9: Media relations
UA.1/12: Alumni relations
UA.1/13: Fundraising
UA.1/15: Strategic planning
UA.1/16: Governance
UA.1/18: Quality management
UA.1/19: Audit
UA.1/20: Legal affairs
UA.1/23: Students' relations
UA.1/24: Organisational development
UA.1/27: Estates management
UA.1/28: Financial management
UA.1/29: Personnel management
UA.1/30: Information services
UA.1/36: Internal services

Newspapers and magazines

Numerous references are made to articles in the national press: see footnotes.

Published sources

Advisory Board for the Research Councils. *Report of the Working Party on Postgraduate Education,* Cmnd. 8537. London: HMSO, 1982.

Advisory Board for the Research Councils, and University Grants Committee. *Report of a Joint Working Party on the Support of University Scientific Research*, Cmnd. 8567. London: HMSO, 1982.

Bain, Andrew. "Private Sector Funding in Higher Education." Bristol: Higher Education Funding Council for England, 1993.

Beloff, Michael. *The Plateglass Universities*. London: Secker & Warburg, 1968.

Berry, Michael, Reid Yuen, and Roderick Braithwaite. *A Sunlit, Intimate Gift ...: Low Wood on Windermere : A Tribute to the Tri-Centenary of the "Low Wood Hotel" 1702–2002*. Low Wood, Windermere: English Lakes Hotels Ltd, 2002.

Birks, Tony. *Building the New Universities*. Newton Abbot: David and Charles, 1972.

Campbell-Savours, Dale. *The Case for the University of the Lakes*. Self published [1995].

Checkland, Peter. *Systems Thinking, Systems Practice*. Chichester: Wiley, 1981.

Committee of Enquiry into the Organisation of Civil Science. *[Report]*, Cmnd. 2171. London: HMSO, 1963.

Committee of Public Accounts. *The Proper Conduct of Public Business: Eighth Report*, 1993–94 Hc154. London: HMSO, 1994.

Committee of Vice-Chancellors and Principals. *External Involvement in the Maintenance and Monitoring of Academic Standards*. London: CVCP, 1984.

Committee of Vice-Chancellors and Principals, and National Union of Students. *Joint Statement from the Committee of Vice-Chancellors and Principals and the National Union of Students*. London: NUS, 1968.

Committee of Vice-Chancellors and Principals of the Universities of the United Kingdom. *University Development in the 1970s: A Statement of Views by the Committee*. s.l.: CVCP, 1970.

Committee on Higher Education. *Higher Education: Report of the Committee Appointed by the Prime Minister under the Chairmanship of Lord Robbins 1961–63*, Cmnd. 2154. London: HMSO, 1963.

Committee on Standards in Public Life. *Standards in Public Life [the Nolan Report]*. Vol. 1: report, Cm. 2850-I. London: HMSO, 1995.

Craig, David M. *An Introduction to University*. Lancaster: Lancaster University, 1965.

Dahrendorf, Ralf. *LSE: A History of the London School of Economics and Political Science, 1895–1995*. Oxford: Oxford University Press, 1995.

Daiches, David. *The Idea of a New University: An Experiment in Sussex*. London: A. Deutsch, 1964.

Department of Education and Science. *Higher Education: A New Framework*, Cm. 1541. London: HMSO, 1991.

Department of Education and Science. *Shifting the Balance of Public Funding of Higher Education to Fees: A Consultation Paper*. London: DES, 1989.

The Development of Higher Education into the 1990s. Cmnd. 9524. London: HMSO, 1985.

DTZ Pieda Consulting. *Higher Education in Cumbria*. s.l.: Advisory Group for Higher Education in Cumbria, 2000.

Education, Science and Arts Committee. *Higher Education: Minutes of Evidence*, 1988–89 HC 87 I. London: HMSO, 1988.

Further Education Unit. *FEU Response to Academic Validation of Degree Courses for Higher Education [the Lindop Report]*. London: FEU, 1985.

The Government's Expenditure Plans 1981–82 to 1983–84. Cmnd. 8175. London: HMSO, 1981.

Griffith, John. *Research Assessment: As Strange a Maze as E'er Men Trod*. London: Council for Academic Freedom and Academic Standards, 1995.

Hartwell, Clare, and Nikolaus Pevsner. *Lancashire: North*, The Buildings of England. New Haven: Yale University Press, 2009.

Higher Education Funding Council for England. "1996 Research Assessment Exercise: The Outcome." RAE 96 1/96 (Bristol: HEFCE, 1996), http://www.rae.ac.uk/1996/c1_96.html.

Higher Education Funding Council for England. "2001 Research Assessment Exercise: The Outcome." RAE 4/01 (Bristol: HEFCE, 2001), http://www.rae.ac.uk/2001/Pubs/4_01/.

Higher Education Funding Council for England. "Assessment Panels' Criteria and Working Methods." RAE Circular 5/99 (Bristol: HEFCE, 1999), http://www.rae.ac.uk/2001/Pubs/5_99/.

Higher Education Funding Council for England. "The Impact of the 1992 Research Assessment Exercise on Higher Education Institutions in England." M 6/97 (Bristol: HEFCE, 1997), http://www.hefce.ac.uk/pubs/hefce/1997/m6_97.htm.

Higher Education Funding Council for England. "Model Financial Memorandum between HEFCE and Institutions: Terms and Conditions for Payment of HEFCE Grants to Higher Education Institutions." 2010/19 (Bristol: HEFCE, 2010), http://www.hefce.ac.uk/pubs/hefce/2010/10_19/.

Higher Education Funding Council for England. "RAE 1996: Conduct of the Exercise: RAE Manager's Report." RAE 96 1/97 (Bristol: HEFCE, 1997), http://www.rae.ac.uk/1996/c1_97.html.

Higher Education Funding Council for England. "Research Excellence Framework: Second Consultation on the Assessment and Funding of Research." 2009/38 (Bristol: HEFCE, 2009), http://www.hefce.ac.uk/pubs/hefce/2009/09_38/09_38.pdf.

Higher Education Funding Council for England, and Higher Education Quality Council. " Joint Statement on Quality Assurance." http://www.hefce.ac.uk/pubs/hefce/1994/m1_94.htm.

Higher Education Funding Council for England, Scottish Higher Education Funding Council, Higher Education Funding Council for Wales, and Department for Employment and Learning Northern Ireland. "Guidance on Submissions." RAE 03/2005 (Bristol: HEFCE, 2005), http://www.rae.ac.uk/pubs/2005/03/rae0305.pdf.

Higher Education Funding Council for England, Scottish Higher Education Funding Council, Higher Education Funding Council for Wales, and Department for Employment and Learning Northern Ireland. "Initial Decisions by the UK Funding Bodies." RAE 01/2004 (Bristol: HEFCE, 2004), http://www.rae.ac.uk/pubs/2004/01/rae0401.pdf.

Higher Education Funding Council for England, Scottish Higher Education Funding Council, Higher Education Funding Council for Wales, and Department for Employment and Learning Northern Ireland. "RAE 2008 Panel Criteria and Working Methods: Panel A." RAE 01/2006 (Bristol: HECFE, 2006), http://www.rae.ac.uk/pubs/2006/01/docs/aall.pdf.

Higher Education Quality Council. *University of Lancaster: Quality Audit Report*, Quality Audit Report. Birmingham: HEQC, 1993.

Iles, Peter, and D. C. A. Shotter. *Lancaster's Roman Cemeteries*. Lancaster: Centre for North-West Regional Studies, 2009.

Inman, J. P. *Charlotte Mason College*. Winchester: Cormorant, 1985.

Johnes, Jill, and Jim Taylor. *Performance Indicators in Higher Education: UK Universities*. Buckingham: Society for Research into Higher Education and Open University Press, 1990.

Jones, Hycel C., G. Lockwood, and Norman MacKenzie. "The University of Sussex." In *Planning the Development of Universities*, edited by Victor G. Onushkin, 173–275. Paris: Unesco, 1971.

Kelly, Thomas. *For Advancement of Learning: The University of Liverpool, 1881–1981*. Liverpool: Liverpool University Press, 1981.

Kissack, Elizabeth. *The Life of Thomas Hayton Mawson: Landscape Architect 1861–1933*. Windermere: privately published, 2006.

Koc, W. T. *Annual Report of the Research Fellow in University Teaching Methods.* Lancaster: University of Lancaster Department of Higher Education, 1965.

Kwon, Winston. "Reputational Objects: A Critical Re-Evaluation of Corporate Brand Management." PhD thesis, Lancaster University, 2006.

Kynaston, David. *Family Britain, 1951–1957.* New York: Walker & Co., 2010.

Lambert Review of Business-University Cooperation: Final Report. London: HM Treasury, 2003.

Martin, Graham. *From Vision to Reality: The Making of the University of Kent at Canterbury.* Canterbury: University of Kent at Canterbury, 1990.

Mawson, Thomas Hayton. *The Life and Work of an English Landscape Architect: An Autobiography.* London: Richards Press, 1927.

McClintock, Marion E. *The University of Lancaster: The First Thirty Years.* Lancaster: Lancaster University, 1994.

McClintock, Marion E. *University of Lancaster: Quest for Innovation (a History of the First Ten Years, 1964–1974).* Lancaster: University of Lancaster, 1974.

McClintock, Marion E., and David C. A. Shotter. *Serving the Region: A History of the Centre for North-West Regional Studies at Lancaster University 1970–2006.* Lancaster: Centre for North-West Regional Studies, 2006.

McMillan, Professor Trevor, Tom Norton, Justin B. Jacobs, and Rosanagh Ker. *Enterprising Universities: Using the Research Base to Add Value to Business.* London: 1994 Group, 2010.

Muthesius, Stefan. *The Postwar University: Utopianist Campus and College.* New Haven: Yale University Press for Paul Mellon Centre for Studies in British Art, 2000.

Nash, Sally, and Martin Sherwood. *The University of Southampton: An Illustrated History.* London: James & James, 2002.

National Audit Office. *Investigation of Misconduct at Glasgow Caledonian University: Report by the Comptroller and Auditor General*, 1997–98 HC 680. London: Stationery Office, 1998.

National Audit Office. *University of Portsmouth: Report by the Comptroller and Auditor General*, 1997–98 HC 4. London: Stationery Office, 1997.

National Committee of Inquiry into Higher Education. *Higher Education in the Learning Society: Main Report [the Dearing Report].* London: HMSO, 1997.

National Union of Students. *Student Participation in College Government.* London: NUS, 1966.

Onushkin, Victor G., ed. *Planning the Development of Universities.* Vol. III. Paris: Unesco, 1974.

Perkin, H. J. *New Universities in the United Kingdom*, Case Studies on Innovation in Higher Education. Paris: O.E.C.D, 1969.

Polytechnics and Colleges Funding Council and Universities Funding Council. *Capital Funding and Estate Management in Higher Education.* Bristol: PCFC, 1992.

Quality Assurance Agency for Higher Education. *Lancaster University: Institutional Audit*, RG 504 06/09. Gloucester: QAA, 2009.

Quality Assurance Agency for Higher Education. *University of Lancaster Collaborative Provision Audit*, RG 264 08/06. Gloucester: QAA, 2006.

Quality Assurance Agency for Higher Education. *University of Lancaster Institutional Audit*, RG 092 10/04. Gloucester: QAA, 2004.

Quality Assurance Agency for Higher Education. "University of Lancaster Quality Audit Report." http://www.qaa.ac.uk/reviews/reports/institutional/lancaster/lancaster.asp#47.

Realising Our Potential: A Strategy for Science, Engineering and Technology. Cm. 2250. London: HMSO, 1993.

Ritchie, William, and Marion E. McClintock. "Capital Building and Cash Flow at the University of Lancaster." In *Managing Crisis*, edited by David Warner and David Palfreyman. Maidenhead: Open University Press, 2003.

Rowe, P. J. *Review of Institutional Lessons to Be Learned, 1994 to 1996 [the Crill Report]*. Lancaster: Lancaster University, 1997.

Sanderson, Michael. *The History of the University of East Anglia, Norwich*. London: Hambledon and London, 2002.

Science and Innovation Investment Framework 2004–2014. London: HM Treasury, 2004.

Science and Innovation Investment Framework 2004–2014: Next Steps. London: HM Treasury, 2006.

Scott, Peter. *The Crisis of the University*. London: Croom Helm, 1984.

"Securing a Sustainable Future for Higher Education: An Independent Review of Higher Education Funding and Student Finance [the Browne Report]." 2010. http://www.bis.gov.uk/assets/biscore/corporate/docs/s/10–1208-securing-sustainable-higher-education-browne-report.pdf.

Shattock, Michael. *Derby College, Wilmerton: Report of an Enquiry into the Governance and Management of the College*. London: Further Education Funding Council, 1994.

Shattock, Michael. *Managing Good Governance in Higher Education*. Maidenhead: Open University Press, 2006.

Shotter, D. C. A. "The Thirty-Fifth Archaeology Forum." *CeNtre WoRds* New Series No. 7 (2008): 87–94.

Smith, Brian, and Vanessa Cunningham. "Crisis at Cardiff." In *Managing Crisis*, edited by David Warner and David Palfreyman. Maidenhead: Open University Press, 2003.

Steering Committee for Efficiency Studies in Universities. *National Data Study [the Jarratt Report]*. London: Committee of Vice-Chancellors and Principals, 1985.

Temple, P., and C. Whitchurch, eds. *Strategic Choice: Corporate Strategies for Change in Higher Education*. Reading: Conference of University Administrators, 1989.

Tight, Malcolm. *The Development of Higher Education in the United Kingdom since 1945*. Maidenhead: Open University Press/McGraw-Hill, 2009.

Trowler, Paul. "Beyond Epistemological Essentialism: Academic Tribes in the 21st Century." In *The University and Its Disciplines: Teaching and Learning within and Beyond Disciplinary Boundaries*, edited by Carolin Kreber, 181–95. New York: Routledge, 2009.

University Grants Committee. *A Strategy for Higher Education into the 1990s*. London: HMSO, 1984.

University Grants Committee. *University Development 1957–1962*, Cmnd. 2267. London: HMSO, 1964.

University Grants Committee. *University Development 1962–67*, Cmnd. 3820. London: HMSO, 1968.

Warnock, Mary. *Universities: Knowing Our Minds*. London: Chatto & Windus, 1989.

Watson, Nigel. *The Durham Difference: The Story of Durham University*. London: James & James, 2007.

Waymark, Janet. *Thomas Mawson: Life, Gardens and Landscapes*. London: Frances Lincoln, 2009.

Wright, Peter. "Learning through Enterprise: The Enterprise in Higher Education Initiative." In *Learning to Effect*, edited by Ronald Barnett. Buckingham: Society for Research into Higher Education, Open University Press, 1992.

Other relevant material

Carter, C. F. *On Having a Sense of All Conditions*, Swarthmore Lecture 1971. London: Friends Home Service Committee, 1971.

Gedge, P. S. and L. M. R. Louden. *S. Martin's College, Lancaster 1964–89*. Lancaster: CNWRS, University of Lancaster, 1993.

Montgomery, F. and M. Flinn. *A Vision of Learning: Edge Hill University 1885–2010*. London: Third Millennium Publishing, 2010.

Mountford, J. *Keele: An Historical Critique*. London: Routledge and Kegan Paul, 1996.

Pope, R. and K. Phillips, *University of Central Lancashire: A History of the Development of the Institution since 1828*. Preston: University of Central Lancashire, 1995.

Rees, H., *A University is Born: The Story of the Foundation of the University of Warwick*. Coventry: Avalon Books, 1989.

Sloman, A. E., *A University in the Making*. London: British Broadcasting Corporation, 1963.

Abbreviations

ABRC	Advisory Board for the Research Councils
AHRC	Arts and Humanities Research Council (2003–)
AHUA	Association of Heads of University Administration
APB	Academic Planning Board (1963–64)
APC	Academic Planning Committee
AUT	Association of University Teachers
BES	Business expansion schemes
BESRES	Business Expansion Schemes for Residences
BGS	Board of Graduate Studies
BIS	Department for Business, Innovation and Skills
BREEAM	Building Research Establishment Environmental Assessment Method
BZW	Barclays de Zoete Wedd Ltd
CABE	Commission for Architecture and the Built Environment
CATS	Credit accumulation and transfer scheme
CEH	Centre for Ecology and Hydrology
CETAD	Centre for Training and Development
CETL	Centre for Excellence in Teaching and Learning
CIDB	Commercial and Industrial Development Bureau
CNAA	Council for National Academic Awards (1964–92)
CRILL	Rowe, *Crill Report*: see Bibliography
CSR	Comprehensive Spending Review
CUC	Committee of University Chairmen
CVCP	Committee of Vice-Chancellors and Principals (to 2000)
DES	Department of Education and Science (to 1992)
DFE	Department for Education (1992–95)
DfEE	Department for Education and Employment (1995–2000)
DfES	Department for Education and Skills (2001–07)
DIUS	Department for Innovation, Universities and Skills (2007–08)
DTI	Department of Trade and Industry
EHE	Enterprise in Higher Education
ELH	English Lakes Hotels
EPSRC	Engineering and Physical Sciences Research Council

ERDF	European Regional Development Fund
ESRC	Economic and Social Research Council
FSSU	Federation Superannuation System for Universities
FTE	Full-time equivalent (students or staff)
HEFCE	Higher Education Funding Council for England (1992–)
HEIF	Higher Education Investment Fund
HEQC	Higher Education Quality Council
HEROBAC	Higher Education Reach-out to Business and the Community
HESA	Higher Education Statistics Agency
ICRA	International Centre for Research in Accounting
ICT	Information and Communications Technologies
IENS	Institute of Environmental and Natural Sciences
IEPPP	Institute for Environment, Philosophy and Public Policy
IMPM	International Masters Programme in Practicing [sic] Management
INSET	In-Service Education and Training
ISS	Information Systems Services
ITE	Institute of Terrestrial Ecology
ITT	Initial teacher training
JIF	Joint Infrastructure Fund
JISC	Joint Information Systems Committee
KBC	Knowledge business centre
LEC	Lancaster Environment Centre
LICA	Lancaster Institute for the Contemporary Arts
LUSU	Lancaster University Students' Union
LUVU	Lancaster University Volunteering Unit (now called Involve)
MASN	Maximum aggregate student number
MJP	MacCormac, Jamieson, Prichard (architectural practice)
MSGS	Management School Graduate School
NERC	Natural Environment Research Council
NSS	National Student Survey
NTFS	National Teaching Fellowship Scheme
NUS	National Union of Students (1922–)
NWDA	Northwest Regional Development Agency
NWUA	North West Universities Association
OECD	Organisation for Economic Cooperation and Development
OFFA	Office for Fair Access
OFSTED	Office for Standards in Education
OJEC	Official Journal of the European Community
PRCS	Premature retirement compensation scheme
Pro-Chancellor	The pro-chancellor in post at the time (see Appendix C)
QAA	Quality Assurance Agency for Higher Education

QR	Quality-related research (funding)
RAE	Research assessment exercise
RCIF	Research Capital Investment Fund
REF	Research Excellence Framework
SME	Small and medium enterprise
SORP	Statement of Recommended Practice
SPARC	Senate Planning and Resources Committee
SRC	Student Representative Council
SRIF	Science Research Investment Fund
STEM	Science, technology, engineering and mathematics (subject clusters)
TQA	Teaching Quality Assessment
UCAS	Universities and Colleges Admissions Service
UCEA	Universities and Colleges Employers Association
UCU	University and College Union
UFC	Universities' Funding Council (1989–92)
UGC	University Grants Committee (1919–89)
UMAG	University Management Advisory Group
USS	Universities Superannuation Scheme
UUK	Universities UK (2000–)
VCSAG	Vice-Chancellor's Strategy Advisory Group
Vice-Chancellor	The vice-chancellor in post at the time (see Appendix C)

List of Illustrations

Index

Emboldened numbers denote figures or plates

sabbatical student officers, 11, 14, 109–10, 136

St Andrews, University of, 27, 150

St Leonard's House, x, 2, 12, 85: facilities at, 84; lease of, 83; physical condition of, 83; second-hand bookshop, 100; Shakespeare (public house), 99; table tennis at, 87; *see also* Centenary Church

S. Martin's College, x, xi, xv, xvi, 85, 86, 266: accredited status, 68, 69–70; Charlotte Mason College, 63, 211–12; founding of, 65, 84; health research, 165; university status, xix, 77–78; *see also* Cumbria, University of

Salford, University of, 38, 196

Salmon, H., 110

Savory, C. J., 205, 208, 209

Scan, 101, 109, 132, 136, 196, 260, **111**

Science and Technology (faculty), 64, 79

Scotforth, ix, 226: Green Lane, 235, 297, 299

Scott, P. F., 37, 189

Secretariat, 78

Secretary, University, 16, 18, 30, 93, 106, 212, 213, 255

Senate, 9, 237, 275: academic authority of, 52; academic standards and, 72–77; associated institutions, 67–68; board of, 13, 106; Chamber, 14, 105, 212; Committee of, 13, 61, 137; conferences of, 35, 60, 111, 245; Courses Committee, 60; effectiveness of, 23; and faculties, 63–64; heads of departments, 14; inauguration role, 10; membership, 11–12, 21; relationship to Council, 20; reserved business, 13; Shadow, x, 31, 32, 33–34; Steering Committee of, 72–73; strategic planning, 35, 41, 43–44

Senate Planning and Resources Committee (SPARC), 16, 40, 43, 62, 156, 157, 200

severance, voluntary, 47, 215–16

Shattock, M., 13–14, 19

Sheffield, University of, 28, 59, 173

Shennan, J. H., 201

Shepheard, P., 231–32

Shine, W. B., 188

shops and banks, 105, 197, 260: in Alexandra Square, 235–36; Post Office, 190, 236

Short, M. H., 49

Sibley, F. N., x, 104

Slaidburn House, xvi, 260–61

Small Firms Club, 284

small and medium enterprises (SMEs), 274, 285–87

Smart, N., 34, 36

Smethurst, W., 100–01

Smith, D. B., x, 30, 204, 233

Smith, H. W., 232, 241, 243

Smoker, P., 146

Snow, C. P., 28, 32, 50

Social Administration (department), xiii, 55–56

Sociology (department), xii, 55, 56, 77: research in, 154, 160, 167, 171; and women's studies, 162

Sommerville, I., 269

Soothill, K., 292

Soper, R., 115

Southampton, University of, 37, 141, 187

South-West Campus, xvi, 119, 207, 209, 212, 251–52, 258–62, 267–68, 290–99

Space Allocation Committee, 248–49

Spanish (section), xv, 55, 56

Spine, 236, 243, 260, 273, 277–79

Sports Centre, xix, 224, 280, **278**

staff: donations/loans of salary by, 39, 213; hours of work of, 195; numbers at Lancaster, **2**; profile of, 1–2; reductions in, 167, 216–17, 220; research, 138–40; significance of contribution of, 4

staff, academic: appointment of, 28, 146; contact and office hours, 121; development of, 74–75, 129; as examiners, 137; fixed term contracts of, 18; inaugural lectures, 141; membership of boards of studies and colleges, 52; office space for, 276; profile of, 1–2, 47, 141; publications of, 142, 146, 150, **178**; qualifications of, 141, 146; quality of, 162; recruitment and renewal of, 47, 112; reductions in, 198; research role, 138–40, 144, 150; research students as, 52; sabbatical leave, 141; shift to faculties, 63; significance of contribution of, 4, 223; and Statute 20, 18; and tenure, 18; terms and conditions of, 20, 23–24; travel funds, 189; training of, 129

staff, assistant: members of Council, 17; technical, 141; terms and conditions of service, 23–24, 190

Staff Learning Centre, xvii

Staff/Student Committee, 12, 89, 92, 93

Stamp, E., 154

Standard & Poor's, xx, 220, 221, 224

Standing Academic Committee, 54, 130

Statute Revision Committee, 11, 12, 15–17, 20

statutes: Commissioners' Statute, 18; and Transitional Provisions, 10, 14; 1971 revisions, 12–14

Stephenson, D. B., 238, 246

Stephenson, P., 233

Stirling, University of, 29, 150

Storey, H. L., 227

Storey Institute, xv , 254–55

Strategy Committee, 40–42, 43, 44

strategic planning process, 17, 26–27: conferences on, 35–36, 41, 44–45; and faculty structures, 63

student counsellors, 15, 109, 132

student finance: advice on, 131; loans for, 41; means-tested grants, 84, 186; rents, 113–15; tuition fees, 122

Student Learning Development Centre, 75

student numbers: arts versus science, 194–95; cap on, 242; at Lancaster, 12, 36, 42, 83, 97, 120, **118**; national, 1, 37, 192–94; reduction in, 39–39, 116, 198–99; targets for, 36, 194–95, 229

Student Registry, 127, 128

student representation, 11–14

Student Representative Council, xii, 12–13: annual cycle of, 109; costs of, 196; Film Society, 113; Graduation Ball, 109; Grants Action Committee, 113; meetings of, 86–87,104, **86**; offices of, 105; president of, 13; rent strikes, 113; relationship to junior common rooms, 109; and student gigs, 112–13

student social facilities, 15, 90, 91, 103–04, 132; in Lancaster, 132; and social manager, 112–13; Town Hall ball, 101

student unrest, 11: boundaries of protest, 116; occupations, 105, 115, 116

students: age of majority, 11; arts versus science, 195, 199; clubs and societies, 87; contact hours, 121; debts of, 122–24, 135–36; disabilities of, 131–32; earnings of, 122–24, 136; electronic communication and, 121; fourth cohort, 102; non-resident, 229, 245; parents of, 121, 122; preference for flats, 91–92; press coverage of, 84, 104–05, 116; profiles of, 80, 121; second cohort, 98–99; study habits of, 96; third cohort, 101; views on facilities and services, 128

Students' Union, xiii, 8: Academic Council, 25, 136; Alternative Prospectus, 128; educational charity, 25; e-voting, 25; Freshers' Fair; funding of, 196–97; General Meetings, 25; Graduate Students' Association, 119; Housing Office, 127; Job Shop, 124; president of, 41, 136, 292; referenda, 25; Slaidburn House, xvi, 260; training of representatives, 14; Union Council, 25; welfare services of, 136–37; *see*